Touring SCOTLAND

Editor
Libby Anderson

CONTENTS

ii	Introduction
iii	How to use this book
iv	Useful addresses
iv–v	Information for disabled visitors
vii–xix	Maps
1–261	Touring Guide to Scotland
262	Index

ACKNOWLEDGMENTS

The Scottish Tourist Board would like to thank everyone who has helped in the provision of information for this publication, especially Historic Scotland, the National Trust for Scotland and the staff of area Tourist Boards throughout Scotland. The information quoted in this book is as supplied to the Scottish Tourist Board and to the best of the Board's knowledge was correct at the time of going to press. The Scottish Tourist Board can accept no responsibility for any error or omission.

August 1993

INTRODUCTION

With over 1300 entries, this latest listing of things to see and do in Scotland is a varied selection from the country's enormous range of visitor attractions. From the original title, **400 Things to See**, the publication has grown in size with every new edition, reflecting the ever-increasing availability of activities for visitors all over Scotland. Here you will find natural wonders, from our ancient mountains and forests, to lochs, country parks and estates; wildlife in remote, undisturbed habitats; rare breeds, both native and foreign, on farms devoted to their conservation. There is the man-made heritage, from mysterious standing stones to castles and great houses, cottages and industrial sites, beautiful and historic gardens.

Boat trips and steam trains offer a leisurely view of the scenery; heritage centres recall Scots famous in all kinds of fields, from David Livingstone to Jim Clark, from Bonnie Prince Charlie to Robert Burns; while smaller statues and monuments pay tribute to characters from Alexander III to Robinson Crusoe, marking the sites of births, deaths and battles.

Museums display exhibits from Scotland and the rest of the world: some concentrate on special subjects such as fishing and whaling, social work and psychiatry, transport, military relics, fire fighting, musical instruments, childhood, Christianity and world religions, our Pictish forebears ... others offer a fascinating glimpse into local history and personalities. ... Art galleries feature permanent exhibitions of international stature, from Old Masters to Scottish colourists, while others have changing exhibitions by contemporary artists, sculptors and craftsmen.

Scotland can be seen at work in distilleries, potteries and crystal works, wood turneries, jewellery studios, tanneries and many other places, large and small; and at play in parks, swimming pools, leisure centres, ice rinks, theatres .. not forgetting the playgrounds and 'hands-on' features provided for children in a growing number of attractions.

MAPS

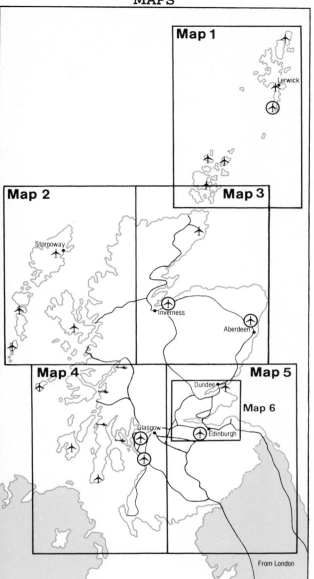

Map 1

Lerwick

Map 2

Map 3

Stornoway

Inverness

Aberdeen

Map 4

Map 5

Dundee

Map 6

Glasgow

Edinburgh

From London

——— Railway routes

⊕ Major airports

✦ Airports with
scheduled flights

→ Heliports

Produced for the Scottish Tourist Board by Baynefield Carto-Graphics Ltd. 1993

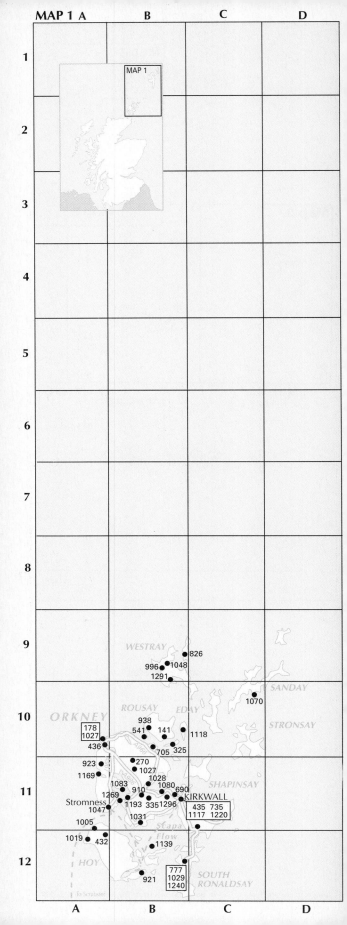

MAP 1

	A	B	C	D
1		MAP 1		
2				
3				
4				
5				
6				
7				
8				

9 WESTRAY ● 826
996 ●●1048
1291 ●
SANDAY
● 1070
10 ORKNEY ROUSAY EDAY STRONSAY
938 ●
178 541● ● 141
1027 ● 325 ● 1118
436 ● 705 ●
923 ●● 270
1169 ● ● 1027
11 1083 ● 1028 SHAPINSAY
1269 ● 910● 1080
Stromness 1193 335 1296 ● 690
1047 ● ● KIRKWALL
1005 ● 1031 435 735
1019 ● ● 432 1117 1220
12 HOY Scapa ● 1139
Flow
921 ● 777
1029
1240
SOUTH
RONALDSAY
To Scrabster

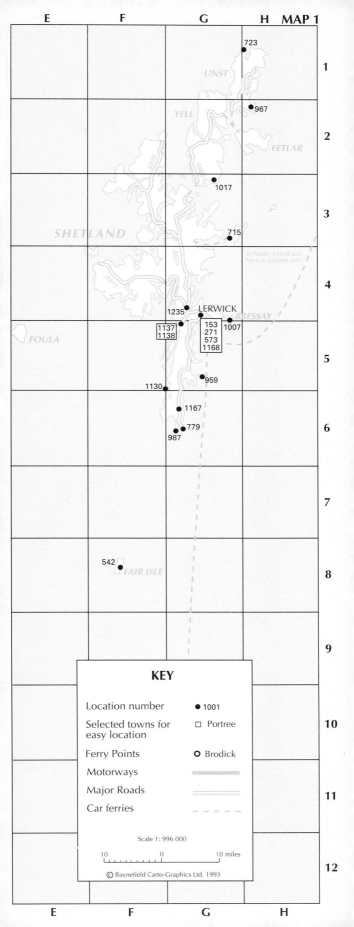

MAP 1

	E	F	G	H

1

723

UNST

YELL

967

FETLAR

2

A970

A968

1017

3

SHETLAND

715

To Faroes, Iceland and
Norway (Summer only)

4

A971

A970

1235

LERWICK

BRESSAY

1137
1138

153
271
573
1168

1007

5

FOULA

959

1130

1167

779

987

6

7

542

FAIR ISLE

8

9

KEY

Location number   ● 1001

Selected towns for   □ Portree
easy location

Ferry Points   ○ Brodick

Motorways

Major Roads

Car ferries

10

11

Scale 1: 996 000

10   0   10 miles

© Baynefield Carto-Graphics Ltd. 1993

12

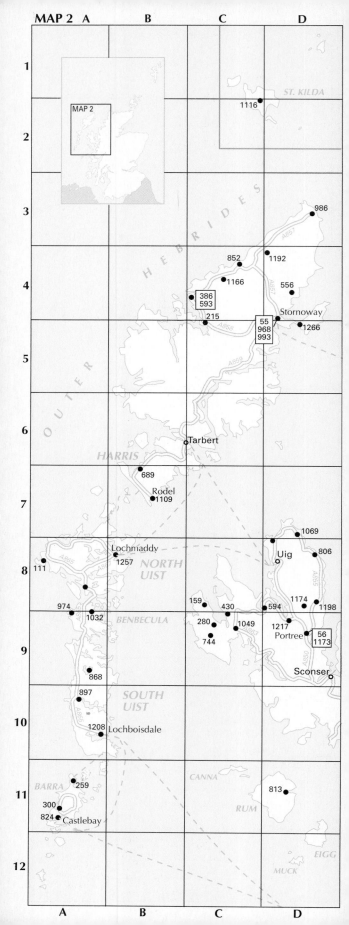

MAP 2

A   B   C   D

1

ST. KILDA

1116

2

3

HEBRIDES

986

A857

4

852   1192

1166

556

386
593

Stornoway

A867

215

A858

55
968
993

1266

5

A858

6

OUTER

Tarbert

HARRIS

689

7

Rodel

1109

1069

8

Lochmaddy

806

A865

1257

NORTH
UIST

Uig

111

A855

159   430

1174

594

1198

974

280

1049

1217

56
1173

9

1032

BENBECULA

744

Portree

868

A950

Sconser

SOUTH
UIST

897

10

A865

1208 Lochboisdale

CANNA

11

BARRA

259

813

300

RUM

824 Castlebay

EIGG

12

MUCK

A   B   C   D

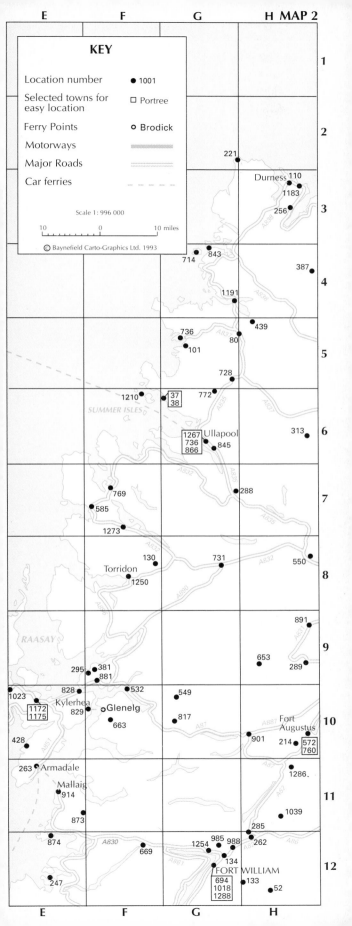

E   **F**   **G**   **H MAP 2**

1

KEY

Location number ● 1001

Selected towns for
easy location □ Portree

Ferry Points ○ Brodick

Motorways

Major Roads

Car ferries

Scale 1: 996 000

10   0   10 miles

© Baynefield Carto-Graphics Ltd. 1993

2

221

Durness 110
1183
256

3

387

714 843

4

1191

439

736 80
101

5

728

1210 772

37
38

SUMMER ISLES

313

1267 Ullapool
736 845
866

6

288

769
585
1273

7

130 731

Torridon
1250

550

8

891

653 289

9

RAASAY

295 381
881

828 532 549

1023 817

1172 Kylerhea
1175 829 Glenelg
663

Fort
Augustus

901 214 572
760

428

10

263 Armadale

1286.

Mallaig
914

11

873

1039

285

874 669 1254 985 988 262
134

247 FORT WILLIAM
694 133
1018 52
1288

12

E   **F**   **G**   **H**

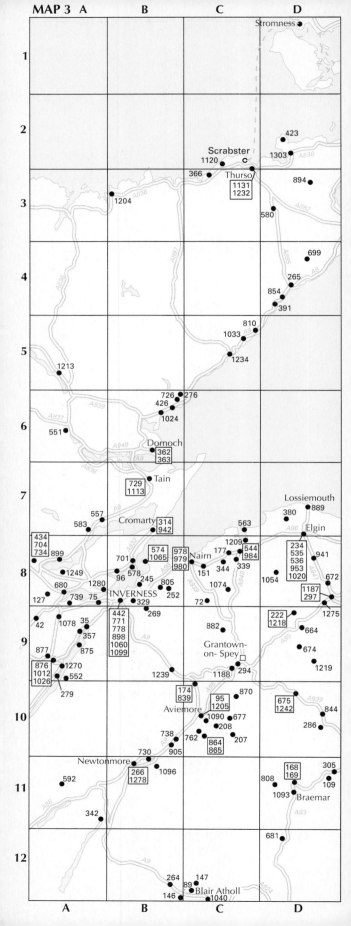

MAP 3

A   **B**   **C**   **D**

1

Stromness

2
423
1303   *A836*
Scrabster
1120   **C**

3
366   Thurso
1131
1232
894
1204   *A836*
580   *A882*

4
699
A95
265   *A9*
854
391

5
810
1033   *A9*
1213
1234

6
726   276
426
A837   *A839*
1024
551
A949
Dornoch
362
363

7
729   Tain
1113
Lossiemouth
557   380   889
583   563   Elgin
Cromarty   314   *A96*
942
434   978   234
704   899   574   979   Nairn   535
734   1065   980   177   1209   536
701   151   344   339   544   953
96   578   984   1020
680   245   805   1074   1054   941
127   1280   252   72   672
739   75   INVERNESS   329   1187
297
1275

9
442   882   222   664
42   1078   35   771   1218
877   357   778   Grantown-   674
875   898   on-Spey   1219
876   1060   1188   294
1012   1270   1099
1026   552   1239
279

10
174   870
839   95   675   844
738   1090   1205   1242   286
Aviemore   762   677
730   905   864   207
865   208

11
Newtonmore   305
592   266   168   169
1278   1096   808   109
1093   Braemar
342

12
681
A9   264   147
89   *A924*
146   1040   Blair Atholl

A   **B**   **C**   **D**

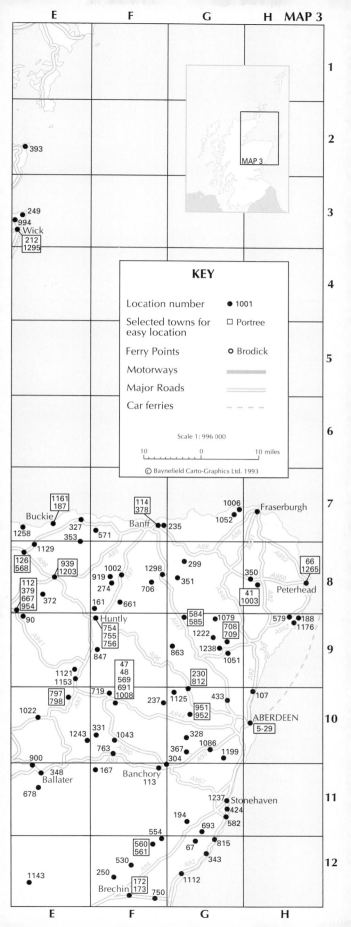

MAP 3

| | E | F | G | H |

1

2

393

3

249
994
Wick
212
1295

4

KEY

Location number	● 1001
Selected towns for easy location	□ Portree
Ferry Points	○ Brodick
Motorways	
Major Roads	
Car ferries	

Scale 1 : 996 000

10   0   10 miles

© Baynefield Carto-Graphics Ltd. 1993

5

6

7

1161
187
Buckie
1258
1006
Fraserburgh
1052
327
571
Banff
235
114
378
353

8

126
568
1129
A96
939
1203
1002
919
274
1298
706
299
351
A98
350
A950
66
1265
Peterhead
112
379
667
954
372
161
661
41
1003
A948

9

90
A941
Huntly
754
755
756
847
584
585
863
1079
1222
708
709
1238
1051
579
188
1176
A92

10

1121
1153
797
798
1022
A97
47
48
569
691
1008
719
237
1125
230
812
433
951
952
107
ABERDEEN
5-29
1243
331
1043
763
A93
328
1086
1199

11

900
348
Ballater
678
167
Banchory
113
A857
1237
Stonehaven
424
582
194
693

12

1143
530
250
560
561
Brechin
172
173
750
A94
67
343
1112
815
554

| | E | F | G | H |

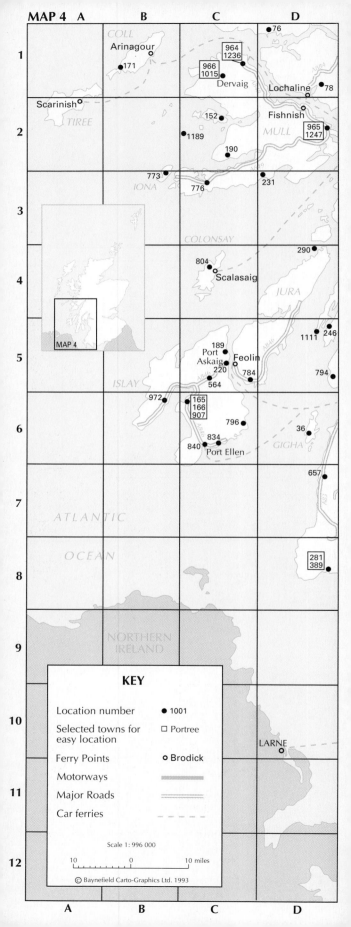

MAP 4

	A	B	C	D

1
COLL
Arinagour ○
● 171
964 / 1236
966 / 1015
Dervaig
● 76
Lochaline ○ ● 78

2
Scarinish ○
TIREE
● 152
● 1189
● 190
Fishnish ○
MULL
965 / 1247

3
● 773
● 776
IONA
● 231

COLONSAY

4
● 290
804 ●
Scalasaig ○
JURA

5
189 ●
Port Askaig
Feolin ○
220 ●
● 784
564 ●
ISLAY
1111 ● ● 246
● 794

6
972 ●
165 / 166 / 907
● 796
834 ●
840 ●
Port Ellen
● 36
GIGHA

7
ATLANTIC
● 657

8
OCEAN
281 / 389 ●

9
NORTHERN IRELAND

10
LARNE ○

KEY

Location number	● 1001
Selected towns for easy location	□ Portree
Ferry Points	○ Brodick
Motorways	
Major Roads	
Car ferries	

Scale 1 : 996 000

10   0   10 miles

© Bayfield Carto-Graphics Ltd. 1993

11

12

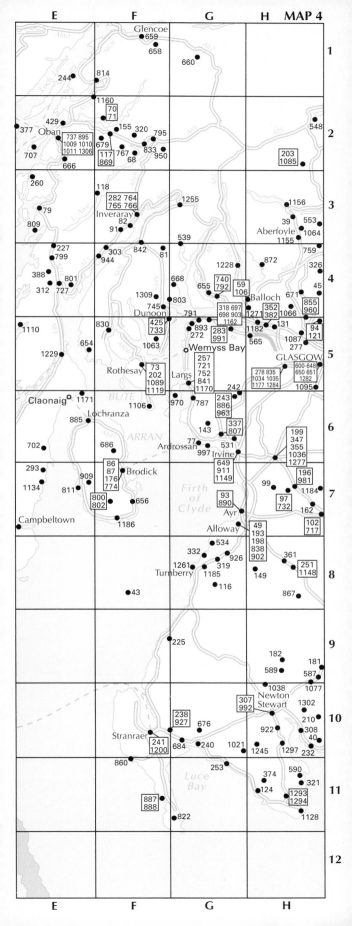

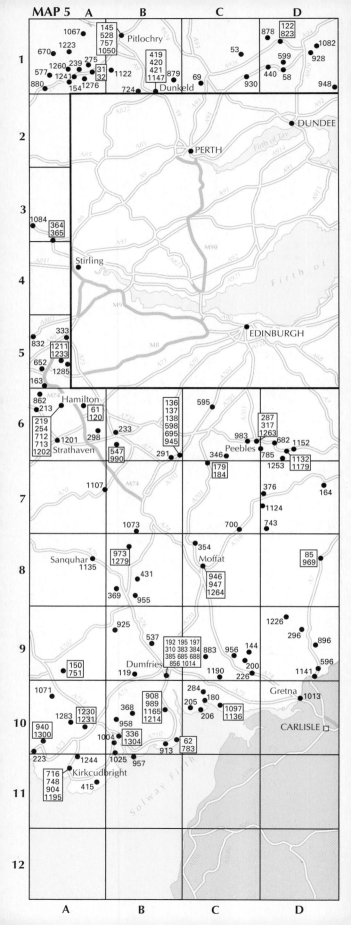

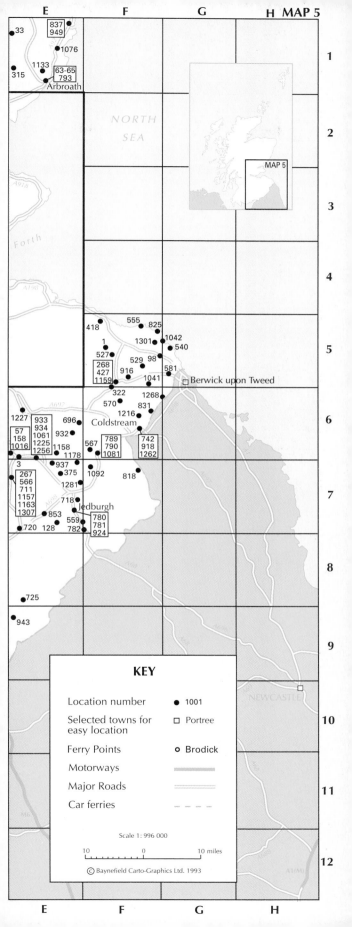

MAP 5

E F G H

1

33
837
949
1076
1133
315
63-65
793
Arbroath

2

NORTH
SEA

MAP 5

3

A918

Forth

A198

4

418
555
825
1301
1042
1
540
527
529
98
268
427
1159
916
581
1041
Berwick upon Tweed

5

322
1268
570
831
1227
1216
933
696
Coldstream
57
934
932
158
1061
1158
567
789
790
1081
742
918
1262
1016
1225
1256
1178
3
937
375
1092
818
267
566
1281
711
718
1157
1163
1307
Jedburgh
720
853
128
559
782
780
781
924

6

7

8

725

9

943

KEY

Location number   ● 1001

Selected towns for   □ Portree
easy location

Ferry Points   ○ Brodick

Motorways

Major Roads

Car ferries   – – –

NEWCASTLE

10

11

Scale 1: 996 000

10   0   10 miles

© Baynefield Carto-Graphics Ltd. 1993

12

E F G H

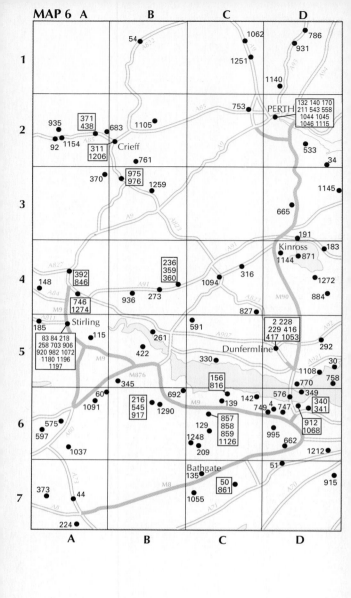

MAP 6

	A	B	C	D
1		54	1062 1251	786 931 1140
2	935 92 1154	371 438 683 1105 311 1206 Crieff 761	753	PERTH 132 140 170 211 543 558 1044 1045 1046 1115 533 34
3		370 975 976 1259		1145 665 191
4	148 392 846 746 1274	236 359 360 936 273	1094 316 827	Kinross 183 1144 871 1272 884
5	185 Stirling 83 84 218 258 703 906 920 982 1072 1180 1196 1197 115	261 422	591 330 Dunfermline 156 816	2 228 229 416 417 1053 292 1108 770 30 758
6	60 1091 575 597 1037	345 216 545 917 1290 692	139 142 129 857 858 859 1126 1248 209	576 349 4 747 340 341 749 912 1068 995 662 1212
7	373 44 224	Bathgate 135	50 861 1055	51 915

MAP 6

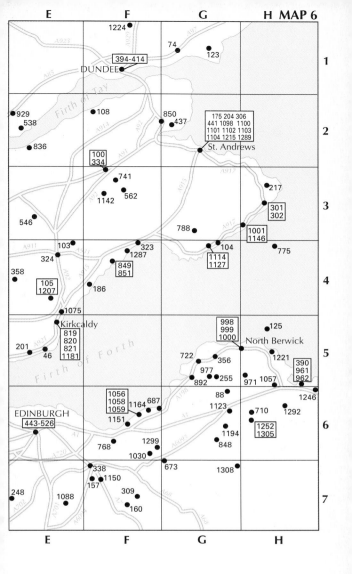

MAP 6

	E	F	G	H

1
1224
74
123
394-414
DUNDEE

2
929
538
108
850
437
175 204 306
441 1098 1100
1101 1102 1103
1104 1215 1289
St. Andrews
836
100
334

3
741
562
1142
546
788
217
301
302
1001
1146

4
103
324
323
1287
104
1114
1127
775
358
849
851
105
1207
186
1075

5
Kirkcaldy
819
820
821
1181
201
46
125
North Berwick
1221
998
999
1000
722
356
390
961
962
977
892
255
971 1057
1246

6
1056
1058
1059
1164 687
1151
88
1123
EDINBURGH
443-526
710
1292
1252
1305
768
1299
1030
1194
848

7
338
157 1150
673
1308
248
1088
309
160

Firth of Tay
Firth of Forth

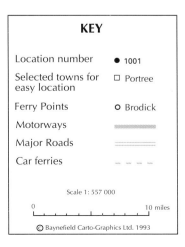

KEY

Location number	● 1001
Selected towns for easy location	□ Portree
Ferry Points	○ Brodick
Motorways	
Major Roads	
Car ferries	

Scale 1: 557 000

0   10 miles

© Baynefield Carto-Graphics Ltd. 1993

TOURING
◄ GUIDE TO ►
SCOTLAND

1 ABBEY ST BATHANS TROUT FARM 5F5

&. A T

Turn off A1 at Grantshouse (A6112 to Duns), take 1st or 2nd unclassified road to right. Signposted Abbey St Bathans thereafter. Easter-Sept. Apr May, Sept: Open weekends and bank holidays, 1300-1700. June July, Aug: Open daily, 1300-1700. Entrance charge (includes feed for fish). Parking available. Gift shop. Restaurant.
Tel: (036 14) 203.

Trout farm and shop selling fresh and smoked trout, and other products. Gallery with display of work by Scottish craftsmen and artists. Pictish broch and site of Cistercian priory. Riverside walks through oak woodlands up to moorland.

2 ABBOT HOUSE HERITAGE CENTRE 6D5

NB. Expected to open Spring 1994.
Maygate, Dunfermline. All year, daily 1000-1700. Abbot's Kitchen restaurant. Book and gift shop. Tel: (0383) 733266.

A new heritage centre in one of Scotland's oldest town houses, parts of which date from 1460, in the heart of Scotland's ancient capital. Abbot House, beside historic Dunfermline Abbey where kings and queens including St Margaret and Robert the Bruce are buried, has been restored and developed to tell the story of Dunfermline and Scotland in an entertaining and interesting way.

3 ABBOTSFORD HOUSE 5E6

&. P T

A7, 2½m SSE of Galashiels. Mid Mar-end Oct. Mon-Sat 1000-1700, Sun 1400-1700. Entrance charge. Concessions for groups over 8. Parking available. Bus from Galashiels. Gardens, tearoom, gift shop. Tel: (0896) 2043.

Sir Walter Scott purchased the Cartley Hall farmhouse on the banks of the Tweed in 1812. In 1822 the old house was demolished, and replaced with the main block of Abbotsford as it is today. His collection of historic relics includes armour and weapons, Rob Roy's gun, Montrose's sword and Prince Charlie's quaich. Visitors see his study, library with over 9,000 rare volumes, armouries, and the dining room where Sir Walter died on 21 September 1832.

4 ABERCORN CHURCH 6D6

&.

Off unclassified road 2m N of A904, by Hopetoun, South Queensferry. All year, daily. Free. Parking available. Tel: 031-331 1869.

Ancient church dedicated to St Serf, founded in 5th century. Abercorn was the first bishopric in Scotland, dating from AD 681. Present building, on site of 7th century monastery, dates from 12th century (see Norman Arch in S wall), reconstructed in 1579 and 1893. Fragments and broken 8th century Anglian crosses and hogback burial monuments; Duddingston aisle 1603; Binns aisle 1618. Also Hopetoun gallery and retiring rooms: 1704.

5 ABERDEEN AMUSEMENT PARK 3H10

Beach Boulevard, Aberdeen. Easter-Sept. Open daily during Easter holidays, July, Aug. Entrance charge. Parking available. Beach bus. Gift shop. Tel: (0224) 581909.

Largest amusement park in Scotland with ten major rides, eight children's rides, large adventure playground, arcades, video games, roller coaster. Wristband ticket gives use of all rides and attractions.

6 ABERDEEN ARTS CENTRE GALLERY   3H10

♿ P T

33 King Street. Jan-Dec. Mon-Sat, 1000-1700. Inductive loop.
Tel: (0224) 635208.

Exhibitions, mainly by local artists, photographers and craftsmen. Exhibitions change monthly, additional smaller displays from time to time.

---

7 ABERDEEN ART GALLERY   3H10

Schoolhill. All year. Mon-Sat 1000-1700 (Thu 1000-2000), Sun 1400-1700. Free. Lift for disabled visitors to the first floor galleries and gives access to McBey print room and reference library. Guide dogs permitted. Gallery shop. Coffee shop. Tel: (0224) 646333.

Permanent collection of 18th, 19th and 20th century art with the emphasis on contemporary works. A full programme of special exhibitions. Music, dance, poetry, events, film, reference library, print room.

---

8 ABERDEEN, BEACH LEISURE COMPLEX   3H10

♿ T

Beach Promenade. Jan-Dec. Daily. Parking available. Public transport. Beach Leisure Centre: Creche, cafe and bar. Inductive loop. Tel: (0224) 647647.
Linx Ice Arena: Skate-in cafeteria, lounge bar. Tel: (0224) 649930.

Beach Leisure Centre has exotic leisure pool, jacuzzi, four flumes, including one of the longest enclosed flumes in the world. Health suite and fully-equipped sports hall including 25ft practice climbing wall. Linx Ice Arena, 56 metres by 26 metres, provides curling, discos, professional instruction, ice hockey and skating clubs, as well as open skating. Spectator seating for 1,000.

---

9 ABERDEEN, BRIDGE OF DEE   3H10

Built in 1520s by Bishop Gavin Dunbar in James V's reign. Its seven arches span 400 feet and it formerly carried the main road south. The medieval solidity of the structure is enlivened by heraldic carvings.

Brig O' Balgownie

10 ABERDEEN, BRIG O' BALGOWNIE   3H10

At Bridge of Don, N of Aberdeen, upstream of main A92 bridge.

Also known as the 'Auld Brig o' Don', this massive arch, 62 feet wide, spans a deep pool of the river and is backed by fine woods. It was completed c. 1320 and repaired in 1607. In 1605 Sir Alexander Hay endowed the bridge with a small property, which has so increased in value that it built the New Bridge of Don (1830), a little lower down, at a cost of £26,000, bore most of the cost of the Victoria Bridge, and contributed to many other public works. Now closed to motor vehicles.

**11 ABERDEEN, CROMBIE
WOOLLEN MILL**   **3H10**

*Signposted off Great Northern Road (A96) at Woodside. Open 7 days,
Mon-Sat 0900-1630, Sun 1200-1630. Closed Christmas and New Year.
Free. Licensed restaurant and coffee shop. Parking available.
Tel: (0224) 483201.*

Visit the original home of the famous Crombie cloth,
coats etc. Award-winning museum and visitor centre.
Audio-visual display. A chance to buy cloth, wool and
ready-made clothes at the picturesque former mill by the
River Don in Aberdeen. Fishing and riverside walks.

**12 ABERDEEN, CRUICKSHANK
BOTANIC GARDEN**   **3H10**

& *Chanonry, Old Aberdeen. Jan-Dec, Mon-Fri 0900-1630, May-Sep,
P Sat and Sun 1400-1700. Free.
Tel: (0224) 272704.*

Extensive collection of shrubs, herbaceous and Alpine
plants, heather and succulents. Rock and water
gardens.

---

13 ABERDEEN, JAMES DUN'S HOUSE   **3H10**

*Schoolhill. All year. Mon-Sat 1000-1700. Free.
Tel: (0224) 646333.*

This former residence of James Dun, master and rector
of Aberdeen Grammar School, is now a museum
featuring special temporary exhibitions of particular
interest to families. Museum shop.

**14 ABERDEEN, DUTHIE PARK
AND WINTER GARDENS**   **3H10**

& *Polmuir Road/Riverside Drive. Jan-Dec, daily, 1000 until 30 minutes
T before dusk. Free. Restaurant and dining room. Plant shop.
Tel: (0224) 585310.*

Beautifully laid out 50-acre park with floral displays in
all seasons including a 'rose mountain'. Children's
play area. Two boating ponds and many interesting
sculptures and monuments. The modern
conservatories known as the Winter Gardens feature
exotic plants, flowers, birds, fish and turtles. Cactus
house with some 600 species and varieties of cacti and
succulents, and a Japanese Garden designed in
traditional style. Three-house conservatory with a
major collection of ferns, plus shrubs, alpine plants,
water and sculpture features and a sunken bandstand.

---

15 ABERDEEN FAMILY HISTORY SHOP   **3H10**

*152/164 King Street. Jan-Dec. Mon-Fri 1000-1600, Sat 1000-1300.
Tel: (0224) 646323.*

Bookshop and advice centre for members of the public
starting research into family history, attached to library
(private) of Aberdeen and North-East Scotland Family
History.

---

16 ABERDEEN, FISHMARKET   **3H10**

Off Market Street. Tel: (0224) 897744.

Aberdeen is one of the major fishing ports of Britain,
landing hundreds of tons of fish daily. Every morning
(Mon-Fri) the fishing fleets unload their catches,
which are auctioned off amid tense bustle. Best visited
between 0700-0800 (Mon-Fri only).

17 ABERDEEN, GORDON HIGHLANDERS' REGIMENTAL MUSEUM   3H10

Viewfield Road. May-Sept. Tues & Thurs, 1300-1630, third Sun in month, 1400-1600. Other times by appointment. Free (donation box). Car parking available. Shop. Tel: (0224) 318174.

Displays of regimental uniforms, colours, weapons, silver and pictures.

18 ABERDEEN, HIS MAJESTY'S THEATRE   3H10

Rosemount Viaduct in city centre. Entrance charges vary according to performance. Parking nearby. Inductive loop. Tel: Box Office (0224) 641122.

Fine theatre building, designed by Frank Matcham and opened in 1906. Wide range of productions from opera and ballet to summer revue and the annual pantomime. Organised tours for schools, workshops and talks.

19 ABERDEEN, JONAH'S JOURNEY   3H10

Rosemount Place, Aberdeen. Apr-Sept, Mon-Fri 1000-1600; Oct-Mar, Mon-Fri 1000-1400. Sat/Sun by arrangement. Closed public holidays. July, please check with Aberdeen Tourist Information Centre. Parking available. Coffee lounge. Shop. Tel: (0224) 647614.

Activity-based learning centre on aspects of life in Bible times; ideal for children as they can dress-up, grind grain, spin, weave. Also they can visit a well, a nomad's tent, Israelite house, workshop, etc.

King's College

20 ABERDEEN, KING'S COLLEGE   3H10

High Street, Old Aberdeen. Free. (University of Aberdeen).

Founded 1494. The chapel, famous for its rich woodwork, is 16th century and the notable 'crown' tower is 17th century.

21 ABERDEEN, KIRK OF ST NICHOLAS 3H10

&

A

P

T

On a site bounded by Back Wynd, Schoolhill, Correction Wynd and Union Street. May-Sept (main door access) Mon-Fri 1200-1600, Sat 1300-1500. Oct-Apr (access through office) Mon-Fri 1000-1300. Sunday service, Jan-Dec 1100. Free (donation box). Small shop. Tel: (0224) 643494.

St Nicholas, the original parish church (locally known as 'the mither kirk'), is still an active place of worship. Although much damaged at the Reformation, the fabric of the church still incorporates 12th century masonry in the transepts, a 15th century vaulted lower church, the rebuilt nave (part of the West Kirk, designed by James Gibbs in 1755), the rebuilt choir (East Kirk, 1837-1874). Features include medieval effigies, wall and floor monuments, 17th century needlework panels, woodwork from the 16th to the 20th centuries. The north transept was refurbished in 1990 by the oil industry, winning a Saltire Society award. The 48-bell carillon is regularly heard throughout the city centre.

22 ABERDEEN, MARISCHAL MUSEUM 3H10

Marischal College, Broad Street. Jan-Dec, Mon-Fri 1000-1700, Sun 1400-1700. Free. Tel: (0224) 273131.

An imposing granite structure of the 19th century. In the quadrangle, entered by a fine archway, are older buildings of 1836-44, with the graceful Mitchell Tower. The Marischal Museum houses local, classical, Egyptian and Chinese antiquities, and a general ethnographic collection.

23 ABERDEEN, PEACOCK PRINTMAKERS 3H10

&

T

21 Castle Street. Jan-Dec, exc 2 weeks over Christmas. Mon-Sat 0930-1730. Free. Shop. Tel: (0224) 639539.

Printmaking workshop, gallery showing art related to North-East Scotland, small museum, shop selling prints and maps. Tours and demonstration of printmaking facilities on request.

24 ABERDEEN, PROVOST ROSS'S HOUSE/ MARITIME MUSEUM 3H10

&

T

Shiprow. NTS Visitor Centre open May-Sept, Mon-Sat 1000-1600. Free. Tel: (0224) 572215.
Maritime Museum open Jan-Dec, Mon-Sat 1000-1700. Shop. Special exhibitions Oct-Mar. Tel: (0224) 585788.

Built in 1593, Provost Ross's House is the third oldest house in Aberdeen. NTS Visitor Centre includes a presentation on the Trust's Grampian properties. Aberdeen Maritime Museum, within Provost Ross's House, uses models, paintings and audio-visual displays to tell the story of local shipbuilding, the fishing industry, and North Sea oil and gas developments.

Provost Ross's House: see No 24

Provost Skene's House

**25 ABERDEEN, PROVOST SKENE'S
HOUSE**   3H10

*Guestrow, off Broad Street. Jan-Dec. Mon-Sat 1000-1700. Free.
Parking available. Refreshments in Provost Skene's Kitchen.
Tel: (0224) 641086.*

Erected in the 16th century, this house bears the name
of its most notable owner, Sir George Skene, Provost
of Aberdeen 1676-1685. Remarkable painted ceilings
and interesting relics. Period rooms suitably furnished
and displays of local history. A video gives an
introduction to the house and its history.

**26 ABERDEEN, ST MACHAR'S
CATHEDRAL**   3H10

*Chanonry, Old Aberdeen. Jan-Dec. Daily, 0900-1700. Free.
Parking available. Tel: (0224) 485988.*

The building, mainly 15th century, is a granite
structure of simple, austere grandeur. Two notable
features are the West Front with its twin castellated
towers, and the painted wooden Heraldic Ceiling in
the nave, dated 1520. The nave is in use as a parish
church.

**27 ABERDEEN,
ST MARY'S CATHEDRAL**   3H10

*20 Huntly Street. Jan-Dec. Daily, 0830-1600 (winter), 0830-1700
(summer). Bookshop.*

Dedicated in 1860 as a church for all the Catholics in
Aberdeen, the architecture of St Mary's is Gothic in
style, with a single elegant spire. The High Altar and
four Side Altars are embellished with tapestries and
paintings by contemporary Scottish artists, depicting
the church's involvement in the community. Stained
West Window depicts the fifteen mysteries of the
Rosary. Fine 19th century organ. Entrance includes a
modern engraved glass window by David Gulland,
depicting the martyr St John Ogilvie.

**28 ABERDEEN, SATROSPHERE,
THE DISCOVERY PLACE**   3H10

*West end of Union Street in Justice Mill Lane. Open all year. Mon-Sat
1000-1600, Sun 1330-1700, closed Tues during school term. Entrance
charge, group discount on application. Small café and seating area. Shop
selling science-based toys and gifts. Parking available. Tel: (0224) 213232.*

'Hands-on' science & technology centre with between
70 and 100 do-it-yourself experiments, exploring
sound, light, energy and the environment. Special
events every two to three months.

29 ABERDEEN, UNIVERSITY ZOOLOGY MUSEUM 3H10

Along King Street, left at roundabout, situated at corner of Tillydrone Avenue and St Machar's Drive. Jan-Dec (exc Christmas and New Year), Mon-Fri 0900-1700. Free. Parking available. Tel: (0224) 272850.

A general collection of exhibits on the animal kingdom, with particular emphasis on British birds and insects. The Botany Department gardens are adjacent. Disabled visitors welcome, but prior notice required.

30 ABERDOUR CASTLE 6D5

At Aberdour, on A921, 5m E of Forth Bridge. Opening standard, except closed Thurs pm & Fridays in winter. Entrance charge. Group concessions. (HS) Tel: 031-244 3101.

ASVA

Overlooking the harbour at Aberdour, the oldest part is the tower, which dates back to the 14th century. To this other buildings were added in succeeding centuries. A fine circular doocot stands nearby, and here also is St Fillans Parish Church, part Norman, part 16th century. Disabled access to grounds only.

31 ABERFELDY DISTILLERY 5A1

On A827 E of Aberfeldy. Jan-Dec (exc Christmas and New Year). Mon-Fri, 0930-1630. Restricted opening in winter. Free. Parking available. Tel: (0887) 820330.

Distillery in a natural landscape on the banks of the River Tay, opened in 1898 by John and Thomas Dewar, sons of John Dewar, one of the early pioneers of whisky blending. Tours from reception centre illustrate processes of malt whisky distillation and maturation.

32 ABERFELDY WATER MILL 5A1

Mill Street. Easter-Oct. Mon-Sat 1000-1730, Sun 1200-1730. Entrance charge. Parking available. Shop. Restaurant. Tel: (0887) 820803.

Working oatmeal mill with interpretative gallery and video presentation. Tours stress the importance of mills and milling in the social history of Scotland.

33 ABERLEMNO SCULPTURED STONES 5E1

At Aberlemno, B9134. 6m NE of Forfar. All times. Free. (HS) Tel: 031-244 3101.

In the churchyard is a splendid upright cross-slab with Pictish symbols; three other stones stand beside the road.

34 ABERNETHY ROUND TOWER 6D2

At Abernethy, A913, 9m SE of Perth. Free: apply Keykeeper. (HS) Tel: 031-244 3101.

A round tower, 74 feet high, dating from the 11th century. Tradition has it that Malcolm Canmore did homage to William the Conqueror here. Beside it is a Pictish symbol stone. (See also No 173).

35 ABRIACHAN GARDEN NURSERY 3A9

North shore of Loch Ness, 9 miles west of Inverness on A82. Jan-Dec (exc Christmas and New Year). 0900-1900 or dusk. Parking available. Plants for sale in nursery. Tel: (046 386) 232.

Extensive gardens on shores of Loch Ness. Interesting and careful plantings in beds terraced up hillside. Woodland walks. St Columba's Font (historic stone) on site.

Achamore House Gardens

36 ACHAMORE HOUSE GARDENS 4D6

&
A
P
T

Isle of Gigha, W of Kintyre. All year, daily, 1000-dusk.
Entrance charge. (Gardens only — house not open to the public).
Parking available. Car and passenger ferry from Tayinloan.
Tel: (058 35) 254/(058 35) 267.

Rhododendrons, camellias and many semi-tropical
shrubs and plants may be seen at these gardens
developed over the past 40 years. Elsewhere on this
fertile island, see the ruined church at Kilchattan,
which dates back to the 13th century.

Achnaba Church: see No 71.

37 ACHILTIBUIE HYDROPONICUM 2G6

&
A
P
T

Achiltibuie, 26 miles NW of Ullapool. Easter-Sept. Daily tours at 1000,
1200, 1400, 1700. Entrance charge. Parking available. Shop.
Refreshments. Tel: (085 482) 202.

Guided tours tell the story of Robert Irvine's 'Garden
of the Future' — a garden without soil. Strawberries
hang overhead, bananas, figs, grapes, lemons, flowers,
herbs and vegetables all grow happily in this remote
corner of Scotland. Tours last approximately 45
minutes. Hydroponic growing kits and souvenirs
available.

38 ACHILTIBUIE SMOKEHOUSE 2G6

Altandhu, 5 miles west of Achiltibuie, NW of Ullapool. Jan-Dec. Mon-
Sat 0930-1700. Parking available. Shop selling Summer Isles Foods.
Tel: (085 482) 353.

Operating salmon/kipper smokehouse with viewing
gallery, so that visitors can learn about salmon
filleting, salmon/kipper smoking, slicing and packing.

39 ACHRAY FOREST DRIVE 4H3

Off A821, 4m N of Aberfoyle. Easter-Oct. Daily 1000-1800.
Entrance charge per car. Tel: (087 72) 258.

Drive on Forest Enterprise roads into the heart of
woodlands offering panoramic views of the Trossachs.
This mixed woodland of conifers, oak and birch
combines conservation and recreation with large-scale
landscaping and timber production. Picnic sites, walks
and car parks. Toilets and play area midway along
drive. Guided tours during Trossachs Festival—details
from Queen Elizabeth Forest Park Visitor Centre.
(See No 1064).

**40 KATHRYN ADE
DESIGNER JEWELLERY** 4H10

  ♿
A

*From A75, follow signs to Cairnholy Monument. Jan-Dec. Daily
1000-1900. Car parking available. Jewellery for sale. Tel: (055 724) 249.*

Working jewellery studio, specialising in handmade,
ethnic and exclusive beads.

---

41 ADEN COUNTRY PARK 3H8

♿
P
T

*On A950 between Old Deer and Mintlaw, 30m N of Aberdeen.
Jan-Dec. Daily, 0700-2200. Wildlife Centre, May-Sept, weekends only,
1400-1700. Free. Tearoom. Parking available.
Tel: (0771) 22857.*

Country park of 230 acres containing woodland
walks, nature trail, wildlife centre, ranger service,
orienteering course, garden for partially sighted,
adventure playground, picnic areas. Other facilities
include cafeteria, craft shop, tourist information centre
and "Best Caravan Park in Scotland" 1992. It is home
of the award-winning North East of Scotland
Agricultural Heritage Centre (See No 1003).

---

42 AIGAS DAM FISH LIFT 3A8

✖

*Aigas Power Station, 3 miles W of Beauly on A831 to Cannich.
June-Oct exc public holidays. Mon-Fri 1000-1100, 1445-1545. Free.
Car parking only. Tel: (0463) 782412.*

Hydro Electric's Aigas Power Station and Dam are
situated on the River Beauly. This river is known for
migratory salmon which return from the Atlantic
Ocean to spawn in the autumn. The Borland type fish
lift is a feature of Aigas Dam that allows migratory
fish free access to the upper river. This one is fitted
with a viewing chamber, so that the salmon can be
seen effortlessly rising from the lower portion of the
river to the upper reservoir to reach the spawning
grounds.

---

43 AILSA CRAIG 4F8

✖

*Island in Firth of Clyde, 10m W of Girvan. Visitors must obtain
permission from the Marquess of Ailsa, the Factor, Cassillis Estates,
Maybole Castle, 4 High Street, Maybole. Tel. (0655) 82103.*

A granite island rock, 1,114 feet high with a
circumference of 2 miles. The rock itself was used to
make some of the finest curling stones and the island
has a gannetry and colonies of guillemots and other
seabirds.

---

44 AIRDRIE OBSERVATORY 5A6

✖

*Public Library, Wellwynd. Meetings of ASTRA every Friday exc public
holidays, in Airdrie Arts Centre, Anderson Street, with access to
Observatory on clear nights. Visits at other times by arrangement.
Entrance free to visitors, charge for ASTRA membership. Parking
available. Shop. Refreshments at meetings. Tel: (0236) 763221.*

Original observatory with 3-inch refractor, founded
1895. After the new Airdrie Library opened in 1920, a
6-inch Cook refractor was donated anonymously, and
set up in 1936. A new dome was fitted after storm
damage in 1987. The telescope was refurbished by
members of the Association in Scotland to Research
into Astronautics Ltd (ASTRA), and the society
became curators of the observatory for the district
council.

45   ALDESSAN GALLERY   4H5

&
T

The Clachan, Campsie Glen, 3 miles east of Strathblane on A891. Jan-Dec, exc Christmas and New Year. Mon-Fri 1100-1730, Sat & Sun 1100-2000. Parking available. Shop. Coffee shop with light meals.

Gallery and batik studio in Grade B listed building shows monthly exhibitions of contemporary art. Craft area specialising in Scottish goods. Silk batik is produced in the studio, and workshop classes can be arranged. Campsie Glen has walks and waterfalls, historic graveyard. Conservation area. Adjoining craft workshops include stained glass, jewellery, violin and guitar-making, sculptor-in-residence.

46   ALEXANDER III MONUMENT   6E5

By A921 S of Kinghorn at Pettycur Promontory. All times. Free. Parking available.

On the King's Crag, a monument marks the place where Alexander III was killed in a fall from his horse in 1286.

47   ALFORD HERITAGE CENTRE   3F10

&
T

Mart Road, Alford. 25 miles W of Aberdeen on A944. Apr-Sep, Mon-Sat 1000-1700, Sun 1300-1700. Entrance charge. Parking available. Refreshments. Tel: (097 55) 62906.

Extensive exhibition of agricultural and rural life, mounted by Alford and Donside Heritage Association.

48   ALFORD VALLEY RAILWAY   3F10

&
A
T

Alford Station. Apr, May, Sept, weekends only. June, July, Aug, daily. First train 1100, last train 1630. Parking available. Tel: (097 55) 62326.

Narrow gauge railway running from restored Alford Station to Haughton Country Park, approx 1 mile (see No 719) and Haughton Country Park to Murray Park (1 mile). Each trip takes around 30 mins. The station building itself forms part of Grampian Transport Museum, with memorabilia, preserved ticket office, and tourist information centre (see No 691).

49   ALLOWAY AULD KIRK   4G7

In Alloway, 2½m S of Ayr. All reasonable times. Tours by prior arrangement. Free. Tel: (0292) 441252 (mornings).

Ancient church, a ruin in Burns' day, where his father William Burns is buried. Through its window, Tam saw the dancing witches and warlocks in the poem *Tam o' Shanter.*

50 ALMOND VALLEY HERITAGE CENTRE 6C7

Millfield, Kirkton North, at western edge of Livingston off A705. Jan-Dec. Daily 1000-1700. Entrance charge. Group discount. Parking available. Shop. Tearoom. Tel: (0506) 414957.

Through museum displays and a range of open-air features extending over 16 acres, the Heritage Centre brings West Lothian's past to life. Traditional farm steading with friendly animals, working watermill, oil worker's cottage and 'mine' in the shale oil museum. Old farm machinery and narrow gauge railway. Horse-drawn cart rides to outlying fields, nature trail, play park, picnic area.

51 ALMONDELL AND CALDERWOOD COUNTRY PARK 6D7

On B7015 (A71) at East Calder or off A89 at Broxburn. 12m SSW of Edinburgh. Park open Jan-Dec, daily. Visitor Centre opening hours: Apr-Sep Mon-Wed 0900-1700, Thur 0900-1600, Sun 1030-1800. Oct-Mar Mon-Thur. 0900-1700, Sun 1000-1630. Closed for lunch 1200-1300. Free except for barbecues (small booking charge). Parking available. Tel: (0506) 882254.

Extensive riverside and woodland walks in former estate, with large picnic and grassy areas. Visitor Centre housed in old stable block has large freshwater aquarium, displays on natural and local history, and short slide show. Ranger Service, guided walks programme.

52 THE ALUMINIUM STORY (KINLOCHLEVEN VISITOR CENTRE & LIBRARY) 2H12

Linnhe Road, Kinlochleven. 21 miles S of Fort William on B863 — turn off A82 at North Ballachulish. Mid-April-mid Oct, Mon-Fri 1000-1700, Sat & Sun 1200-1630. Mid-Oct-mid-Apr, Tues & Thur 1000-1200, 1300-1700, Wed, Fri, Sat 1000-1200, 1300-1500. Free. Tel: (085 54) 663.

Imaginative audio-visual display and video presentation telling the story of an industry and a community — how the combination of hilly terrain, water and human ingenuity brought aluminium smelting to Kinlochleven over 80 years ago. Outside, a giant sundial.

53 ALYTH MUSEUM 5C1

Off A94, 3m N of Meigle. May-Sep, Wed-Sun 1300-1700. Free. Tel: (0738) 32488 (Perth Museum).

A collection of rural agricultural and domestic artefacts.

54 AMULREE PARISH CHURCH 6B1

On A822 between Crieff and Dunkeld or Aberfeldy. Jan-Dec. Daily, during daylight hours. Door is at end of church furthest from gate. From July-Sept, Sunday services weekly at 0945; from Oct-June, fortnightly at 1415. Free. Parking available.

Amulree Parish Church was founded in 1743 as a Mission Church by the Society for the Propagation of Christian Knowledge (SPCK), when it was realised there was no regular preacher and no place of worship for 12 miles in any direction. Over the years, the population has shrunk — some emigrated to Ontario, Canada, and a display in the church, together with family lists, helps people looking for family roots.

55 AN LANNTAIR GALLERY 2D4

Town Hall, South Beach Street, Stornoway. All year, Mon-Sat 1000-1730. Coffee shop closes 1630. Free. Parking available. Tel: (0851) 703307.

The gallery operates a lively contemporary and traditional exhibitions programme, which changes monthly. The visual arts programme is supplemented by musical, literary and performing events with a strong emphasis on traditional Gaelic culture.

56 AN TUIREANN ARTS CENTRE 2D9

Struan Road, Portree, Isle of Skye. Jan-Dec. Tues-Sat 1000-1700, later in summer. Charges for performances, exhibitions free. Parking available. Restaurant. Tel: (0478) 3306.

A community arts centre established in 1991, promoting indigenous work as well as exhibitions, performing arts and workshops from beyond the local area. Residential arts schools are staged in other venues on the island. Cafeteria in the gallery, landscaped picnic area. Children and disabled visitors welcome.

57 PETER ANDERSON OF SCOTLAND CASHMERE WOOLLEN MILL AND MUSEUM 5E7

Nether Mill, Huddersfield Street, Galashiels. Jan-Dec, exc Christmas & New Year. Shop & museum: Mon-Sat 0900-1700, Sun (Jun-Sep only) 1200-1700. Tours: Mon-Fri (exc Fri pm), 1030, 1130, 1330, 1430. Entrance charge. Group discount. Parking available. Mill shop. Tel: (0896) 2091.

From small beginnings in a weaving shop at the back of a church, Peter Anderson has expanded over a century to the present mill complex where the whole process of tweed manufacture — except for carding and spinning — is carried out. In a 40-minute tour, visitors can see all aspects of production from spun yarn to the finished article. The museum shows the involvement of Galashiels in the woollen trade, using photographs, traditional artefacts and machinery. Refurbished Leffell water turbine wheel is harnessed to run a weaving loom within the museum.

58 ANGUS FOLK MUSEUM 5D1

Kirkwynd, Glamis, off A94, 5m SW of Forfar. Easter weekend, May-Sept. Daily 1100-1700, last tour 1630. Entrance charge. Group discount. Parking available. (NTS) Tel: (0307) 840288.

ASVA

Kirkwynd Cottages, a row of 19th century cottages with stone-slabbed roofs, containing relics of domestic and agricultural life in the county in the 19th century and earlier. In the agricultural section are farming implements and an exhibition, 'Life on the Land'.

59 ANTARTEX VILLAGE 4H4

Lomond Industrial Estate, Balloch, Alexandria. Just off A82, opposite Vale of Leven Hospital down Heather Avenue. Jan-Dec, exc Christmas & New Year. Daily 1000-1800. Free. Parking available. Public transport. Shops. Spinning Wheel coffee shop/restaurant. Tel: (0389) 52393.

At Antartex Village, visitors can enjoy a factory tour and see sheepskin coats being made. The British Antarctic Survey Exhibition charts the advances made by explorers at the South Pole. Loch Lomond Crafts Centre allows local craftspeople to demonstrate their skills and sell direct to the public. Mill and factory shops retail classic Scottish knitwear, tartans, gifts and souvenirs from the Edinburgh Woollen Mill.

60 ANTONINE WALL 6A6

From Bo'ness to Old Kilpatrick, best seen off A803 E of Bonnybridge, 12m S of Stirling. All reasonable times. Free. (HS) Tel: 031-244 3101.

This Roman fortification stretched from Bo'ness on the Forth to Old Kilpatrick on the Clyde. Built about AD 142-143, it consisted of a turf rampart behind a ditch, with forts about every two miles. It was probably abandoned about AD 163. Remains are probably best preserved in the Falkirk/Bonnybridge area, notably Rough Castle (see No 1091 and at Bearsden, see No 1087).

61 AQUATEC 5A6

ASVA

1 Menteith Road, Motherwell. Jan-Dec, exc Christmas & New Year. Charges for activities. Group discount. Parking available. Shop. Restaurant, refreshments. Tel: (0698) 276464.

Built in 1989, Aquatec has a well-designed leisure pool with flume tyre ride, water cannon, air beds, children's beach area, lagoon, wild water channel. Leisure Ice Rink has the only Ice Tunnel in Britain, and a log fire. Health suite, gym.

62 ARBIGLAND GARDENS 5B10

By Kirkbean, off A710, 12m S of Dumfries. May-Sept. Tue-Sun, Bank holiday Mons, 1400-1800. House open afternoons Whit Week. Entrance charge, groups by arrangement. Parking available. Shop. Tearoom. Tel: (038 788) 283.

Arbigland House was built in 1755, replacing an older house nearby, so that the gardens, which extend to 15 acres, have been evolving since around 1700. Admiral John Paul Jones, 'Father of the American Navy', was the son of a gardener and worked in the gardens as a boy. His birthplace cottage is now a museum. (See No 783).

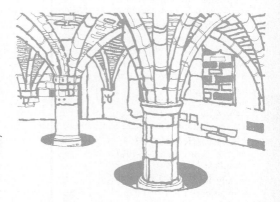

Arbroath Abbey

63 ARBROATH ABBEY 5E1

In Arbroath. Opening standard. Entrance charge. Group concessions. (HS) Tel: 031-244 3101.

Founded in 1178 by William the Lion and dedicated to St Thomas of Canterbury, it was from here that the famous Declaration of Arbroath asserting Robert the Bruce as King was issued in 1320. Important remains of the church survive; these include one of the most complete examples of an abbot's residence.

64 ARBROATH ART GALLERY 5E1

Arbroath Library, Hill Terrace. Jan-Dec, Mon, Wed 0930-2000. Tues, Thurs 0930-1800. Fri, Sat 0930-1700. Free. Shop. Tel: (0241) 75598.

Art Gallery with a permanent and touring exhibition facility, displays works from the Arbroath Collection, including watercolours and pastels by James Watterston Herald, and two fine oils by Peter Breughel II. Regularly changing programme of touring exhibitions includes contemporary works by local artists and others.

65 ARBROATH MUSEUM 5E1

Signal Tower, Ladyloan, Arbroath. Jan-Dec. Mon-Sat 1000-1700. Free. Pre-booking for groups essential. Shop. Tel: (0241) 75598.

Exhibits feature flax, engineering and fishing, the industries which made Arbroath. Shank's lawnmowers, the Arbroath Smokie and the Bellrock lighthouse are specialities. Wildlife room exhibits animals and plants from the cliffs, the shore and under the waves.

66 ARBUTHNOT MUSEUM 3H8

St Peter Street, Peterhead. Jan-Dec, exc public holidays. Mon-Sat 1000-1200, 1400-1700. Free. Shop. Tel: (0779) 77778.

Local history museum with whaling and fishing displays. Interesting coin collection, excellent Inuit collection. Exhibitions in gallery change every six weeks.

67 ARBUTHNOTT HOUSE AND GARDENS 3G12

By Laurencekirk, 3 miles W of Inverbervie on B967. Gardens open Jan-Dec, house by arrangement. Entrance charge. Group discount. Tel: (0561) 61226.

Home of the Arbuthnott family since 1160, Arbuthnott House is part 15th, part 17th and part 18th century. 17th century gardens with parterre on steep slope. Woodlands and river valley.

68 ARDANAISEIG GARDENS 4F2

E of B845, 22m E of Oban. End March-Oct, daily 1000-dusk. Entrance charge. Parking available. Tel: (086 63) 333.

Woodland Garden with fine trees and a great variety of rhododendrons, azaleas and other flowering shrubs, surrounding a Walled Garden of about one acre with a large herbaceous border. Magnificent views across Loch Awe and of Ben Cruachan.

69 ARDBLAIR CASTLE 5C1

On A923 1m W of Blairgowrie. Jan-Dec, by appointment only. Entrance charge. Parking available. Tel: (0250) 873155.

Mainly 16th-century castle on 12th-century foundations, home of the Blair Oliphant family. Jacobite relics and links with Charles Edward Stuart. Room containing relics of Lady Nairne (née Oliphant), author of *Charlie is My Darling* and other songs.

70 ARDCHATTAN GARDEN   4F2

    Adjoining Ardchattan Priory, 5 miles E of Connel Bridge. Apr-Nov.
P *Daily, dawn to dusk. Entrance charge. Parking available. Refreshments/*
T *light lunches. Tel: (063 175) 274.*

A lochside garden, restructured by the present owner
in 1950, and before that, by his mother in 1904. It
now comprises a 2-acre wild garden to the west of
Ardchattan House, with over 200 different shrubs,
including shrub roses and 30 species of sorbus, with
wild flowers. A formal garden in front of the house
leads down to Loch Etive, with two herbaceous
borders, three shrub borders, rock garden, and fine
views of Mull to the west and Ben Cruachan to the
east.

71 ARDCHATTAN PRIORY   4F2

On the N side of Lower Loch Etive, 6½m NE of Oban. Open all times.
Free. (HS) Tel: 031-244 3101.

One of the Valliscaulian houses founded in Scotland in
1230, and the meeting place in 1308 of one of Bruce's
Parliaments, among the last at which business was
conducted in Gaelic. Burned by Cromwell's soldiers in
1654, the remains include some carved stones.
Achnaba Church, near Connel, has notable central
communion pews.

72 ARDCLACH BELL TOWER   3C8

Off A939, 8½m SE of Nairn. Open all reasonable times. Free: apply
keykeeper. (HS) Tel: 031-244 3101.

A two-storey tower of 1655 whose bell summoned
worshippers to the church and warned the
neighbourhood in case of alarm.

73 ARDENCRAIG GARDENS   4F5

    At Ardencraig, by Rothesay, Isle of Bute. May-Sept, Mon-Fri 0900-1630,
A *Sat and Sun 1300-1630. Free. Parking available. Shop. Tearoom.*
T *Tel: (0700) 504644.*

Bought by the Royal Burgh of Rothesay in 1968, this
garden now produces plants for floral displays
throughout Bute. Contains propagation, educational
and show unit, aviaries containing many foreign bird
species. Ornamental ponds with interesting varieties of
fish.

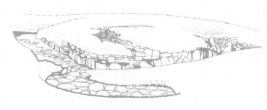

Earth - Houses

**74 ARDESTIE AND CARLUNGIE
EARTH-HOUSES**   6G1

N of A92. Ardestie: about 6m E of Dundee, at junction with B962.
Carlungie: 1m N on unclassified road to Carlungie. All times. Free. (HS)
Tel: 031-244 3101.

Two examples of large earth-houses attached to surface
dwellings. At Ardestie the gallery is curved and 80 feet
in length: the Carlungie earth-house is 150 feet long,
and is most complex; used in first centuries AD.

75 ARDFEARN NURSERY   3A8

*Bunchrew, 4 miles W of Inverness on A863. Jan-Dec. Daily 0900-1700.
Free. Parking available. Tel: (0463) 243250.*

Horticultural adviser and broadcaster Jim Sutherland
and his son Alasdair have created a small family
nursery on the shores of the Beauly Firth. Wide
variety of plants of extreme hardiness, attractive display
beds containing over 1,000 species and cultivars, with
easy access for all including wheelchairs. Sales area
with shrubs, trees, heathers, rhododendrons, conifers
and alpines.

**76 ARDNAMURCHAN NATURAL HISTORY
AND VISITOR CENTRE**   4D1

*From Salen take the B8007 for 7m to Glenborrodale. The Centre is 2m
further on. Apr-Oct, Mon-Sat 1030-1730; Sun 1200-1730. Admission
free. Parking available. Coffee shop, books and gifts.
Tel: (097 24) 254 or (097 24) 263.*

Designed for the Glasgow Garden Festival, this
attractive Douglas fir building houses static displays of
local geology and wildlife. Live television transmission
shows wildlife activity such as nesting and feeding.

77 ARDROSSAN CASTLE   4G6

*Ardrossan, on a hill overlooking Ardrossan Bay. All year, all reasonable
times. Free. Tel: (0294) 602617.*

Mid 12th-century castle on a hill with fine views of
Arran and Ailsa Craig. Castle was destroyed by
Cromwell and only part of the north tower and two
arched cellars remain.

78 ARDTORNISH ESTATE   4D1

*Morvern, Argyll. 40 miles SW of Fort William on Sound of Mull. Mar-
Oct. Estate open all day, gardens 0900-1800. Entrance charge for gardens.
Car parking only. Shop. Tel: (0967) 421288.*

Interesting Victorian Highland estate. Castle, gardens,
market garden.

79 ARDUAINE GARDEN   4E3

*20m S of Oban on the A816, joint entrance with Loch Melfort Hotel.
Jan-Dec. Daily, 0930-sunset. Entrance charge. Group concessions.
Parking available. (NTS). Tel: (085 22) 366.*

Outstanding lochside woodland garden of particular
interest to plantsmen and garden enthusiasts. Planted
early this century, Arduaine contains a noted collection
of rhododendron species, range of flowering shrubs
and trees. Lower garden displays herbaceous plantings
among ponds and streams, enhanced by marginal
plants and water lilies.

80 ARDVRECK CASTLE   2H5

A837, 11m E of Lochinver, on Loch Assynt. All reasonable times. Free.

Built c. 1490 by the MacLeods, who in the mid-13th
century obtained Assynt by marriage; the three-
storeyed ruins stand on the shores of Loch Assynt.
After his defeat at Culrain, near Bonar Bridge, in
1650, the Marquess of Montrose fled to Assynt but
was soon captured and confined here before being sent
to Edinburgh and executed.

81   ARGYLL FOREST PARK   4F4

*W and NW from Loch Long almost to Loch Fyne: A815, B839, B828
and A83. Parking available. (FC) Tel: (036 984) 666.*

Three forests — Ardgartan, Glenbranter and Benmore
— cover 60,000 acres of superb scenery. There are
scores of forest walks through old estate woodlands,
such as the famous waterfall walks of Puck's Glen and
Lauder. (See Nos 1063 and 842). The Lauder Walks,
once an outstation for the rhododendron collection for
the Royal Botanic Garden, are best viewed in late
spring when the shrubs are in bloom. Guided walks in
summer. Guidebook available in local shops.

82   ARGYLL WILDLIFE PARK   4F3

*Dalchenna. On A83, 2 miles from Inveraray. Open all year
0930-1800/dusk. Entrance charge. Tearoom. Tel: (0499) 2264/2284.*

60 acre site, with one of Europe's largest collections of
wildfowl, a large owl collection, with an emphasis on
Scottish wildlife.

83   ARGYLL'S LODGING   6A5

Castle Wynd, Stirling. Seen from the outside.

This fine example of an old town residence was built
c. 1632 by Sir William Alexander of Menstrie, later
Earl of Stirling, who eleven years earlier helped to
found Nova Scotia (New Scotland). It is now a youth
hostel.

**84   ARGYLL AND SUTHERLAND
       HIGHLANDERS' MUSEUM**   6A5

*In Stirling Castle. Easter-end Sep, Mon-Sat 1000-1730,
Sun 1100-1730. Oct-Easter, Mon-Fri 1000-1600, Sun 1100-1600. Free.
Parking available. Shop. Restaurant in Castle. Tel: (0786) 75165.*

Museum tells the story of the regiment from 1794 to
the present. Exhibits include colours, medals, silver,
weapons, uniforms, pictures and memorabilia. The
history of the Argylls is illustrated by story boards,
commentaries and slides. (See No 1197).

Armadale Castle and Gardens: see No 263.

**85   JOHNIE ARMSTRONG OF GILNOCKIE
       MEMORIAL**   5D8

*Carlanrig, Teviothead. Take the A7 S from Hawick for 9m then turn
right on to unclassified road. Memorial is 100yds on left next to
churchyard. All year. Free access. Parking available.*

A stone marker marks the mass grave of Laird of
Gilnockie and his men hanged without trial by King
James V of Scotland, 1530. Information plaque.
Wheelchair access via nearby field gate.

**86   ARRAN & ARGYLL
       TRANSPORT MUSEUM**   4F7

*Anchor Hotel Park, Corrie Road, Brodick, Isle of Arran. Apr-Oct, 4 days
per week. Entrance charge. Group discount. Parking available. Sales stall.
Refreshments. Tel: (0770) 2150.*

Independent museum run by enthusiasts, with displays
of public transport in Arran and Argyll, from
luxurious paddlesteamers to mailcarts and early motor
buses. One section is housed in a converted bus, ex-
Guernsey Railway Albion No 70. Photographs,
uniforms, advertisements, fittings and equipment from
early transport of all kinds.

87 ARRAN VISITOR CENTRE 4F7

 T

Home Farm, Brodick, Isle of Arran. 1 mile from Brodick Pier on road N to Lochranza. Easter-Oct. Daily, 0930-1715. Free. Parking available. Shop. Tel: (0770) 2831.

Cheese factory and set of specialist shops stocking locally made foodstuffs, natural body care products, books, clothing, toys, jewellery on an environmental theme.

88 ATHELSTANEFORD CHURCH 6G6

Off B1343, 4m N of Haddington. Approach also from A1 and B1347 turn-off. All reasonable times. Sunday worship 1000. Free; donations. Parking available. Tel: (062 088) 249 or (062 088) 378.

The plaque by the church tells the story of the origins of St Andrew's Cross (the Saltire), which was first adopted as the Scottish flag at this place. A floodlit flag flies permanently on the site. The Book of the Saltire exhibited in the church. Detailed history of the Saltire and Church.

89 ATHOLL COUNTRY COLLECTION 3C12

 T

Blair Atholl. Easter, June-mid Oct. Daily, 1330-1730. From 0930, Mon-Fri, July-Sept. Entrance charge. Group discount. Parking available. Tel: (0796) 481232.

Folk museum with lively displays showing village and glen life in the past, including blacksmith's 'smiddy', crofter's stable, byre and living-room. Road, rail and postal services, the school, the kirk, the vet and gamekeeper are all featured. Attractions include the Trinafour Post Office and Shop, the Caledonian Challenge Shield for Rifle Shooting, and photographic display of wild flowers.

90 AUCHINDOUN CASTLE 3E9

In Glen Fiddich, 3m SE of Dufftown, ½m off A941. All times: viewed from the outside only. Free. (HS) Tel: 031-244 3101.

A massive ruin on the summit of an isolated hill, enclosed by prehistoric earthworks. The corner stones were removed to Balvenie (see No 112). In Queen Mary's wars the castle was the stronghold of the redoubtable 'Edom o' Gordon' who burned Corgarff (see No 286). Jacobite leaders held a council of war there after Dundee's death at Killiecrankie.

91 AUCHINDRAIN OLD HIGHLAND TOWNSHIP 4F3

 A
 T

On A83, 5½m SW of Inveraray on A83. Apr-Sept. Daily, 1000-1700 (exc. Sat in Apr, May, Sept). Entrance charge. Group discount. Parking available. Shop. Refreshments. Tel: (049 95) 235.

Auchindrain is an original West Highland township, or village, of great antiquity and the only communal tenancy township in Scotland to have survived on its centuries-old site much in its original form.
The township buildings, which have been restored and preserved, are furnished and equipped in the style of various periods to give the visitor a living experience of what life was really like for the Highlander in past centuries. Museum shows Highland life through more traditional displays.

92 AUCHINGARRICH WILDLIFE CENTRE   6A2

Glascorrie Road, Comrie. 2 miles S of Comrie on Braco road. Jan-Dec. Daily 1000-dusk. Entrance charge. Group discount, special rates for handicapped people. Parking available. Shop. Coffee shop. Tel: (0764) 679469.

Set in 100 acres of Perthshire hill scenery, Auchingarrich has one of the largest bird collections in Scotland, with 17 ponds and over 100 species of waterfowl, ornamental and game birds. Highland cattle, wild deer, goats, 47-stone Rosie the pig, wallabies, llamas and a host of smaller animals. Visitors can handle young chicks in wild bird hatchery. Play areas include 'child-sized' rabbit burrow. Woodland walks, viewpoints, picnic benches and barbecue sites.

93 AULD KIRK   4G7

Off High Street, Ayr. Open Tues & Thurs in July & August between 1930-2030. Free. Tel: (0292) 262938.

A fine church, dating from 1654, with notable lofts inside. Robert Burns was baptised and sometimes attended church there.

Aultroy Cottage: see No 130.

94 AULD KIRK MUSEUM   4H5

Take A803 through Springburn and Bishopbriggs to Kirkintilloch Cross. Jan-Dec. Tues, Wed, Fri, 1000-1200, 1400-1700. Thurs 1000-1700. Sat 1000-1300, 1400-1700. Free. Tel: 041-775 1185.

The Auld Kirk Museum, formerly the parish church for Kirkintilloch dating back to 1644, houses changing temporary exhibitions featuring local history, art, craft and photography.

95 AVIEMORE MOUNTAIN RESORT   3C10

Off A9, 32m S of Inverness. Jan-Dec. Daily. Free (charge for facilities). Parking available. Tel: (0479) 810624.

Leisure, sport and conference centre with wide range of recreational and entertainment facilities, including: cinema/theatre, swimming pool, ice rink, saunas, solarium, artificial ski slope, go-karts, discos, restaurants, bars, chalets, and many more.

96 AVOCH HERITAGE ASSOCIATION   3B8

Old Post Office, Bridge Street/High Street. Jul-Sep, Mon-Sat 1000-1700. Entrance charge. Parking available. Tel: (0381) 20823.

'Schooldays' — a photographic display with artefacts relating to education in Avoch and the surrounding area over a period of 200 years.

Avondale Castle: see No 1201.

97 AYR GORGE WOODLANDS 4G7

At Failford, S of A758 Ayr-Mauchline road. Jan-Dec. Free.
Parking available. (SWT)

Gorge woodland, partly semi-natural, dominated by
oak and some coniferous plantation. Situated by the
River Ayr. Historic sandstone steps and viewing
platform. Extensive network of well-maintained
footpaths.

98 AYTON CASTLE 5F5

A
P
T

At Ayton, by Eyemouth, on A1, 7m N of Berwick. May-Sept, Sun
1400-1700, or by appointment. Entrance charge. Parking available.
Tel: (089 07) 81212.

Historic castle, built in 1846, important example of the
Victorian architectural tradition. Ayton Castle has
been restored in recent years and is fully lived in as a
family home.

99 BACHELORS' CLUB 4H7

Tarbolton, off B743, 7½m NE of Ayr off A758. Apr-Oct. Daily,
1200-1700. Entrance charge. Group discount. Parking available.
Tel: (0292) 541940.

A 17th-century house where in 1780 Robert Burns
and his friends founded a literary and debating society,
the Bachelors' Club. In 1779, Burns attended dancing
lessons here, and in 1781 he was initiated as a
Freemason. Period furnishings, with reminders of
Burns' life at Lochlea Farm.

100 SIR DOUGLAS BADER GARDEN FOR
THE DISABLED 6F3

Duffus Park, Cupar, Fife. Daily during daylight hours.
Tel: (0334) 53722 ext 437.

A garden designed and constructed to inform and
display the various uses of man-made and natural
materials in the construction of raised beds, water
features, aviary, paths, rock gardening, seating, etc. all
complimented by the colour of trees and shrubs. New
sale products and varieties of plants are included in the
garden, to keep disabled gardeners up to date.

101 BADNABAN CRUISES 2G5

Badnaban, 2½ miles S of Lochinver, just off the coastal road to
Achiltibuie/Ullapool. Jan-Dec (weather permitting). May-June best time
for seabirds nesting. Sailings at 1000, 1300, 1500. Charge. Car parking
available. Passengers may embark/disembark at Lochinver Pier by previous
arrangement. Tel: (057 14) 358.

Small boat (up to 8 passengers) cruises to seal colonies
and seabird nesting sites on islands in Enard Bay, views
of Assynt peaks from an unusual angle. All sailings
depend on weather and tides, and are at skipper's
discretion.

102 BAIRD INSTITUTE MUSEUM 4H7

A
P

Centre of Cumnock, off the Square. All year, Fri 0930-1300, 1330-1600,
Sat 1100-1300. Free. Groups by arrangement. Parking available.
Tel: (0290) 22111.

The Baird Institute dates back to 1891 when it was
built from money bequeathed by a local draper named
John Baird. Now a local history museum with a
varied programme of temporary exhibitions. Major
collections include Cumnock pottery, Mauchline box
ware, Ayrshire embroidery. James Keir Hardie Room
is dedicated to the early Scottish Labour leader's links
with Cumnock.

103   BALBIRNIE CRAFT CENTRE   6E4

♿
P

*In Balbirnie Park, Markinch, on eastern outskirts of Glenrothes
New Town. Jan-Dec. Exact times vary, but usually Mon-Fri, 1000-1700;
Sat 1200-1700; Sun 1300-1700. Free. Parking available.
Tel: (0592) 755975.*

Housed in fine 18th century complex of coach
buildings, individually owned craft workshops feature
pottery, fashion, stained glass, furniture, jewellery,
leatherwork and an art gallery. The centre is situated
in extensive Balbirnie Park, with walks, golf course,
Bronze Age stone circle, and play area.

104   BALCASKIE HOUSE AND GARDENS   6G4

♿
T

*2 miles W of Pittenweem on B942. Jun-Aug, Sat-Wed 1400-1800 (last
entry 1700). Entrance charge. Parking available. Refreshments.
Tel: (0333) 311202.*

Owned by Sir Ralph Anstruther of That Ilk, Bart.,
Balcaskie has been in the Anstruther family for nine
generations since 1698. The architect Sir William
Bruce bought the estate and the existing tower house
in 1665. He built the present house and terraced
garden, which offers fine views of the Firth of Forth
and the Bass Rock, and laid out the formal park and
avenues along strong axial vistas.

105   BALGONIE CASTLE   6E4

♿
P

*By Markinch, Fife. 2 miles E of Glenrothes on B921 off A911. Jan-Dec.
Daily, any reasonable time. Entrance charge. Group discount. Parking
available. Shop. Tel: (0592) 750119.*

14th-century castle with additions to 1702. 17th-century
home of Field Marshall Sir Alexander Leslie, made
Lord General of the Scottish Covenanting Army and
1st Earl of Leven. Garrisoned by Rob Roy McGregor
with 200 clansmen in January 1716. 14th-century
chapel, used for weddings. 2-acre wildlife garden.
Leather carver's workshop and tapestry weaver's
studio. Continuing restoration of this family home,
and living museum. Educational centre for school
visits (no charge).

Balhousie Castle: see No 140

106   BALLOCH CASTLE COUNTRY PARK   4H4

♿
P
T

*E of Balloch at S end of Loch Lomond. Easter-Sep weekend. Daily
1000-1800. Free. Parking available. Trains from Glasgow. Shop.
Refreshments. Tel: (0389) 58216.*

Balloch Castle sits in 200 acres of woodland, parkland
and ornamental gardens on the shore of Loch
Lomond. The Visitor Centre on the ground floor tells
the story of the park and the surrounding region
through slides and stained glass display panels. Loch
Lomond Park Authority ranger service organises walks
and events in the area. Picnic and barbecue sites, toilets
for disabled people.

107 BALMEDIE COUNTRY PARK 3H10

*Balmedie, 8 miles N of Aberdeen. Country park open Jan-Dec, daily.
Visitor Centre: Apr-Sep, daily, Oct-Mar, Mon-Fri only 0900-1700. Free.
Only Park barbecues may be used, book in advance through Ranger
Service. Parking available. Tel: (0358) 42396.*

Country park on the Don-Ythan coastline, a section of
the attractive North-East coast with its long stretches
of unbroken mobile dunes. Two large car parks, three
barbecue sites, play areas, picnic sites and easy access to
the beach using boardwalks. Ranger Service, based in
Visitor Centre, provides information on the physical,
social and natural history of the area.

108 BALMERINO ABBEY 6F2

*On S shore of River Tay on unclassified road 5m SW of Newport.
View from outside only. Entrance charge (honesty box). (NTS).
Tel: 031-336 2157.*

Cistercian abbey founded in 1229 by Queen
Ermingade, second wife of William Lyon. Ruined
during period of Reformation. Gardens.

109 BALMORAL CASTLE 3D11

*On A93, 8m W of Ballater. Grounds. Carriage Exhibition, Royal Travel
Exhibition and Estate Wildlife Exhibition in the Carriage Room.
Exhibition of paintings and works of art in the Castle Ballroom. May-Jun-
Jul. Daily except Sun 1000-1700. Entrance charge. Children free. Parking
available. Gardens, refreshment room. Souvenir shops. Donations from
entry fee to charities. Wheelchairs available free of charge.
Tel: (033 97) 42334.*

ASVA

The family holiday home of the Royal Family for over
a century. The earliest reference to it, as Bouchmorale,
was in 1484. Queen Victoria visited the earlier castle in
1848; Prince Albert bought the estate in 1852; the
castle was rebuilt by William Smith of Aberdeen with
modifications by Prince Albert and was first occupied
in 1855. Souvenir shops, refreshment room, country
walks and pony-trekking, pony cart rides, when ponies
available.

110 BALNAKEIL CHURCH 2H3

At Balnakeil, ¹/₂m W of Durness. All reasonable times. Free.

This old church (1619) has a monument to Rob
Donn, the famous Celtic Bard, erected in the
churchyard. Although now ruinous the site is very
attractive. There are many local tales relating to the
Church. Nearby, Balnakeil Craft Village has a group
of craft workers and shops to visit.

111 BALRANALD NATURE RESERVE 2A8

*3m NW of Bayhead, North Uist, turn off main road. Reception cottage
at Goular near Hougharry. Apr-Sep, daily. Donation cairn. Parking
available. (RSPB) Tel: 031-557 3136.*

Hebridean marsh, machair and shore. Important for
plants and nesting birds. Warden on site from April to
August.

112 BALVENIE CASTLE 3E8

*At Dufftown, A941, 16m SSE of Elgin. Apr-Sep, standard opening; closed
Oct-Mar. Entrance charge. Group concessions. Parking available. (HS)
Tel: 031-244 3101.*

Picturesque ruins of 13th-century moated stronghold
originally owned by the Comyns. Visited by Edward I
in 1304 and by Mary Queen of Scots in 1562.
Occupied by Cumberland in 1746. The corner stones
came from Auchindoun (see No 90).

113 BANCHORY MUSEUM   3F11

*Bridge Street, Banchory. Free. Contact North East Scotland Museums
Service for details of hours. Tel: (0779) 77778.*

New museum (opening 1993) in library complex,
features local history and natural history. Large
collection of Royal commemorative china, items
connected with noted fiddler Scott Skinner. Highland
dress display and fine silverware by Robb of Ballater.

114 BANFF MUSEUM   3F7

*On A98 at Banff. Jun-Sep, 1400-1715 (not Thu). Free.
Tel: (0779) 77778.*

Displays of Banff silver, arms and armour, local history
and relics of James Ferguson, the 18th century
astronomer. Ground floor, accessible to wheelchairs,
has award-winning natural history display.

Robert the Bruce, Bannockburn Heritage Centre

115 BANNOCKBURN HERITAGE CENTRE   6A5

♿
T

*Off M80/M9, 2m S of Stirling. (Heritage Centre). Apr-Oct. Daily
1000-1800. Audio-visual presentation (last showing 1730). Entrance
charge. Group discount. Parking available. (NTS)
Tel: (0786) 812664.*

ASVA

The audio-visual presentation tells the story of the
events leading up to the most significant victory in
Scottish history, the Battle of Bannockburn (1314). In
June 1964, Her Majesty The Queen inaugurated the
Rotunda and unveiled the equestrian statue of Robert
the Bruce. Exhibition 'The Kingdom of the Scots'.
Induction loop for the hard of hearing.

116 BARGANY GARDENS   4G8

♿

*4m from Girvan, 18m S of Ayr on B734. Mar-Oct, 0900-1900 or sunset.
Parking available, coaches by advance contact. Tel: (046 587) 249.*

Woodland garden centred on a lily pond surrounded
by azaleas and rhododendrons. Daffodils and
snowdrops in spring. Fine trees, rock garden and
extensive walled garden. Small picnic area near the car
park.

The Scottish Tourist Board would like to hear from disabled visitors who have made use of the information - your experiences will enable us to help others.

The sites have not been personally inspected by Scottish Tourist Board staff.

DEAF PEOPLE   We assume that all operators of sites in this book will be sympathetic to visitors with hearing problems. Any special facility will be mentioned in the text.

BLIND PEOPLE   We assume that all sites in this book will welcome guide dogs. If they do not, this will be mentioned in the text. Any special facility will also be mentioned in the text.

EASY WHEEL CHAIR ACCESS   Most or all of the site easily accessible. No more than one step, but entrance may be by a side door. No rough terrain, but not all the footpaths may be suitable.

ACCESS WITH ASSISTANCE   Two or more steps, but not as many as a flight. It has been evaluated as 'possible with strong help'. This help may sometimes be available on site. Please ring - it may be easy.

PARTIAL ACCESS   (Partial Access with Assistance) Easy access to part of the site, but the rest may not be possible because of stairs. Please ring for advice on how much you will be able to see.

VERY DIFFICULT/NO ACCESS Knowing the determination of some of our visitors, we hesitate to say impossible, but from the information supplied to us we can say daunting, strenuous, dangerous, for example with spiral staircase, stiles, rocky paths ... Your comments on these sites would be welcomed.

TOILET DOOR   26 inch/700 mm OR MORE Some toilets have been specially adapted for disabled visitors, some are known to be large and easily accessible. Please ring the sites if this is essential.

Comments on these or any other aspect of your visit will be welcome. Write to the Scottish Tourist Board, 23 Ravelston Terrace, Edinburgh EH4 3EU.

117 BARGUILLEAN GARDEN 4F2
Glen Lonan, 3m W of Taynuilt. Jan-Dec. Daily, 0900-dusk. Entrance charge, children free. Parking available. Refreshments for groups by arrangement. Tel: (086 62) 254.

Eleven acres of lochside woodland gardens, particularly attractive from May to July. The garden was created, starting in 1956, by Mr & Mrs Neil Macdonald as a memorial to their elder son Angus. Now run by younger son Sam Macdonald, Barguillean features daffodils, azaleas, rhododendrons, flowering shrubs and heathers.

118 BARNALINE WALKS 4F3
Dalavich, on unclassified road along W shore of Loch Awe. Jan-Dec. Daily. Free. Parking available.

Three walks starting from Barnaline Car Park and Picnic Site, taking in Dalavich Oakwood Forest Nature Reserve (an interpretative trail with old stable information point), Avich Falls and Loch Avich. Panoramic views of Loch Awe.

119 BARNSOUL FARM 5B9
1½ miles from Shawhead village, off A75 from Dumfries. Apr-Oct. Free. Car parking only. Tel: (038 773) 249.

Farm with wide variety of nature and bird life which visitors can watch.

120 BARON'S HAUGH 5A6
North Lodge Avenue, Adele Street, Motherwell. Jan-Dec. Daily. Donation cairn. Parking available. (RSPB) Tel: 031-557 3136.

Nature reserve with floods, marches, woodland. Of interest all year round, particularly winter.

121 BARONY CHAMBERS MUSEUM 4H5
Take A803 through Springburn and Bishopbriggs to Kirkintilloch Cross. Jan-Dec, Tues, Thurs, Fri 1400-1700; Sat 1000-1300 and 1400-1700. Free. Tel: 041-775 1185.

Barony Chambers is a museum of local life. It looks at the domestic and working life of the people in the area.

122 BARRIE'S BIRTHPLACE 5D1
9 Brechin Road, Kirriemuir. Easter weekend, May-Sept, Mon-Sat 1100-1730, Sun 1400-1730. Entrance charge. Group discount. Tearoom. Books and souvenirs for sale. (NTS). Tel: (0575) 72646.

ASVA

Birthplace of author and playwright J. M. Barrie, best known for his creation 'Peter Pan'. The house is furnished as it may have been when the Barrie family was in residence. Exhibition 'The Genius of J. M. Barrie' contains manuscripts, personal possessions, costumes and mementoes.

123 BARRY MILL 6G1
Barry, off A930, 2 miles W of Carnoustie. Easter weekend, May-mid-Oct. Daily 1100-1300, 1400-1700. Entrance charge. Group discount. Parking available. (NTS). Tel: (0241) 56761.

A working water mill running on a demonstration basis, where visitors can follow the milling process from the arrival of the oats to the bagging of the meal. Displays highlight the importance of the mill in the local community, on a site where there has been milling since the 15th century. Orchard picnic area and lade-side walkway.

124 BARSALLOCH FORT   4H11

Off A747, 7½m WNW of Whithorn. All reasonable times.
Free. (HS) Tel: 031-244 3101.

Remains of an Iron Age fort on the edge of a raised
beach bluff. 60-70 feet above the shore, enclosed by a
ditch 12 feet deep and 33 feet wide.

125 BASS ROCK   6H5

Off North Berwick. Boat trips from North Berwick go round the
Bass Rock. Parking available. Tel: (0620) 2838 (boat trips) or
(0620) 2197 (Tourist Information Centre).

A massive 350-feet-high rock whose many thousands
of raucous seabirds include the third largest gannetry
in the world.

126 BAXTERS VISITORS CENTRE   3E8

♿
P
T
1m W of Fochabers on main Inverness-Aberdeen road (A96). Jan-Dec.
Mon-Fri 0930-1630. Last tour on Fri, 1400. Also Sat and Sun from
mid-Apr-Christmas, 1100-1600. Coaches please book in advance for
afternoons July-Aug. Tel: (0343) 820393, ext 241.

ASVA

Restaurant, woodland walk, audio-visual theatre,
Victorian Kitchen, Old Shop and Cellar, picnic area.

127 BEAULY PRIORY   3A8

At Beauly, A9, 12m W of Inverness. Open all reasonable times. Free.
Parking available. (HS) Tel: 031-244 3101.

Ruins of a Valliscaulian Priory founded in about 1230.
Notable windows and window-arcading.

128 BEDRULE CHURCH   5E7

Bedrule, nr Denholm, off A698, Bedrule/Chesters Road.
Tel: (0450) 87518.

Bedrule Church, with its remarkable stained glass and
armorial bearings and picturesque location, high above
Rule Water and at the foot of Rubers Law, is the focus
of the area from which 'fighting Turnbulls' came.
William Turnbull, born 1400, became Bishop of
Glasgow and founder of Glasgow University (1451).
More recently, a magnificent stained glass window by
Roland Milton commemorates the 1992 centenary of
Bedrule Women's Guild. Although nothing remains
of Bedrule Castle, the mound of Fulton Tower still
dominates this reach of the Rule.

Beech Hedge: see No. 931

---

129 BEECRAIGS COUNTRY PARK   6C6

♿
T
From Linlithgow take Preston Road S for 2m, signposted on left. Country
Park open all year; Visitor Centre all year, 0830-1700. Free.
Parking available. Restaurant. Tel: (0506) 844516.

1,000-acre country park with woodland walks, deer
farm, fish farm, forestry, outdoor pursuit courses and a
'trim' course. Restaurant facilities, barbecue and visitor
centre. Caravan and camping park.

130 BEINN EIGHE NATIONAL NATURE RESERVE 2F8

W of A896/A832 junction at Kinlochewe. (SNH)
Tel: (044 584) 258.

The first National Nature Reserve in Britain, of great natural history and geological interest. Car park, woodland trail and mountain trail on A832 NW of Kinlochewe. Aultroy Cottage Visitor Centre on A832, 1m nearer Kinlochewe. Car park, toilets.

131 BELL OBELISK 4H5

Off A82 W of Bowling. All times. Free.

The obelisk at Douglas Point erected to commemorate Henry Bell, who launched the *Comet*, the first Clyde passenger steamer. Bowling is where the Forth and Clyde Canal enters the Clyde, and where the first practical steamboat, Symington's *Charlotte Dundas* was tried out in 1802 and in 1812.

132 BELL'S CHERRYBANK GARDENS 6D2

In Perth off A9 Glasgow Road at Arthur Bell Distillers office.
Free. Parking available. Tel: (0738) 27330/21111.

Beautifully landscaped garden. Children's play area, café facility (light refreshments).

133 BEN NEVIS 2H12

Near Fort William. Parking available.

Britain's highest mountain (4,406 ft/1,344 m) and most popular mountain for both rock-climber and hillwalker. It is best seen from the north approach to Fort William, or from the Gairlochy Road, across the Caledonian Canal. (See No 214).

134 BEN NEVIS DISTILLERY VISITOR CENTRE 2G12

Lochy Bridge, 2 miles N of Fort William on A82. Jan-Dec exc 2 weeks at Christmas. Mon-Fri 0900-1700 (July & Aug, 1930), also Sat, Apr-Sept. Last tour one hour before closing. Free. Parking available. Gift shop. Tearoom. Tel: (0397) 700200.

Small exhibition, audio-visual display, guided tours for groups up to 15, whisky tasting. Guided tours are not suitable for disabled visitors due to the large number of steps in the distillery.

135 BENNIE MUSEUM 6C7

9-11 Mansefield Street, Bathgate. 3 miles W of Livingston, near M8. Jan-Dec exc Christmas & New Year. Mon-Sat. Apr-Sep 1000-1600, Oct-Mar 1100-1530. Free. Parking available. Gift shop. Tearoom next door. Tel: (0506) 534944.

Museum with some 4,500 artefacts illustrating social, industrial, religious, military history of Bathgate, a former Royal Burgh. Postcards and photographs of town from 1890s onwards. Fossil material, glass bottles, Roman coin found in Bathgate, relics of Prince Charles Edward Stuart and the Napoleonic Wars.

136 BIGGAR GASWORKS MUSEUM   5B6
♿ *Gasworks Road, near the War Memorial, Biggar. Daily. May-Sept. Limited car parking. Working exhibits and live steam on special occasions. Free. For details please phone. (National Museums of Scotland). Tel: 031-225 7534.*

Biggar Gasworks was built in 1839 and closed in 1973 on the arrival of natural gas. It is now the only surviving coal gasworks in Scotland. The buildings, plant and associated displays give a concise picture of the coal-gas industry. Working machinery and gas lights, guided tours, display of gas appliances, video show.

137 BIGGAR KIRK   5B6
♿ *Kirkstyle, Biggar. Daily till dusk. Sunday services 1100, also 0930 on last Sun of month. Refreshments at Gillespie Centre, 72 High Street, Biggar. (Church of Scotland). Tel: (0899) 20227.*

Collegiate Church built in 1545 (on site of earlier building) by Malcolm, Lord Fleming of Biggar, uncle of Mary, Queen of Scots.

138 BIGGAR PUPPET THEATRE   5B6
♿ T   *On the B7016 E of Biggar. All year, Mon-Sat 1000-1700; closed Wed; Sun 1400-1700. Entrance charge. Group concessions (over 20). Parking available. Tearoom. Licensed. Tel: (0899) 20631 (Box Office); (0899) 20521 (Administration).*

Complete Victorian theatre in miniature seating 100. Puppets, performances, displays and guided tours backstage. Attractive grounds with tearoom, shop, games, picnic area and car park. Disabled visitors welcome but prior notice required. Induction loop.

The Binns: see No 749.

139 BIRKHILL FIRECLAY MINE   6C6
From Bo'ness take A706 towards Linlithgow, right at crossroads at top of hill, 2m to Upper Kinneil Farm, turn right down unclassified signposted road. Early Apr-late Oct, weekends only. Mid-Jul-Aug, daily 1100-1600 (last tour). Entrance charge. Group concessions. Openings coincide with Bo'ness & Kinneil Railway. Parking available. Tel: (0506) 825855 (24 hrs)

Fireclay mine. Discover the secrets of fireclay deep in the underground tunnels at the heart of the mine. See 300-million-year-old fossils, learn how mines worked the clay. Meadow walk, ancient woodlands. Mine tour not accessible to disabled visitors. (See also No 156).

Bishop's Palace: see No 435.

140 BLACK WATCH REGIMENTAL MUSEUM   6D2
⚔ *Balhousie Castle, Perth. Entrance from Hay Street or North Inch. Jan-Dec exc Christmas & New Year period. Easter-Sep, Mon-Fri 1000-1630, Sun & public holidays 1400-1630, Oct-Easter, Mon-Fri 1000-1530. Free. Parking available (Hay Street). Garden. Shop. Advance notice required for groups. Tel: (0738) 21281, ext 8530.*

Balhousie Castle houses the Regimental Headquarters and Museum of the Black Watch (Royal Highland) Regiment, and displays the history of this famous regiment from 1740 to the present.

141 BLACKHAMMER CAIRN 1B10

N of B9064, on the south coast of the island of Rousay (Orkney).
All times. Free. (HS) Tel: 031-244 3101.

A long cairn containing a megalithic burial chamber
divided into seven compartments or stalls; probably
third millennium BC.

Black Watch Memorial: see No 1276.

Blackness Castle

142 BLACKNESS CASTLE 6C6

B903, 4m NE of Linlithgow. Opening standard, except Oct-Mar closed
Thurs afternoon and Fri. Entrance charge. Group discount (over 11).
Parking available. (HS) Tel: 031-244 3101.

This 15th-century stronghold, once one of the most
important fortresses in Scotland, was one of the four
castles which by the Articles of Union were to be left
fortified. Since then it has been a state prison in
Covenanting time, a powder magazine in the 1870s,
and more recently, for a period, a youth hostel.

---

143 BLACKSHAW FARM PARK 4G6

Å
P
T

On the B781 between West Kilbride and Dalry. End Mar-mid-Aug, daily.
Mid-Aug-end Sep, Sat, Sun, Mon only 1030-1700. Entrance charge.
Group discount (over 10). Family ticket. Parking available.
Tel: (0563) 34257.

Working farm with seasonal demonstrations of
clipping and shearing sheep, milking, cows, feeding
calves, etc. Nature trails. Cup and ring stone of
historic interest. Four-wheel all-terrain motorbikes,
tractor and trailer rides, grass sledging, aerial cableway.

144 BLACKWOODRIDGE POTTERY 5C9

Å

Waterbeck, on B722, 1 mile N of Eaglesfield. Jan-Dec, Sun-Fri
1000-1700. Free. Car parking only. Tel: (046 16) 600.

Pottery producing handmade domestic stoneware in
brightly coloured enamel designs.

Blair Athol Distillery

**145 BLAIR ATHOL DISTILLERY
VISITOR CENTRE**   5B1

*S of Pitlochry centre. Open all year round, Mon-Sat 0930-1700.
Sundays, Easter to Oct 1200-1700. Seating up to 90 persons. Licensed.
Parking available. Shop. Restaurant. Tel: (0796) 472234.*

ASVA

The home of Bell's whisky, the famous blend. Blair
Athol presents a tranquil collection of old distillery
buildings with an attractive courtyard. All traditional
processes are shown on guided tours, from burn water
to cask. New visitor centre houses exhibition, function
area, shops and audio-visual.

146 BLAIR ATHOLL MILL   3C12

*Turn off A9 for Blair Atholl, 5 miles N of Pitlochry. Apr (or Easter)-Oct,
Mon-Sat 1030-1730, Sun 1200-1730. Entrance charge. Group discount.
Parking available. Shop. Tearoom, uses mill products.
Tel: (0796) 481321 or (0796) 483317.*

Built in 1613, this water mill produces oatmeal and
flour which are on sale, and some is used in the small
wholemeal bakery at the mill. Guide dogs in tearoom
only.

147 BLAIR CASTLE   3B12

&
P
T

*Near A9, 7m NNW of Pitlochry. Apr-late Oct. Daily, 1000-1800. (Last
entry 1700). Entrance charge. Group discount. Parking available. Family
ticket. Shop. Restaurant. Tel: (0796) 481207.*

ASVA

A white turreted baronial castle, seat of the Duke of
Atholl, chief of Clan Murray. The oldest part is
Cumming's Tower, 1269. Mary, Queen of Scots,
Prince Charles Edward Stuart and Queen Victoria
stayed here. When the castle was in Hanoverian hands
in 1746, General Lord Murray laid siege to it on the
Prince's behalf, making it the last castle in Britain to
be besieged. The Duke is the only British subject
allowed to maintain a private army, the Atholl
Highlanders. There are fine collections of furniture,
portraits, lace, china, arms, armour, Jacobite relics and
masonic regalia. Licensed restaurant, gift shop, deer
park, pony-trekking, nature trails, picnic areas and
caravan park.

148 BLAIR DRUMMOND SAFARI AND
LEISURE PARK 6A4

Exit 10 off M9 N of Stirling, 4 miles towards Callander. Apr-early Oct. Daily, 1000-1730 (last admission 1630). Entrance charge. Discount for groups over 15, paid in advance; discount for handicapped visitors and helpers. Parking available. Bus from Stirling. Transport in park available for visitors without cars. Shops. Ranch Kitchen restaurant, Watering Hole Bar, kiosks, picnic and barbecue areas.

ASVA

Park with drive-through wild animal reserves to see and photograph animals close at hand. Boat safari around Chimpanzee Island and Waterfowl Sanctuary, walks around Pets' Farm. Performing sea lions; giant slide and adventure playground; cable slide across lake; pedal boats and splash cats; face painting and amusements.

149 BLAIRQUHAN CASTLE 4H8

Straiton, Maybole, 14 miles S of Ayr on B7045. Mid July-mid Aug. Tues-Sun, 1330-1615. Entrance charge. Group discount. Tearoom. Parking available. Tel: (065 57) 239.

Blairquhan was a castle built in 1820-24 for Sir David Hunter Blair, 3rd Baronet, replacing an earlier one which dated from the 14th century, part of which is included in the new castle. It was designed by the well known Scottish architect, William Burn.

Belted Galloway Cattle

150 BLOWPLAIN OPEN FARM 5A9

Balmaclellan, Castle Douglas, 13 miles W of Castle Douglas on A713, turn off on A712 (Balmaclellan). Signposted 1 mile on right. Easter-end Oct, 1400 every day except Sat. Other times by arrangement. Entrance charge. Group discount. Parking available. Tel: (064 42) 206.

A Galloway hill farm with animals in picturesque surroundings. Pedigree and cross-breed sheep, cattle, suckler cows, Belted Galloways and Dougal, the friendly 'Highlander'. Visitors can meet and feed animals, including lambs in spring and summer. Pheasants, peacocks, ducks and hens.

151 BOATH DOOCOT 3C8

Off A96 at Auldearn, 2m E of Nairn. Donation box (NTS) Tel: (0463) 232034.

A 17th-century doocot (dovecote) on the site of an ancient castle where Montrose flew the standard of Charles I when he defeated the Covenanters in 1645. The plan of the battle is on display.

152 BOATHOUSE VISITOR CENTRE   4C2

*Ulva Ferry, Isle of Ulva, by Aros, Isle of Mull. 8 miles W of Salen on
B8035 and B8073. Short ferry crossing. Mid Apr-mid Oct, limited
opening other months. Mon-Fri 0800-1700. Also Sun, Jun-Aug. Other
times by arrangement. Ferry runs all year, Visitor Centre open but
unmanned outside above times. Entrance charge. Family ticket. Car
parking only. Shop. Tearoom.*

ASVA

Small island off Mull with lovely scenery, abundant
wildlife and fascinating history. The Boathouse has
interpretative displays of Ulva's history from Stone
Age to the present. Five signposted walks, from one to
five hours long.

153 BOD OF GREMISTA   1G4

*Gremista, on N outskirts of Lerwick, Shetland. May-Sep. Tue, Wed,
Thur, Sat, Sun afternoons. Entrance charge. Parking available. Tel: (0595)
5057.*

Museum in restored 18th century fishing booth.
Famous as the birthplace of Arthur Anderson, co-
founder of the Peninsular and Oriental Steam
Navigation Company, now P & O.

154 BOLFRACKS GARDEN   5A1

*2m W of Aberfeldy on A827 to Kenmore. Gates on left. Apr-Oct. Daily
1000-1800. Donation box. Parking available. Tel: (0887) 820207.*

Garden overlooking Tay Valley. Good collection of
trees, shrubs and perennials. Open under Scotland's
Gardens Scheme.

Bonawe Iron Furnace

155 BONAWE IRON FURNACE   4F2

*At Bonawe, 12m E of Oban, off A85. Opening standard, Apr-Sep only.
Entrance charge. Parking available. (HS) Tel: 031-244 3101.*

ASVA

The restored remains of a charcoal furnace for iron-
smelting, established in 1753, which worked until
1876. The furnace and ancillary buildings are in a
more complete state of preservation than any other
comparable site.

156 BO'NESS & KINNEIL RAILWAY   6C6

*Off Union Street, Bo'ness. Leave M9 at junction 3 or 5. Open weekends,
Apr-Oct, Dec. Also holiday Mons, Apr, May, Aug. Also Wed-Fri, June.
Daily, mid July-Aug. Check timetable for exact dates and times. Entrance
charge. Family tickets. Group discount. Bufferstop Cafe. Sales stand.
Picnic area. Parking available. Tel: (0506) 822298.*

Victorian railway centre with steam-hauled trains on
3½ mile journey from Bo'ness to Birkhill. At Birkhill,
walks around Avon Gorge, and Birkhill Fireclay Mine
(see No 139). At Bo'ness, guided tours of Scotland's
largest collection of locomotives, rolling stock and
historic railway buildings, including Haymarket train
shed of 1842. New wagon display opening 1993.

157 BONNYRIGG LEISURE CENTRE 6F7

  ♿
T *King George V Park, off main street, opposite supermarket. 5 miles S of Edinburgh on A768, B704. Jan-Dec. Daily 0900-2200 exc Christmas & New Year. Entrance charges. Parking available. Refreshments. Tel: 031-663 7579.*

Modern centre with leisure pool with two lagoons, spa bath, flume, water cannons, fountains and grotto. Function hall, two artificial turf outdoor pitches, health and fitness suite with sauna and solarium. Enclosed soft play area for younger children.

Border Country Life Exhibition: see No 1227.

158 BORDERS WOOL CENTRE 5E6

  ♿
T *North Wheatlands Mill, Wheatlands Road, off A72 NW of Galashiels town centre. Mar-Oct, Mon-Fri 0900-1700, Sat 0900-1600. Suns in Aug, 0900-1600. Free. Shop. Parking available. Tel: (0896) 4293 or 4774.*

Housed beside a large stone-built wool grading mill, the centre tells the story of British sheep and wool. During the season there are live sheep in the enclosure, wool fleece display, information panels, video. Continuous fleece grading in mill, hand spinning demonstrations on Tuesdays and Thursdays.

**159 BORRERAIG PARK
EXHIBITION CROFT** 2D9

  ♿ *By Dunvegan, Isle of Skye. Take B884 towards Glendale, turn off for Husabost & Borreraig. Jan-Dec. Mon-Sat 1000-dusk. Entrance charge. Parking for cars/minibuses. Shop. Tel: (047 081) 311.*

On a remote working croft, the largest collection of horse-drawn mowers in Scotland is part of an outside display of agricultural implements and machinery once used in the surrounding townships. Museum in converted blackhouse houses unusual and varied collection of local exhibits, and a natural history display. Visitors are welcome to ask proprietors about aspects of crofting, past and present. Various animals to be seen, depending on season.

160 BORTHWICK CHURCH 6F7

Off A7, 13m SE of Edinburgh. Parking available. Tel: (0875) 20653.

Nearby is Borthwick Castle (seen from outside only), built about 1430, with twin towers and two wings, one of the strongest and biggest of Scotland's tower houses. Mary, Queen of Scots visited the castle after her marriage to Bothwell. Borthwick Church, largely Victorian with an aisle and a vault dating from the 15th century, an apse originating in the 12th century, 18th and 19th century memorials (particularly Dundas family), and two 15th century effigies thought to be the best preserved in Scotland. Association with Borthwick family and Clan.

161 BORVE BREW HOUSE 3F8

  ♿
T *Ruthven, 6 miles W of Huntly. Jan-Dec. Daily 1300-2000. Free. Car parking only. Refreshments. Tel: (046 687) 343.*

Guided tours and displays of small family specialist brewery.

162 BOSWELL MUSEUM AND MAUSOLEUM 4H7

In Auchinleck. A76, 17m E of Ayr. Seen from outside at all times. For entry and guided tour, contact Mrs Wilson, Chrissie's Shop, 86 Main Street, Auchinleck; prior notice appreciated. Free: donations welcome. Parking available. Tel: (0290) 20931.

The ancient Parish Church, formerly a Celtic cell, was enlarged by Walter fitz Alan in 1145-65, and again by David Boswell in 1641-43. It is now a museum of the Boswell family, and also contains a memorial to William Murdoch (1745-1839), a pioneer of lighting and heating by gas. The Boswell Mausoleum, attached, built by Alexander Boswell (Lord Auchinleck) in 1754, is the burial place of five known generations, including James Boswell, Dr Johnson's famous biographer. Boswell's home, Auchinleck House, is nearby, under restoration. 2 miles away at Lugar a walking tour on Murdoch, including his birthplace at Belo Mill, opened in 1984.

163 BOTHWELL CASTLE 5A5

At Uddingston on A74, 7m SE of Glasgow. Opening standard, except Oct-Mar closed. Thurs afternoon and Fri. Entrance charge. Parking available. (HS) Tel: 031-244 3101.

Once the largest and finest stone castle in Scotland, dating from the 13th century and reconstructed by the Douglases in the 15th century. In a picturesque setting above the Clyde Valley.

164 BOWHILL 5D7

    ♿
P
T

Off A708, 3m W of Selkirk. Grounds and Playground open 1st Sat in May-Aug bank holiday (not Fri). House open 1-31 Jul. Daily (incl Fri) 1200-1700, Sun 1400-1800. (House 1300-1630). Dates subject to slight alteration each year. Please telephone for precise information. Conference/Study facilities. Licensed restaurant. Parking available. Tel: (0750) 20732.

For many generations Bowhill has been the Border home of the Scotts of Buccleuch. Inside the house, begun in 1812, there is an outstanding collection of pictures, including works by Van Dyck, Reynolds, Gainsborough, Canaletto, Guardi, Claude Lorraine, Raeburn, etc. and a selection of the world-famous Buccleuch collection of portrait miniatures. Also porcelain and furniture, much of which was made in the famous workshop of André Boulle in Paris. Restored Victorian kitchen. In the grounds are an adventure woodland play area, a riding centre, garden, nature trails, licensed tearoom and gift shop, bicycle hire. Audio-visual presentation, theatre, visitor centre.

165 BOWMORE DISTILLERY, 4C6

    ♿
A
T

Nr centre of Bowmore village, Isle of Islay. Jan-Dec. Mon-Fri, from 1000. Individuals and groups accepted (please phone in advance). Children admitted. Guided tours and shop. Car and limited coach parking. Tel: (046 681) 671.

ASVA

Malt whisky distillery, licensed since 1779, owned by Morrison Bowmore Distillers since 1963. Traditional floor maltings are a major feature. Extensive renovations completed in 1992 improved the tour route through the distillery. Across the entrance yard, a former warehouse, gifted to local community, is now a swimming pool heated by waste energy from the distillery. (See No 907).

Bowmore Round Church

166   BOWMORE ROUND CHURCH   4C6

Bowmore, Isle of Islay. Daily. 0900-dusk. Parking available. Free.
Tel: (049 681) 254 (TIC).

Also known as Kilarrow Parish Church, was built by
the Campbells of Shawfield as part of Daniel
Campbell's planned village in 1769. Believed to be a
copy of an Italian design, it possibly owes its shape to
the belief that no evil spirits could hide in any corners.
The builder was Thomas Spalding.

167   BRAELOINE CENTRE   3F11

  Glen Tanar, 3 miles SW of Aboyne on B976. Apr-Sept. Daily,
A *1000-1700. Donations to Glen Tanar Charitable Trust. Parking available.*
  Tel: (033 98) 86072.

Centre contains a display of natural and cultural
history of Glen Tanar. Waymarked walks from centre
to points of interest, viewpoints, picnic areas. Hills,
woods, riverside. Glen Tanar Charitable Trust Ranger
service will provide guided walks by arrangement.

168   BRAEMAR CASTLE   3D11

A93, at Braemar. May-mid Oct. Daily exc Fri 1000-1800. Entrance
charge. Group discount. Parking available. Shop. Tel: (033 97) 41219.

A turreted stronghold, built in 1628 by the Earl of
Mar, Braemar Castle was burned in 1689 by the Black
Colonel (John Farquharson of Inverey). Repaired by
the Government after the 1745 Rising, it was
garrisoned by Hanoverian troops. Later transformed
into a private residence by the Farquharsons of
Invercauld who had purchased it in 1732. L-plan with
central round tower and spiral stair. Barrel vaulted
ceilings, massive iron "yett", underground prison.
Star-shaped defensive curtain wall. Fully furnished
residence.

169   BRAEMAR HIGHLAND
       HERITAGE CENTRE   3D11

  Mar Road, Braemar. Jan-Dec. Daily 1000-1800. Extended hours Jul-Sep.
T *Entrance charge. Parking available. Shop. Tel: (033 97) 41944.*

Static displays and specially-commissioned film telling
the story of Braemar through three themes — a
journey over hills explaining the history of the land, a
journey through time and the history of the Braemar
Royal Highland Gathering, and the building of
Balmoral Castle and Royal links with the area.

170   BRANKLYN GARDEN   6D2

&   *Dundee Road (A85). Perth. Mar-Oct. Daily 0930-sunset.*
A   *Entrance charge. Group concessions. Limited parking. No dogs. (NTS)*
    Tel: (0738) 25535.

Described as the finest two acres of private garden in
the country, this outstanding collection of plants,
particularly rhododendrons, alpines, herbaceous and
peat garden plants, attracts gardeners and botanists
from all over the world.

---

171   BREACACHADH CASTLE   4B1

Isle of Coll. Open by appointment only. Tel: (087 93) 444.

The best example of a 15th century west coast castle.
Seat of the Macleans of Coll until 1750. Restored by
Major & the Hon Mrs Maclean-Bristol as their family
home.

---

172   BRECHIN MUSEUM   3F12

&   *In Library, St-Ninian's Square. Jan-Dec. Mon, Wed 0930-2000. Tues,*
P   *Thurs 0930-1800. Fri, Sat 0930-1700. Free. Car parking only.*
    Tel: (0307) 68813/64123.

Local museum exhibiting Brechin's history from
prehistoric times up to local government re-
organisation in 1975. The stories of Brechin Round
Tower, Brechin at War, local industries and the
administration of the town are illustrated with
artefacts and photographs. Small exhibition of local
artist David Waterson R.A.

---

173   BRECHIN ROUND TOWER   3F12

At Brechin. Viewed from the churchyard. All reasonable times. (HS)
Tel: 031-244 3101.

One of the two remaining round towers of the Irish
type in mainland Scotland, dating back to the 11th or
12th century. Now attached to the cathedral (c 1150,
partially demolished 1807, restored 1900-02;
interesting tombstones. (See also Abernethy, No 34).

Bridge of Carr

174   BRIDGE OF CARR   3C10

Carrbridge. All times.

High and narrow single-arch bridge. Built by John
Niccelsone, mason, in summer 1717, for Sir James
Grant.

---

175   BRITISH GOLF MUSEUM   6G2

&   *Opposite Royal & Ancient Golf Club in St Andrews. May-Oct, daily,*
T   *1000-1730; Nov, Thurs-Tues 1000-1600; Dec-Feb, Thurs-Mon,*
    1100-1500; Mar-Apr, Thurs-Mon, 1000-1700. Entrance charge.
    Parking available. Shop. Tel: (0334) 78880.

Visitors can trace 500 years of golf history, stroke for
stroke, with visual and touch-screen displays in this
museum which has won seven awards since opening in
1990. History and atmosphere of great matches,
famous moments are re-lived.

Brodick Castle

176 BRODICK CASTLE, GARDEN AND COUNTRY PARK 4F7

& P T

2m N of Brodick Pier, Isle of Arran. Garden and Country Park: Jan-Dec, daily 0930-sunset. Castle: Easter holidays, May-Sep. Daily 1300-1700. Also open between Easter and May, early-mid Oct, Mon, Wed, Sat, 1300-1700. Shop, restaurant, dates as Castle, also open mornings. Please check exact dates and times. Entrance charge. Group concessions. Parking available. Tel: (0770) 2202.

Ancient seat of the Dukes of Hamilton. Contains superb silver, porcelain and paintings. Country Park includes formal and woodland gardens. Ranger/naturalist centre, woodland walks, adventure playground.

177 BRODIE CASTLE AND GARDENS 3C8

& A P T

Off A96, 4½m W of Forres. Apr-Oct. Mon-Sat 1100-1800. Sun 1400-1800. Last admission 1715. Entrance charge. Group concessions. Shop. Small tearoom. Entry to grounds only by donation. Parking available. (NTS) Tel: (030 94) 371.

ASVA

Home of the Brodie family, the castle was largely rebuilt after the earlier structure was burned in 1645; it is based on the 16th century 'Z' plan, with additions made in the 17th and 19th centuries. The house contains fine French furniture, English, Continental and Chinese porcelain, and a major collection of paintings. Extensive grounds with woodland walks, four-acre pond, wild garden with fine daffodil collection, picnic area and adventure playground.

178 BROUGH OF BIRSAY 1A10

At Birsay, N end of mainland, 11m N of Stromness, Orkney. Tides permitting. Open all reasonable times. Free. Parking available. (HS) Tel: 031-244 3101.

The remains of a Romanesque church and a Norse settlement on an island accessible only at low tide. A replica of a Pictish sculptured stone discovered in the ruins is in the grounds (original in the Museum of Antiquities, Queen Street, Edinburgh, No 487).

179 BROUGHTON GALLERY 5C7

& A P

On the A701 just N of Broughton village. End Mar-mid Oct. mid Nov-mid Dec. Daily 1030-1800 (incl Sun); closed Wed. Free. Parking available. Tel: (089 94) 234.

An imposing building designed by Basil Spence in 1938 in the style of a 16th-century Scottish fortified tower house. Contains continuous exhibitions of paintings and crafts by living British artists for sale. The walled garden contains dovecote and knot garden with fine views of the Tweeddale Hills. Nearby in Broughton village at the corner of Biggar road is a garden which contains no less than 14,000 bedding plants.

180 BROW WELL   5C10

On B725, 1m W of Ruthwell. All times. Free.

Ancient mineral well visited by Robert Burns in July
1796, when at Brow sea bathing under his doctor's
orders.

181 BRUCE'S STONE   4H9

6m W of New Galloway by A712. All reasonable times. Free. (NTS)

This granite boulder on Moss Raploch records a
victory by Robert the Bruce over the English in
March 1307, during the fight for Scotland's
independence.

Bruce's Stone

182 BRUCE'S STONE   4H9

*N side of Loch Trool, unclassified road off A714. 13m N of Newton
Stewart. All times. Free.*

A massive granite memorial to Robert the Bruce's first
victory over the English leading to his subsequent
success at Bannockburn. Fine views of Loch Trool and
the hills of Galloway. Start of hill climb to The
Merrick (2,764ft), highest hill in southern Scotland.

183 MICHAEL BRUCE'S COTTAGE   6D4

& *Kinnesswood, off A911, 4m E of Milnathort. Apr-Sep, daily 1000-1800.*
A *(Keys at The Garage, Kinnesswood.) Admission by donation.
(Michael Bruce Memorial Trust)*

A cottage museum in the birthplace of the Gentle
Poet of Loch Leven (1746-1767), who wrote and
improved some of the Scottish Paraphrases.

184 JOHN BUCHAN CENTRE   5C7

& *S end of Broughton, 6m E of Biggar. Easter-Sept, daily 1400-1700.*
T *Entrance charge. Group concessions. Parking available. (Biggar Museum
Trust). Tel: (0899) 21050.*

The Centre tells the story of John Buchan, 1st Lord
Tweedsmuir, author of 'The 39 Steps' and also lawyer,
politician, soldier, historian and Governor-General of
Canada. Broughton village was his mother's
birthplace, and a much-loved holiday home.

185 BUCHLYVIE POTTERY SHOP   6A5

& *15 miles W of Stirling on A811. Jan-Dec. Mon-Sat 0930-1700, Sun
1230-1630. Car parking only. Tel: (036 085) 405.*

Fine porcelain pottery hand cast and hand painted on
the premises, designed by Alison Borthwick. Some of
the processes can be seen from the shop.

186 BUCKHAVEN MUSEUM   6F4

Above Buckhaven Library, College Street, Buckhaven. All year, Mon 1400-1900, Tue 1000-1200, 1400-1700, Thu 1000-1200, 1400-1900, Fri 1400-1700, Sat 1000-1230. Parking available. Free. (Kirkcaldy District Museums). Tel: (0592) 260732.

Buckhaven was once described as 'a full-flavoured fisher town' and its past importance in the East Coast fisheries is reflected in displays on the fisherfolk themselves, their lifestyle and their fishing techniques.

187 BUCKIE MARITIME MUSEUM   3E7

Town House West, Cluny Place, Buckie. All year, Mon-Fri 1000-2000, Sat 1000-1200. Free. Parking available. Sales point. Tel: (0309) 673701.

Displays on fishing methods, coopering, lifeboats, navigation, local history and the herring trade. The Peter Anson Gallery houses watercolours of the development of fishing on the East Coast of Scotland.

188 BULLERS OF BUCHAN   3H9

Off A975, 7m S of Peterhead. Parking available. Tel: (0261) 812789 (Tourist Information).

Vast sea chasm 200 feet deep where the sea rushes in through a natural archway open to the sky. The surrounding cliff scenery is spectacular and seabirds of many species proliferate. Great care is required.

189 BUNNAHABHAIN DISTILLERY   4C5

Port Askaig, Isle of Islay (The Highland Distilleries Co.) Open all year, Mon-Fri 1000-1600. Visits by appointment. Parking available. Small reception room and shop. Tel: (049 684) 646.

Visitors can see malt whisky distillation. Individuals and groups welcome.

190 BURG   4C2

5m W on track from B8035 on N shore of Loch Scridain, Isle of Mull. Only accessible at low tide. Free. (NTS) Tel: (041) 552 8391.

The area contains MacCulloch's fossil tree, possibly 50 million years old, which can be reached at low water. Cars inadvisable beyond Tiroran. 5-mile walk, very rough in places.

191 BURLEIGH CASTLE   6D3

Off A911, 2m NE of Kinross. Opening standard. Free: key-keeper at farm opposite. (HS) Tel: 031-244 3101.

A fine tower house dating from about 1500. The seat of the Balfours of Burleigh, several times visited by James VI.

192 ROBERT BURNS CENTRE   5B9

Mill Road, Dumfries. Apr-Sep, Mon-Sat 1000-2000, Sun 1400-1700. Oct-Mar, Tue-Sat 1000-1300, 1400-1700. Entrance charge for audio-visual, rest of centre free. Parking available. Shop. Jean Armour's Cafe, open Apr-Sept. Tel: (0387) 64808.

Award-winning centre illustrates the connection between Robert Burns, Scotland's national poet, and the town of Dumfries. Situated in the town's 18th century watermill on the west bank of the River Nith, the centre tells of Burns' last years spent in the busy streets and lively atmosphere of Dumfries in the 1790s. Film theatre shows feature films in the evening.

193 BURNS COTTAGE AND MUSEUM 4G7

&

T

B7024, at Alloway, 2m S of Ayr. All year. Jun-Aug 0900-1800, Sun 1000-1800, Apr, May, Sep, Oct 1000-1700 (Sun 1400-1700); Nov-Mar 1000-1600 (not Sun). Entrance charge. Family tickets. Tearoom. Shop. Museum and gardens. Parking available (includes Burns Monument). Tel: (0292) 441215.

In this thatched cottage built by his father, Robert Burns was born, 25 January 1759, and this was his home until 1766. Adjoining the cottage is a museum containing many relics, song and poetry manuscripts which belonged to Burns. Entrance charge includes admission to the nearby Burns Monument (see No 198) and gardens.

194 BURNS FAMILY TOMBSTONES AND CAIRN 3G11

Off A94, 8m SW of Stonehaven at Glenbervie Church. All times. Free.

The Burnes (Burns) family tombstones in the churchyard were restored in 1968 and a Burns memorial cairn is nearby.

195 BURNS HOUSE, DUMFRIES 5B9

Burns Street. All year. Mon-Sat 1000-1300, 1400-1700, Sun 1400-1700. Closed Sun and Mon, Oct-Mar. Entrance charge. Parking nearby. Tel: (0387) 55297.

It was in this ordinary sandstone house in a back street of Dumfries that Robert Burns spent the last three years of his short life, and died in 1796. The house retains its 18th century character and contains many items connected with the poet, including letters and manuscripts, Kilmarnock and Edinburgh editions of his works, and the chair where he sat to write his last poems and songs.

196 BURNS HOUSE MUSEUM, MAUCHLINE 4H7

Castle Street, Mauchline, 11m ENE of Ayr. Easter-30 Sept, Mon-Sat 1100-1230, 1330-1730, Sun 1400-1700 (or by arrangement). Entrance charge. Parking available. Tel: (0290) 50045.

On the upper floor is the room which Robert Burns took for Jean Armour in 1788. It has been kept intact and is furnished in the style of that period. Models of Robert and Jean hold a five-minute taped conversation. The remainder of the museum contains Burnsiana and a collection of folk objects. There is a large collection of Mauchline boxware and an exhibition devoted to curling and curling stones which are made in the village. Nearby is Mauchline Kirkyard (scene of *The Holy Fair*) in which are buried four of Burns' daughters and a number of his friends and contemporaries. Other places of interest nearby are 15th-century Mauchline Castle and Poosie Nansie's Tavern.

197 BURNS MAUSOLEUM 5B9

St Michael's Churchyard, Dumfries. All reasonable times. Free. Tel: (0387) 53862.

Burns was buried in St Michael's Churchyard near to the house in Mill Vennel where he died in 1796 (see No 195). In 1815 his remains were moved into the present elaborate mausoleum.

Burns Monument

198 BURNS MONUMENT, ALLOWAY   4G7

B7024 at Alloway, 2m S of Ayr. Open all year. June-Aug 0900-1800;
April, May, Sept, Oct 1000-1700 (Sun 1400-1700), Nov-Mar 1000-1600
(not Sun). Entrance charge includes Burns' Cottage. Family tickets.
(Trustees of Burns Monument). Tel: (0292) 41321.

Grecian monument (1823) to the poet with relics
dating back to the 1820s. Nearby is the attractive
River Doon, spanned by the famous Brig o' Doon,
a single arch (possibly 13th century), central to Burns'
poem *Tam o' Shanter*. Museum, gift shop, gardens.
(See also No 193).

199 BURNS MONUMENT AND MUSEUM,
KILMARNOCK   4H6

Kay Park. Closed till further notice. View from outside only.
Tel: (0563) 26401.

The Monument has a statue by W G Stevenson,
offering fine views over the surrounding countryside.

200 BURNSWARK HILL   5C9

By unclassified road, 1½m N of B725, Ecclefechan-Middlebie road.
All reasonable times. Free.

A native hill fort (around 6th century BC) with
extensive earthworks, flanked by a Roman artillery
range. Thought to have been a series of Roman
practice siege works, best seen from the hilltop. The
excavated ditches and ramparts of Birrens fort are
nearby.

201 BURNTISLAND MUSEUM   6E5

Above library, High Street. Jan-Dec. Open library hours. Car parking
nearby. Free. Tel: (0592) 260732.

''Burntisland Edwardian Fair'' recreates the sights and
sounds of the town's Fair as it was in 1910. Also small
local history gallery.

202   BUTE MUSEUM   4F5

Stuart Street, Rothesay. Apr-Sep, Mon-Sat 1030-1630 (June-Sep, Sun 1430-1630); Oct-Mar, Tue-Sat 1430-1630. Entrance charge. Lecture room. Parking available. (Buteshire Natural History Society). Tel: (0700) 502248.

Exhibits relating to the Island of Bute, including geology, prehistory, Clyde steamers, recent bygones, birds and mammals.

203   BYGONES MUSEUM AND BALQUHIDDER VISITOR CENTRE   4H2

Stronvar House, Balquhidder, 2½ miles W of A84 between Lochearnhead and Strathyre. Follow Thistle signs to Rob Roy's Grave. Mar-Oct. Daily 1030-1700. Free car park open all year for walkers. Entrance charge. Group concessions. Shop. Tearoom. Tel: (087 74) 688.

A collection of everyday items and curios of yesteryear, displayed in a Scottish laird's baronial mansion overlooking Loch Voil and the Braes o' Balquhidder. Stronvar House was built by David Bryce in 1850, for David Carnegie. Balquhidder was the home of Rob Roy Macgregor, and his grave can be seen in the village churchyard. (See No 1085).

The Byre Theatre

204   THE BYRE THEATRE   6G2

Abbey Street, St Andrews. Group concessions available for performances. Theatre seats 174. Parking available. Bar, coffee bar. Evening meals for groups, by arrangement. Inductive loop. Sign language performance. Tel: (0334) 76288.

Resident professional repertory company during the summer months.

205   CAERLAVEROCK CASTLE   5C10

Off B725, 9m S of Dumfries. Opening standard. Entrance charge. Group concessions. Parking available. (HS) 031-244 3101.

ASVA

This seat of the Maxwell family dates back to 1270. In 1330, Edward I laid siege to it and in 1638 it capitulated to the Covenanters after a siege lasting 13 weeks. The castle is triangular with round towers. The heavy machicolation is 15th century and over the gateway between two splendid towers can be seen the Maxwell crest and motto. The interior was reconstructed in the 17th century as a Renaissance mansion, with fine carving.

206 CAERLAVEROCK NATIONAL NATURE RESERVE   **5C10**

♿ P

B725, S of Dumfries, by Caerlaverock Castle and Wildfowl & Wetland Trust Refuge. All year. Free. Parking available. (SNH) Tel: (038 777) 275.

An internationally important reserve covering 7,710 hectares of salt marsh and inter-tidal foreshore on the north Solway. Noted haunt of wintering wildfowl, including up to 13,000 barnacle geese, and the most northerly colony of natterjack toads in Britain. Access unrestricted except in sanctuary area. Care must be taken in relation to tides and quicksands. Wildfowling on parts of the reserve, by permit only. Leaflets from Reserve Office, Hollands Farm Road, Caerlaverock, Dumfries DG1 4RS.

Cairn Baan: see No 800.

207 CAIRNGORM CHAIRLIFT   **3C10**

A951 from A9 at Aviemore, then by Loch Morlich to car park at 2,000 feet. All year, daily 0900-1630, depending on weather. Prices vary according to journey. Group rates. Tel: (047 986) 1261.

At the car park is a large Day Lodge containing bar, shop and snack bar. At the top of the chairlift is the Ptarmigan snack bar, the highest observation building in Great Britain at 3,600 feet with magnificent views to west and north-east.

208 THE CAIRNGORM REINDEER CENTRE   **3C10**

Reindeer House, Glenmore. A951 from Aviemore. All year, daily 1000-1700. Herd visits, 1100 departure. Extra afternoon trips at peak times. Parking available. Tel: (0479) 861 228.

Britain's only herd of reindeer, free-ranging on the northern slopes of the Cairngorms. Visitors join the guide for a walk to the reindeer's hillside grazing. Exhibition with audio-visual and gift shop.

209 CAIRNPAPPLE HILL   **6C6**

Off B792, 3m N of Bathgate. Apr-Sep, standard opening, closed Oct-Mar. Entrance charge. Group concessions. (HS) Tel: 031-244 3101.

Sanctuary and burial cairns. Originally a Neolithic sanctuary remodelled in the Early Bronze Age (c 1800 BC) as a monumental open-air temple in the form of a stone circle with enclosing ditch. Later (c 1500 BC) it was despoiled and built over by a Bronze Age Cairn, considerably enlarged several centuries later. Now excavated and laid out.

210 CAIRNSMORE OF FLEET RESERVE   **4H10**

♿ A P

Buckshead, Gatehouse of Fleet. Take B796 from Gatehouse for 6 miles, turn right at junction for 1 mile, then gates to Dromore Farm Steading. All year. Free. Car parking, limited coach parking. (SNH) Tel: (0557) 814435 or (0671) 3440.

Internationally important reserve of 2,370 hectares of mountain moorland rising to over 700 metres and home to a wide range of wildlife and upland plants. Traditional hill sheep farming is part of the site management centred around the reserve office which sits close to the scenic back-drop of the Clints of Dromore, the old "Paddy" line and the big Fleet viaduct and the river. On the open hill, no paths and difficult terrain. No restrictions on access-only climbing.

211 CAITHNESS GLASS (PERTH) 6D2

& T

Inveralmond, Perth. On A9 north of the town. All year. Free. Factory Shop: Mon-Sat 0900-1700, Sun 1300-1700, Sun 1100-1700 (Easter-end Sept). Factory viewing: Mon-Fri 0900-1630. Parking available. Shop. Restaurant. (Caithness Glass Plc.) Tel: (0738) 37373.

ASVA

Visitors are welcome at the factory to see the fascinating process of glass-making. Factory shop, paperweight museum and gallery, and licensed restaurant.

212 CAITHNESS GLASS (WICK) 3E3

& T

Airport Industrial Estate, Wick. Jan-Dec. Mon-Sat 0900-1700, Sun 1100-1700. (Winter, closed Sun). Free. Restaurant and factory shop. Tel: (0955) 2286.

ASVA

Glass making seen from upper and lower viewing galleries, also engraving and jewellery departments. Exhibition showing history of the company.

213 CALDERGLEN COUNTRY PARK 5A6

& T

Strathaven Road, East Kilbride. Park: all times, Visitor Centre (summer): Mon-Fri 1030-1700, Sat and Sun, public holidays, 1130-1830; winter 1130-1600. Free. Tel: (03552) 36644.

Park consists of over 300 acres of wooded gorge and parkland 5km in length. Extensive path system, nature trails, picnic sites, woodland and river with large waterfalls. Visitor Centre gives history of the landscape in the area and includes 'hidden worlds' natural history display. Ornamental garden, children's zoo and adventure playground. Ranger service.

214 CALEDONIAN CANAL 2H10

&

Canal Office, Seaport Marina, Muirtown Wharf, Inverness. Tel: (0463) 233140.

Designed by Thomas Telford and completed in 1822, the Caledonian Canal links the lochs of the Great Glen (Loch Lochy, Loch Oich and Loch Ness). It provides a coast to coast shortcut between Corpach near Fort William and Clachnaharry at Inverness. The Canal has been described as the most beautiful in Europe—the spectacular Highland scenery of lochs, mountains and glens is unusual for a canal. A wide variety of craft on the canal throughout the year and can usually be seen at close quarters as they pass through locks and bridges. There are a number of pleasure cruises available on the canal and small boats are available. (See also No 778).

215 CALLANISH STANDING STONES   2C5

Callanish, off A858, 12m W of Stornoway, Lewis. All times. Free. (HS) Tel: 031-244 3101.

A unique cruciform setting of megaliths second in importance only to Stonehenge. It was probably carried out in a series of additions between 3000 and 1500 BC. An avenue of 19 monoliths leads north from a circle of 13 stones, with rows of more stones fanning out to south, east and west. Inside the circle is a small chambered tomb.

216 CALLENDAR HOUSE   6B6

♿
P
T
Callendar Park, Falkirk. Jan-Dec. Mon-Sat 1000-1700, Sun (Apr-Sep) 1400-1700. Entrance charge. Shop. Tel: (0324) 614031.

Mansion set in beautiful parkland close to centre of Falkirk. Exhibition tells the 900-year history of the house, costumed interpreters describe early 19th century life in the restored kitchens. Temporary exhibition gallery in restored dining room.

217 CAMBO GARDENS   6H3

♿
1m S of Kingsbarns on the A917, 2½m N of Crail. All year, Mon-Fri 1000-1600. Entrance charge. Parking available. Tel: (0333) 50313.

Charming Victorian walled garden designed around the Cambo Burn, with a small waterfall spanned by an oriental bridge set against a weeping willow. Provides flowers, fruit and vegetables to mansion house (not open). Acres of snowdrops and daffodils in spring, followed by lilac, peonies and irises. Old fashioned roses in summer, crocus, chrysanthemums and dahlias in autumn.

218 CAMBUSKENNETH ABBEY   6A5

1m E of Stirling. Open all reasonable times. Free. (HS) Tel: 031-244 3101.

Ruins of an abbey founded in 1147 as a house of Augustinian Canons. Scene of Bruce's Parliament, 1326.

219 CAMERONIANS (SCOTTISH RIFLES) REGIMENTAL MUSEUM   5A6

♿
Mote Hill, off Muir Street, Hamilton. All year. Mon-Sat 1000-1300, 1400-1700, closed all day Thursday. Free. Parking available. Tel: (0698) 428688.

Display of uniforms, medals, banners, and documents, relating to the regiment and also to Covenanting times.

220 CAOL ILA DISTILLERY   4C5

Port Askaig, Isle of Islay. Ferries from Kennacraig and (summer) Oban. Jan-Dec exc Christmas & New Year. Mon-Fri, by appointment. Parking available. Shop. Tel: (049 684) 207.

Built in 1846, Caol Ila Distillery looks out over the Sound of Islay towards Jura. Water from Loch nam Ban flows to supply the distillery, finishing in an attractive waterfall which was once the main source of power. The main buildings were replaced in the early 1970s and how house six stills producing a fine traditional Islay malt whisky.

221   CAPE WRATH   2G2

12m NW of Durness. Ferry: Tel: (0971) 511376.
Minibus: Tel: (0971) 511287 or 511343.

The most northerly point of Scotland's north-west
seaboard. A passenger ferry (summer only) connects
with a minibus service to the cape. Also some of
mainland Britain's highest sea cliffs at Clo Mor which
stand 920 ft high.

222   CARDHU DISTILLERY
VISITOR CENTRE   3D9

On the B9102 on north bank of River Spey. Jan-Dec. Mon-Fri
0930-1630. Sat 0930-1630 (May-Sept). Parking available. Shop.
Tearoom. Landscaped gardens, picnic area; cafeteria for snacks.
Tel: (034 06) 204.

The origins of Cardhu go back to the heyday of illicit
distilling, when farmers made use of their own barley
and local water. Licensed since 1824, the Cumming
family expanded and improved the distillery over many
years. Now a major element in the famous Johnnie
Walker company. New visitor centre with exhibition
depicting the history of Cardhu and Johnnie Walker.

Cardoness Castle.

223   CARDONESS CASTLE   5A10

On A75, 1m SW of Gatehouse of Fleet. Opening standard Apr-Sept,
weekends only Oct-Mar. Entrance charge. Group concessions.
Parking available. (HS) Tel: 031-244 3101.

This 15th-century tower house was long the home of
the McCullochs of Galloway. It is four storeys high,
with a vaulted basement. Features include the original
stairway, stone benches and elaborate fireplaces.

224   CARFIN GROTTO   6A7

Carfin Village, 2m N of Motherwell. Daily. Free. Parking available.
Tel: (0698) 263308.

Replica of the Grotto of Our Lady of Lourdes and a
place of pilgrimage, created in 1920 by local
volunteers. Reliquary with relics of a number of saints
can be viewed.

225   CARLETON CASTLE   4F9

Off A77, 6m S of Girvan. All reasonable times. Free.

One in a link of Kennedy watchtowers along the
coast. Now a ruin, it was famed in ballad as the seat of
a baron who got rid of seven wives by pushing them
over the cliff, but was himself disposed of by May
Culean, his eighth wife.

226 CARLYLE'S BIRTHPLACE 5C9

A74 at Ecclefechan, 5½m SE of Lockerbie. Apr-late Oct, daily 1200-1700 (last tour 1630). Entrance charge. Group concessions if booked in advance. (NTS) Tel: (057 63) 666.

Thomas Carlyle (1795-1881) — historian, essayist and social reformer — was born in this little arched house built by his father and uncle, both master masons.

227 CARNASSERIE CASTLE 4E4

Off A816, 9m N of Lochgilphead. All reasonable times. Free. (HS) Tel: 031-244 3101.

The house of John Carswell, first Protestant Bishop of the Isles, who translated Knox's *Liturgy* into Gaelic, and published it in 1567, the first book printed in that language. The castle was captured and partly blown up during Argyll's rebellion in 1685.

228 ANDREW CARNEGIE BIRTHPLACE MUSEUM 6D5

Moodie Street, Dunfermline, close to Abbey. Apr-Oct, Mon-Sat 1100-1700 Sun 1400-1700; Nov-Mar, daily 1400-1600. Free. Parking available. Tel: (0383) 724302.

Weaver's cottage, birthplace of Andrew Carnegie in 1835, and linked Memorial Hall. The displays tell the fascinating story of the weaver's son who emigrated to Amercia and became one of the world's richest men and who then gave away 350 million dollars for the benefit of mankind. Demonstrations of handloom weaving, May to October, first Friday of month.

229 CARNEGIE LEISURE CENTRE 6D5

Pilmuir Street, Dunfermline. Jan-Dec. Times and charges vary according to activity. Parking available. Cafeteria/bar. Tel: (0383) 723211.

Major leisure centre attracting over 800,000 visits per year. Original building donated by Andrew Carnegie at the turn of the century, but added to and modernised since then. Latest attraction is a large indoor climbing wall.

230 CARNEGIE MUSEUM 3G9

The Square, Inverurie. Jan-Dec. Mon, Tues, Thurs, Fri 1400-1700, Sat 1000-1300. Free. Shop. Tel: (0779) 77778 (NE Scotland Museums Service).

Permanent display of local archaeology, with thematic exhibitions three times a year. Just outside the town on B993 is the Bass, a 60 foot high motte.

231 CARSAIG ARCHES 4D3

On shore 3m W of Carsaig, South Mull. All times. Free.

A 3-mile walk from Carsaig leads to these remarkable tunnels formed by the sea in the basaltic rock. Reached only at low tide. On the way is the Nun's Cave, with curious carvings; it is said that nuns driven out of Iona at the time of the Reformation sheltered here.

232 CARSLUITH CASTLE 4H10

A75, 7m W of Gatehouse-of-Fleet. Open all reasonable times. Free. Parking available. (HS) Tel: 031-244 3101.

A roofless 16th-century tower house on the L-plan, built in the 1560s for the Browns.

233 CARTLAND BRIDGE   5B6

On: A73 W of Lanark. All times. Free.

An impressive bridge built by Telford in 1822 over a gorge, carrying the Mouse Water. It is one of the highest road bridges in Scotland.

Castle Balliol: see No 867.

234 CASHMERE VISITOR CENTRE/
JOHNSTONS OF ELGIN   3D8

& *Turn off A96, follow signs for Elgin Cathedral, cross River Lossie,*
T *entrance 150yds on right. Mill Shop: Mon-Sat 0900-1730. Mill tours*
Mon-Thurs 1000-1630. Free. Parking available. Shop. Tel: (0343) 549319.

ASVA

Cashmere from China and lambswool are dyed, spun and woven by Johnstons. Established in 1798 at Newmill, Elgin, this is the only British mill where raw natural materials are converted into the final product. Mill shop.

235 MV CAST - A - WAY   3F7

Macduff Harbour. For times and charges contact Moray Firth Leisure Ltd,
Station Brae, Macduff, Banffshire AB44 1UL. Tel: (0261) 32877.

Pleasure cruises head east from Macduff harbour passing the notorious Collie Rocks, Tarlair, Melrose, Greenside Beach, Mohr Head, Gamrie Bay, Gardenstown, Crovie, Troup Head, Cullykhan and Pennan.

Castle Campbell

236 CASTLE CAMPBELL   6B4

In Dollar Glen, 1m N of Dollar. Opening standard, except Oct-Mar
closed Thurs afternoon and Fri. Entrance charge. Group concessions. (HS)
Tel: 031-244 3101.

On a steep mound with extensive views to the plains of the Forth, this castle was built towards the end of the 15th century by the first Earl of Argyll, and it was at one time known as Castle Gloom. It was burned by Cromwell's troops in the 1650s. The courtyard, great hall, and the great barrel roof of the third floor are well worth seeing. The 60 acres of woodland of Dollar Glen (NTS) make an attractive walk to the castle. The glen has a variety of steep paths and bridges through spectacular woodland scenery. (See No 359).

237   CASTLE FRASER   3F10

*Sauchen, Inverurie. Off A944, 4m N of Dunecht and 16 m W of
Aberdeen. Weekends in April and October 1400-1700; May, Jun, Sept,
daily 1400-1800; Jul, Aug 1100-1800. Grounds open all year
0930-sunset. Entrance charge. Group concessions booked in advance.
Parking available. Shop. Tearoom. (NTS) Tel: (033 03) 463.*

ASVA

Castle Fraser belongs to the same period of native
architectural achievements as Crathes Castle, and is the
most sophisticated example of this indigenous style
owned by the National Trust for Scotland. One of
the Castles of Mar, it was begun around 1575 by the
6th Laird, Michael Fraser, and incorporates earlier
building. Two great families of master masons, Bel and
Leiper, took part in the work which was completed in
1636. The armorial panel high on the north side is
signed "I Bel". A formal garden has been made in the
old walled garden. Plant sales, tearoom, children's
adventure playground, picnic area, publications.

Castle Girnigoe: see No 249.

Castle Gloom: see No 236.

238   CASTLE KENNEDY GARDENS   4F10

*5 miles E of Stranraer on A75, opposite Castle Kennedy village.
Apr-Sep, daily 1000-1700. Entrance charge. Group concessions. Plant
centre and tearoom. Parking available. Tel: (0776) 2024.*

Historic gardens laid out between two natural lochs,
with ruined Castle Kennedy and Lochinch Castle at
either end. The gardens are landscaped with impressive
terraces, earthworks and avenues around a two-acre lily
pond. Castle Kennedy, known to exist in the 14th
century, was destroyed by fire in the 18th century.
Lochinch Castle privately occupied and not open to
the public. Gardens famous for rhododendrons,
azaleas, embothriums and many other specimen plants.

239   CASTLE MENZIES   5A1

*Weem, 1½m W of Aberfeldy on B846. Apr-mid Oct. Mon-Sat
1030-1700, Sun 1400-1700. Last entry 1630. Entrance charge.
Group concessions. Parking available. Gift shop. Tearoom.
Tel: (0887) 820982.*

Imposing 16th century castle restored by the Menzies
Clan Society, a fine example of the transition between
Z-plan clan stronghold and later mansion house. Seat
of the clan chiefs for over 400 years, Castle Menzies
was involved in a number of historic occurrences.
Bonnie Prince Charlie stayed here on his way to
Culloden in 1746. Small clan museum.

240   CASTLE OF PARK   4G10

*Off A75, by Glenluce, 9m ESE of Stranraer. Not yet open to the public;
may be viewed from the outside. Parking available. (HS) Tel: 031-244 3101.*

A tall, imposing castellated mansion, still entire, built
by Thomas Hay of Park in 1590.

241   CASTLE OF ST JOHN   4F10

*In Stranraer town centre, Castle Street. Mid Apr-mid Sept, Mon-Sat
1000-1300, 1400-1700. Entrance charge. Shop. Tel: (0776) 5088.*

16th-century towerhouse later used as the town jail.
Now open as a visitor centre with displays on
Stranraer and Wigtown District. Information point.

242 CASTLE SEMPLE COLLEGIATE CHURCH   4G6

At Castle Semple, 3m W of Howwood. Not open to the public; may be viewed from the outside. (HS) Tel: 031-244 3101.

The church is a rectangular structure. A square tower projects from the west gable. The apse is three-sided, each side having three windows of debased Gothic form.

243 CASTLE SEMPLE COUNTRY PARK   4G6

&
P
T

Off Largs Road, Lochwinnoch, 9m SW of Paisley. Jan-Dec. 0900-dusk in summer; 0900-1630 winter. Free, but charges for use of loch. Parking available. Snack trailer in summer. Picnic areas and information centre. Tel: (0505) 842882.

Part of Clyde-Muirshiel Regional Park, based on Castle Semple Loch. New lochside interpretative centre, display centre. Rangers lead guided walks and give illustrated talks. Loch open to non-powered craft for sailing, canoeing, windsurfing, rowing. Rescue cover is available. Woodland walks, school water safety tests, orienteering. Cycle track in centre of Lochwinnoch.

Castle Sinclair: see No 249.

244 CASTLE STALKER   4E1

On a tiny island offshore in Loch Linnhe, 25m NNE from Oban on A828. Apr-Aug. open by appointment. Entrance charge includes boat trip. Car parking only. Tel: (063 173) 234.

Picturesque ancient seat of the Stewarts of Appin dating back to the 14th century. Used as a hunting lodge by James IV, it gave shelter to refugees from the Glencoe massacre, was garrisoned by Government troops during the '45 Rebellion, and was fully restored during the 1960s by Lieutenant Colonel Denis Raymond Stewart Allward, whose family now occupies it.

245 CASTLE STUART   3B8

5m E of Inverness on B9039. Jan-Dec. 1000-1700 in summer, 1000-1600 winter. Entrance charge. Group concessions. Gift shop. Parking available. Tel: (0463) 790 745.

Built in 1625 by James Stuart, 3rd Earl of Moray, on land bestowed by Mary Queen of Scots to her half-brother James, Regent and 1st Earl of Moray. Small, attractive garden.

246 CASTLE SWEEN   4D5

On E shore of Loch Sween, 15m SW of Lochgilphead. All reasonable times. Free. (HS) Tel: 031-244 3101.

This is probably the oldest stone castle on the Scottish mainland, built in the mid-12th century. It was destroyed by Sir Alexander Macdonald in 1647.

247 CASTLE TIORAM   2E12

On an islet in Loch Moidart, reached by unclassified road N of A861, 6m NNW of Salen.

The ancient seat of the Macdonalds of Clan Ranald, built in the early 14th century, well situated on a small island and accessible at low tide. It was burned by the orders of the then chief when he joined the 1715 Rising, fearing it might be taken by his enemies the Campbells.

248 CASTLELAW FORT 6E7

Off A702, 7m S of Edinburgh. Open all reasonable times. Free. (HS)
Tel: 031-244 3101.

A small Iron Age hill fort consisting of two concentric
banks and ditches. In the older rock-cut ditch an
earth-house is preserved. Occupied into Roman times
(2nd century AD).

249 CASTLES GIRNIGOE AND SINCLAIR 3E3

3m N of Wick. Take road to Staxigoe and follow signs to castle.
All times. Free. Care to be taken in wet weather. Parking available.

Two adjacent castles on a cliff-edge above Sinclair's
Bay, one time strongholds of the Sinclairs, Earls of
Caithness. Girnigoe is the older, dating from the end
of the 15th century; Sinclair was built 1606-07. Both
were deserted around 1679 and twenty years later were
reported in ruins.

250 THE CATERTHUNS 3F12

5m NW of Brechin. All times. Free. (HS)
Tel: 031-244 3101.

These remains of Iron Age hill forts stand on hills on
either side of the road from Balrownie to Pitmudie,
beyond Little Brechin. The Brown Caterthun has four
concentric ramparts and ditches; the White Caterthun
is a well-preserved hill fort with massive stone
rampart, defensive ditch and outer earthworks.

251 CATHCARTSTON VISITOR CENTRE 4H8

Centre of Dalmellington 15 miles SE of Ayr on A713. Jan-Dec. Mon-Fri
1000-1700. Easter-Oct, also open Sat & Sun 1400-1700. Free.
Tel: (0292) 550633.

Interpretation centre containing weaving tableau with
taped commentary. Changing exhibitions of local
industries in the past such as mining and iron-making,
and showing the heritage site being created at
Waterside. (No 361).

252 CAWDOR CASTLE 3B8

At Cawdor, between Inverness and Nairn on B9090 (off A96). May-first
Sun in Oct. Daily 1000-1730, last admission 1700. Entrance charge.
Group concessions. Gift shop, book shop, wool shop. Parking available.
Restaurant, snack bar, picnic area. Tel: (066 77) 615.

ASVA

The old central tower of 1372, fortified in 1454 (a
family home for over 600 years), is surrounded by
16th-century buildings, remodelled during the
following century. Notable gardens surround the
castle. Shakespeare's Macbeth was Thane of Cawdor,
and the castle is one of the traditional settings for the
murder of Duncan. Licensed restaurant, snack bar and
picnic area in grounds; beautiful gardens and extensive
nature trails; 9-hole pitch and putt golf course and
putting green.

253 CHAPEL FINIAN 4G11

5m NW of Port William. All reasonable times. Free. (HS)
Tel: 031-244 3101.

A small chapel or oratory probably dating from the
10th or 11th century, in an enclosure about 50 feet
wide.

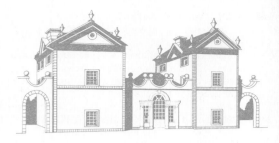

Chatelherault

254   CHATELHERAULT COUNTRY PARK   5A6

*At Ferniegair, 1m S of Hamilton off A72. Visitor Centre: 1 Apr-30 Sept
1030-1800; 1 Oct-31 Mar 1030-1700 daily. Last admission ½ hour
before closing. House: All year, daily 1100-1600 (last admission 1545)
closed for functions—check. Parking available. House free. Visitor Centre,
entrance charge. Gift shop. Tearoom.
Tel: (0698) 426213.*

Magnificent hunting lodge and kennels built in 1732
by William Adam for the Duke of Hamilton. The
buildings have been restored and there are extensive
country walks and a fascinating visitor centre giving a
vivid portrayal of the 18th century characters who
helped to build it. Restored 18th century gardens,
terraces and parterre. Facilities for disabled visitors.

255   THE CHESTERS FORT   6G5

*1m S of Drem, unclassified road to Haddington, East Lothian. All times.
Free. (HS) Tel: 031-244 3101.*

The Chesters is one of the best examples in Scotland
of an Iron Age fort with multiple ramparts.

256   CHORAIDH CROFT   2H3

♿
P
T

*10 miles E of Durness on A838, halfway along W shore of Loch Eriboll.
May-Oct. Daily 1000-2030. Entrance charge, accompanied children free.
Parking available. Crafts and wool for sale. Tearoom. Tel: (0971) 511235.*

Working croft with rare breeds of domestic farm
animals, aquariums and pond containing sea life.
Exhibition of crofting life past and present. Pets'
corner, croft walk taking in animal enclosures and
pointing out features of interest on the croft and in the
surrounding countryside.

257   CHRISTIAN HERITAGE MUSEUM   4G5

♿
A
P

*Benedictine Monastery, Mackerston Place, Largs. Apr-Sep. Mon-Sat
1000-1230, 1400-1700, Sun 1400-1700. Other times by appointment.
Groups by prior arrangement. Free. Parking available. Gift shop. Tearoom.*

Display boards tell the story of the spread of
Christianity and monasticism. Illustrations depict
monastic life — the Rule, the Community and the
Crafts. There are examples of Church needlework and
a collection of beautifully embroidered vestments,
religious items on display and models of ancient
monasteries in south-west Scotland. The Monastery
Chapel is also open and visitors are welcome.

258 THE CHURCH OF THE HOLY RUDE   6A5

*St John Street, Stirling. May-Sep, weekdays 1000-1700. Free. Sundays
1100 (worship). Tel: 0786 747154.*

The only church in Scotland still in use which has
witnessed a coronation, when in 1567, the infant
James VI, age 13 months, was crowned. John Knox
preached the sermon. The church dates from 1414,
and Mary, Queen of Scots worshipped there. Notable
pipe-organ; extensive restoration now ending.

259 CILLE BHARRA   2A11

At Eolaigearraidh (Eoligarry), at N end of Isle of Barra. All times. Free.

The ruined church of St Barr, who gave his name to
the island, and the restored chapel of St Mary formed
part of the medieval monastery. Among the gravestones
preserved there was a unique stone carved with a Celtic
cross on one side and Norse runes on the other. A
replica of this stone now stands in Cille Bharra.

260 CLACHAN BRIDGE   4E3

B844 off A816, 12m SW of Oban. All times. Free.

This picturesque single-arched bridge, built in 1792,
which links the mainland with the island of Seil, is
often claimed to be the only bridge to 'span the
Atlantic' (though there are others similar). The waters
are actually those of the narrow Seil Sound, which
joins the Firth of Lorne to Outer Loch Melfort, but
they can with some justification claim to be an arm of
the Atlantic.

Clackmannan Tower

261 CLACKMANNAN TOWER   6B5

*On a hill W of Clackmannan (A907). No facilities for entry whilst
restoration work is in progress; may be closely viewed from the outside.
(HS) Tel: 031-244 3101.*

Before the partial collapse of this tower with its
14th-century nucleus, it was one of the most complete
of Scottish tower houses. In Clackmannan itself, see
the old Tolbooth, the ancient 'Stone of Mannan' and
the stepped Town Cross.

262 CLAN CAMERON MUSEUM   2H12

  *Achnacarry, Spean Bridge. Turn off A82 at Commando Monument,
turn right after crossing canal. Easter-mid Oct, 1400-1700. Other times by
appointment. Entrance charge. Group concessions. Parking available. Gift
shop. Refreshments. Tel: (0397) 772473/81741.*

Museum shows the history of the Cameron Clan, its
involvement with the Jacobite Risings, the subsequent
resurgence of the clan; also the story of Achnacarry
and its wildlife. Sections on the Queen's Own
Cameron Highlanders, and the Commandos, who
trained at Achnacarry during the last war. Building on
site of a croft burned by Cumberland in 1746.

**263   CLAN DONALD CENTRE
AND ARMADALE GARDENS**   2E11

*At Armadale, Isle of Skye, on A851, ½ m N of Armadale Pier. Apr-Oct,
daily 0930-1730. Entrance charge. Group concessions. Family tickets.
Licensed restaurant and tea room. Tel: (047 14) 305.*

ASVA

Skye's award-winning visitor centre includes the
Museum of the Isles in a restored section of Armadale
Castle, telling the story of the Macdonalds and the
Lords of the Isles; 40 acres of restored 19th century
woodland gardens; several miles of nature trails and
access to a Highland estate; a countryside ranger
service offering guided walks, talks and children's
events; programme of arts events; and self-catering
accommodation.

264   CLAN DONNACHAIDH MUSEUM   3B12

&   *Bruar Falls, Calvine, 4m W of Blair Atholl. Mid-Apr-mid Oct, weekdays
(exc Tues) 1000-1300, 1400-1700, Sun 1400-1700. At other times by
arrangement. Free. Parking available. Shop. Tel: (0796) 483264.*

Clan Donnachaidh comprises Reid, Robertson,
MacConnachie, Duncan, MacInroy and others. Old
and new exhibits include items associated with the
Jacobite Risings of 1715 and 1745.

**265   CLAN GUNN HERITAGE CENTRE
AND MUSEUM**   3D4

&   *Latheron, 16m SW of Wick. June-Sep, Mon-Sat 1100-1700. Also Sun,*
T   *July and Aug, 1400-1700. Entrance charge. Group concessions by
arrangement. Parking available. Gift shop. Tel: (059 32) 325.*

Clan Gunn Heritage Centre at Latheron Old Parish
Church shows the dramatic story of this ancient
Scottish clan from its Norse origins to the present.
Links with America — before Columbus — are traced
by way of the effigy of a 14th century knight on a
rock ledge in Massachusetts.

Clan MacAlister Centre: see No 657.

266   CLAN MACPHERSON MUSEUM   3B11

&   *In Newtonmore on A9/A86, 15m S of Aviemore. May-Sep, Mon-Sat
1000-1730, Sun 1430-1730. Free. Parking available. Tel: (0540) 673332.*

Relics and memorials of Clan Chiefs and other
Macpherson families. Exhibits include a letter to
Prince Charles Edward Stuart from his father, a
massive silver epergne depicting an incident in the life
of Cluny of the '45 after the Battle of Culloden, green
banner of the clan, Victorian royal warrants, crests,
James Macpherson's fiddle and other historic relics.

Clan Tartan Centre: see No 657.

**267   CLAPPERTON DAYLIGHT
PHOTOGRAPHIC STUDIO**   5E7

&   *Scott's Place, E of Selkirk town centre on right near Police Station.
Apr-Oct, Sat and Sun 1400-1630; other times by arrangement.
Entrance charge. Tel: (0750) 20523.*

One of the oldest original daylight photographic
studios in existence, still in family hands. With
changing displays of photographs dating back to the
1860s.

**268 JIM CLARK MEMORIAL TROPHY
ROOM**   5F5

*44 Newtown Street, Duns. Easter-Oct, Mon-Sat 1000-1300, 1400-1700,
Sun 1400-1700. Entrance charge. Parking available.
Tel: (0361) 82600, ext 36/37.*

A memorial to the late Jim Clark, twice world motor
racing champion, with a large number of his trophies.

269 CLAVA CAIRNS   3B9

*Near Culloden, off B9006, 6m E of Inverness. All reasonable times.
Free. (HS) Tel: 031-244 3101.*

An extensive group of standing stones and cairns
dating from the Bronze Age.

270 CLICK MILL   1B11

*At Dounby, Orkney. All reasonable times. Free. (HS)
Tel: 031-244 3101.*

The only working example of the traditional
horizontal water mill of Orkney.

271 CLICKHIMIN BROCH   1G5

*About 1m SW of Lerwick, Shetland. Open all reasonable times. Free. (HS)
Tel: 031-244 3101.*

This site was fortified at the beginning of the Iron
Age with a stone-built fort. Later a broch (which still
stands to a height of 17 feet) was constructed inside
the fort.

Cloch Lighthouse

272 CLOCH LIGHTHOUSE   4G5

A770, 3m SW of Gourock. Seen from the outside only.

This notable landmark stands at Cloch Point with fine
views across the Upper Firth of Clyde estuary. The
white-painted lighthouse was constructed in 1797.

273 CLOCK MILL HERITAGE CENTRE 6B4

Upper Mill Street, Tillicoultry. Apr.-Oct. Daily, 1000-1700. Parking available. Free. Shop with crafts and woollens. Tel: (0259) 752176.

Housed in an impressive former mill building of 1824, at the foot of Mill Glen, the Clock Mill Heritage Centre introduces the long tradition of woollen mills and textile production in the ''Wee County'' of Clackmannan. Exhibition looks at life in the mills during the Industrial Revolution and includes examples of old spinning and weaving machinery. Story boards, audio-visual. Starting point for the Mill Trail, linking several mills and factory shops in Clackmannan.

Llama

274 CLOVERLEAF FIBRE STUD 3F8

Mill of Kinnaindy, Bridge of Marnoch, 8m N of Huntly. Take A97, then take turning to Netherdale on right. The farm is 300 yds from junction. Jan-Dec. Guided tours at 1100, 1300 and 1500; other times by arrangement. Entrance charge. Group concessions. Parking available. Gift shop. Tel: (0466) 780879.

Working farm breeding llamas, alpacas, guanacos, goats bearing cashmere, cashgora and mohair. Friesland milk sheep. Garments for sale on display together with spinning and knitting fibres obtained from the animals.

275 CLUNY HOUSE GARDENS 5A1

3½ miles from Aberfeldy on Weem-Strathtay road. Mar-Oct. Daily 1000-1800. Entrance charge. Car parking available, coaches by arrangement. Plant stall. Tel: (0887) 820795.

Cluny is a 2.5 hectare wild woodland garden growing mainly Himalayan plants. The garden holds the National Collection of Asiatic primulas and has a wide range of other groups of plants such as meconopsis, lilies, nomocharis, trilliums and rhododendrons. There are fine examples of specimen trees including the widest sequoia gigantea in Britain. April, May and June are spectacular flowering months, while September and October bring lovely autumn colours.

276 CLYNELISH DISTILLERY 3B6

Just off A9 at northern outskirts of Brora. Jan-Dec exc Christmas & New Year. Mon-Fri 0930-1630. Parking available. Shop. Tel: (0408) 621444.

The first Clynelish Distillery was built in 1819, as part of a scheme of economic improvement by the Marquess of Stafford, husband of the heiress to the Sutherland estates. These were early days for purpose-built distilleries, but the aim was to reduce illicit distilling by giving local farmers a legitimate market for their barley. The whisky is now produced at a new distillery with six stills, which was built alongside the original premises in 1967.

277 CLYDEBANK DISTRICT MUSEUM 4H5

Old Town Hall, Dumbarton Road, Clydebank. 3 miles N of Glasgow on A814. Jan-Dec exc public holidays. Mon & Wed 1400-1630, Sat 1000-1630. Free. Parking available. Shop. Tel: 041-941 1331 ext 402.

Community-based local history museum located within Clydebank Town Hall and forming part of the district council's libraries and museums department. Collections reflect early prehistory and the Roman period, but the main emphasis is on the last two centuries of social, economic, political and industrial history. Famous Singer collection of sewing machines, shipbuilding and engineering material, and several items surviving from the Clydebank Blitz.

278 COATS OBSERVATORY 4H5

Coats Observatory, Oakshaw Street West, Paisley. Mon, Tue and Thur 1400-2000, Wed, Fri and Sat 1000-1700. Free. Groups by prior arrangement. (Renfrew District Council). Tel: 041-889 2013.

There has been a continuous tradition of astronomical observation and meteorological recording since the observatory was built in 1882. The recent updating of seismic equipment and the installation of a satellite weather picture receiver has made it one of the best equipped observatories in the country. (See No 1035).

279 COBB MEMORIAL 3A9

Between Invermoriston and Drumnadrochit by A82. All times. Free.

A cairn commemorates John Cobb, the racing driver, who lost his life near here in 1952 when attempting to beat the water speed record, with his jet speedboat, on Loch Ness.

280 COLBOST FOLK MUSEUM 2C9

3m W of Dunvegan, Isle of Skye. Daily 1000-1800. Entrance charge. Group concessions. Parking available. Tel: (047 022) 296.

Thatched traditional 'black house', typical of living conditions in the 19th century.

281 COLUMBA'S FOOTSTEPS 4D8

W of Southend at Keil.

Traditionally it is believed that St Columba first set foot on Scottish soil near Southend. The footsteps are imprinted in a flat topped rock near the ruin of an old chapel.

282 COMBINED OPERATIONS MUSEUM 4F3

Cherry Park, in grounds of Inveraray Castle, Inveraray. First Sat in Apr-second Sun in Oct. Mon-Sat, 1000-1800, Sun 1300-1800, closed Fri. except in Jul-Aug. Last admissions: 1730. Entrance charge. Group concessions. Parking available. Tel: (0499) 2203.

The museum covers the work of No. 1 Combined Training Centre at Inveraray during World War II, where 250,000 troops were trained in beach assault landing techniques. Displays also cover Commando raids and landings from Dieppe to D-Day. Scale models of ships, and landing craft.

283 PS "COMET" REPLICA 4G5

Port Glasgow town centre, adjacent to A8. May be viewed from outside. Jan-Dec. Car parking available.

Replica of the first sea-going paddle steamer in Europe which was built in Port Glasgow in 1812, to carry freight and passengers between Greenock, Helensburgh and Glasgow.

284 COMLONGON CASTLE 5C10

Situated in Clarencefield, midway between Dumfries and Annan on B725. Apr-Sept, by appointment only. Entrance charge. Group concessions by arrangement. Gardens not open to public. Parking available. Tel: (038 787) 283.

15th century restored castle furnished with period artefacts. Great Hall is decorated with arms and heraldic displays.

Commando Memorial

285 COMMANDO MEMORIAL 2H12

Off A82, 11m NE of Fort William. Parking available.

An impressive sculpture by Scott Sutherland, erected in 1952 to commemorate the Commandos of World War II who trained in this area. Fine views of Ben Nevis and Lochaber.

286 CORGARFF CASTLE 3D10

Off A939, 15m NW of Ballater. Opening standard, key-keeper in winter. Entrance charge. Group concessions. Parking available. (HS) Tel: 031-244 3101.

ASVA

A 16th-century tower house, converted into a garrison post and enclosed within a star-shaped loopholed wall in 1748. The castle was burned in 1571 by Edom o' Gordon and the wife, family and household of Alexander Forbes, the owner, perished in the flames. (See also No 90).

287 THE CORNICE MUSEUM OF ORNAMENTAL PLASTERWORK 5D6

Innerleithen Road, Peebles. Entrance opposite Park Hotel main entrance. Apr-Oct. Mon-Fri 1400-1600, Sat 1030-1230, or by arrangement. Entrance charge. Group concessions. Tel: (0721) 20212.

Re-creation of a plasterer's casting workshop from around the turn of the century, illustrating main methods of creating ornamental plasterwork used in Scotland at that time. Large collection of "masters".

288 CORRIESHALLOCH GORGE 2G7

A835 at Braemore, 12m SSE of Ullapool. All times. Free.
Parking available. (NTS) Tel: (0463) 232084.

Spectacular mile-long gorge, one of the finest examples
in Britain of a box canyon, is 200 feet deep, and
contains the Falls of Measach which plunge 150 feet.
Suspension bridge viewpoint.

289 CORRIMONY CAIRN 2H9

At Glen Urquhart, 8½m W of Drumnadrochit, Loch Ness. All times.
Free. (HS) Tel: 031-244 3101.

This neolithic chambered cairn is surrounded by a slab
kerb, outside which is a circle of standing stones.

290 CORRYVRECKAN WHIRLPOOL 4D4

Between the islands of Jura and Scarba.

This treacherous tide-race, very dangerous for small
craft, covers an extensive area and may be seen from
the north end of Jura or from Craignish Point. The
noise can sometimes be heard from a considerable
distance.

291 COULTER MOTTE 5B6

Off A72, 2m N of Coulter, 1½m SW of Biggar (A702). Open all
reasonable times. Free. (HS) Tel: 031-244 3101.

Early medieval castle mound, originally moated and
probably surrounded by a palisade enclosing a timber
tower.

292 COWDENBEATH LEISURE CENTRE 6D5

Pitt Road, Cowdenbeath. 6 miles from Dunfermline. Jan-Dec. Mon-Fri
0700-2100. Sat & Sun 0900-1630. Entrance charge. Group concessions.
Parking available. Tel: (0383) 514520.

Opened in June 1987, Centre has 25-metre main
swimming pool and 11-metre toddlers' pool kept at a
constant 84°. Multi-gym with free weights and life
rower, life cycle power jog and climbmax; sunbeds and
sauna.

293 CRAFT CENTRE
AND KINTYRE ALPINE NURSERY 4E7

Torrisdale. 12 miles from Campbeltown on B842 to Carradale. Apr-Dec.
Mon-Sat 1000-1800, Sun 1400-1800. Free. Parking available. Plants,
books, crafts, paintings for sale. Tearoom. Tel: (058 33) 317.

Picturesque crofthouse converted to craft
shop/tearoom and alpine nursery. Panoramic views,
overlooks seal colony on shore. Landscaped garden
with alpine trough display. Alpine plants, unusual
rhododendrons and choice herbaceous plants for sale.

294 CRAGGAN FISHERY 3C9

1 mile S of Grantown-on-Spey on A95. Apr-Oct, daily. Oct-Mar,
Wed-Sun, weather permitting. 1000-1800, also Thurs 1800-2200.
Entrance charge. Car parking only. Snack bar. Tel: (0479) 2120.

Two trout fishing lochs. Main loch, fly only, brown
and rainbow trout. Small loch has bait fishing for
under-15s. Rod hire, permits sold on site.

295 CRAIG HIGHLAND FARM 2F9

Two miles E of Plockton on shore road to Stromeferry. Mar-Oct. 1000-dusk. Entrance charge. Group concessions by arrangement. Car parking only. Tel: (059 984) 205.

Rare breeds farm on the shores of Loch Carron, dedicated to the conservation of domestic farm animals, poultry and waterfowl. Visitors meet and may feed animals including pigs, sheep, rabbits, pheasants, goats, pony, llama. Much stock is now critically rare, especially ancient breeds of Highland sheep, some of which are now fewer than 100 in number. Site overlooks seals, a heronry, pine woodland towards the Applecross hills over the loch. Private shore and coral strand.

296 CRAIGCLEUCH CASTLE COLLECTION 5D9

    2m NW of Langholm on B709. Easter, May-Sept, daily 1000-1700, or by arrangement. Entrance charge. Gift shop. Woodland Walks. Parking available. Tel: (038 73) 80137.

Baronial Scottish stone mansion exhibiting the Craigcleuch collection, hundreds of superb selected curiosities. Fine rare tribal ethnographic carvings, sculptures, masks, paintings on silk. Prehistoric American Indian carved stone animals and birds. Exquisite red coral carving. Chinese Jade animals, Japanese Ivories. Unspoiled panoramic views over mountains of Southern Uplands 'Gates of Eden', woodlands.

297 CRAIGELLACHIE BRIDGE 3D8

Near A941, just N of Craigellachie, 12m SSE of Elgin. Parking available.

One of Thomas Telford's most beautiful bridges. Opened in 1814, it carried the main road till 1973 when a new bridge was built alongside. It has a 152 ft main span of iron, cast in Wales, and two ornamental stone towers at each end.

298 CRAIGNETHAN CASTLE 5A6

2½m W of A72 at Crossford, 5m NW of Lanark. Apr-Sept, opening standard. Closed Oct-Mar. Entrance charge. Group concessions. Parking available. (HS) Tel: 031-244 3101.

This extensive and well-preserved ruin, chief stronghold of the Hamiltons who were supporters of Mary, Queen of Scots, was repeatedly assailed by the Protestant party and partly dismantled by them in 1579. The oldest, central portion is a large tower house of unusual and ornate design. Recent excavations have revealed possibly the earliest example in Britain of a *caponier*, a covered gun-looped passageway across a defensive ditch.

299 CRAIGSTON CASTLE 3G8

Turriff-Fraserburgh road, 8m SE of Banff. Can be seen from road. Open by appointment only, June-Sept. Entrance charge. Parking available. Tel: (088 85) 228.

Castle built by John Urquhart around 1602, and still owned by same family. Interesting library and carved wooden panels from 16th century. Adjacent woodlands have interesting species. (See No 1298).

Craigston Museum

300 CRAIGSTON MUSEUM 2A11

Craigston, Isle of Barra. Side road branches off A888 NW of Castlebay. Park at end of tarred road and walk half mile up track. July & Aug, 4 days per week, advertised at Castlebay TIC. Other times by appointment. Exterior of cottage may be viewed at any reasonable time. Entrance charge. Refreshments.

This, the last thatched house in Barra, has been restored by a local committee as a small croft museum, simply but fittingly furnished. It stands in a remote and beautiful location in a glen on the west side of the island and makes an interesting contrast with two nearby chambered cairns. Related exhibition each summer at Castlebay Community School.

301 CRAIL MUSEUM AND HERITAGE CENTRE 6H3

62-64 Marketgate, Crail. Easter period, Jun-mid Sept. Mon-Sat, 1000-1230, 1430-1700. Sundays and weekends outside main opening period, afternoons only. Free. Parking available. Tel: (0333) 50869.

Exhibits illustrate history of Royal Burgh, its Collegiate Church, old harbour and fishing heritage, 200-year-old Golf Club and HMS *Jackdaw* (Fleet Air Arm station during World War II). Tourist Information Centre.

302 CRAIL TOLBOOTH 6H3

Marketgate, Crail. 9m SE of St Andrews. Tel: (0333) 50310.

The Tolbooth, now a library and town hall, dates from the early 16th century, displaying a fish weather vane, and a coat of arms dated 1602. In the striking Dutch Tower is a bell dated 1520, cast in Holland. There have been 18th and 19th century additions. Elsewhere in this picturesque fishing village which is the oldest Royal Burgh in the East Neuk of Fife, see the Collegiate Church dating back to the 13th century, the Mercat Cross topped by a unicorn, the harbour and the crowstepped, red-tiled houses.

303 CRARAE GLEN GARDEN 4F4

A83, 10m SW of Inveraray. All year, daily 0900-1800 (dusk in winter). Entrance charge. Visitor Centre, Crafts, information area, refreshment service. (Crarae Garden Charitable Trust). Tel: (0546) 86614.

Among the loveliest open to the public in Scotland, these gardens of Crarae Lodge, beside Loch Fyne and set in a Highland glen, are noted for rhododendrons, azaleas, conifers and ornamental shrubs.

304   CRATHES CASTLE AND GARDENS   3F11

    P
    T

*Off A93, 3m E of Banchory. Castle, Visitor Centre, Shop and
Restaurant. Apr-Oct, daily 1100-1800. Garden and Grounds all year
0930 to sunset. Entrance charges. Group concessions. Trust shop, plant
sales, restaurant, wayfaring course, adventure playground, picnic area,
dog walks. Parking available. Ranger Service. Tel: (033 044) 525.*

ASVA

Royal historic associations date from 1323, when the
Lands of Leys were granted to the Burnett family by
Robert the Bruce. The Horn of Leys, said to have been
gifted by Bruce, is in the Great Hall. The castle's
features include remarkable late 16th century painted
ceilings. The large walled garden is a composite of
eight separate areas which include herbaceous borders
with many unusual plants. The great yew hedges date
from 1702, fascinating examples of topiary. Six nature
trails including one suitable for wheelchairs. Visitor
Centre with two permanent exhibitions.

305   CRATHIE CHURCH   3D11

*Crathie, 8m W of Ballater. 1 Apr-31 Oct, daily 0930-1730, Sun
1400-1700 (services held at 1130, Sun). Free.*

This small church, built in 1895, is attended by the
Royal Family when in residence at Balmoral.
(See No 109).

306   CRAWFORD ARTS CENTRE   6G2

    A

*93 North Street, St Andrews. Gallery: Jan-Dec. Mon-Sat 1000-1700,
Sun 1400-1700. Craft shop, refreshments. Theatre programme varies.
Galleries free, theatre charges vary. Tel: (0334) 74610.*

Founded in 1977, the centre has a changing
programme of art exhibitions from painting and
sculpture to photography and crafts. Children's
activities during school holidays, lectures and adult
classes throughout the year. Studio theatre used for
performance by a variety of groups.

**307   CREEBRIDGE MOHAIR
AND WOOLLENS**   4H10

    P
    T

*Creebridge Mill, Newton Stewart. Jan-Dec. 0900-1700. Free. Parking
available. Mill shop. Tel: (0671) 2868.*

Mohair and woollen weavers with retail outlet.
Processes include winding, warping, weaving, brushing.

**308   CREETOWN GEM ROCK MUSEUM
AND GALLERY**   **4H10**

&
T

*Approach by A75 to Creetown, turn up opposite clock tower. Apr-Oct,
daily, 0930-1800. Nov-Dec, closed Thurs-Fri. Closed Christmas-early Jan.
Other times, weekends only, 1000-1600 or by appointment. Entrance
charge. Group concessions. Family ticket. Parking available. Tearoom.
Shop. Tel: (067 182) 357.*

A beautiful collection of gems and minerals from
around the world. This large worldwide collection has
taken over 50 years to gather together and is
recognised as being one of the most comprehensive of
its type. Audio-visual display and ''Crystal Cave''.
Gemstone polishing demonstrations in new workshop.
Gift shop specialises in gemstones, jewellery, geological
speciments and lapidary equipment.

309   CRICHTON CASTLE   **6F7**

*B6367, 7m SE of Dalkeith. Opening standard Apr-Sept. Closed
Oct-Mar. Entrance charge. Group concessions. Parking available. (HS)
Tel: 031-244 3101.*

The keep dates from the 14th century, although
today's ruins are mostly 15th/17th century. This
castle, elaborate in style, has an arcaded range, the
upper frontage of which is wrought with faceted
stonework, erected by the Earl of Bothwell in the 16th
century. The little Collegiate Church, ½m north,
dating from 1499 and still in use, is notable for its
tower and barrel vaulting.

310   CRICHTON ROYAL MUSEUM   **5B9**

&
A
T

*Off B725 Glencaple road, 1m S of Dumfries centre in hospital grounds.
Square building with clock face behind church. All year, Thurs, Fri
1330-1630, Easter-Oct Thurs, Fri, Sat 1330-1630. Outwith these times,
open for parties by appointment. Free. Parking available. Garden shop and
tearoom. Tel: (0387) 55301 ext 2360.*

Museum highlights, in a spacious setting, developments
in one of Britain's leading hospitals. Special features
include operating theatre, patients' art 1839-61; topical
displays; library and reading room. Beautiful grounds
with splendid rock garden and arboretum.

311   CRIEFF VISITORS' CENTRE   **6B2**

*On the A822 leading south from Crieff on Muthill Road. All year, daily
0900-late, (0900-1700 winter). The factories are only open on working
days. Free. Plant centre. Children's play area. Tel: (0764) 4014.*

ASVA

A large modern visitor centre containing 180 seat
restaurant, adjoining showroom with two walk round
craft factories enabling visitors to see paperweights and
pottery being made.

312   CRINAN CANAL   **4E4**

Crinan to Ardrishaig, by Lochgilphead. Tel: (0546) 603210/603797.

Constructed between 1793 and 1801 to carry ships
from Loch Fyne to the Atlantic without rounding
Kintyre. The 9-mile stretch of water with 15 locks is
now almost entirely used by pleasure craft. The
towing path provides a very pleasant, easy walk with
the interest of canal activity. There are magnificent
views to the Western Isles from Crinan; where the
Crinan basin, coffee shop, boatyard and hotel make a
visit well worthwhile.

313 CROICK PARLIAMENTARY CHURCH 2H6

   On unclassified road up Strathcarron, 10m W of Ardgay. All reasonable times. Communion service on last Sun in July. Free.

Designed by Thomas Telford, Croick Church is one of 32 'parliamentary' churches built in the Highlands and Islands during the 1820s. During the Clearance of Glencalvie in May 1845, crofters evicted sheltered briefly in the churchyard and left sad messages that can still be seen, scratched on the church's east window.

314 CROMARTY COURTHOUSE 3B7

   P   *Church Street, Cromarty, 25 miles N of Inverness by A9 then A832. Apr-Oct 1000-1800. Nov-Mar 1200-1600. Entrance charge. Group concessions. Parking available. Shop. Tel: (038 17) 418.*

ASVA

Cromarty County Courthouse, built in 1773, has been converted into an award-winning museum with animated figures such as Sir Thomas Urquhart, one of Scotland's great eccentrics. A trial has been reconstructed in the courtroom. Folk tales of the area are told, and the story of Cromarty's remarkable growth in the 18th century. Also available, a personal tape tour of the old town, ''narrated'' by Hugh Miller, Cromarty's most famous son. (See No 942).

315 CROMBIE COUNTRY PARK 5E1

   P   T   *Monikie, near Broughty Ferry. 11½ miles E of Dundee on A92. Turn left at Muirdrum crossroads, signposted thereafter. Jan-Dec, 1000-dusk. Free. Parking available. Tel: (024 16) 360.*

Scenic country park based on Victorian reservoir which supplied Dundee until 1981. Broadleaved and coniferous woodlands. Within the park, a variety of habitats support grebes, coots, ducks and moorhens, pink foot and greylag geese in winter, woodland birds such as green woodpeckers, tree creepers and crossbills, red squirrels, roe deer and foxes. Ranger service. Discovery trail. Hide, trail and other facilities for disabled visitors. Picnic and barbecue areas, play park and conservation areas.

316 CROOK OF DEVON FISH FARM 6C4

   T   *5 miles W of Kinross on A977 to Kincardine Bridge. Mar-Oct, then weekends up to Christmas. Daily 1000-1800 (2000 in summer). Entrance and permit charges. Parking available. Shop. Restaurant. Tel: (0577) 840297.*

Working trout farm stocking 50,000 rainbow trout in ponds. Bank fishing available. Visitors can feed the trout and visit the ''Commando-style'' adventure park.

317 CROSS KIRK 5C6

   Peebles. Open all reasonable times. Key from custodian in nearby house. Free. (HS) Tel: 031-244 3101.

The remains of a Trinitarian Friary, consisting of a nave and west tower. The foundations of the cloistered building have been laid bare.

318 CROSS OF LORRAINE 4G5

   Lyle Hill, Greenock. Access via Newton Street. Jan-Dec, all reasonable times. Free. Parking available.

Monument to the contribution made by the Free French Navy during World War II. The Cross of Lorraine is situated at a popular viewpoint overlooking the Clyde.

Crossraguel Abbey

319 CROSSRAGUEL ABBEY　　　　　　**4G8**

A77, 2m SW of Maybole. Apr-Sept, opening standard. Closed Oct-Mar.
Entrance charge. Group concessions. Parking available. (HS)
Tel: 031-244 3101.

A Cluniac monastery built in 1244 by the Earl of
Carrick during the reign of Alexander II. The Abbey
was inhabited by Benedictine monks from 1244 until
the end of the 16th century, and the extensive remains
are of high architectural distinction.

Croy Brae: see No 534.

**320 CRUACHAN PUMPED STORAGE
POWER STATION**　　　　　　**4F2**

Off A85, 18m E of Oban. Easter-Oct, daily 0900-1630.
Entrance charge. Parking available. Snack bar. Tel: (086 62) 673.

In a vast cavern inside Ben Cruachan is ScottishPower's
400,000 kilowatt pumped storage power station which
utilises water pumped from Loch Awe to a reservoir
1,200 feet up the mountain. New Visitors' Centre,
guided minibus tour, picnic area and snack bar.

---

321 CRUGGLETON CHURCH　　　　　　**4H11**

Cruggleton Farm, 3 miles S of Garlieston on B7004. Jan-Dec.
Key available at farmhouse. Free.

Ancient church containing Norman arch, rebuilt end
of 18th century.

---

322 CRUMSTANE FARM PARK　　　　　　**5F6**

On A6105, 1¾ miles SE of Duns. Easter-Sep. Daily, exc Tues (unless
opened by prior arrangement), 1000-1800. Entrance charge. Group
concessions. Parking available. Tel: (0361) 83268.

Over 60 varieties of farm animals and poultry
including many rare breeds. Picnic areas.

---

323 ROBINSON CRUSOE STATUE　　　　　　**6F4**

Lower Largo. All times.

Bronze statue of Alexander Selkirk, the real life mariner
on whom Daniel Defoe based his famous character. The
statue has stood on the site of his home for over 100 years.

---

324 CRYSTALS ARENA　　　　　　**6E4**

Viewfield Road, Glenrothes. Aug-May. 0900-2400. Entrance charges.
Refreshments. Tel: (0592) 773774.

Leisure centre with ice skating, ice hockey, curling,
carpet bowls, snooker tables.

325 CUBBIE ROW'S CASTLE   1B10

On the island of Wyre, Orkney. Open all reasonable times. Free. (HS)
Tel: 031-244 3101.

Probably the earliest stone castle authenticated in
Scotland. The *Orkneying Saga* tells how (c 1145)
Kolbein Hruga built a fine stone castle in Wyre.
It consists of a small rectangular tower, enclosed
in a circular ditch. In a graveyard near the castle is
St Mary's Chapel, a ruin of the late 12th century.
It is a small rectangular structure of nave and chancel.
The walls are built of local whinstone.

326 CULCREUCH CASTLE
AND COUNTRY PARK   4H4

&   *Fintry, 6 miles S of Kippen on B822. Jan-Dec. 1200-2300. Free. Parking*
P   *available. Shop. Restaurant, tearoom and bar in Castle. Tel: (036 086) 228.*
T

Culcreuch Castle and its 1600-acre parkland lie
between the Campsie Fells and the Fintry Hills at the
head of the Endrick Valley. Visitors are welcome to
explore the grounds including river banks, two small
lochs and a magnificent pinetum planted in 1842. The
castle, now a hotel, dates back to 1296 and is well-
preserved. It is the ancestral home of the Galbraith
clan, and since 1699 has been the home of the Barons
of Culcreuch.

327 CULLEN OLD CHURCH   3E7

&   *Signposted in Cullen. Apr-Sept, daily 1400-1600. Free. Parking available.*
     Tel: (0542) 40757.

12th-century parish church with 16th and 17th
century additions. Although essentially 14th century,
this church with its fine sacrament house still
incorporates some 12th-century work.

328 CULLERLIE STONE CIRCLE   3G10

Off A944, 1m S of Garlogie, 13m W of Aberdeen. All times. Free.
(HS) Tel: 031-244 3101.

The stone circle of eight undressed boulders encloses
an area on which eight small cairns were later
constructed, probably of late second millennium BC.

329 CULLODEN MOOR   3B8

&   *B9006, 5m E of Inverness. Site open all year. Visitor Centre: all year exc*
P   *25/26 Dec and all Jan. Early Feb-Mar, Nov-Dec, 1000-1600; Apr-mid*
T   *May, mid Sept-Oct, 0900-1700; late May-mid Sept, 0930-1800.*
     Entrance charge. (NTS) Tel: (0463) 790607.

ASVA

Here Prince Charles Edward's cause was finally
crushed at the battle on 16 April 1746. The battle
lasted only 40 minutes: the Prince's army lost some
1,200 men, and the King's army 310. Features of
interest include the Graves of the Clans, communal
burial places with simple headstones bearing individual
clan names alongside the main road; the great
memorial cairn, erected in 1881; the Well of the Dead,
a single stone with the inscription 'The English were
buried here'; Old Leanach farmhouse, now restored as
a battle museum; and the huge Cumberland Stone
from which the victorious Duke of Cumberland is
said to have viewed the scene. Visitor Centre has
exhibition, study room, restaurant, bookshop, audio-
visual programme in English, French, German, Gaelic,
Italian, and Japanese. Induction loop.

Culross Palace

330   CULROSS   6C5

7½m W of Dunfermline. Parking available.

Culross, on the north shore of the River Forth, is a
most remarkable example of a small town of the 16th
and 17th centuries which has changed little in 300
years. The small 'palace' (NTS) was built between
1597 and 1611 by Sir George Bruce, who developed
the sea-going trade in salt and coal from Culross.
With crow-stepped gables and pantiled roofs, the
'palace' also has outstanding painted ceilings. Other
buildings which must be seen include the Study, the
Town House, the 13th-century Abbey (HS), the Ark
and the Nunnery.

331   CULSH EARTH HOUSE   3F10

*Access by Culsh Farmhouse, near Tarland on B9119, 13m NE of Ballater.
Open all reasonable times. Free. (HS) Tel: 031-244 3101.*

A well-preserved earth house of Iron Age date with
roofing slabs intact over a large chamber and entrance.

**332   CULZEAN CASTLE AND
         COUNTRY PARK**   4G8

*Near Maybole, 12 miles S of Ayr on A719. Gardens, Country Park: Jan-
Dec, daily 0900-sunset. Castle, Restaurant, Shops: Apr-Oct, daily
1030-1730. Entrance charges to Castle. Group concessions. Parking
available. Plant sales in walled garden. Inductive loop. Tel: (065 56) 274.*

ASVA

Robert Adam's castle, built 1772-1792 for David, 10th
Earl of Cassillis on a cliff-top site associated with the
Kennedy family since the late 14th century, is notable
for the magnificent Oval Staircase and Round
Drawing Room. The Eisenhower Room traces the
General's career and his close association with
Culzean. There is a 40th Anniversary Exhibition,
National Trust Benefactors' Room and a Trust shop.
Scotland's first Country Park, created in 1969 and
consisting of 563 acres, contains a wealth of interest
from shoreline through the Deer Park, Fountain
Court and Swan Pond to mature parklands, gardens,
woodland walks and adventure playground. Visitor
Centre facilities include a shop, restaurant, exhibition,
auditorium and information. Ranger service,
environmental education and interpretative programme.

333 CUMBERNAULD THEATRE 5A5

Kildrum, Cumbernauld. Jan-Dec. 1000-2300. Charges vary according to event. Parking available. Restaurant and bars. Tel: (0236) 737235.

Based in a row of 18th century cottages, this theatre complex houses an arena-style auditorium seating 250, a studio theatre, restaurant and bars. Year-round programme mixes drama, music, comedy, children's theatre and dance.

334 CUPAR SPORTS CENTRE 6F2

Carslogie Road, next to Elmwood College, Cupar. Jan-Dec. Mon-Fri 0900-2200, Sat 0900-1700, Sun 0800-1700. Charges for activities. Car parking only. Shop. Refreshments. Tel: (0334) 54793.

Sports centre with swimming pool, sports hall, squash courts, fitness training room, steam room, two solaria. Access to all areas for disabled users.

335 CUWEEN HILL CAIRN 1B11

A965, ½m S of Finstown, which is 6m WNW of Kirkwall, Orkney. All reasonable times. Apply to key-keeper at nearby farmhouse. Free. (HS) Tel: 031-244 3101.

A low mound covering a megalithic passage tomb. Contained bones of men, dogs and oxen when discovered. Probably mid third millennium BC.

336 DALBEATTIE MUSEUM 5B10

Southwick Road, centre of Dalbeattie. Open from May 1993, most days May-Oct. Free. Gift shop. Tel: (0556) 610437.

The story of Dalbeattie's industrial development, with displays of artefacts produced in the water-powered industries, such as granite memorials, bobbins, paper, brick and tiles, gloves and fertiliser. Over 10,000 photographs, displays of harbour. Gallery featuring work of local artists.

337 DALGARVEN MILL—THE AYRSHIRE MUSEUM OF COUNTRYLIFE AND COSTUME 4G6

On A737, Dalry Road, Kilwinning. Mon-Sat 1000-1700, Sun 1230-1700. Entrance charge. Group concessions. Parking available. Coffee room. Wholemeal bread, oatmeal and flour for sale. Tel: (0294) 52448.

The museum is within a large restored working water mill. There are extensive displays of agricultural and rural life including machinery, hand tools, furnishings and photographs. The costume collection has been gathered locally and there are three display changes per year. The mill has been in the same family since 1883 and was in existence prior to 1602. Riverside walks. Bakehouse supplies bread and home baking for sale and to coffee room.

338 DALKEITH PARK 6F7

At E end of Dalkeith High Street, 7m S of Edinburgh on A68. Apr-Oct, daily 1000-1800. Entrance charge. Group concessions. Parking available. Shop. Tearoom. Tel: 031-663 5684 (1100-1800) or 031-665 3277 outwith these hours.

Woodland walks beside the river in the extensive grounds of Dalkeith Palace (not open to the public), an 18th century planned landscape. Farm animals including working Clydesdale horses, adventure woodland play area, nature trails, 18th century bridge, orangery and ice house. Ranger Service.

339 **DALLAS DHU DISTILLERY**   3C8

ASVA

Off the A940, 2m S of Forres. Opening standard exc closed Thur pm and all day Fri from Oct-Mar. Entrance charge. Parking available. Shop. (HS) Tel: 031-244 3101.

Built at the end of the 19th century, this picturesque little distillery is a perfectly preserved time-capsule of the distiller's craft and a monument to Scotland's most famous product. Visitors may take guided tours or explore at leisure. Multi-lingual video on the history of Scotch whisky, a taste of the 'water of life', exhibition. Shop offering nearly 200 different whiskies. Picnic site.

Dalmeny House

340 **DALMENY HOUSE**   6D6

&
P
T
ASVA

By South Queensferry, 7m W of Edinburgh, take A90 then B924. May-Sep, Sun 1300-1730, Mon & Tues 1200-1730. Last admission 1645. Other times by arrangement only. Entrance charge. Group concessions. Parking available. Tearoom. Tel: 031-331 1888.

The Primrose family, Earls of Rosebery, have lived here for over 300 years. The present house dates from 1815, in Tudor Gothic style, built by William Wilkins. Interior Gothic splendour of hammerbeamed hall, vaulted corridors and classical main rooms. Magnificent collection of 18th century British portraits, 18th century French furniture, tapestries, porcelain from the Rothschild Mentmore collection, the Napoleon collection and other works of art. Lovely grounds and 4½-mile shore walk from Cramond to South Queensferry. Open throughout the year (except Christmas and New Year) for groups by arrangement with the administrator. (See also No 460).

341 **DALMENY KIRK**   6D6

&

Off A90, 7m W of Edinburgh, 2m E of South Queensferry in Dalmeny. All year, daily on request. Free. Tel: 031-331 1869.

Dedicated to St Cuthbert, Dalmeny Kirk has been described as the most complete example of a Romanesque (Norman) church in Scotland. Built c1130-50, the church consists of a modern West Tower (1934); the original nave, chancel and semi-circular apse; the South Doorway with exquisitely carved arches. On the north side is the Rosebery aisle and crypt built in 1671 by Sir Archibald Primrose. The stained glass windows in the apse were gifted by a Polish army officer at the end of World War II. The church was restored in 1927-37, and in 1992.

342 DALWHINNIE DISTILLERY 3A11

Off A9, midway between Perth and Inverness. Jan-Dec exc Christmas & New Year. Mon-Fri 0930-1700. Parking available. Shop. Tel: (052 82) 208.

ASVA

At 1073 feet, Dalwhinnie claims to be the highest distillery in Scotland, exposed to winter blizzards and often cut off by snow, but enjoying a supply of pure water from the Allt an t'Sluic Burn. Opened in 1898 at this Highland crossroads, to benefit from the presence of the railway link. Visitor centre exhibition features James Buchanan, a licensee of the distillery, famed for his Buchanan and Black and White blends, also the history and geography of the area, and the group of Classic Malts.

343 DAMSIDE GARDEN HERBS AND ARBORETUM 3G12

Situated 2 miles inland off the A92 between Montrose and Stonehaven by Johnshaven. Follow signs. Apr-24 Dec. Tues-Sun 1000-1700. Evenings by arrangement, groups. Entrance charge. Group concessions. Parking available. Tearoom and licensed shop. Tel: (0561) 61496.

Herb garden of over 8 acres showing the history of Celtic, Roman, monastic and formal herbs. Newly planted arboretum. Information area.

344 DARNAWAY FARM VISITOR CENTRE 3C8

Off A96, 3m W of Forres. May-mid Sept, daily 1000-1700. Entrance charge. Group concessions. Also available: estate tours including Darnaway Castle—Jul, Aug, Wed, Thurs and Sun 1300 and 1500 with estate ranger. Tearoom. Tel: (0309) 4469.

Exhibition of the farms and forest of Moray Estates, with audio-visual programme. Viewing platform to watch cows being milked. Nature trails and woodland walks, picnic areas, tearoom and play area. Farm animals, hive bees, tractor shed.

345 BARBARA DAVIDSON POTTERY 6B5

Muirhall Farm, Larbert, near Stirling. Jan-Dec exc Christmas & New Year. Mon-Sat 0900-1730, Sun 1400-1730. Free. Car parking only. Pottery shop. Tel: (0324) 554430.

Living and working pottery in a picturesque converted 17th century farm steading has the workshop in the barn, shop in the cowshed, and a place for visitors to try making pots (small charge, July and August) in the cobbled stable.

346 DAWYCK BOTANIC GARDEN 5C6

Stobo, B712, 8m SW of Peebles. 15 Mar-22 Oct inclusive, daily 1000-1800. Entrance charge. Group concessions. Parking available. No animals (except guide dogs). Tel: (072 16) 254.

Rare trees, including many very fine conifers, shrubs, rhododendrons and narcissi, among woodland walks. In the woods is Dawyck Chapel, designed by William Burn. A specialist garden of the Royal Botanic Garden, Edinburgh.

347 DEAN CASTLE AND COUNTRY PARK 4H6

Dean Road, off Glasgow Road, Kilmarnock. Daily 1200-1700. Jan-Dec exc Christmas and New Year. Entrance charge for Castle. Organised parties by arrangement. Country park: All year, Free. Parking available. Tearoom. Tel: (0563) 22702/26401.

ASVA

14th-century fortified keep with dungeon and battlements and 15th-century palace, the ancestral home of the Boyd family. It contains an outstanding collection of medieval arms, armour, tapestries and musical instruments. Display of Burns manuscripts. The country park has 200 acres of woodland with rivers, nature trail, children's corner, picnic areas, lawns, aviary, deer park and riding centre.

348 DEE VALLEY CONFECTIONERS 3E11

Station Square, Ballater. Jan-Dec exc Christmas and New Year. Daily, 0900-2100 summer, 0900-1700 other seasons. Free. Parking available. Confectionery shop with refreshments. Tel: (033 97) 55499.

Sweet-making seen from a viewing area within the factory. Hand-made production takes around 30 minutes to arrive at the finished article, methods relatively unchanged in the company's 25 years of sweet-making.

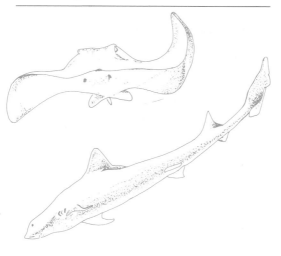

Deep - Sea World

349 DEEP-SEA WORLD 6D6

North Queensferry. Follow signs to Forth Road Bridge. From S, take first exit to North Queensferry. From N, take exit 1 and follow signs to North Queensferry. Jan-Dec exc Christmas & New Year. Daily 0900-1800. Entrance charges. Group concessions. Family tickets. Parking available. Gift shop. Shark Bite Restaurant. Tel: (0383) 411411.

Visitors have a 'diver's eye view' of thousands of fish as they travel along transparent tunnels on an underwater safari beneath the Firth of Forth. Wet and dry interactive exhibits in this, the largest single fish display in the northern hemisphere, include octopus display, corals, tropical fish, rock pools, audio-visual.

350 DEER ABBEY 3H8

At Old Deer, off A950, 10m W of Peterhead. Open all reasonable times. Free. (HS) Tel: 031-244 3101.

Rather scant remains of a Cistercian monastery founded in 1218.

Deer Museum: see Nos 584 and 1250.

351 DELGATIE CASTLE 3G8
Off A947, 2m E of Turriff. Apr-Oct. Daily, 1400-1700. Entrance charge. Tel: (0888) 62750.

Tower house, home of the Hays of Delgatie, dating back to the 11th century with additions up to the 17th century. Its contents include pictures and arms; the notable painted ceilings were installed c 1590. Mary, Queen of Scots stayed here for three days in 1562 after the Battle of Corrichie; a portrait hangs in the room she used. Large turnpike stair of 97 steps.

352 DENNY SHIP MODEL EXPERIMENT TANK 4H5
Building adjacent to Safeway supermarket, access by Castle Street 200yds E of Dumbarton town centre. Jan-Dec. Mon-Sat 1000-1600. Entrance charge. Family tickets. Parking available. Tel: (0389) 63444.

The world's oldest surviving ship model experiment tank. Visitors can witness the process of making wax hull forms, unchanged since 1883.

353 DESKFORD CHURCH 3E8
Off B9018, 4m S of Cullen. Open all reasonable times. Free. (HS) Tel: 031-244 3101.

This ruined building includes a rich carving which bears an inscription telling that *this present lovable work of sacrament house* was provided by Alexander Ogilvy of Deskford in 1551.

354 DEVIL'S BEEF TUB 5C8
A701, 6m N of Moffat. Free. Parking available. Can be seen from the road.

A huge, spectacular hollow among the hills, at the head of Annandale. In the swirling mists of this out-of-the-way retreat Border reivers hid cattle 'lifted' in their raids.

Devorgilla's Bridge: see No 1014.

355 DICK INSTITUTE 4H6
Elmbank Avenue, off London Road, Kilmarnock. Jan-Dec. Mon, Tue, Thur, Fri 1000-2000, Wed & Sat 1000-1700. Free. Parking available. Small shop. Tel: (0563) 26401.

The museum has an important collection of geological specimens, local archaeology, Scottish broadswords, firearms and natural history. The Art Gallery has frequently changing exhibitions.

356 DIRLETON CASTLE 6G5
A198, 8m W of North Berwick. Opening standard. Entrance charge. Group concessions. (HS) Tel: 031-244 3101.

Near the wide village green of Dirleton, these beautiful ruins date back to 1225 with 15th/17th-century additions. The castle had an eventful history from its first siege by Edward I in 1298 until its destruction in 1650. The 'clustered' donjon dates from the 13th century and the garden encloses a 17th-century bowling green surrounded by yews.

357 DOCHFOUR GARDENS   3A9

Approx 6m SW of Inverness on the A82 Inverness-Fort William road. The entrance is near the south end of Loch Dochfour. Apr-Oct, Mon-Fri 1000-1700, Sat & Sun 1400-1700. Honesty Box. Parking available. Plants and fruit for sale. Tel: (046 386) 218.

Fifteen acres of terraced gardens are set against the background of Loch Dochfour in the famous Great Glen. Special features are the magnificent specimen trees, naturalised daffodils, rhododendrons, water garden and extensive yew topiary. The large kitchen garden has soft fruit in season.

358 DOGTON STONE   6E4

Off B922, 5m NW of Kirkcaldy. All reasonable times. Free. Entry by Dogton Farmhouse. (HS) Tel: 031-244 3101.

An ancient Celtic Cross with traces of animal and figure sculpture.

359 DOLLAR GLEN   6B4

Off A91, N of Dollar. Free. Parking available. (NTS)

Beautiful wooded glen providing a spectacular walk to Castle Campbell, which dominates the scene. Great care should be taken: the paths are narrow and steep, and can be dangerous when wet.
(See No 236).

360 DOLLAR MUSEUM   6B4

Castle Campbell Hall, top of Burnside at entrance to Mill Green. Turn off A91 at clock. Apr-Oct. Sat & Sun, other times by arrangement. Museum opening 1993—please check hours with curator. Tel: (0259) 42895.

Permanent display depicting the history and surrounding area. Thematic displays commemorate local events. Changing exhibitions.

361 DOON VALLEY HERITAGE   4H8

Dunaskin Ironworks site, Waterside, 2 miles S of Patna on A713 Ayr-Castle Douglas road. May-Oct, daily 1100-1600. Groups and schools at other times, by arrangement. Entrance charge—allows entry to all sites belonging to Dalmellington & District Conservation Trust. Parking available. Gift shop. Tel: (0292) 531144.

The newest of Scotland's open-air industrial museums, Doon Valley Heritage is situated at the old Dalmellington Iron Company works, and has exhibits illustrating local and social history, countryside and architecture. Nearby, Chapel Row Ironworker's Cottage, a reconstructed dwelling of 1914, may be seen by arrangement with the Conservation Trust.

362 DORNOCH CATHEDRAL   3B6

In Dornoch. All year. 0900-dusk. Free. Parking available. Inductive loop.

Founded in 1224 by Gilbert, Archdeacon of Moray and Bishop of Caithness, this little cathedral was partially destroyed by fire in 1570, restored in the 17th century, in 1835-37, and again in 1924. The fine 13th-century stonework is still to be seen.

363 DORNOCH CRAFT CENTRE   3B6

Town Jail. All year. Summer, Mon-Sat 0930-1700, Sun 1200-1700; Winter, Mon-Fri 0930-1700. Free. Parking available. Coffee room, Apr-Sep. Tel: (0862) 810555.

Weaving of tartans on Saurgr power looms. Small exhibition in Jail cells.

Doune Castle

364 DOUNE CASTLE 5A3

Off A84 at Doune, 8m NW of Stirling. Opening standard except Oct-Mar closed Thur pm and all day Fri. Entrance charge. Group concessions. Parking available. (HS) Tel: 031-244 3101.

Splendid ruins of one of the best preserved medieval castles in Scotland, built late 14th or early 15th century by the Regent Albany. After his execution in 1424 it came into the hands of the Stuarts of Doune, Earls of Moray, in the 16th century, and the 'Bonnie Earl of Moray' lived here before his murder in 1592. The bridge in the village was built in 1535 by Robert Spittal, James IV's tailor, to spite the ferryman who had refused him a passage.

365 DOUNE MOTOR MUSEUM 5A3

&
T

At Doune on A84, 8m NW of Stirling. Apr-Oct, daily 1000-1700. Entrance charge. Group concessions. Parking available. Gift shop. Self-service restaurant. Tel: (0786) 841203.

The Earl of Moray's collection of vintage and post-vintage cars, including examples of Hispano Suiza, Bentley, Jaguar, Aston Martin, Lagonda and the second oldest Rolls Royce in the world.

366 DOUNREAY EXHIBITION CENTRE 3C3

Dounreay, 10m W of Thurso, signposted off A836. Mid May-mid Sept. Exhibition open Tues-Sun (not Mon), 1000-1600. Tours Tues-Sun, 1145, 1300, 1415. Please book in advance. Over 12s only. Free. Parking available. Tel: (0847) 802121 ext 2702.

In operation since 1959, Dounreay Fast Reactor has been supplying grid electricity since the earliest days of the British nuclear industry. The site now provides an international research and development facility. The Dounreay Exhibition Centre has two floors of information, models, videos and hands-on exhibits, suitable for all ages. Tours of the Prototype Fast Reactor, available to visitors over 12 years old, leave the centre each day.

USEFUL ADDRESSES

Many of the properties listed in this book are owned or managed by charities or statutory bodies, and where possible this is mentioned in the text. The Principal bodies are:

Historic Scotland (HS), 20 Brandon Street, Edinburgh EH3 5RA. Tel. 031-244 3101.

Forestry Commission (Scotland) (FC or FE), 231 Corstorphine Road, Edinburgh EH12 7AT. Tel. 031-334 0303.

Scottish Natural Heritage (SNH), 12 Hope Terrace, Edinburgh EH9 2AS. Tel. 031-447 4784.

National Trust for Scotland (NTS), 5 Charlotte Square, Edinburgh EH2 4DU. Tel. 031-226 5922.

Royal Society for the Protection of Birds (RSPB), 17 Regent Terrace, Edinburgh EH7 5BN. Tel. 031-556 5624.

Scottish Wildlife Trust (SWT), 16 Cramond Glebe Road, Edinburgh EH4 6NS. Tel. 031-312 7765.

Many gardens are open occasionally under the auspices of **Scotland's Gardens Scheme,** 31 Castle Terrace, Edinburgh EH1 2EL. Tel. 031-229 1870.

Association Scottish Visitor Attractions (ASVA), 28 Eglinton Street, Irvine, Ayrshire, KA12 8AS. Tel. 0294 313058.

Established in 1988, this organisation aims to maintain high standards among tourist attractions in Scotland, carrying out quality inspections of all aspects from car-parking and toilets to staff service, information and interpretation, and value for money. Entries in this publication displaying the ASVA logo have been inspected and approved.

INFORMATION FOR DISABLED VISITORS

Detailed information for disabled visitors has been requested from all entrants in this publication. Where this was available, we have assessed it and shown by symbol just how easy or difficult it is to gain access to a particular site. Where there is no information in the entry, we have not received a completed questionnaire. If you have any doubts, or enquiries, please telephone the site in advance.

Entries are listed alphabetically according to the **name of the attraction**, eg BURNS MAUSOLEUM. The location is only given when it is part of the name, eg SKYE ENVIRONMENTAL CENTRE. The entries are also **numbered** for cross-referencing and for use on the maps.

Entries in **cities**, however, are listed together under the name of the city - ABERDEEN, DUNDEE, EDINBURGH or GLASGOW. This is because there are many attractions close together in the cities and it is easier to plan a day out when all the attractions can be seen at a glance.

On pages vii - xix , there is a series of **maps** covering the whole of Scotland, with the entries marked by number. Each entry carries a map reference to help you locate it on the correct map.

. The first section of each entry (in italics) gives details of **location**, **opening hours** and **telephone number**. The section also tells you whether you will have to pay an **admission charge**. Distances given are approximate, and are normally the shortest by road, except in a few remote places, where they are 'as the crow flies'.

Opening standard is used in some Historic Scotland entries to denote the following hours: April – September, Mon – Sat 0930 1800, Sun 1400 – 1800; October – march, Mon – Sat 0930 – 1600, Sun 1400 – 1600.

Please check details of properties, opening hours, etc. before making a long journey – things do change.

The second section of the entry describes the attraction, with some history and general details.

There is an index at the end of this book (page 262), breaking down the entries into different interests such as gardens, Folk and Clan Museums, Castles, Scotland for Children and so on.

367 DRUM CASTLE   3G10

Drumoak, by Banchory. Off A93, 10m W of Aberdeen. Apr & Oct, Sat & Sun 1400-1700. May-Sep, daily 1400-1800. Garden of Historic Roses, May-Oct, daily 1000-1800. Grounds open all year, 0930-sunset. Entrance charge to Castle. Group concessions. Play and picnic area. Tearoom. Publications. Parking available. (NTS) Tel: (0330) 811204.

The great square tower of Drum Castle is one of the three oldest tower houses in Scotland. It was the work of Richard Cementarius, first Provost of Aberdeen and King's Master Mason, in the late 13th century. Additions were made in 1619, and during the reign of Queen Victoria, to the fine Jacobean mansion house. In 1323 King Robert the Bruce gave a charter of the Royal Forest of Drum to his faithful armour-bearer, William de Irwyn. Family memorabilia in the Irvine Room. Grounds contain the Old Wood of Drum, coniferous plantations, deciduous woodland, arboretum, Garden of Historic Roses.

368 DRUMCOLTRAN TOWER   5B10

Off A711, 8m SW of Dumfries. Open all reasonable times, apply key-keeper. Free. (HS) Tel: 031-244 3101.

Situated among farm buildings, this is a good example of a Scottish tower house of about the mid-16th century, simple and severe.

**369 DRUMLANRIG CASTLE
AND COUNTRY PARK**   5B8

Off A76, 3m N of Thornhill, Dumfriesshire and 16m off A74 by A702. First Sat in May-late August Bank Holiday. Castle: Mon-Sat 1100-1700, Sun 1300-1700 (closed Thurs). Grounds: Mon-Sat 1100-1800, Sun 1200-1800. Entrance charges for house and grounds. Group concessions. Shop. Tearoom. Tel: (0848) 30248.

Unique example of late 17th century Renaissance architecture in pink sandstone, built on the site of earlier Douglas strongholds. Set in parkland ringed by the wild Dumfriesshire hills. Louis XIV furniture, and paintings by Rembrandt, Leonardo da Vinci, Holbein, Murillo and many others. Adventure woodland play area, extensive garden and woodland walks, gift shop, tearoom, working craft centre and visitor centre in old stable yard. Drumlanrig Bird of Prey Centre has daily free-flying demonstrations. Facilities for disabled visitors include wheelchair lift (unaccompanied).

370 DRUMMOND CASTLE GARDENS   6A3

Muthill, 3 miles S of Crieff on A822. May-Sep. Daily 1400-1800 (last entry 1700). Entrance charge. Cards and brochures for sale. Parking available. Gardens only open to public. Tel: (076 481) 257.

Fine formal garden has magnificent early Victorian parterre with fountains, terracing and topiary. It is laid out in the form of a St Andrew's cross, best viewed from the upper terrace. The multi-faceted sundial by John Mylne, Master Mason to Charles I, has been the centrepiece since 1630.

371 DRUMMOND FISH FARMS   6A2

Aberuchill, 1 mile W of Comrie. Jan-Dec. Jun-Aug 1000-2200. Sep-May 1000-1700. Entrance charges. Group concessions. Car parking, limited coach parking. Farm shop. Picnic facilities. Tel: (0764) 70500.

Fish farm open to view with explanatory notes and boards around farm. Fish feed included in admission charge. Four ponds, including beginners' pond, for fishing. Rods and tuition available.

372 DRUMMUIR CASTLE 3E8

Just off B9014 between Keith and Dufftown. May-Sept, Sun 1400-1600.
Entrance charge. Parking available. Tel: (054 281) 225.

Victorian castle with magnificent Lantern Tower,
recently restored home of the Duff family. Tours
provided by owners. Garden and grounds.
(See No 939).

373 DRUMPELLIER COUNTRY PARK 6A7

&
P
T

From Glasgow leave M8 at junction 8 to A89 to traffic lights, filter left to
B8752 and proceed 1¼m to 'T' junction. Turn right and proceed for
700yds for entrance to Park. Jan-Dec. Visitor Centre (closed Christmas &
New Year) 1030-1930 (summer), 1200-1600 (winter). Butterfly House
open summer only. Free. Parking available. Tearoom. Tel: (0236) 22257.

Extensive park covering loch, heath and woodland
with a good path network, picnic tables and play
areas. Countryside ranger service provides walks and
activities all year round, trail leaflets describe history
and wildlife of park. Woodend Loch has a
birdwatching hide; angling is available all year on
Monklands Canal and on Lochend Loch in summer.
Visitor Centre, Butterfly House, ducks, geese and
swans, orienteering course, golf driving range.
Country fair in June.

374 DRUMTRODDEN 4H11

Off A714, 8m SSW of Wigtown. All times. Free. (HS)
Tel: 031-244 3101.

A group of cup-and-ring markings of Bronze Age
date on a natural rock face. 400 yards south is an
alignment of three adjacent stones.

Dryburgh Abbey

375 DRYBURGH ABBEY 5E7

Off A68, 6m SE of Melrose. Opening standard. Entrance charge. Group
concessions. Parking available. (HS) Tel: 031-244 3101.

ASVA

One of the four famous Border abbeys, founded in the
reign of David I by Hugh de Morville, Constable of
Scotland. Though little save the transepts has been
spared of the church itself, the cloister buildings have
survived in a more complete state than in any other
Scottish monastery, except Iona and Inchcolm (see
Nos 773 and 758). Much of the existing remains are
12th/13th century. Sir Walter Scott is buried in the
church.

376 DRYHOPE TOWER 5D7

Off A708 near St Mary's Loch, 15m W of Selkirk. Access all reasonable
times. Free.

A stout little tower now ruinous, but originally four
storeys high, rebuilt c 1613. Birthplace of Mary Scott,
The Flower of Yarrow who married the freebooter Auld
Wat of Harden, 1576 — ancestors Sir Walter Scott
was proud to claim.

Duart Castle

377   **DUART CASTLE**   4E2

Off A849, on E point of Mull. May-Sept, daily 1030-1800. Entrance charge to Castle. Family ticket. Grounds free. Parking available. Gift shop. Tearoom. Tel: (068 02) 309.

ASVA

Duart is one of the oldest inhabited castles in Scotland, built on a cliff overlooking the Sound of Mull. Home of the 28th Chief of Clan Maclean, the keep was built in 1360 adjoining the original courtyard. The clan supported the Stuarts, and the castle was taken by the Duke of Argyll in 1691. After the 1745 Rising, the castle was used as a garrison by English troops. It fell into ruin and was restored by Sir Fitzroy Maclean in 1911. The keep contains dungeons with figures of prisoners from the Spanish Armada and exhibitions of clan history. Fine views from the wall walk.

378   **DUFF HOUSE**   3F7

At Banff. Under restoration: no access at present. Parking available. (HS) Tel: 031-244 3101.

Although incomplete, William Adam's splendid and richly detailed mansion is among the finest works of Georgian baroque architecture in Britain.

379   **DUFFTOWN MUSEUM**   3E8

The Clock Tower, The Square, Dufftown. Apr, May, Oct, Mon-Sat 1000-1730; June, Sept, Mon-Sat 0930-1800, Sun 1400-1800; July, Aug, Mon-Sat 0930-1830, Sun 1000-1230, 1330-1800. Free. Parking available. Tel: (0309) 673701.

Situated in the Tower at the heart of Dufftown, the museum has displays on local history, distilling, and reconstructed laundry.

380   **DUFFUS CASTLE**   3D7

Off B9012, 5m NW of Elgin. Open all reasonable times. Free. (HS) Tel: 031-244 3101.

Massive ruins of a fine motte and bailey castle, surrounded by a moat still entire and water-filled. A fine 14th-century tower crowns the Norman motte. The original seat of the de Moravia family, the Murrays, now represented by the dukedoms of Atholl and Sutherland.

381 DUIRINISH GARDENS AND NURSERY 2F9

4 miles from Kyle of Lochalsh. Follow the signs for Plockton and turn right at Duirinish. Lodge is on left hand side at the top of the hill. Open Mar-Nov, Mon-Sat, dawn-dusk. Nursery on site—plants for sale. Voluntary contributions go to charity. Limited car parking. Tel: (059 984) 268.

Duirinish Lodge has a wild woodland garden which hosts a wide variety of rhododendrons, azaleas and other tender plants. Native birch, oak and pine woods in sheltered gully site. Viewpoint across to Applecross and the Isles of Skye and Raasay.

382 DUMBARTON CASTLE 4H5

Dumbarton, off A814 on Dumbarton Rock. Opening standard except Oct-Mar, closed Thurs pm and all day Friday. Entrance charge. Group concessions. Parking available. (HS) Tel: 031-244 3101.

Though mainly modern barracks, a dungeon, a 12th-century gateway and a sundial gifted by Mary, Queen of Scots are preserved. It was from Dumbarton that Queen Mary left for France in 1548, at the age of five.

383 DUMFRIES AND GALLOWAY AVIATION MUSEUM 5B9

P
T

Heathhall Industrial Estate, off A701, 3 miles N of Dumfries. Signposted. Easter-Oct. Sat & Sun 1000-1700, other times by arrangement. Entrance charge. Parking available. Gift shop. Tel: (0387) 51895 (Mr R Waugh).

Award-winning museum run by volunteers who have amassed an impressive collection of aeroplane relics and components, including a Spitfire, currently under restoration, recovered from Loch Doon. Visitors can sit in the cockpit of Mystere IVa, one of six complete aircraft. "Firsts" include the first jet-powered aircraft and the first jet trainer to enter RAF service, and the first British-built helicopter. Aero-engines, Air Force uniforms and memorabilia.

384 DUMFRIES ICE BOWL 5B9

King Street, Dumfries. Open 11 months, daily 0900-2300. Entrance charges. Parking available. Refreshments. Tel: (0387) 51300.

New leisure facility with artificial indoor bowling green, ice rink open for skating and curling.

385 DUMFRIES MUSEUM AND CAMERA OBSCURA 5B9

P
T

The Observatory, Dumfries. All year, Mon-Sat 1000-1300, 1400-1700, Sun 1400-1700; closed Sun and Mon Oct-Mar. Camera Obscura closed Oct-Mar. Museum: free, charge for Camera Obscura. Parking available. Gift shop. Tel: (0387) 53374.

Situated in the 18th century windmill tower on the top of Corbelly Hill, Dumfries Museum is the largest museum in south-west Scotland, with collections inaugurated over 150 years ago. Exhibitions trace the history of the people and landscape of Dumfries and Galloway. The Camera Obscura, on the top floor of the tower, was installed in 1836 when the building was converted into an observatory, and gives a table-top panorama of Dumfries and the surrounding countryside.

386 DUN CARLOWAY BROCH 2C4

A858, 16m WNW of Stornoway, Isle of Lewis. Open all reasonable times. Free. (HS) Tel: 031-244 3101.

One of the best presented Iron Age broch towers. Still standing about 30 feet high.

387 DUN DONAIGIL BROCH 2H4

20m N of Lairg. A836, then on Loch Hope road. All reasonable times. Free. (HS) Tel: 031-244 3101.

A notable example of a prehistoric broch.

Dun Telve and Dun Troddan: see No 663.

388 DUNADD FORT 4E4

W of A816, 4m NNW of Lochgilphead. All reasonable times. Free. (HS) Tel: 031-244 3101.

On an isolated once-fortified hillock, Dunadd was one of the ancient capitals of Dalriada (c 500-800), from which the Celtic Kingdom of Scotland sprang. Near its citadel is carved a fine figure of a boar and the sign of a footprint; this is probably where the early kings were invested with royal power.

389 DUNAVERTY ROCK 4D8

At Southend, dominating beach and golf course. All times. Free.

Formerly the site of Dunaverty Castle, a Macdonald stronghold. In 1647, about 300 people were put to death there by Covenanters under General Leslie. The rock is known locally as 'Blood Rock'.

390 DUNBAR LEISURE POOL 6H5

  T
Castlepark, Dunbar. May-Sep, daily 1000-2000. Oct-Apr, 1000-1700 (Thur, Fri 2000). Entrance charges. Parking available. Restaurant/tearoom. Tel: (0368) 65456.

Sited on a clifftop near Dunbar Castle, attractive complex has 25-metre, 6-lane swimming pool with water features, health suite, function and activity hall. Indoor beach area for waterplay for swimmers of all ages, yellow 'banana' flume with speedometer so that swimmers can check the speed of their descent.

391 DUNBEATH HERITAGE CENTRE 3D4

  T
Old School, Dunbeath. Easter-Oct, Mon-Sat 1000-1700, Sun 1100-1800. Entrance charge. Family tickets. Parking available. Bookshop. Tel: (059 33) 233.

Audio-visual, tableaux of sculpted figures, panels and artefacts illustrate the history of the peoples of Dunbeath and their relationship with the land. Stained glass and a mural bring the environment to life. A landscape model is the focus of the geology section, and powerful binoculars scan the Beatrice Oilfield, 12 miles offshore. Displays include local author Neil M Gunn; the running of a Highland estate; the work of Dunbeath Preservation Trust, photographic and geneological archives.

392   DUNBLANE CATHEDRAL   6A4

In Dunblane, A9, 6m N of Stirling. Open all reasonable times. Free. (HS)
Tel: 031-244 3101.

The existing building dates mainly from the 13th
century but incorporates a 12th-century tower. The
nave was unroofed after the Reformation but the
whole building was restored in 1892-95.

393   DUNCANSBY HEAD   3E2

The NE point of mainland Scotland, 18m N of Wick. All times. Free.

The lighthouse on Duncansby Head commands a fine
view of Orkney, the Pentland Skerries and the
headlands of the east coast. A little to the south are
the three Duncansby Stacks, huge stone 'needles' in
the sea. The sandstone cliffs are severed by great deep
gashes (geos) running into the land. One of these is
bridged by a natural arch.

**394   DUNDEE, BARNHILL ROCK
           GARDEN**   6F1

Broughty Ferry Esplanade, via Broughty Ferry town centre and Bridge
Street, off Dalhousie Road. Jan-Dec. Free. Parking available.

Five acres of well-maintained rock garden overlooking
the River Tay and of interest throughout the year with
collections of antipodean plants and an extensive water
feature.

**395   DUNDEE, BARRACK STREET
           MUSEUM**   6F1

City centre. Jan-Dec exc Christmas and New Year. Mon-Sat 1000-1700.
Free (prior notice of groups preferred). Small shop.
Tel: (0382) 23141 ext 65162.

Opened in 1910, Barrack Street Museum now houses
the city's natural history collections for study and
display. Subjects include Scottish wildlife of the
Lowlands and Highlands, geology, and examples from
more exotic locations including the great 'Tay Whale'
skeleton. Gallery for changing exhibitions explores
nature and environmental themes. New displays under
development on ground floor.

**396   DUNDEE, BROUGHTY CASTLE
           MUSEUM**   6F1

Castle Green, Broughty Ferry, 4m E of city centre. Jan-Dec. Mon-Thu &
Sat 1000-1300, 1400-1700 (closed Fri). Sun (Jul-Sep only), 1400-1700.
Free. Booking essential for large groups. Car parking only. Gift shop.
Tel: (0382) 76121.

15th century estuary fort, now a museum, housing
local history displays on fishing, ferries and growth of
the town; Dundee's whaling story; local sea shore life;
military history. An observation room gives excellent
views across the Tay Estuary. Floodlit at night.

**397 DUNDEE, BROUGHTY FERRY
HARBOUR**   6F1

*Adjacent to Broughty Castle Museum on waterfront. Parking available.
Tel: (0382) 23141 ext 4282.*

Recently renovated, the harbour provides a focus for
water-based activities — water skiing, a watering
facility for yachts, sea and river swimming, the
Dundee Water Festival in early August, with raft
races. Water sports equipment for hire. Parking
facilities for disabled visitors.

**398 DUNDEE, CAMPERDOWN HOUSE AND
COUNTRY PARK**   6F1

*Off A923, near junction with A972, 3m NW of city centre.
Tel: (0382) 23141.*

A mansion of c 1829 for the 1st Earl of Camperdown,
son of Admiral Lord Duncan, victor of the Battle of
Camperdown, 1797. The mansion is situated in 395
acres of beautiful parkland containing many rare trees,
(including Camperdown Elm). Golf, tennis,
horseriding, putting. Mansion houses a self-service
restaurant. Award-winning ''Battle of Camperdown''
Adventure Play Park and Wildlife Centre (No 399).

**399 DUNDEE, CAMPERDOWN
WILDLIFE CENTRE**   6F1

*Off A923, near junction with A972, 3m NW of Dundee.
Jan-Dec. Apr-Sep, daily 1000-1630 (last admission 1545). Oct-Mar, daily
1000-1530 (last admission 1445). Entrance charge. Group concessions.
Parking available. Snack bar, souvenir shop, restaurant in park.
Tel: (0382) 623555.*

Indigenous wildlife collection including deer
paddocks, wildcats, pinemartens, European brown
bear, lynx, wolves, arctic foxes, pheasants, golden eagle
and buzzards. Wildfowl ponds, bantams and large
selection of domestic stock. Guided tours for
educational parties.

**400 DUNDEE, CATHEDRAL CHURCH OF
ST PAUL**   6F1

*Castlehill, 1 High Street, Dundee. Jan-Dec. Tours Mon-Fri 1000-1600.
Free, donations welcome. Souvenirs. Refreshments. Tel: (0382) 202200.*

Built in 1853, this landmark cathedral is an
outstanding example of the work of Sir George
Gilbert Scott. The tower and spire are 210 feet high;
inside, a reredos by Salviati of Venice and one of the
finest organs in the country. St Paul's is the Cathedral
Church of the ancient Diocese of Brechin. Notable
Victorian stained glass windows. Guided tours
available, school visits welcome.

401 DUNDEE, CLATTO COUNTRY PARK   6F1

*Dalmahoy Drive, off A972 from Dundee city centre. All year,
1000-dusk. Free. Parking available. Tel: (0382) 89076.*

Reservoir area with 24 acres of water protected by a
shelter belt of conifers and mixed woodland. Particularly
popular for watersports. Windsurfing, canoeing and
sailing equipment for hire (instruction available).
Coarse fishing, rowing boat hire. Barbecue facilities.
Children's play areas.

Claypotts Castle

402   DUNDEE, CLAYPOTTS CASTLE   6F1

S of A92, 3m E of city centre. Apr-Sep, opening standard. Oct-Mar, closed. Free. (HS) Tel: 031-244 3101.

Now in suburban surroundings, this is one of the most complete of tower houses, laid out on a Z-plan. It bears the dates 1569 and 1588 and was built for the Strachan family.

403   DUNDEE, DISCOVERY POINT   6F1

  ♿
  T

Discovery Quay, close to Tay Bridge.
Jan - Dec (from July 1993).
Mar - Oct, Mon - Sat 10.00 - 17.00, Sun 11.00 - 17.00;
Nov - Feb, Mon - Sat 10.00 - 16.00, Sun 11.00 - 16.00.

ASVA

Major new attraction entertains visitors with the story of the Royal Research Ship *Discovery*, Captain Scott's famous Antarctic exploration vessel, built in Dundee in 1901. The centre tells why she was built in Dundee, of her launching and voyages to Antarctica. Audio-visual recounts the rescue of the *Discovery* from the ice by Dundee whaler *Terra Nova*, and the *Morning*. Visitors can also tour the ship in her new berth — sections never before seen by the public have been opened up.

**404   DUNDEE, DUNTRUNE
DEMONSTRATION GARDEN**   6F1

Duntrune Terrace, off Claypotts Road, turn off from A85. Jan-Dec. Mon-Fri 0800-1600. Demonstration Apr-Sep, every Wed pm and alternate Sat am. Parking available. Tel: (0382) 23141 ext 4299.

A year-round display and advice centre on all aspects of gardening.

Frigate Unicorn

405 DUNDEE, FRIGATE UNICORN   6F1

Victoria Dock, just E of Tay Road Bridge. Jan-Dec exc Christmas and New Year. Daily, 1000-1700. Entrance charge. Group concessions. Refreshments available. (The Unicorn Preservation Society). Tel: (0382) 200900.

The Frigate *Unicorn* is a 46-gun wooden warship launched at Chatham in 1824. She is the oldest British-built warship afloat and the fourth oldest ship afloat in the world. Guns, models and displays reveal the facts about life in the Royal Navy in the golden age of sail.

406 DUNDEE, HOWFF BURIAL GROUND   6F1

Meadowside. Daily, closes 1700 or dusk if earlier. Tel: (0382) 23141.

Formerly the gardens of the Greyfriars' Monastery, the Howff was granted to Dundee as a burial ground by Mary, Queen of Scots. Used as a burial ground between the 16th and 19th centuries, it contains many finely carved tombstones. It was also used as a meeting place by Dundee's Incorporated Trades until 1778, hence the name 'howff'.

407 DUNDEE LAW   6F1

All reasonable times. Car park at top of hill. Floodlit at night.

The Law is the highest point in the city, and takes its name from the old Scots word for a hill. It is the remains of a volcanic plug and was later the site of an ancient hill fort. Atop the Law is Dundee's War Memorial with a beacon which is lit four times a year. Magnificent panoramic views across Dundee and the surrounding countryside to Fife and the northern mountains.

408 DUNDEE, McMANUS GALLERIES   6F1

Albert Square, city centre. Jan-Dec exc Christmas and New Year. Mon-Sat 1000-1700. Free (prior notice of groups preferred). Shop. Tel: (0382) 23141 ext 65136.

Dundee's principal museum and art gallery. Local history displays include major galleries on trade and industry, social and civic history. Archaeology gallery, costume gallery, magnificent Albert Hall with its fine stained glass window and vaulted roof. Art galleries contain important collection of Scottish and Victorian paintings. Also silver, glass, ceramics, furniture. Regular touring exhibitions.

409 DUNDEE, MILLS OBSERVATORY   6F1

Balgay Park. Approach by Perth Road/Blackness Avenue/Balgay Road. Apr-Sep, Mon-Fri 1000-1700, Sat 1400-1700; Oct-Mar, Mon-Fri 1500-2200, Sat 1400-1700. Closed Christmas and New Year. Free (booking essential for large groups and for entry into the Planetarium). Parking available. Shop. Tel: (0382) 67138.

Full-time public astronomical observatory, opened 1935. Magnificent Victorian ten-inch refracting telescope available for viewing the Moon, planets etc on clear winter evenings. Small telescopes; exhibition on astronomy and space science; audio-visual. Regular public lectures and planetarium shows; summer activities for children.

410 DUNDEE, SHAW'S SWEET FACTORY 6F1

♿
T

Fulton Road, west end of the Kingsway by NCR Factory. May-Sep, Mon-Fri 1130-1600 (closed last week Jul/first week Aug). Oct-Apr (exc Christmas and New Year). Wed only 1330-1700. Free. Coach parties or large groups Mon-Fri any time by phone (1 hour's notice). Factory shop. Parking available. Tel: (0382) 610369.

1940s style sweet factory, producing old fashioned sweets using traditional methods such as striping and sugar-pulling. The sweet-maker will demonstrate and explain the procedure. Small museum of sweet-making.

Tay Bridges

411 DUNDEE, TAY BRIDGES 6F1

The present Railway Bridge carries the main line from Edinburgh to Aberdeen. Built between 1883 and 1887, it replaces the first Tay Railway Bridge which was blown down by a storm in 1879 with the loss of a train and 75 lives after being in use for less than two years. The Rail Bridge is the longest in Europe.
The Road Bridge was opened in 1966, spanning the River Tay from Dundee to Newport-on-Tay, a distance of 1½ miles. It is made of box girders resting on 42 concrete piers, and took over three years to build. No disabled access to Road Bridge walkway.

412 DUNDEE, TEMPLETON WOODS 6F1

Signposted, N off A923 Coupar Angus road, opposite Camperdown Park. Jan-Dec. Ranger Centre open daylight hours in winter, 1000-1700 Apr-Sep. Parking available. Picnic and barbecue tables. Tel: (0382) 623555.

150 acres of mixed woodland is a major focus for the Dundee Countryside Ranger Service, who operate out of the award-winning Ranger Centre. The centre has an ongoing ecology-based exhibition, and is the start for a wide variety of guided walks.

413 DUNDEE, UNIVERSITY BOTANIC GARDEN 6F1

♿
T

Off Riverside Drive. Mar-Oct, Mon-Sat 1000-1630, Sun 1100-1600. Nov-Feb, Mon-Sat 1000-1500, Sun 1100-1500. Entrance charge. Parking available. Refreshments. Tel: (0382) 66939.

Designed and inaugurated in 1971, this young botanic and teaching garden has a good collection of trees and shrubs, landscaped naturalistically. Two large tropical and temperate plant houses. Award-winning visitor centre.

414 DUNDEE, VERDANT WORKS 6F1

♿

27 West Henderson's Wynd. Jun-Aug. Mon-Fri, 1200-1700 (last admission 1600). Car parking only. Refreshments. Tel: (0382) 26659.

A typical example of an early 19th century Dundee jute mill. Built in 1833, and very little changed since then, the mill is now in the process of conversion into a living museum of Dundee's textile industry. The first stage has brought restoration of the Victorian office and lodge, which can be visited along with the courtyard and boiler room.

415   DUNDRENNAN ABBEY   5A11

A711, 7m SE of Kirkcudbright. Apr-Sep, opening standard. Oct-Mar,
closed. Entrance charge. Group concessions. Parking available. (HS)
Tel: 031-244 3101.

A Cistercian house founded in 1142 whose ruins
include much late Norman and transitional work.
Here it is believed Mary, Queen of Scots spent her last
night in Scotland, 15 May 1568.

416   DUNFERMLINE ABBEY AND PALACE   6D5

Monastery Street, Dunfermline. Opening standard exc Oct-Mar, closed
Thur pm and all day Fri. Entrance charge. Group concessions. (HS)
Tel: 031-244 3101.

This great Benedictine house owes its foundation to
Queen Margaret, wife of Malcolm Canmore (1057-93)
and the foundations of her modest church remain
beneath the present nave, a splendid piece of late
Norman work. At the east end are the remains of
St Margaret's shrine, dating from the 13th century.
Robert the Bruce is buried in the choir, his grave
marked by a modern brass. Of the monastic buildings,
the ruins of the refectory, pend and guest-house still
remain. The guest-house was later reconstructed as a
royal palace, and here Charles I was born.

**417   DUNFERMLINE DISTRICT MUSEUM
AND SMALL GALLERY**   6D5

Viewfield Terrace, Dunfermline. All year except public and local holidays.
Mon-Sat 1100-1700. Free. Small Shop. Parking available.
(Dunfermline District Council). Tel: (0383) 721814.

A 'memory museum' telling the story of Dunfermline
District — its social, natural and industrial history.
Special displays of Damask linen, the industry that
made Dunfermline famous in the last century. The
Small Gallery has monthly exhibitions of paintings,
prints, photographs and crafts.

418   DUNGLASS COLLEGIATE CHURCH   5F5

On estate road, W of A1 (signposted Bilsdean) 1m N of Cockburnspath.
All reasonable times. (HS) Free. Tel: 031-244 3101.

Founded in 1450, the church consists of nave, choir,
transepts, sacristy and a central tower; richly
embellished interior, in an attractive estate setting.

419   DUNKELD BRIDGE   5B1

Over the River Tay at Dunkeld. Free access at all times. Parking available.

One of Thomas Telford's finest bridges, built in 1809.
An attractive riverside path leads from here downstream
to the famous Birnam Oak, last relic of Macbeth's
Birnam Wood, and then around the village of Birnam.
Best view is from riverside garden. Wheelchair users
should approach from the square through the archway.
Riverside path not suitable for wheelchairs.

420 DUNKELD CATHEDRAL   5B1

High Street, Dunkeld, 15m NNW of Perth. Opening standard. Free. (HS)
Tel: 031-244 3101.

Refounded in the early 12th century on an ancient
ecclesiastical site, this cathedral has a beautiful setting
by the Tay. The choir has been restored and is in use as
the parish church. The nave and the great north-west
tower date from the 15th century.

421 DUNKELD LITTLE HOUSES   5B1

   Dunkeld A9, 15m N of Perth. Tourist Information Centre with
audio-visual presentation open Apr-Dec. Free. Parking available. (NTS)
Tel: (0350) 727460.

The houses date from the rebuilding of the town after
the Battle of Dunkeld, 1689. Charmingly restored by
NTS and Perth County Council, they are not open to
the public but may be seen from the outside and
information on them gained from the Visitor Centre
or from the National Trust for Scotland's representative
at the Ell Shop.

Dunmore Pineapple

422 DUNMORE PINEAPPLE   6B5

N of Airth, 7m E of Stirling off A905, then B9124. Not open to public,
viewed from the outside only. Parking nearby. (NTS, leased to the
Landmark Trust) Tel: (0738) 31296.

This curious structure, built as a 'garden retreat' and
shaped like a pineapple, stands in the grounds of
Dunmore Park, and bears the date 1761. It is the focal
point of the garden and is available for holiday and
other short lets by phoning the Landmark Trust
(0628) 825925.

423 DUNNET HEAD   3D2

B855, 12m NE of Thurso. Parking available.

This bold promontory of sandstone rising to 417 feet
is the northernmost point of the Scottish mainland
with magnificent views across the Pentland Firth to
Orkney and a great part of the north coast to Ben
Loyal and Ben Hope. The windows of the lighthouse
are sometimes broken by stones hurled up by the
winter seas.

Dunnottar Castle

424 DUNNOTTAR CASTLE   3G11

Off A92, S of Stonehaven. Mid Mar-Oct, Mon-Sat 0900-1800, Sun 1400-1700. Nov-mid Mar, Mon-Fri 0900-dusk. Last entry half an hour before opening. Entrance charge. Group concessions. Parking available. Cards and guides for sale. Tel: (0569) 62173.

An impressive ruined fortress on a rocky cliff 160 feet above the sea, a stronghold of the Earls Marischal of Scotland from the 14th century. Montrose besieged it in 1645. During the Commonwealth wars, the Scottish regalia were hidden here for safety. Cromwell's troops occupied the castle but in 1652 this treasure was smuggled out by the wife of the minister at Kinneff, 7 miles south, and hidden under the pulpit in his church. The original site has early religious connections with St Ninian in the 5th century. (See also No 815).

425 DUNOON CERAMICS   4F5

Hamilton Street, Dunoon. ½ mile N of town on A815. Jan-Dec exc Christmas and New Year. Mon-Fri, 0900-1230, 1300-1630. Free. Parking available. Gift shop. Tearoom (mornings only). Tel: (0369) 4360.

Factory site of the famous Dunoon mug. Production processes can be viewed from start to finish, including clay making and decorating. Visitors learn about design, manufacture and quality control.

426 DUNROBIN CASTLE AND GARDENS   3B6

Off A9, 12½m NNE of Dornoch, 1 mile N of Golspie. May, Mon-Thurs 1030-1230. 1-15 Oct, Mon-Sat 1030-1630, Sun 1300-1630. Last admission 1600. June-Sept, Mon-Sat 1030-1730, Sun 1300-1730. Last admission 1700. Other times by arrangement. Gardens open all year round. Parking available. Gift shop. Tearoom. Tel: (0408) 633177.

Magnificently set in a great park and formal gardens, overlooking the sea. Dunrobin Castle was originally a square keep built about 1275 by Robert, Earl of Sutherland, from whom it got its name Dun Robin. For centuries this has been the seat of the Earls and Dukes of Sutherland. The present outward appearance results from extensive changes made 1845-50. Fine paintings, furniture and a steam-powered fire engine are among the miscellany of items to be seen. Gift shop, tearoom and museum in grounds.

427 DUNS CASTLE   5F5

16 miles W of Berwick-upon-Tweed on A6105. Open by private arrangement, groups of 8 or more. Charge for tour and refreshments. Parking available. Tel: (0361) 83211.

Duns Castle is a 14th century peel tower with Georgian additions, inhabited by the same family for 300 years. Its Gothic stone and plasterwork are of the finest quality, and its furnishings reflect the Scottish, Dutch and French influences of its history. The castle is set in beautiful landscaped grounds with a lake, now a nature reserve, to the north.

428 DUNSCAITH CASTLE   2E10

At Tokavaig, on unclassified road 20m SSW of Broadford, Isle of Skye.
All reasonable times. Free.

Well-preserved ruins of a former Macdonald stronghold.

**429 DUNSTAFFNAGE CASTLE AND
CHAPEL**   4E2

Off A85, 4m N of Oban. Apr-Sep, opening standard. Oct-Mar, closed.
Entrance charge. Group concessions. Parking available. (HS)
Tel: 031-244 3101.

A fine, well-preserved example of a 13th-century castle
with curtain wall and round towers. The ruins of a
chapel of exceptional architectural refinement are nearby.

**430 DUNVEGAN CASTLE
AND GARDENS**   2C9

Dunvegan, Isle of Skye. Mar-end Oct. Mon-Sun 1000-1730.
(Restaurant, shops, garden. Castle closed Sun morning.) Entrance charge.
Tel: (047 022) 206.

Historic stronghold of the Clan Macleod, set on the
sea loch of Dunvegan, still the home after 700 years of
the chiefs of Macleod. Possessions on view, books,
pictures, arms and treasured relics, trace the history of
the family and clan from the days of their Norse
ancestry through thirty generations to the present day.
Boat trips from the castle jetty to the seal colony,
castle water gardens, audio-visual theatre, Clan
exhibitions, items belonging to Bonnie Prince Charlie.

**431 DURISDEER PARISH CHURCH
(QUEENSBERRY AISLE)**   5B8

& *6 miles N of Thornhill, unclassified road off A702. All reasonable times.*
Free.

A post-Reformation 'T' church, a major monument
in the Scottish Baroque style. The Queensberry Aisle,
with its elaborate monument by Van Nost,
commemorates the second Duke of Queensberry
(d. 1711) and his Duchess (d. 1709).

432 DWARFIE STANE   1A12

On island of Hoy, Orkney. All reasonable times. Free. (HS)
Tel: 031-244 3101.

A huge block of sandstone in which a burial chamber
has been quarried. No other tomb of this type is
known in the British Isles. Probably third millennium
BC.

433 DYCE SYMBOL STONES   3G10

At Dyce Old Church, 5m NW of Aberdeen. All reasonable times. Free.
(HS) Tel: 031-244 3101.

Two fine examples of Pictish symbol stones.

434 EAGLE STONE   3A8

By A834 on east side of village of Strathpeffer. All reasonable times. Free.

A Pictish stone which has two symbols etched into its
surface. One is the shape of a horseshoe and the other
is of an eagle. Several theories as to the stone's origin
exist — one of which is that it is a marriage stone.

Earl Patrick's Palace

435 EARL PATRICK'S PALACE AND BISHOP'S PALACE 1B11

Kirkwall, Orkney. Apr-Sep, opening standard. Oct-Mar, closed. Entrance charge. Group concessions. Parking available. (HS) Tel: 031-244 3101.

ASVA

Earl Patrick's Palace has been described as *the most mature and accomplished piece of Renaissance architecture left in Scotland*; it was built in 1607. The Bishop's Palace nearby dates back to the 13th century, with a 16th century round tower.

436 EARL'S PALACE, BIRSAY 1A10

At Birsay, N end of Mainland, 11m N of Stromness, Orkney. All reasonable times. (HS) Tel: 031-244 3101.

The impressive remains of the palace built in the 16th century by the Earls of Orkney.

Earlshall Castle and Gardens

437 EARLSHALL CASTLE AND GARDENS 6G2

♿ A P *1m E of Leuchars, off A92, 6 miles from St Andrews. Apr-Oct, daily 1300-1800. Entrance charge. Group concessions. Free admission to garden for visitors in wheelchairs. Gardens, gift shop, tearoom, picnic facilities, woodland walks. Parking available. Tel: (0334) 839205.*

ASVA

Earlshall is a fine example of a 16th century Scottish castle, very strongly built with 5-feet-thick walls, battlements and gun loops. Richly fitted main rooms, including the long gallery with its magnificent painted ceiling and wealth of old timber panelling. Still a family home with permanent display of Scottish weapons. Yew topiary gardens, nature trail, gardens. Earlshall is the family home of the Baron and Baroness of Earlshall.

438 EARTHQUAKE HOUSE 6A2

Off A85 just W of Comrie. Apr-Oct. Free. Exhibits can be seen through window and glazed doors at any reasonable time. Car parking only.

The village of Comrie lies close to the Highland boundary fault and has a history of earth tremors. Tiny Earthquake House was built in 1874 as a recording station, but a period of low seismic activity and the installation of more sophisticated equipment elsewhere in Scotland meant that it gradually fell into disrepair. Restored in 1986, this is one of the nation's smallest listed buildings. It contains a model of the original seismometer, and modern seismological equipment provided by the British Geological Survey. Records of recent local, national and international earthquakes are on display.

439 EAS COUL AULIN FALLS 2H5

At the head of Loch Glencoul, 3m W of A894. Contact: Mr Watson, Tel: (057 14) 446.

The tallest waterfall in Britain, dropping 658 feet (200 metres). Cruises to the waterfall daily in summer. (See No 1191).

440 EASSIE SCULPTURED STONE 5D1

In Eassie Kirkyard, 7m WSW of Forfar. All reasonable times. Free. (HS) Tel: 031-244 3101.

A fine example of an early Christian monument, elaborately carved.

441 EAST SANDS LEISURE CENTRE 6G2

In St Andrews immediately adjacent to East Sands beach. Jan-Dec, Mon-Fri 0900-2200, Sat & Sun 0900-1800. Entrance charges. Shop. Restaurant. Parking available. Tel: (0334) 76506.

Leisure centre and pool with 50-metre water slide, squash courts, steam room, jacuzzi, solaria, fitness room. All areas accessible to disabled users. Swimming pool access by special chair in sloping beach area.

442 EDEN COURT THEATRE 3B8

Bishops Road, Inverness. Concessions for parties of 10 or more persons (depends on show). Restaurant and bar. Parking available. Tel: (0463) 221718.

An 800-seat, multi-purpose theatre, conference centre and art gallery, completed in 1976 and situated on the banks of the River Ness. Part of the complex is the 19th-century house built by Robert Eden which houses the new luxury cinema, The Riverside Screen. There is a wide variety of entertainment throughout the year including classical concerts, drama, variety shows, films, pantomime and art exhibitions.

443 EDINBURGH, ADAM POTTERY 6E6

76 Henderson Row, corner of Saxe-Coburg Street. Jan-Dec exc Christmas, New Year and Easter periods. Mon-Sat 1000-1800. Charge for talk and throwing demonstration (3 days' notice). Pottery showroom and sales. Tel: 031-557 3978.

'One-woman' pottery where Janet Adam's wheelthrown stoneware and porcelain is made and sold. Delicate porcelain vases and bowls, large planters, bread crocks, jugs and decorative platters are all reduction-fired to 1300°C, giving a wide palette of subtly colourful glazes. Visitors can watch the potter at work — advance notice is required for throwing demonstrations.

444 EDINBURGH, AINSLIE PARK LEISURE CENTRE 6E6

Off Ferry Road, ¼m E of Crewe Toll roundabout. Centre is on left after Northern General Hospital into Pilton Drive. All year. Charges variable according to activity. Parking available. Tel: 031-551 2400.

Opened in 1989; superbly equipped, brightly designed building on leisure theme with swimming pools, flumes and a leisure complex. Function room for 150. Bar, café and audio-visual library.

445 EDINBURGH, BRASS RUBBING CENTRE 6E6

Trinity Apse, Chalmers Close, Royal Mile (opposite Museum of Childhood). Jun-Sep, weekdays 1000-1800; Oct-May, weekdays 1000-1700; Suns during Festival 1400-1700. Free. A charge is made for every rubbing, which includes cost of materials and a royalty to the churches where applicable. Tel: 031-556 4364.

Housed in the surviving part of the 15th century Trinity College church, replicas of the brass commemorating Robert the Bruce and the Burghead Bull, a Pictish incised stone c AD 700 are among the selection available. Instruction and materials supplied.

446 EDINBURGH BUTTERFLY AND INSECT WORLD 6E7

Melville Nursery, 5m S of Edinburgh on A7 towards Dalkeith. Early Mar-Jan exc Christmas and New Year. 1000-1700 summer, 1000-1600 winter. Entrance charges. Group concessions. Parking available. Gift shop. Tearoom. Tel: 031-663 4932.

ASVA

An exotic rainforest landscaped with tropical plants, cascading waterfalls and lily ponds, provides the setting for butterflies from all over the world to fly freely around. See also the fascinating world of strange insects, spiders and scorpions in perfect safety. Apiary, large live honey bee exhibit. Tearoom, garden centre, tropical fish shop, children's playground and picnic area. Bird of Prey Centre nearby.

447 EDINBURGH, CALTON GALLERY 6E6

10 Royal Terrace, NE shoulder of Calton Hill. Jan-Dec exc 24 Dec-5 Jan. Mon-Fri 1000-1800, Sat 1000-1300. Tel: 031-556 1010.

Family firm of fine art dealers established in 1980 in an elegant Georgian townhouse. Royal Terrace, on the northern face of Calton Hill, was designed by William Playfair around 1820 and is the longest unbroken facade in the New Town. Visitors see 19th and early 20th-century Scottish oil paintings, watercolours and prints in room settings on three floors. Landscapes and seapieces, still-life and figurative paintings. English and European paintings and bronzes.

448 EDINBURGH, CALTON HILL 6E6

Off Regent Road at E end of city centre. All times. Free. Tel: 031-225 2424. (Edinburgh District Council)

A city centre hill, 350 feet above sea level, with magnificent views over Edinburgh and the Firth of Forth. The monumental collection on top includes a part reproduction of the Parthenon, intended to commemorate the Scottish dead in the Napoleonic Wars; it was begun in 1824 but ran out of funds and was never completed. The 102 feet high Nelson Monument (completed 1815) improves the view from its high parapets. (See No 463).

449 EDINBURGH, CAMERA OBSCURA 6E6

         Castlehill, at top of Royal Mile, next to Castle. Jan-Dec. Apr-Oct, daily 0930-1800 (later in Jul & Aug). Nov-Mar, daily 1000-1700. Entrance charges. Group concessions. Family tickets. Gift shop. Tel: 031-226 3709.

ASVA

High in the unusual Outlook Tower, an 1850s 'cinema' shows live images of Edinburgh. The scene changes as the guide operates the Camera's system of revolving lenses and mirrors, and tells the story of the city's historic past. Also 3-D International Holography Exhibition, Pinhole Photography, Victorian Edinburgh and Artists' Edinburgh exhibitions. Award-winning centre.

450 EDINBURGH, CAMMO ESTATE 6E6

Approx 4 miles from city centre, NW off Queensferry Road. Jan-Dec. Visitor Centre, May-Sep, Mon-Fri 0800-1700. Free. Parking available. Tel: 031-317 8797.

Forty acres of mature woodland, pond and ruined buildings illustrate the fascinating history of a once-private estate. Owned by National Trust for Scotland, managed by Edinburgh District Council. Pleasant walks, River Almond walkway adjoins for walk to Cramond.

Edinburgh Canal Centre

451 EDINBURGH CANAL CENTRE 6E6

Baird Road, Ratho, 8 miles W of Edinburgh. Signposted. Jan-Dec. Charges for use of facilities. Parking available. Restaurant and bars. Tel: 031-333 1320/1251.

Based at the Bridge Inn at Ratho, two luxury canal boat restaurants cruise the Union Canal. Exhibits of canal life in the past on view in Bridge Inn, souvenirs and canalware for sale. New dry dock and reception centre opened by the Seagull Trust in 1993 — free cruising for disabled visitors.

452 EDINBURGH, CANONGATE KIRK 6E6

On the Canongate, Royal Mile.

The church, built by order of James VII in 1688, is the Parish Church of the Canongate and also the Kirk of Holyroodhouse and Edinburgh Castle. The church silver dates from 1611. Restored in 1951, the church contains much heraldry. The burial ground contains the graves of Adam Smith, the economist, 'Clarinda', friend of Robert Burns, and Robert Fergusson, the poet.

453 EDINBURGH CASTLE   6E6

*Castle Rock, top of the Royal Mile. Apr-Sep, daily 0930-1715 (last entry).
Oct-Nov, daily 0930-1615 (last entry). Castle closes 45 mins after last
entry. Entrance charges. Parking available. (HS) Tel: 031-244 3101.*

One of the most famous castles in the world, whose
battlements overlook the Esplanade where the floodlit
Military Tattoo is staged each year, late August to early
September. The castle stands on a rock which has been
a fortress from time immemorial. The oldest part of
the buildings which make up the castle is the
12th-century chapel dedicated to St Margaret. In
addition to the Great Hall built by James IV, with fine
timbered roof, and the Old Palace, which houses the
Regalia of Scotland and the Military Museum, the
castle also holds the Scottish National War Memorial,
opened in 1927. Royal Scots Dragoon Guards Display
Room.

454 EDINBURGH, CITY ART CENTRE   6E6

&
T

*Market Street. Open Jun-Sep, Mon-Sat, 1000-1800, Sun during Festival,
1400-1700. Oct-May, Mon-Sat, 1000-1700. Usually free, occasionally
charges for special exhibitions. Gift shop. Refreshments.
Tel: 031-225 2424 ext 3541.*

The City of Edinburgh's Art Gallery. A converted
warehouse on six floors with a programme of
temporary changing exhibitions and displays from the
City's collection of paintings.

**455 EDINBURGH, CLAN TARTAN
CENTRE**   6E6

&
T

*70-74 Bangor Road, Leith. Jan-Dec. Daily, 0900-1730. Free. Parking
available. Shop. Restaurant. Courtesy taxi service from city.
Tel: 031-553 5100/5161.*

Exhibition of Scottish history and audio-visual display.
Computer tracing of clan histories and tartan prints.
Large shop with extensive range of clan crest shields,
brooches, full Highland dress, cashmeres, knitwear and
clothing for ladies and men.

**456 EDINBURGH, COLLECTIVE
GALLERY**   6E6

&

*Cockburn Street, near Waverley Station. Jan-Dec exc Christmas and New
Year. Tues-Sat 1100-1700, extended hours at peak times. Free. Shop.
Tel: 031-220 1260.*

'New Art' venue, showing contemporary Scottish
work in exhibitions that change monthly. Educational
programme of workshops, classes, talks and tours.
Works available for sale, gallery shop specialising in
innovative applied art and design.

**457 EDINBURGH, CORSTORPHINE OLD
PARISH CHURCH**   6E6

&
A
T

*Kirk Loan, Corstorphine, signposted at A8/Kirk Loan junction. Feb-Nov.
Wed only, 1030-1200. Extended opening during Festival, by arrangement.
Sunday services 1000-1130. Free, donations accepted. Limited car parking.
Tea and coffee. Tel: 031-334 7864 (mornings).*

Interesting 15th century church with pre-Reformation
relics and medieval tombs.

**458   EDINBURGH, CRABBIE'S HISTORIC
WINERY TOUR**   6E6

*From Princes Street, straight down Leith Walk to traffic lights and turn left
into Great Junction Street. June-Sept, Mon-Thurs 1000-1600; other times
by appointment. Free. Tel: 031-554 3216.*

Crabbie's Green Ginger has been made for centuries in
the ancient Port of Leith to the same traditional family
recipe, a unique process involving cowslips, elderflowers,
cloves, cinnamon, lemons, oranges, raisins and ginger.
Large historic Visitor Centre.

Craigmillar Castle

459   EDINBURGH, CRAIGMILLAR CASTLE   6E6

*A68, 3½m SE of city centre. Opening standard exc Oct-Mar, closed
Thu pm and all day Fri. Entrance charge. Group concessions.
Parking available. (HS) Tel: 031-244 3101.*

Imposing ruins of massive 14th century keep enclosed
in the early 15th century by an embattled curtain wall;
within are the remains of the stately ranges of
apartments dating from the 16th and 17th centuries.
The castle was burnt by Hertford in 1544. There are
strong connections with Mary, Queen of Scots, who
frequently stayed here. While she was in residence in
1566 the plot to murder Darnley was forged.

Cramond

460   EDINBURGH, CRAMOND   6E6

*5m NW of city centre, on the shores of the Firth of Forth.
Exhibition at The Maltings, Jun-Sep, Sat & Sun 1400-1700. Walks from
The Maltings, Jun-mid Sep, Sun 1500. Free. Car parking only. Gift shop.*

This picturesque 18th century village is situated at the
mouth of the River Almond. See particularly the
Roman fort and medieval tower, the kirk, kirkyard
and manse, the old schoolhouse and the iron mills.
Conducted walks around the village in summer are led
by members of Cramond Heritage Trust.

**461 EDINBURGH CRYSTAL
VISITOR CENTRE**   6E7

*Eastfield, Penicuik, 10m S of Edinburgh. Jan-Dec. Tours Mon-Fri
0900-1530. Shop, Restaurant and Audio-Visual, 0900-1700 Mon-Sat and
Sun 1100-1700. Entrance fee to Visitor Centre. Charge for tour (free for
disabled visitors). Group concessions. Children under 8 years not admitted
to factory tour. Parking available. Tel: (0968) 675128.*

Factory tours (30 mins) reveal the secrets of glassmaking
from glassblowing through cutting to engraving.
Extended Activity Tours include the chance to try
glassblowing and cutting (6-12 persons, booking
essential). In the Visitor Centre, world's largest
selection of Edinburgh Crystal, coffee shop, woollen
mill shop and a new display of the company's history
entitled "The Story of Edinburgh Crystal".

Edinburgh, Dean Village

462 EDINBURGH, DEAN VILLAGE   6E6

Bell's Brae, off Queensferry Street, on Water of Leith.

There was grain milling in this notable village of
Edinburgh for over 800 years. The view is among the
most picturesque in the city. A walk along the
waterside leads to St Bernard's Well.

463 EDINBURGH EXPERIENCE   6E6

*City Observatory, Calton Hill. Car park at summit; pedestrian access
by steps from Regent Road. Early Apr-late Oct. Mon-Fri 1400-1700.
Sat & Sun 1030-1700. Jul & Aug, daily 1030-1700. Other times by
arrangement. Entrance charge. Family tickets. Group concessions.
Parking available. Tel: 031-556 4365.*

Twenty-minute full-colour three-dimensional slide
show, viewed through 3-D glasses. The story of
Scotland's capital is told, from its volcanic birth to the
present day. (See No 448).

**464 EDINBURGH, FLYING COLOURS
GALLERY**   6E6

*William Street, central Edinburgh. Feb-Dec. Tue-Fri 1100-1800, Sat
1000-1300. Free. Tel: 031-225 6776.*

Flying Colours Gallery shows work by living Scottish
artists in a succession of solo exhibitions changing
monthly. Lively and colourful work from established
artists as well as young, unknown talent. All works
for sale.

465   EDINBURGH, FOUNTAIN BREWERY   6E6

Scottish & Newcastle Breweries plc, Gilmore Park. Tours Mon-Fri 1015 & 1415. Entrance charges. No children under 8 on tour. Parking available. Tel: 031-229 9377 (1000-1600).

A tour of the complete brewing process and high-speed canning line, where cans are filled at a rate of 1500 per minute in one of the most fully automated breweries in Europe.

466   EDINBURGH, FRUITMARKET GALLERY   6E6

♿
T

29 Market Street, near Waverley Station. Jan-Dec. Tues-Sat 1100, also Sun during Festival, 1200-1800. Free. Bookshop. Restaurant. Tel: 031-225 2383.

Leading venue for the exhibition of international contemporary art, design and architecture. The programme balances national and international artists, working with other British galleries to organise touring exhibitions. The gallery produces high quality publications associated with the exhibitions, and runs an ancillary events and education programme.

467   EDINBURGH GALLERY   6E6

18a Dundas Street, N of Hanover Street. Jan-Dec. Mon-Fri 1100-1700, Sat 1000-1300. Free. Tel: 031-557 5227.

The Edinburgh Gallery holds regular exhibitions of contemporary works of art, with a bias towards Scottish figurative, landscape and still life.

468   EDINBURGH, GEORGIAN HOUSE   6E6

No 7 Charlotte Square. Apr-Oct, Mon-Sat 1000-1700, Sun 1400-1700. Last tour 1630. Entrance charges. Group rates for parties over 20. (NTS). Tel: 031-225 2160.

ASVA

The lower floors have been furnished as they might have been by their first owners, showing the domestic surroundings and reflecting the social conditions of that age. Charlotte Square itself was built at the end of the 18th century and is one of the most outstanding examples of its period in Europe. Bute House is the official residence of the Secretary of State for Scotland. The west side of the square is dominated by the green dome of St George's Church, now West Register House. (See No 524). Audio-visual and Induction loop.

469   EDINBURGH, GENERAL REGISTER HOUSE   6E6

♿
P

E end of Princes Street. Jan-Dec. Legal: 0930-1630. Historical: 0900-1645 (last admission 1625). Exhibitions: 1000-1600. Free. Tel: 031-556 6585.

This fine Robert Adam building, founded 1774, is the headquarters of the Scottish Record Office and the home of the national archives of Scotland. There is a branch repository at West Register House in Charlotte Square. (See No 524). In front is a notable statue of the Duke of Wellington (1852). Alternative wheelchair access. Guide dogs admitted to exhibition area.

470   EDINBURGH, GLADSTONE'S LAND   6E6

477B Lawnmarket, Royal Mile. Apr-Oct, Mon-Sat 1000-1700, Sun 1400-1700. Last admission ½ hr before closing. Entrance charges. Group concessions. Trust Shop. (NTS). Tel: 031-226 5856.

Completed in 1620, the six-storey tenement contains remarkable painted ceilings, and has been refurbished as a typical home of the period. Reconstructed shop booths display replicas of 17th century goods.

471   EDINBURGH, GORGIE CITY FARM   6E6
&   T

51 Gorgie Road. Jan-Dec exc Christmas & New Year. Free. Car and minibus parking only. Tearoom. Tel: 031-337 4202.

A 2½ acre site in the centre of the city with a wide range of animals kept in farm conditions (cow, sheep, goats, pigs, ducks, hens, Shetland pony and other small animals). Large organic vegetable garden. Set up in 1982 as a community project, the farm is now particularly popular with children.

Greyfriars Bobby

472   EDINBURGH, GREYFRIARS BOBBY   6E6

Corner of George IV Bridge and Candlemaker Row. All times. Free.

Statue of Greyfriars Bobby, the Skye terrier who, after his master's death in 1858, watched over his grave in the nearby Greyfriars Churchyard for 14 years.

473   EDINBURGH, GREYFRIARS KIRK   6E6
&   T

Greyfriars Place, S end of George IV Bridge. Easter-Sept Mon-Fri 1000-1600, Sat 1000-1400. Kirkyard 0900-1800. Free. Gift bookshop. Tel: 031-225 1900.

The Kirk, dedicated on Christmas Day, 1620, was the scene of the adoption and signing of the National Covenant on 28 February 1638. The Covenant is displayed at the church. The kirkyard, inaugurated in 1562, is on the site of a 15th century Franciscan Friary, and contains a fine collection of 17th century Scottish monuments. In 1679, 1,400 Covenanters were imprisoned in the kirkyard. There is a Martyrs' Monument and a memorial to Greyfriars Bobby.

**474   EDINBURGH, GEORGE HERIOT'S   6E6
SCHOOL**
&   A   P

Lauriston Place. May be viewed from the grounds. Gates close 16.30. Tel: 031-229 7263 (Trust Office).

Now a school, the splendid building was begun in 1628, endowed by George Heriot, goldsmith and jeweller to James VI and I, the 'Jingling Geordie' of Scott's novel *Fortunes of Nigel*.

475 EDINBURGH, HERMITAGE OF BRAID 6E6

   Braid Road, 2½ miles S of city centre. Jan-Dec. Visitor Centre Mon-Fri
P *0900-1700, park open all reasonable times. Tel: 031-447 7145.*

Tranquil woodland walks in 130 acres of ancient
mature woodland, including Blackford Hills with
excellent views across Blackford Pond and the
surrounding city. Good area for birdwatching. Guided
walks from May-Sept, environmental and educational
activities are bookable.

Edinburgh High Kirk: see No 506.

---

476 EDINBURGH, HILLEND SKI CENTRE 6E6

   Biggar Road, S outskirts of Edinburgh. Apr-Sept, Mon-Fri 0930-2100.
P *Oct-Mar, daiy, 0930-2200. Closed Christmas Day & New Year's Day.*
T *Charge for chairlift. Session tickets for skiers are also available. Parking*
available. Restaurant. Tel: 031-445 4433.

Europe's largest dry ski slope has been in operation
since 1964. Two main slopes of 400m are served by
chairlift, T-bar and button tows. Nursery slope of
50m. Ski and boot hire for both Hillend and snow
skiing, ski maintenance workshop. Instruction
available. Chairlift gives access to Pentland walks and
fine views.

---

477 EDINBURGH, HUNTLY HOUSE
MUSEUM 6E6

   Canongate, Royal Mile. Jun-Sep, Mon-Sat 1000-1800; Oct-May,
P *Mon-Sat 1000-1700; Sun during Festival 1400-1700. Free.*
Tel: 031-225 2424, ext 6689.

Built in 1570, this fine house is now a city museum
illustrating Edinburgh life down the ages, and contains
important collections of Edinburgh silver and glass and
Scottish pottery.

---

478 EDINBURGH, KINGFISHER GALLERY 6E6

   5 Northumberland Street Lane NW, right turn off Northumberland
T *Street. Jan-Dec. Mon-Fri 1030-1630. Also Sat 1030-1630 from Jun-Aug.*
Free. Tel: 031-557 5454.

Small mews art gallery specialising in Scottish and
international contemporary art — paintings, sculpture,
ceramics and jewellery.

---

479 EDINBURGH, KINLOCH ANDERSON
HERITAGE ROOM 6E6

   Commercial Street/Dock Street, Leith. Jan-Dec. Mon-Sat 0900-1730.
T *Free. Parking available. Courtesy taxi service. Woollen shop.*
Tel: 031-555 1371/1390.

The Heritage Room is a museum of historic items
made or collected by Kinloch Anderson since the
company's foundation in 1868. One cabinet features
the Royal Tartans, others regimental and civilian
uniforms and the history of kiltmaking. A viewing
window allows visitors to see manufacturing in
progress. A talk on the origin of the kilt and how it is
made today can be arranged. Retail shop specialises in
cashmeres and woollens, high quality clothing from
Scotland, accessories and gifts. Highland Dress Room
for men's kilt outfits.

480 EDINBURGH, KING'S THEATRE 6E6

2 Leven Street. Tel: 031-229 1201.

Opened 1906. Completely restored 1985. Producing ballet, opera, comedy, farce, variety, drama, dance.

Edinburgh, John Knox House

481 EDINBURGH, JOHN KNOX HOUSE 6E6

45 High Street, Royal Mile. All year, Mon-Sat 1000-1700. Last entry 1630. Entrance charge. Tel: 031-556 9579/2647.

A picturesque 15th-century house associated with John Knox, the religious Reformer, and James Mossman, Keeper of The Royal Mint to Mary Queen of Scots. The house contains many original features including a painted ceiling and an exhibition on the life and times of John Knox and James Mossman.

482 EDINBURGH, LADY STAIR'S HOUSE 6E6

Off Lawnmarket, Royal Mile. Jun-Sept, Mon-Sat 1000-1800; Oct-May, Mon-Sat 1000-1700; Sun during Festival 1400-1700. Free. Gift shop. Tel: 031-225 2424 ext 6593.

Built in 1622, Lady Stair's House is now a museum containing objects, photographs, paintings and manuscripts relating to three of Scotland's greatest writers — Robert Burns, Sir Walter Scott and Robert Louis Stevenson.

483 EDINBURGH, LAMB'S HOUSE 6E6

Burgess Street, Leith. Visits by prior arrangement. (NTS) Tel: 031-554 3131.

The restored residence and warehouse of Andrew Lamb, a prosperous merchant of the 17th century. Now an old people's day centre.

Lauriston Castle

484 EDINBURGH, LAURISTON CASTLE   6E6

     N of A90 at Cramond Road South, 4m WNW of city centre. Apr-Oct,
P   *daily except Fri 1100-1300, 1400-1700; Nov-Mar, Sat and Sun only,*
T   *1400-1600. Entrance charge. Parking available.*
     Tel: 031-336 2060/225 2424, ext 6682.

The original tower house built by Sir Archibald Napier,
father of the inventor of logarithms was much extended
by William Burn in the 1820s. The last occupant,
W. R. Reid, owner of the prestigious Edinburgh
furnishing firm of Morison & Co., completely
refurbished the castle in 1903 and his Edwardian
interior has been carefully preserved. It includes a fine
collection of eighteenth century Italian furniture,
oriental rugs etc. Now administered by the City of
Edinburgh.

485 EDINBURGH, LEITH WATERWORLD   6E6

     377 Easter Road. Also accessible from bottom of Leith Walk. Jan-Dec.
T   *Mon-Fri 1200-2130 (community programmes from 0900-1200). Sat &*
     Sun 0900-1700. Entrance charge. Family ticket. Group concessions.
     Parking available. Cafe. Tel: 031-555 6000.

Two flumes, a river run, bubble beds, spa pool, wave
machine, shower curtains, waterfall, mushrooms, fast
flow channel, beach area add up to water play for all ages.

486 EDINBURGH, MAGDALEN CHAPEL   6E6

     Cowgate, off the Grassmarket. Jan-Dec. Mon-Fri 0930-1630. Other times
     by arrangement. Free. Gift shop. (Scottish Reformation Society).
     Tel: 031-220 1450.

The chapel was founded in 1541 and has been used in
various ways — as an ecclesiastical building by various
denominations, and as Guildhall for the Incorporation
of Hammermen who were patrons of the hospital
which adjoined the chapel in the early days. Important
stained glass windows are the only pre-Reformation
examples in their original setting. Opened in March
1993, after extensive renovations, as headquarters of
the Scottish Reformation Society.

Edinburgh: Mercat Cross: see No 496.

487 EDINBURGH, MUSEUM OF ANTIQUITIES 6E6

Jan-Dec. Mon-Sat 1000-1700; Sun 1400-1700. Tel: 031-225 7534.

An intriguing and comprehensive collection of the history and everyday life of Scotland from the Stone Age to modern times. Also 'Dynasty'—the Royal House of Stewart exhibition traces 300 years of Stewart rule in Scotland through portraits and objects from the Scottish National Collection.

488 EDINBURGH, MUSEUM OF CHILDHOOD 6E6

42 High Street, Royal Mile. Jun-Sep weekdays 1000-1800; Oct-May weekdays 1000-1700; Sun during Festival 1400-1700. Free. Tel: 031-225 2424 ext 6645/6647.

This unique museum has a fine collection of childhood-related items including toys, dolls, dolls' houses, costumes and nursery equipment. It has a programme of changing exhibitions and activities.

489 EDINBURGH MUSEUM OF FIRE 6E6

Lauriston Place. Visits by arrangement with Fire Brigade Headquarters. Free. (Lothian & Borders Fire Brigade). No Parking. Tel: 031-228 2401.

Guided tours round the museum, with its collection of old uniforms, equipment and engines, subject to the availability of a Fireman Guide.

490 EDINBURGH, NATIONAL GALLERY OF SCOTLAND 6E6

The Mound, Mon-Sat 1000-1700 (extended hours during Festival); Sun 1400-1700. Free. Tel: 031-556 8921.

One of the most distinguished of the smaller galleries of Europe, the National Gallery of Scotland contains a comprehensive collection of Old Masters, Impressionist and Scottish paintings. This includes masterpieces by Raphael, El Greco, Rembrandt, Constable, Titian, Velazquez, Raeburn, Van Gogh and Gauguin. Drawings, watercolours and original prints (Turner, Goya, Blake etc) are shown on request (Mon-Fri 1000-1200, 1400-1630).

491 EDINBURGH, NATIONAL LIBRARY OF SCOTLAND 6E6

George IV Bridge. All year exc first week in Oct. Reading Room: Mon, Tues, Thur, Fri 0930-2030, Wed 1000-2030, Sat 0930-1300. Exhibitions: Mon-Fri 1000-1700 (1000-2030 during Festival), Sat 1000-1700, Sun 1400-1700. Free. Publications counter. Tel: 031-226 4531.

Founded in 1689, this is one of the four largest libraries in Great Britain. Its unparalleled collection on Scottish history and culture are available to researchers, and its frequently changing exhibitions are open to the general public.

Edinburgh, Nelson Monument: see No 448.

**492 EDINBURGH, NETHERBOW ARTS
CENTRE**   6E6

*43 High Street. All year, Mon-Sat 1000-1630 (also in evenings for theatre).
Free. Cafe/restaurant. Tel: 031-556 9579/2647.*

A modern arts centre in Edinburgh's Old Town
offering a range of exhibitions and performances with
an emphasis on the Scottish arts. Open-air courtyard.

**493 EDINBURGH, NEW TOWN
CONSERVATION CENTRE**   6E6

*13A Dundas Street. All year. Mon-Fri. 0900-1300, 1400-1700. Free.
Tel: 031-557 5222.*

Headquarters of committee which administers grants
for the conservation of the Georgian New Town.
There is an exhibition area and a conservation
reference library. Publications are on sale.

494 EDINBURGH, OPEN EYE GALLERY   6E6

*75/79 Cumberland Street. Jan-Dec. Mon-Fri 1000-1800, Sat 1000-1600.
Free. Tel: 031-557 1020.*

Contemporary and fine arts gallery, with 17 exhibitions
per year showing work by established artists as well as
young contemporaries. Regular exhibitions of
ceramics, sculpture and innovative jewellery. Print
room specialising in early 20th century etchings.

**495 EDINBURGH, PALACE OF
HOLYROODHOUSE**   6E6

*Canongate. Foot of the Royal Mile. Apr-Oct 0930-1715, Sun 1030-1630;
Nov-Mar 0930-1545 (not Sun). The Palace is also closed during Royal
and State Visits, for periods before and after visits, and occasionally at other
times; check dates on 031-556 1096. Entrance charge. Family tickets.
Group concessions. Tearoom for small groups. Parking available. Gift shop.
Tel: 031-556 7371 (office)/031-556 1096 (recorded information).*

The Palace of Holyroodhouse is the official residence of
The Queen in Scotland. The oldest part is built against
the monastic nave of Holyrood Abbey, little of which
remains. The rest of the palace was reconstructed by
the architect Sir William Bruce for Charles II. Here
Mary Queen of Scots lived for six years; here she met
John Knox; here Rizzio was murdered, and here
Prince Charles Edward Stuart held court in 1745. State
apartments house tapestries and paintings; the picture
gallery has portraits of over 80 Scottish kings, painted
by De Wet in 1684-86.

496 EDINBURGH, PARLIAMENT HOUSE   6E6

*Parliament Square, behind the High Kirk of St Giles, Royal Mile.
Jan-Dec. Tue-Fri 1000-1600. Free. Restaurant.
Tel: 031-225 2595.*

Built 1632-39 this was the seat of Scottish government
until 1707, when the governments of Scotland and
England were united. Now the Supreme Law Courts
of Scotland. Parliament Hall has fine hammer beam
roof and portraits by Raeburn and other major
Scottish artists. Access (free) to the splendid Signet
Library on an upper floor is by prior written request
only, to: The Librarian, Signet Library, Parliament
House, Edinburgh. Outside is the medieval Mercat
Cross, which was restored in 1885 by W E Gladstone.
Royal proclamations are still read from its platform.

497 **EDINBURGH, THE PEOPLE'S STORY**   6E6

Housed in the Canongate Tolbooth, near the foot of Royal Mile. Mon-Sat 1000-1700 (June to Sept 1000-1800). During the Edinburgh Festival: Sun 1400-1700. Free. Tel: 031-225 2424, ext 4057.

The Canongate Tolbooth, which was built in 1591, now houses The People's Story. The museum tells of the lives, work and leisure of ordinary people in the Scottish capital from the late 18th century to the present day. It has reconstructions of a cooper's workshop, a steamie, a 1940s kitchen and many more displays based on first hand accounts of Edinburgh life. Lift and adapted toilets for disabled visitors.

Edinburgh, Royal Botanic Gardens

498 **EDINBURGH, ROYAL BOTANIC GARDEN**   6E6

Inverleith Row; Arboretum Place (car parking). Jan-Dec exc Christmas and New Year. Daily. Sept-Oct 1000-1800. May-Aug 1000-2000. Mar-Apr 1000-1800. Nov-Feb 1000-1600. Free. Plant houses 1000 (Sun 1100) to 1700, summer; 1000 (Sun 1100) to 30 minutes before sunset, winter. Free. Parking available. Terrace cafe. Specialist gifts and plants for sale. Tel: 031-552 7171.

SVA

The Royal Botanic Garden has a world famous rock garden and probably the biggest collection of rhododendrons in the world. The 'Glasshouse Experience' shows a great range of exotic plants displayed as eleven indoor landscapes. Exhibitions, behind-the-scenes tours and educational activities.

499 **EDINBURGH, ROYAL COMMONWEALTH POOL & NAUTILUS FLUME COMPLEX**   6E6

From Princes Street turn onto North Bridge, follow road for about 1m, turn left onto Salisbury Place, then right into Salisbury Road; pool is on left. All year. Entrance charge. Parking available. Cafeteria. Tel: 031-667 7211.

50m swimming pool, diving pool, teaching pool, Nautilus Flume Complex (Europe's largest indoor flume). Fitness centre.

500 **EDINBURGH, ROYAL LYCEUM THEATRE COMPANY**   6E6

Grindlay Street. All year. Group rates. Tel: 031-229 9697.

Resident company in fine Victorian theatre. Up to twelve plays a year. Bars, restaurant, easy booking, disabled access, concessions, tours.

**501   EDINBURGH, ROYAL MUSEUM OF
SCOTLAND**   6E6

&   *Chambers Street. Jan-Dec. Mon-Sat 1000-1700, Sun 1200-1700. Free.*
T   *Tearoom. Inductive loop. Tel: 031-225 7534.*

Part of the National Museums of Scotland in a fine
Victorian building. Houses the national collections of
decorative arts of the world, ethnography, natural
history, geology, technology and science. Special
exhibitions, lectures, gallery talks, films and other
activities for adults and children.

502   EDINBURGH, ROYAL OBSERVATORY   6E6

&   *Blackford Hill. Apr-Sep, Mon-Fri 1000-1600, Sat, Sun, holidays*
P   *1200-1700. Oct-Mar, daily 1300-1700. Entrance charge. Group*
T   *concessions. Parking available. Gift shop. Tel: 031-668 8405.*

Situated in a pleasant public park on the south side of
Edinburgh and commanding fine views of the city, the
Observatory Visitor Centre explores the exciting
world of modern astronomy and space research.
Spectacular photographs of deep space, videos and
computer games, Scotland's largest telescope and a
well-stocked astronomy shop.

**503   EDINBURGH, ROYAL SCOTTISH
ACADEMY**   6E6

&
A   *At the foot of the Mound, on Princes Street. Mon-Sat 1000-1700,*
T   *Sun 1400-1700. Entrance charge. Tel: 031-225 6671.*

The Academy has annual exhibitions from late April
to July, and special Festival exhibitions. Ramped
wheelchair entrance at side.

504   EDINBURGH, ST CECILIA'S HALL   6E6

&
A   *The Cowgate, at foot of Niddry Street. Jan-Dec. Wed, Sat 1400-1700.*
P   *During Festival, Mon-Sat 1030-1230. Entrance charge. Parking available.*
    Gift shop. Tel: 031-667 1011, ext 4577/4415.

Scotland's oldest concert hall, built to a design by
Robert Milne in 1762, for the Edinburgh Musical
Society. After many alterations and changes of use, it
was acquired by the University of Edinburgh and
restored to its original use in 1968. It is the home of
the Russell Collection of Early Keyboard Instruments,
which is of international importance. Publications,
recordings, postcards, technical information available.

**505   EDINBURGH, ST CUTHBERT'S
CHURCH**   6E6

&   *Lothian Road. Open with guides Jun-Sep, Mon-Fri 1030-1530; other*
T   *times by arrangement. Free. Coffee served Tues mornings. Inductive loop.*
    Tel: 031-229 1142.

An ancient church, the 'West Kirk', rebuilt by
Hippolyte Blanc in 1894. The tower is 18th century,
and there is a monument to Napier of Merchiston,
inventor of logarithms. Thomas de Quincey is buried
in the churchyard.

Edinburgh, St Giles' Cathedral

506 **EDINBURGH, ST GILES' CATHEDRAL** 6E6

 ♿
A
T

High Street, Royal Mile. Winter, Mon-Sat 0900-1700, Sun 1200-1700. Summer, Mon-Sat 0900-1900, Sun 1300-1700. Also open for services. Occasionally closed for weddings, ceremonies etc. Please check before travelling any distance. Free (donation for Thistle Chapel). Gift shop. Restaurant. Inductive loop. Tel: 031-225 9442.

St Giles' Cathedral is also known as the High Kirk of Edinburgh. Dating from around 1120, the cathedral was almost destroyed by the English army in 1385, but after much rebuilding became the centre of the Reformation in Scotland, during the ministry of John Knox. Only briefly elevated to the status of Cathedral by Charles I in 1633, the building has undergone many changes. One of the most recent was the addition of the exquisite Thistle Chapel. This is used for ceremonial occasions by the Knights of the Most Ancient and Most Noble Order of the Thistle, of which the Queen is the head.

507 **EDINBURGH, ST JOHN'S CHURCH** 6E6

W end of Princes Street. All reasonable times. Free. Tel: 031-229 7565.

An impressive 19th-century church, the nave of which was built in 1817 by William Burn. There is a fine collection of Victorian stained glass. The Church's art collection features, outside, sculpture in granite by Ronald Rae, and inside, a controversial painting of the deposition and crucifixion of Christ by Ian Hughes., Peace and Justice Resource Centre, One World Shop, Corner Stone vegetarian restaurant and Bookshop, International Voluntary Service.

508 **EDINBURGH, ST MARY'S CATHEDRAL** 6E6

In Palmerston Place, West End. Mon-Sat 0730 (Morning prayers) 1815, Sun 0800-1900. Occasionally later in summer. Tours can be arranged. Shop. Tel: 031-225 6293.

Built 1879, with the western towers added in 1917. The central spire is 276 feet high and the interior is impressive. Nearby is the charming Easter Coates House, built in the late 17th century with some stones filched from the old town; it is now St Mary's Music School. Gardens with seats.

**509 EDINBURGH, ST TRIDUANA'S
CHAPEL**   **6E6**

*At Restalrig Church, in Restalrig district, 1½m E of city centre. Open all
reasonable times. Keykeeper. Free. (HS) Tel: 031-244 3101.*

From the late 15th century the shrine of St Triduana
was situated in the lower chamber of the King's
Chapel built by James III, adjacent to Restalrig
Church. The design, a two storey vaulted hexagon, is
unique. The lower chapel of St Triduana survives
intact but the upper chamber was demolished in 1560.

**510 EDINBURGH, THE SCOTCH WHISKY
HERITAGE CENTRE**   **6E6**

& *354 Castlehill, Royal Mile. Jan-Dec exc Christmas and New Year's Day.*
T *Daily, 1000-1700. Extended hours Jun-Sep. Entrance charge. Family
tickets. Group concessions. Whisky and gift shop. Tel: 031-220 0441.*

ASVA

The Scotch Whisky Heritage Centre brings the story
of Scotland's national drink vividly to life with the
equivalent of a distillery tour in the heart of Edinburgh's
Old Town. An explanation of the whisky-making
process is followed by an audio-visual, then a journey
in a whisky barrel through dramatic sets depicting the
history of whisky with figures, sound effects and
commentary in a choice of languages.

Scott Monument

511 EDINBURGH, SCOTT MONUMENT   **6E6**

*East Princes Street Gardens. Oct-Mar, Mon-Sat 1000-1500; April-Sept,
Mon-Sat 1000-1800. Entrance charge. Small shop. Tel. 031-225 2424.*

One of Edinburgh's most famous landmarks, the
150-year-old monument commemorates one of
Scotland's greatest writers, Sir Walter Scott. Steep
climb to the top rewards the visitor with superb views
of Edinburgh and its surroundings.

**512 EDINBURGH, SCOTTISH AGRICULTURAL
MUSEUM**   **6E6**

& *Ingliston, nr Edinburgh Airport. May-Sep, Mon-Fri 1000-1700. Jun-Aug,*
T *also Sat 1000-1700. Oct-Apr, Wed only 1000-1700. Open to groups
outside normal hours/season. Parking available. Shops. Tearoom. (NMS)
Tel: 031-333 2674 or 031-225 7534, ext 313.*

Scotland's national museum of country life. Farming,
old trades and skills, social and home life. Fascinating
displays, old photographs, audio visual presentation.
Disabled facilities and access.

513 EDINBURGH, SCOTTISH EXPERIENCE AND LIVING CRAFT CENTRE   6E6

High Street, opposite John Knox's House. Jan-Dec exc Christmas and New Year. Daily, 1000-1800. Entrance charge. Family tickets. Group concessions. Shops. Restaurant. Tel: 031-557 9350.

Scottish craftspeople in a small complex of workshops, weaving tartan, making kilts and Aran sweaters, making pottery — visitors can try throwing a pot — working Scottish jewellery and sgian dhubhs. Bagpipe workshop shows how pipes are made and how to play them — pipes and chanters for sale. Ancestral research undertaken, information about Scottish clans and tartan history. Exhibition of Highland dress through the ages. Film theatre and Scottish fare.

514 EDINBURGH, SCOTTISH NATIONAL GALLERY OF MODERN ART   6E6

Belford Road. All year, Mon-Sat 1000-1700, Sun 1400-1700 (extended hours during Festival). Prints and Drawings room open by arrangement between 1000-1200, 1430-1630 Mon-Fri. Free. Parking available. Cafe. Tel: 031-556 8921.

Scotland's collection of 20th-century painting, sculpture and graphic art, with masterpieces by Derain, Matisse, Braque, Picasso and Giacometti; and work by Hockney, Caulfield and Hepworth. Also Scottish School. Walled sculpture garden.

515 EDINBURGH, SCOTTISH NATIONAL PORTRAIT GALLERY   6E6

E end of Queen Street. Mon-Sat 1000-1700 (extended hours during Festival), Sun 1400-1700. Free. Print Room and Reference Section open 1000-1200, 1430-1630 Mon-Fri. Café. Tel: 031-556 8921.

Illustrates the history of Scotland through portraits of the famous men and women who contributed to it in all fields of activity from the 16th century to the present day, such as Mary, Queen of Scots, James VI and I, Flora Macdonald, Robert Burns, Sir Walter Scott, David Hume and Ramsay MacDonald. The artists include Raeburn, Ramsay, Reynolds and Gainsborough. Reference section of engravings and the national collection of photography.

516 EDINBURGH SCOUT MUSEUM   6E6

Valleyfield Street, Tollcross. Jan-Dec exc public holidays. Mon-Fri 0930-1630. Please check opening times by telephone. Free. Donation box. Tel: 031-229 3756.

Based within Area Scout offices, an exhibition of the history of the Scout movement in Edinburgh and worldwide, with photographs, books, uniforms and badges.

517 EDINBURGH, STILLS 6E6

105 High Street, halfway down Royal Mile. Up small flight of steps.
Jan-Dec exc public holidays. Tues-Sat 1100-1730. Free. Tel: 031-557 1140.

Stills is a photography gallery showing Scottish and international photography, with an emphasis on contemporary work. Education activities support exhibitions, and there is a specialist photography bookshop.

518 EDINBURGH, TALBOT RICE GALLERY 6E6

University of Edinburgh, Old College, South Bridge. Tues-Sat 1000-1700.
Usually free. Closed certain Sats if no special exhibition, check press or
Tel: 031-667 1011, ext 4308/031-650 2210/1/2/3

Edinburgh University's Torrie Collection and changing exhibitions are on public display in the Talbot Rice Gallery, within the fine Old College building, part of the University of Edinburgh, begun by Robert Adam in 1789 and completed by William Playfair around 1830.

519 EDINBURGH, SIR JULES THORNE HISTORICAL MUSEUM 6E6

At rear of Royal College of Surgeons of Edinburgh, 18 Nicolson Street.
Jan-Dec exc public holidays. Mon-Fri 1400-1600. Free. Donations invited.
Tel: 031-556 6206.

Historic exhibition of ''Edinburgh and Medicine''. Lower floor of the hall illustrates the history of surgery in general, and Edinburgh's special contribution from 1505 to the present. Facsimiles of many precious records are displayed, such as the Queen Mary Charter of 1567, and artefacts connected with notable Edinburgh figures in early medical history. Sections are devoted to distinguished surgeons such as Sir Charles Bell, Liston and Syme, and to less worthy personalities such as Burke and Hare.

520 EDINBURGH, 369 GALLERY 6E6

233 Cowgate. Jan-Dec. Tues-Sat 1200-1800. Free. Tel: 031-225 3013.

Art gallery, mounting new exhibitions every month.

Traverse Theatre

521 EDINBURGH, TRAVERSE THEATRE 6E6

Cambridge Street, next to Usher Hall and Lyceum. Jan-Dec. Daily.
1000-0100. Bar 1200-1200 (Fri, Sat 0100). Charge for performances.
Group concessions. Restaurant and bar. Inductive loop. Tel: 031-228 1404.

Britain's acclaimed theatre for new writing has pioneered work by new writers for the last thirty years, and has launched the careers of many actors, directors and writers. Now in a new theatre in the heart of the city.

**522 EDINBURGH UNIVERSITY COLLECTION
OF HISTORIC MUSICAL INSTRUMENTS** 6E6
*Reid Concert Hall, Bristo Square. All year, Wed 1500-1700,
Sat 1000-1300. Free. Tel: 031-447 4791 or 031-650 2423.*

The collection now consists of over 1,500 instruments
and is maintained by the University for the purposes
of research, performance and support for teaching.
Some 700 are woodwind, over 300 are brass, about
250 stringed and the rest percussion, bagpipes,
ethnographic and acoustical instruments. Study room,
specialist visits by arrangement. (See also No 504).

523 EDINBURGH, USHER HALL 6E6
*From West End of Princes Street, turn onto Lothian Road; Usher Hall is
on left. Please contact the Usher Hall for further details. Prices on
application. Tel: 031-228 1155.*

Fine 19th-century concert hall which offers a wide
range of concerts and performances.

**524 EDINBURGH, WEST REGISTER
HOUSE** 6E6
*W side of Charlotte Square. Mon-Fri. Exhibitions: 1000-1600.
Search Room: 0900-1645. Free. Tel: 031-556 6585.*

Formerly St George's Church, 1811, this now holds the
more modern documents of the Scottish Record Office
(see No 469). Permanent exhibition on many aspects
of Scottish history, including the Declaration of
Arbroath, 1320. Guide dogs in exhibition area only.

525 EDINBURGH, WHITE HORSE CLOSE 6E6
Off Canongate, Royal Mile.

A restored group of 17th-century buildings off the
High Street. The coaches to London left from White
Horse Inn (named after Queen Mary's Palfrey), and
there are Jacobite links.

526 EDINBURGH ZOO 6E6
*Corstorphine Road, 3 miles W of city centre on A8. Open every day of
the year. April-Sept 0900-1800, Oct-Mar 0900-1630. (Sundays open
0930). Entrance charges. Group concessions. Parking available. Gift shops.
Restaurant. Tearoom. Cafeteria. Kiosks in summer months. Bar.
Children's play area. Tel: 031-334 9171.*

Established in 1913 by the Royal Zoological Society of
Scotland, this is one of Britain's leading zoos, with
over 1,500 mammals, birds and reptiles — including
many endangered species — all set in 80 acres of
attractive hillside parkland. Famous for its knowledge
and care of penguins, Edinburgh Zoo now has the
world's largest penguin enclosure, with a spectacular
deep water pool and underwater viewing windows.
The 'Penguin Parade' takes place daily at 1400 from
April to September.

527 EDINSHALL BROCH 5F5
*On the NE slope of Cockburn Law, off A6112 4m N of Duns. All
reasonable times. Free. (HS) Tel: 031-244 3101.*

Listed among the ten Iron Age brochs known in
lowland Scotland, its dimensions are exceptionally
large. The site was occupied into Roman times.

528   **EDRADOUR DISTILLERY**   5B1

*2½m E of Pitlochry. Mar-Oct, Mon-Sat, 0930-1700. Nov-Feb,
Sat 1000-1600 (shop only). Other times by arrangement. Parking
available. Tel: (0796) 472095.*

The smallest distillery in Scotland, established 1825.
A visit includes a guided tour, audio-visual presentation
ASVA   and tasting.

---

529   **EDROM NORMAN ARCH**   5F5

*Off A6105, 3m ENE of Duns. All reasonable times. Free. (HS)
Tel: 031-244 3101.*

Fine Norman chancel arch from church built by Thor
Longus c 1105, now standing behind recent parish
church.

---

530   **EDZELL CASTLE AND GARDEN**   3F12

*Off B966, 6m N of Brechin. Opening standard except Oct-Mar, closed
Thurs pm and all day Friday. Entrance charge. Group concessions. (HS)
Tel: 031-244 3101.*

ASVA

The beautiful pleasance, a walled garden, was built by
Sir David Lindsay in 1604; the heraldic and symbolic
sculptures are unique in Scotland, and the flower-
filled recesses in the walls add to the outstanding
formal garden, which also has a turreted garden house.
The castle itself, an impressive ruin, dates from the
early 16th century, with a large courtyard mansion of
1580.

---

531   **EGLINTON COUNTRY PARK**   4G6

*2m N of Irvine off A78 at Eglinton interchange. Park: Jan-Dec, daily,
dawn-dusk. Visitor Centre: Easter-Oct, daily, 1000-1630. Free. Parking
available. Gift shop. Tearoom. Tel: (0294) 51776.*

This is a major country park built around the former
Eglinton Montgomery Estate and ruined castle.
Displays in the visitor centre explain the natural
history and the history of the area, including material
on the Eglinton tournament of 1839. The centre is the
base of the Irvine Ranger Service who run guided
walks and events in summer.

Eilean Donan Castle

532   **EILEAN DONAN CASTLE**   2F10

*Off A87, 9m E of Kyle of Lochalsh. Easter-Sep, daily 1000-1800.
(Last admission 1730). Entrance charge. Parking available. Gift shop.
Tel: (0599) 85 202.*

On an islet (now connected by a causeway) in Loch
Duich, this picturesque castle dates back to 1220. It
passed into the hands of the Mackenzies of Kintail
who became Earls of Seaforth. In 1719 it was
garrisoned by Spanish Jacobite troops and was blown
up by an English man o'war. Now completely
restored, it incorporates a war memorial to the Clan
Macrae, who held it as hereditary Constables on behalf
of the Mackenzies.

533 ELCHO CASTLE 6D2

On River Tay, 3m SE of Perth. April-Sept, opening standard. Oct-Mar, closed. Entrance charge. Group concessions. (HS) Tel: 031-244 3101.

A preserved fortified mansion notable for its tower-like jambs or wings and for the wrought-iron grills protecting its windows. An ancestral seat of the Earls of Wemyss; another castle, on or very near the site, was a favourite hide-out of William Wallace.

534 ELECTRIC BRAE 4G8

A719 9m S of Ayr (also known as Croy Brae).

An optical illusion is created so that a car appears to be going down the hill when it is in fact going up.

Elgin Cathedral

535 ELGIN CATHEDRAL 3D8

North College Street, Elgin. Opening standard except Oct-Mar closed Thurs pm and all day Friday. Entrance charge. Group concessions. (HS) Tel: 031-244 3101.

When entire, this was perhaps the most beautiful of Scottish cathedrals, known as the Lantern of the North. It was founded in 1224, but in 1390 it was burned by the Wolf of Badenoch. It did not fall into ruin until after the Reformation. Much 13th-century work still remains; the nave and chapter house are 15th-century. There is a 6th-century Pictish slab in the choir.

536 ELGIN MUSEUM 3D8

High Street, Elgin. Apr-Sept, Mon-Fri (exc Wed) 1000-1700, Sat 1100-1600. Sun 1400-1700. Admission charges. Shop. Tel: (0343) 543675.

An award-winning museum housing a world famous collection of Old Red Sandstone, Permian and Triassic fossils including dinosaurs. Also exhibited are items ranging from pre-historic to modern times, natural history specimens, the history and archaeology of Moray and many other parts of the world.

537 ELLISLAND FARM 5B9

Off A76, 6½m NNW of Dumfries. All reasonable times, but intending visitors are advised to phone in advance. Free. Limited car parking only. (Ellisland Trust). Tel: (0387) 74 426.

Robert Burns took over this farm in June 1788, built the farmhouse, and tried to introduce new farming methods. Unsuccessful, he became an Exciseman in September 1789; in August 1791 the stock was auctioned, and he moved to Dumfries in November 1791. Some of the poet's most famous works were written at Ellisland, including *Tam o'Shanter* and *Auld Lang Syne*. The Granary houses a display showing Burns as a farmer. Farmhouse with museum room; granary building with Burns display; riverside walk.

**538 ERROL STATION RAILWAY
HEREITAGE CENTRE**   6E2

& *Errol Station, between Dundee and Perth. May-Sept. Sun only*
T *1200-1700. Entrance charges. Parking available. Refreshments.
Tel: (057 54) 222.*

Preserved railway station on the Dundee-Perth railway
line, which is still operational. Original building of
1847 has booking office, general waiting room, ladies'
waiting room and porter's house — all restored to
1920s appearance. Slide show of Dundee-Perth railway.

**539 EUROPEAN SHEEP
AND WOOL CENTRE**   4G3

*Drimsynie Estate, Lochgoilhead. A83 to top of Rest and Be Thankful,
B828 to Lochgoilhead. Signposted. Mid Mar-late Oct. Daily, 0900-2300.
Shows: Mon-Fri 1100, 1300, 1500, Sat & Sun 1300, 1500.
Entrance charge. Parking available. Gift shop. Restaurant, snacks.
Tel: (030 13) 247.*

An all-weather indoor attraction in a scenic lochside
setting. Forty-minute live show with 19 different
breeds of sheep, dog obedience trials, sheep shearing.
Sheep are penned indoors and can be seen around the
custom-built theatre. Adjoining is Drimsynie Leisure
Centre, with swimming pool, ice rink and indoor
bowling.

540 EYEMOUTH MUSEUM   5G5

& *Auld Kirk, Market Place, Eyemouth. Easter-Oct, Mon-Fri 1000 to
variable closing times. Sun 1400. Entrance charge. Group concessions. Tel:
(089 07) 50678.*

Opened in 1981 to commemorate the Great East
Coast Fishing Disaster in which 189 fishermen were
lost, 129 of them from Eyemouth. Displays include
Eyemouth tapestry, and the wheelhouse of a modern
fishing boat. Museum reflects the fishing and farming
history of East Berwickshire. Gallery exhibitions.

541 EYNHALLOW CHURCH   1B10

*On island of Eynhallow, Orkney. All reasonable times. Free. (HS)
Tel: 031-244 3101.*

A 12th-century church, now largely in ruins. Close by
is a group of domestic buildings, also ruined.

542 FAIR ISLE   1F8

*Most isolated inhabited island in Britain, halfway between Orkney and
Shetland. Twice-weekly mailboat sailings in summer from Shetland and
scheduled and charter flights from Shetland. Observatory open Mar-Oct.
(NTS) Tel: (035 12) 258/251.*

Home of internationally-famous Bird Observatory,
open March to October. Important breeding ground
for great and Arctic skuas, storm petrel, fulmar,
razorbill, puffin, etc. The Observatory, on main bird
migration routes, notes some 300 species. The island
itself is notable for Fair Isle knitwear in intricate
colourful patterns, a traditional skill of the islanders.
Each summer the NTS organises working holidays on
the island for conservation volunteers, and all-inclusive
breaks can be booked at the Bird Observatory.

543 FAIRWAYS HEAVY HORSE CENTRE 6D2

Walnut Grove, by Perth. 2m E of Perth, off A85. Daily, Apr-Sep, 1000-1800. Entrance charge. Tel: (0738) 32561/25931.

This Centre is both a working and breeding establishment for Clydesdale horses, which can be seen working on the farm most days. Rides in a wagon pulled by a team of Clydesdales. Video show featuring the heavy horses at work throughout the year. A video shows the blacksmith at work at his anvil and the horses being shod.

544 FALCONER MUSEUM 3C8

Tolbooth Street, Forres, 12m W of Elgin. May, June, Sept, Mon-Sat 0930-1800, Sun 1400-1700; July, Aug, Mon-Sat 0930-1830, Sun 1200-1730; Nov-April, Mon-Fri 1000-1230; 1330-1630. Free. Shop. Tel: (0309) 673701.

Displays on local history, natural history, fossils and temporary exhibitions. New display features the Corries folk duo.

545 FALKIRK MUSEUM 6B6

15 Orchard Street, Falkirk. All year, Mon-Fri 1000-1230, 1330-1700. Free. Shop. Tel: (0324) 24911, ext 2202/2472.

Permanent displays on the archaeology of the district, Dunmore Pottery, 19th century foundry products and natural history. Museum shop.

Falkland Palace and Gardens

546 FALKLAND PALACE AND GARDENS 6E3

A912, 11m N of Kirkcaldy. Apr-Sept, Mon-Sat 1000-1800, Sun 1400-1800; Oct, Mon-Sat 1000-1700, Sun 1400-1700. Last tour of Palace 1 hour before closing. Entrance charges. Group concessions. Shops. (NTS). Tel: (033 757) 397.

ASVA

A lovely Royal Palace in a picturesque little town. The buildings of the Palace, in Renaissance style, date from 1501-41. This was a favourite seat of James V, who died here in 1542, and of his daughter Mary, Queen of Scots. The Royal Tennis Court of 1539, the oldest in Britain, is still played on. Exhibition. Visitor Centre, Trust Shop; sacred music played nearby in chapel. Display in Town Hall of the history of the Palace, and the Royal Burgh of Falkland. The gardens are small but charming. Outside viewing only for disabled. The Palace belongs to Her Majesty The Queen.

547 FALLS OF CLYDE CENTRE 5B6

New Lanark. Easter-Oct, Mon-Fri 1100-1700, Sat-Sun 1300-1700; Oct-Easter, weekends only, 1300-1700. Entrance charges. Audio-visual exhibition area. Parking available. (SWT). Tel: (0555) 665262.

Visitor Centre, in the old dyeworks building in New Lanark (see No 990), for the nature reserve and nearby waterfalls. Ancient gorge woodland, spectacular falls, dippers.

Falls of Dochart

548 FALLS OF DOCHART   4H2

Killin. Free.

Dramatic waterfalls rushing through the centre of this picturesque Highland village. On the island of Inchbuie on the river is the burial ground of Clan McNab. Access key to this island and to the graveyard available from Tourist Information Centre in Killin.

549 FALLS OF GLOMACH   2G10

NE off A87, 18m E of Kyle of Lochalsh. Parking available. (NTS).

One of the highest falls in Britain, 370 feet, set in a steep narrow cleft in remote country. The best approach is from the Dorusdain car park (Forestry Commission), 2 miles off the north section of the loop in the old A87. Path 5 miles: allow 5 hours for round trip. Stout footwear, protective clothing, food and compass essential.

Falls of Measach: see No 288.

550 FALLS OF ROGIE   2H8

2m W of Strathpeffer. Open at all times. Parking available. Free.

The word 'Rogie' comes from the Norse language and means 'splashing foaming river'. From the suspension bridge which spans the Falls, salmon may be seen leaping.

551 FALLS OF SHIN   3A6

A836, 5m N of Bonar Bridge.

Spectacular falls through a rocky gorge famous for salmon leaping. Display board about the life cycle of salmon near car park.

552 FARIGAIG FOREST CENTRE   3A9

Off B862 at Inverfarigaig, 17m S of Inverness. Easter-Oct. Daily 0800-1800. Free. Parking available. (FC) Tel: (0463) 791 575.

A Forestry Commission interpretation centre in a converted stone stable, showing how forest wildlife can be conserved and encouraged. Displays of birds and animals, wide range of forest activities, mainly conservation-oriented. Details of local walks supplied.

Farr Church: see No 1204.

553 **FARM LIFE CENTRE** 4H3

 ♿
P
T
Dunaverig, Ruskie, Thornhill. 8 miles E of Aberfoyle on A873.
June-Oct. Daily, 1000-1800. Entrance charges. Group concessions.
Parking available. Gift shop. Farm tearoom. Shop. Tel: (078 685) 277.

Dunaverig is a small family farm of the enclosure
period, circa 1800, traditionally run with sheep, cattle
and crops The Farm Life Centre traces the history of
Dunaverig from earliest times using models,
photographs, charts, tools and implements housed in
the original buildings. Animals indoors and outdoors,
adventure playground, picnic areas, nature walk with
fine views.

554 **FASQUE** 3F12

 ♿
P
T
Approx ½m N of Fettercairn on the Edzell-Banchory road (B974).
May- Sep, daily (not Fri) 1330-1730. Entrance charge. Group concessions.
Parking available. Small shop. Refreshments by arrangement.
Tel: (056 14) 569.

Bought by Sir John Gladstone in 1829, Fasque was
home to William Gladstone, four times Prime
Minister to Queen Victoria, for much of his life.
Today, the sixth generation of the family live in the
house. Downstairs very little has changed — the
kitchen, sculleries, washroom, knives hall, bakery and
buttery contain a wealth of domestic articles.
Magnificent cantilever staircase leads to state rooms,
vast drawing room, library and bedrooms. Red deer
roam in the park in front of the house. The family
church in the grounds, St Andrews, welcomes visitors.

555 **FAST CASTLE** 5F5

Off A1107, 4m NW of Coldingham. Parking available.

The scant, but impressive remains of a Home
stronghold, perched on a cliff above the sea. Care
should be taken on the cliffs.

556 **FEAR AN EICH** 2D4

 ♿
T
Coll Pottery, Back, Isle of Lewis. 6 miles from Stornoway on B895.
Jan-Dec. 0900-1800. Parking available. Shop.
Tearoom. Tel: (0851) 82219.

Pottery making range of marbled ware, figures from
Highland and island history, badges, and a range of
animals and birds.

557 **FEARN ABBEY** 3A7

Take A9 N from Alness for 12m, turn right onto B9165.

The Abbey was founded in the 13th century. It was
converted into a parish church, but in 1742 the roof
fell in during a service killing 42 people, a disaster
prophesied by the Brahan Seer. The restored church
(the nave and choir of the Abbey) is still a parish
church, but the North and South Chapels are still
roofless.

558 **FERGUSSON GALLERY** 6D2

 ♿
P
T
Marshall Place, by South Inch, Perth. Jan-Dec. Mon-Sat, 1000-1700. Free.
Gift shop. Tel: (0738) 441944.

Art Gallery devoted to the works of the famous
Scottish Colourist painter J D Fergusson, housed in a
converted historic water works.

Ferniehirst Castle

559 FERNIEHIRST CASTLE 5E7

  ♿
  T

1½m S of Jedburgh. Information centre: open May-Oct, Wed 1330-1630. Entrance charge. (Private apartments in castle, open by arrangement only. Additional fee. Contact Lothian Estates Office, Jedburgh.) Tel: (0835) 62201.) Parking available. Gift shop. Tel: (0835) 62201.

Scotland's frontier fortress, 16th-century Border Castle, ancestral home of the Kerr family, recently restored by the Marquess of Lothian, Chief of the Kerrs. A 17th century stable has been adapted to incorporate an information centre giving details on Border families and Border history.

560 FETTERCAIRN ARCH 3F12

In Fettercairn. On B9120, 4m W of Laurencekirk. All times. Free.

Stone arch built to commemorate the visit by Queen Victoria and the Prince Consort in 1861.

561 FETTERCAIRN DISTILLERY VISITORS' CENTRE 3F12

5m W of the A94 Perth to Aberdeen road at Fettercairn. ½m W of Fettercairn square. Mon-Sat 1000-1630 (last tour 1600). Free. Parking available. Gift shop. Tel: (056 14) 205.

Fettercairn is one of the oldest licensed distilleries in Scotland. Tours describe the processes involved in distilling malt whisky and the lives of the people in the Mearns. Audio-visual presentation.

562 FIFE FOLK MUSEUM 6F3

  ♿

At Ceres, 3m SE of Cupar. Apr-Oct, daily (except Fri) 1415-1700. Entrance charge. Group concessions. Small museum shop. Parking available. Tel: (033 482) 380 (outwith opening hours).

Situated in the 17th-century Weigh House, near an old bridge in an attractive village, this museum and two adjoining weavers' cottages house a growing collection in an atmospheric setting, showing the domestic and agricultural past of Fife. Countryside annexe. Nearby is the attractive Ceres Church (1806) with a horse-shoe gallery. Alternative wheelchair entrance.

563   **FINDHORN FOUNDATION**   3C7

   P

From Forres take B9011 to Kinloss and Findhorn for 1 mile, turn left immediately after Esso Seapark garage to Findhorn and just after Kinloss Air Base on right is Findhorn Foundation. Sign also says Findhorn Bay Caravan Park. Visitor Centre open all year, afternoons only in winter. Free. Parking available. Green Room Cafe open all day in summer, pm only in winter. Apothecary snack bar. Tel: (0309) 690311.

The Findhorn Foundation Community was founded in 1962 and has grown into an established community of resident members based on the spiritual beliefs of living in co-operation with nature and the planet. There are energy efficient buildings and a 75kw wind generator. There are weaving and pottery studios, a performing arts centre, and gardens at the Park and at Cullerne.

Fingal's Cave: see No 1189.

564   **FINLAGGAN CENTRE**   4C5

Off A846 Post Askaig-Ballygrant road. Isle of Islay. April (Easter), Thurs & Sun 1430-1700. May-Sept, Tues, Thurs, Sun 1430-1700. Oct, Thurs & Sun 1400-1600. Access to Eilean Mor by boat, except during lambing (April/May). Entrance charge. Car parking. Gift shop. Tel: (049 684) 644.

In Loch Finlaggan there are two islands, on the larger of which, Eilean Mor, are the remains of a chapel, residential buildings and fortifications, some of which date from the time of the Lords of the Isles (mainly 14th/15th centuries). On nearby Eilean na Comhairle (Council Isle) they had their administrative centre. The Finlaggan Trust has an information/interpretative centre in a cottage near Loch Finlaggan.

565   **FINLAYSTONE**   3H5

   T

By A8 W of Langbank, 17m W of Glasgow. Woods and gardens open daily 1030-1700. House: Apr-Aug, Sun afternoon, or by arrangement. Entrance charges. Lunches and teas, daily Apr-Sept, weekends Oct-Mar. Tel: (047 554) 285 (1230-1300 or evenings) or (047 554) 505. (Ranger Service.)

Family-run estate, with beautiful formal garden and woodland walks, picnic sites, play areas, visitor centre and ranger service. Celtic art exhibition. House with doll collection and Victorian display, has historic connections with John Knox and Robert Burns.

566   **FLODDEN MONUMENT**   5E7

Town Centre, Selkirk. All times. Free. Tel: (0750) 20096.

The monument was erected in 1913 on the 400th anniversary of the battle and is inscribed 'O Flodden Field'. The memorial is the work of sculptor Thomas Clapperton, and commemorates the lone survivor of the 80 Selkirk men who marched to Flodden.

567 FLOORS CASTLE   5F6

*B6089, signposted 1 mile N of Kelso. Easter weekend. End April, May
June, Sept, Sun-Thurs 1030-1730. July & Aug, daily 1030-1730. Oct,
Sun & Wed 1030-1600. Last admission to house 45 mins before closing.
Coach parties by arrangement in April & Oct. Entrance charges. Group
concessions. Parking available. Gift shop. Licensed restaurant. Garden
Centre open daily for plant sales. Tel. (0573) 223333.*

ASVA

Floors Castle is the home of the Roxburghe family,
and the apartments display an outstanding colleciton
of French 17th-18th century furniture, many fine
works of art and tapestries, Chinese and Dresden
porcelain, and a Victorian collection of birds. The
extensive parkland and gardens overlooking the River
Tweed provide delightful walks and picnic areas. The
walled garden contains splendid herbaceous borders,
best seen in the months of July, August and
September.

568 FOCHABERS FOLK MUSEUM   3E8

& *Fochabers. All year. Winter, daily 0930-1300, 1400-1700. Summer,*
P *daily 0930-1300, 1400-1800. Entrance charge. Family tickets.
Group concessions. Parking available. Tel: (0343) 820362.*

An interesting conversion of an old church housing a
large collection of horse-drawn carts on the top floor,
and on the ground floor a varied collection of local
items, giving the history of Fochabers over the past
200 years.

569 FOGGIELEY SHEEPSKIN RUGS   3F10

& *Craigievar, Alford, on B9119 Aberdeen-Tarland road. Jan-Dec. Mon-Fri
0900-1800. Sat & Sun 1000-1700. Free. Parking available. Shop.
Tel: (033 98) 83317.*

Tannery workshop where skins are taken from their
raw state to finished rugs. Shop sells rugs, leather and
sheepskin goods and clothing.

570 FOGO KIRK   5F6

& *Off B6460 3m SW of Duns. All reasonable times. Free.
Parking available.*

Fogo was founded in the early 12th century. Two
built-up arches, traceable on the north wall, and also
vestry, are probably from these ancient days. Two
laird's lofts are entered by outside stairs, and have
coats-of-arms to commemorate the families — the
Hogs and the Trotters. The kirk was completely
restored in 1755, which is probably when the box-
pews were installed. The lovely Lych Gate is the War
Memorial, and 16 war graves from World War II are
in the kirkyard.

571 FORDYCE JOINER'S WORKSHOP
AND VISITOR CENTRE   3F7

& *1¹/₂ miles off A98, W of Portsoy. Easter-Oct. Daily, 1000-1700.*
T *Garden open all reasonable times. Free. Parking available.*

This attraction describes the trade of the country
joiner/carpenter over the last century and a half,
through video, photographic, tool and machinery
displays. Wood craftsman at work in the former
workshop. As part of the development, a Victorian
garden has been laid out close to the Fordyce Burn.
Fordyce, one of Scotland's best conserved small villages
and largely traffic-free, is built around a 16th century
castle and an early church containing splendid
canopied tombs.

572   **FORT AUGUSTUS ABBEY & FORT**   2H10

&   *S end of Loch Ness, on A82. May-Sep. Mon-Sat 1000-1230, 1330-1700.*
P   *Sun 1330-1700. Entrance charge. Parking available. Gift shop.*
Tel: (0320) 6232.

New development interprets the history of the military
fort and the monastery on this site, tells the story of
monks in the Highlands since Celtic times. Historical
link with Scottish monasteries in Germany from the
16th to 19th centuries.

573   **FORT CHARLOTTE**   1G4

Lerwick, Shetland. Opening standard. Free. (HS) Tel: 031-244 3101.

A fort roughly pentagonal in shape with high walls
containing gun ports pointing seawards. Designed by
John Mylne and begun in 1665 to protect the Sound
of Bressay, it was burned in 1673 with the town of
Lerwick by the Dutch, but repaired in 1781.

574   **FORT GEORGE**   3B8

*B9039, off A96 W of Nairn, Opening standard. Entrance charge. Group
concessions. Parking available. (HS) Tel: 031-244 3101.*

ASVA

Begun in 1748 as a result of the Jacobite rebellion, this
is one of the finest late artillery fortifications in
Europe. There is also the Regimental Museum of the
Queen's Own Highlanders. (See No 1065).

575   **FORTH AND CLYDE CANAL**   6A6

&   *Between the Rivers Forth and Clyde.*
Tel: (0324) 612415 or 041-332 6936.

Opened in 1790, the Canal linked the industrial towns
of West Central Scotland with the east coast at
Grangemouth. The surrounding scenery varies widely
from the impressive industrial monuments near the
centre of Glasgow to the remains of the Antonine
Wall still visible in the more rural areas. Although
closed to navigation in 1963, the Canal is beginning to
enjoy a renaissance through recreation activity. The
towing path provides delightful walks through town
and country with plenty of interest for both nature
and history enthusiasts. Excursions by Canal boat are
available from the Stables Inn, Glasgow Road near
Kirkintilloch and a restaurant boat also operates from
this point. Canal Society boats from Auchinstarry,
near Kilsyth. Fishing, canoeing etc. by permit.
Countryside Ranger Service. Guided Walks and Canal
events during summer months.

576   **FORTH BRIDGES**   6D6

Queensferry, 10m W of Edinburgh.

For over 800 years travellers were ferried across the
Firth of Forth. Queensferry was named from Queen
Margaret who regularly used this passage between
Dunfermline and Edinburgh in the 11th century. The
ferry ceased in 1964 when the Queen opened the
Forth Road Bridge, a suspension bridge then the
longest of its kind in Europe (2,753 yards). Also here
is the rail bridge of 1883-90, one of the greatest
engineering feats of its time. It is 2,765 yards long.

577 FORTINGALL YEW 5A1

Fortingall, 9m W of Aberfeldy. All reasonable times. Parking available.

The surviving part of the great yew in an enclosure in the churchyard is reputedly over 3,000 years old, perhaps the oldest tree in Europe. The attractive village, which was rebuilt in 1900 with many thatched cottages, is claimed to be the birthplace of Pontius Pilate and has been a religious centre since St. Columban times.

Fortrose Cathedral

578 FORTROSE CATHEDRAL 3B8

At Fortrose, 8m SSW of Cromarty. Open all reasonable times. Free. (HS) Tel: 031-244 3101.

The surviving portions of this 14th century cathedral include the south aisle with its vaulting and much fine detail.

579 FORVIE NATURE RESERVE/VISITOR CENTRE 3H9

&
T

Off A974, 4m N of Newburgh turn at crossroads to Collieston, 1m turn right to Visitor Centre. Weekends all year, 1000-1700; weekdays, May-Aug 1000-1700. Free. Prior booking for group visits. Parking available. (SNH) Tel: (036 887) 330.

The nature reserve is an area of dunes, moorland and cliffs on an estuary. The visitor centre has an exhibition and audio-visual programme. There is a wildlife garden, a pond and a tree nursery.

580 FOSSIL VISITOR CENTRE 3D3

&
P
T

Village Hall, Spittal, 10 miles S of Thurso on A895. Jun-Sep. Tues-Sat 1000-1600. Entrance charge. Group concessions. Entrance to hall is free. Parking available. Gift shop. Tearoom. Tel: (Jun-Sep) (084 784) 266.

Spittal village hall has exhibitions of local history, the Flows, and the wildlife of the area. The Fossil Centre has displays of fossils, geology and the flagstone industry.

581 FOULDEN TITHE BARN 5G5

A6105, 5m NW of Berwick-upon-Tweed. May be viewed from the roadside. (HS) Tel: 031-244 3101.

A two-storeyed tithe barn, with outside stair and crow-stepped gables.

582 FOWLSHEUGH NATURE RESERVE   3G11

Access along cliff-top path N from small car park at Crawton, signposted from A92, 3m S of Stonehaven. All times. Donation cairn. Parking available. (RSPB) Tel: 031-557 3136.

Large and spectacular seabird colony, best seen April-July. Information warden sometimes present, April to August.

583 FYRISH MONUMENT   3A7

Above village of Evanton on Fyrish Hill, off A9. All times. Free.

Curious monument erected in 1782 by Sir Hector Munro who rose from the ranks and distinguished himself at the relief of Seringapatam. The monument is a replica of the Indian gateway and was built to provide work at a time of poverty and unemployment in the Evanton area.

584 FYVIE CASTLE   3G9

T

Off A947, 8m SE of Turriff and 25m NW of Aberdeen. Easter, weekends Apr & Oct, 1400-1700. May, daily 1400-1800. Jun-Aug, daily 1100-1800. Sept, daily 1400-1800. Grounds open all year, 0930-sunset. Entrance charges. Group concessions. Parking available. Exhibition. Shop. Tearoom. (NTS) Tel: (0651) 891266.

The five towers of Fyvie Castle enshrine five centuries of Scottish history, each being named after one of the five families who owned the castle. The oldest part dates from the 13th century and it is now one of the grandest examples of Scottish baronial architecture. Apart from the great wheel stair, the finest in Scotland, and the 17th-century morning room, with its contemporary panelling and plaster ceiling, the interior as created by the first Lord Leith of Fyvie reflects the opulence of the Edwardian era. There is an exceptionally important collection of portraits including works by Batoni, Raeburn, Ramsay, Gainsborough, Opie and Hoppner. In addition, there are arms and armour and 16th-century tapestries. Picnic areas and walks in grounds.

584 FYVIE CHURCH   3G9

Off A947, 7m NW of Oldmeldrum. Open by arrangement. Parking available. Free. Tel: (065 16) 230 or 335.

An attractive church with notable stained glass by Tiffany, Celtic stones and 17th-century panelling inside. 'Tifty's Annie' of local ballad fame is buried in the churchyard, and nearby a cross marks the site of a 12th-century monastery.

585 GAIRLOCH HERITAGE MUSEUM   2F7

T

In Gairloch, on A832. Easter-Sep, Mon-Sat 1000-1700. Entrance charge. Gift shop. Licensed restaurant. Parking available. Tel: (0445) 2287.

ASVA

Heritage centre displaying all aspects of life in a typical West Highland parish from the Stone Age to the present day, including archaeology, fishing, agriculture and the domestic arts. Reconstructed croft house room, schoolroom, dairy and shop. The local lighthouse, and preserved fishing boats outside.

586 GALLOWAY DEER MUSEUM   4H10

On A712, by Clatteringshaws Loch, 6m W of New Galloway.
Apr-Sep, daily 1000-1700. Free. Tearoom. Shop. Parking available
(charge). (FC) Tel: (064 42) 285/(0556) 3626.

The centre, in a converted farm steading, features deer
and other aspects of Galloway wildlife, geology and
history. Audio-visual room. Bruce's Stone (See No
181) on Raploch Moss is a short walk away. Mountain
bike routes start from centre, forest walks nearby,
fishing permits available. Picnic site overlooks
Clatteringshaws Loch.

587 GALLOWAY FOOTWEAR CO-OP LTD   4H10

From Castle Douglas travel N on A713 (Ayr) for 13 miles, take right turn
onto A712, Balmaclellan village ½m on left. Follow signs from bottom of
village. Easter-Oct, Mon-Fri 0900-1700. Other times by appointment.
Parking available. Shoes, leather goods for sale and to order.
Tel: (064 42) 465.

Visitors can watch footwear being made — 16 styles
of boots, shoes, sandals and clogs — in the workshop.
It is also the site of the school where Old Mortality's
wife taught.

589 GALLOWAY FOREST PARK   4H9

Off A714, 10m NW of Newton Stewart. Cafe. Parking available.
Free. (FC). Free leaflet is available from the Forestry Commission,
Creebridge, Newton Stewart DG8 6AJ, and Kirroughtree Visitor Centre.
Tel: (0671) 2420.

250 square miles of magnificent countryside in
Central Galloway, including the Merrick (2,765 feet)
the highest hill in southern Scotland. The land is
owned by the Forestry Commission and there is a
wide variety of leisure facilities including forest trails,
fishing, a red deer range, a wild goat park, a forest
drive (see No 1071), a deer museum (see No 587).
Murray's Monument dominates a hillside off the
A712. It was erected to commemorate the son of a
local shepherd who became a Professor at Edinburgh
University.

590 GALLOWAY HOUSE GARDENS   4H11

At Garlieston, 8m S of Wigtown. Mar-Oct, daily 0900-1730. Admission
by collection box, in aid of Scotland's Gardens Scheme and Sorbie Church
Organ Fund. Tel: (098 86) 680.

Galloway House was built in 1740 by Lord Garlies,
eldest son of the 7th Earl of Galloway, and later
enlarged by Burn, and the hall decorated by Lorimer.
Not open to the public.
The grounds cover some 30 acres and go down to the
sea and sandy beach. There are fine old trees, and as a
speciality in May/June there is a well-grown
handkerchief tree. In season there are many snowdrops,
pretty old-fashioned daffodils and a good collection of
rhododendrons and azaleas. Also a walled garden with
greenhouses and a camellia house.

Galloway Forest Park

**591 GARTMORN DAM COUNTRY PARK
        AND NATURE RESERVE**   6C5

*By Sauchie, 2m NE of Alloa off A908. (Park) All year at all times.
(Visitor Centre) Apr-Sept, daily 0830-1930; Oct-Mar, Sat & Sun
1400-1600. Free. (Clackmannan District Council).
Tel: (0259) 214319.*

The oldest dam in Scotland, with reservoir. The park
is an important winter roost for migratory duck, there
are pleasant walks and fishing is available. Visitor
Centre has exhibits, information and slide shows. Talks
and escorted walks can be arranged through the ranger
service.

592 GARVAMORE BRIDGE   3A11

*6m W of Laggan Bridge, on unclassified road, 17m SW of Newtonmore.
All times. Free.*

This two-arched bridge at the south side of the
Corrieyairack Pass was built by General Wade in 1735.

593 GEARRANNAN VILLAGE   2C4

*Carloway, Isle of Lewis. On side road. 1 mile from bridge at Carloway.
Jan-Dec.*

A group of black houses, mostly now in ruins,
evacuated in 1974 and subject to a conservation order.
The village overlooks a beautiful bay on the west coast
of Lewis. One of the houses has been converted into a
Gatliff Trust Hostel, used by hostellers from all over
the world, and can be visited for a small admission
charge.

594 GIANT MACASKILL MUSEUM   2D8

*Centre of Dunvegan village near public car park. Easter-Oct. Mon-Sat
0930-1800; Sun 1230-1700. Entrance charge. Group concessions.
Parking available. Tel: (047 022) 296.*

The museum contains a life-sized model of Angus
MacAskill, listed in the *Guinness Book of Records* as the
tallest Scotsman and tallest 'true' giant at 7' 9". Panels
depict the story of his life and feats of great strength.

595 LADY GIFFORD STATUE   5C6

*Village clock, in West Linton, 17m SSW of Edinburgh. All reasonable
times. Tel: (0968) 60346*

Statue on the front of the village clock at West Linton,
carved in 1666 by the Laird Gifford, a Covenanter and
skilled stonemason. The clock is on the site of a well,
disused since Victorian times. Laird Gifford also
executed panels (1660 and 1678) on a house opposite,
depicting Lady Gifford and the entire family genealogy.

596 GILNOCKIE TOWER   5D9

*A7, 5m S of Langholm. All reasonable times. Free. Can only be viewed
from outside. Tel: (03873) 80976.*

Also known as Holehouse, the tower dates from the
16th century and has walls 6 feet thick. It was once
the home of the 16th-century Border freebooter, Johny
Armstrong. (See also Nos 85 and 943).

597   MV 'GIPSY PRINCESS'   6A6

&♿ *Auchinstarry Canal Basin, B802, 1m S of Kilsyth. May-Oct. Guided*
A *cruises are advertised in local press. Group bookings by arrangement.*
Charges on application. Parking available. Gift shop. Tel: (0236) 721856
or (0236) 822437.

The *Gipsy Princess* is a new (1990) custom-built,
36-seater passenger boat with open air and covered
accommodation, designed and operated by the Forth
& Clyde Canal Society. She follows the route of the
former 'Gipsy Queen' which cruised in the early part
of the century beneath the wooded slopes of
Craigmarloch Hill through the historic Kelvin Valley.
(See No 575).

598   GLADSTONE COURT MUSEUM   5B6

&♿ *A702 North Back Road, Biggar, 26m from Edinburgh, 12m from A74*
A *(South). Easter-Oct, daily 1000-1230, 1400-1700; Sun 1400-1700; other*
times by arrangement. Parking available. (Biggar Museum Trust).
Tel: (0899) 21050.

An indoor street museum of shops and windows.
Grocers, photographer, dressmaker, bank, school,
library, ironmonger, chemist, china merchant,
telephone exchange, etc.

Glamis Castle

599   GLAMIS CASTLE   5D1

A94, 5m SW of Forfar. Easter, Early Apr-early Oct, daily 1030-1730,
other times by prior arrangement only. Entrance charge. Group concessions.
Parking available. Gift shop. Gallery shop. Garden produce stall. Self-
service restaurant. Tel: (030 784) 242/243.

ASVA

This famous Scottish castle, childhood home of Her
Majesty Queen Elizabeth The Queen Mother and
birthplace of The Princess Margaret, owes its present
appearance to the 17th century. Portions of the high
square tower, with walls 15 feet thick, are much older.
There has been a building on the site from very early
times and Malcolm II is said to have died there in
1034. One of the oldest parts of today's castle is
Duncan's Hall, legendary setting for Shakespeare's
famous play 'Macbeth'. There are also fine collections
of china, painting, tapestry and furniture.

600 GLASGOW, ART GALLERY AND MUSEUM 4H5

In Kelvingrove Park. Jan-Dec exc Christmas and New Year. Mon-Sat 1000-1700, Sun 1100-1700. Free. Parking available. Gift shop. Restaurant. Tel: 041-357 3929.

This fine municipal art collection contains superb French Barbizon, Impressionist, Post-Impressionist paintings as well as a good range of Old Master and British pictures including magnificent works by Giorgione and Rembrandt. Galleries devoted to temporary exhibitions. Other areas include sculpture, furniture designed by Charles Rennie Mackintosh and his contemporaries, silver, pottery, glass and porcelain, an important collection of European arms and armour and displays of archaeological, historical and ethnographic material. The natural history displays illustrate geology, with minerals, dinosaurs and other fossils. The natural history of Scotland is treated in depth. Alternative entrance for wheelchairs.

601 GLASGOW, THE BARRAS 4H5

¼m E of Glasgow Cross. All year, Sat and Sun 0900-1700. Free. Tel: 041-552 7258 (Wed-Sun 1000-1600).

Glasgow's world famous weekend market, with an amazing variety of stalls and shops. Founded one hundred years ago, the Barras is now home to over 800 traders each weekend. Look out for the Barras archways, children's creche and buskers. Numerous licensed premises and cafes. All markets are covered.

Glasgow Botanic Gardens

602 GLASGOW BOTANIC GARDENS 4H5

Entrance from Great Western Road (A82). Gardens 0700-dusk; Kibble Palace 1000-1645; Main Range 1300 (Sun 1200)-1645. Closes 1615. Oct-Mar. Free. Tel: 041-334 2422

The glasshouses contain a wide range of tropical plants including an internationally recognised collection of orchids and the National Collection of begonias. The Kibble Palace, an outstanding Victorian glasshouse, has a unique collection of tree ferns and other plants from temperate areas of the world. Outside features include a Systematic Garden, Herb Garden, Chronological Border, and Arboretum.

603 GLASGOW, THE BURRELL COLLECTION 4H5

Pollok Country Park. Jan-Dec exc Christmas and New Year. Mon-Sat 1000-1700, Sun 1100-1700. Free. Parking available. Gift shop. Restaurant and bar. Tel: 041-649 7151.

Housed in a new building opened in 1983, a world famous collection of textiles, furniture, ceramics, stained glass, art objects and pictures (especially 19th century French) gifted to Glasgow by Sir William and Lady Burrell. Temporary exhibition gallery, parking and facilities for handicapped.

604 GLASGOW, CATHCART CASTLE 4H5

In Linn Park. All reasonable times. Free. Tel: 041-637 1147.

Sparse ruins of a 15th-century castle now in a city
park. Nearby is the Court Knowe, associated with
Mary, Queen of Scots.

605 GLASGOW CATHEDRAL 4H5

*At E end of Cathedral Street. Opening standard. Free. (HS)
Tel: 031-244 3101.*

The Cathedral, dedicated to St Mungo, is the most
complete survivor of the great Gothic churches of
south Scotland. A fragment dates from the late 12th
century, though several periods (mainly 13th century)
are represented in its architecture. The splendid crypt
of the mid-13th century is the chief glory of the
cathedral, which is now the Parish Church of
Glasgow.

606 GLASGOW, CITIZENS' THEATRE 4H5

*119 Gorbals Street, S bank of Clyde, just over George V Bridge. Sept-
July. Box Office: Mon-Sat 1000-1800 (2100 on performance nights.)
Sun 1700-2100, performance nights only. Charge for performances.
Group concessions. Parking available. Bars, confectionery stalls, coffee.
Inductive loop. Sign language performance.
Tel: 041-429 0022 (1000-2000, box office), 041-429 5561 (admin).*

Opened in 1878 originally as a Music Hall and now a
listed building. Main 600-seat auditorium and two
studio theatres. Alternative wheelchair entrance.

607 GLASGOW, CITY CHAMBERS 4H5

*George Square. Jan-Dec. Mon-Fri, guided tours at 1030 and 1430 or by
arrangement. Sometimes restricted owing to Council functions. Free.
Gift shop open after tours. Tel: 041-221 9600.*

Grade 'A' listed building, headquarters of City of
Glasgow district council. Built in Italian Renaissance
style, and opened in 1888 by Queen Victoria. The
interiors, particularly the banqueting hall, Council
Chambers and the marble staircases, reflect all the
opulence of Victorian Glasgow.

608 GLASGOW, COLLINS GALLERY 4H5

*University of Strathclyde, Richmond Street, off George Street.
Open during exhibitions, Mon-Fri 1000-1700, Sat 1200-1600.
Free. Car parking only. Sales desk. Refreshments.
Tel: 041-552 4400, ext 4145.*

Modern gallery which presents a lively programme of
contemporary exhibitions throughout the year,
ranging from contemporary painting and sculpture,
crafts and photography to local history and
architecture. Most exhibitions include demonstrations,
talks, workshops or films with special events for
children.

609 GLASGOW, COMPASS GALLERY 4H5

*178 West Regent Street. Jan-Dec exc public holidays. Mon-Sat
1000-1730. Free. Tel: 041-221 6370.*

Long established contemporary gallery with changing
exhibitions of contemporary Scottish and international
art. Paintings, original prints, sculpture and ceramics.

Crookston Castle

610 GLASGOW, CROOKSTON CASTLE   4H5

4m SW of city centre. Open all reasonable times. Keykeeper. Free. (HS) Tel: 031-244 3101.

On the site of a castle built by Robert Croc in the mid-12th century, the present tower house dates from the early 15th century. Darnley and Mary, Queen of Scots stayed here after their marriage in 1565.

611 GLASGOW, CUSTOM HOUSE QUAY   4H5

N shore of the Clyde, between Glasgow Bridge and Victoria Bridge.

The Quay is part of the Clyde Walkway, an ambitious project to give new life to the riverside. There is a fine view of Carlton Place on the opposite bank.

Glasgow, Fossil Grove: see No 650.

612 GLASGOW, DESIGN COUNCIL SCOTLAND   4H5

Ca d'Oro Buildings, 45 Gordon Street. Jan-Dec. Mon-Fri 0900-1700. Tel: 041-221 6121.

Design exhibitions and information. Publications for business, industry, designers, students and teachers.

613 GLASGOW, GEORGE SQUARE   4H5

Glasgow city centre.

The heart of Glasgow with the City Chambers (see No 607) and statues of Sir Walter Scott, Queen Victoria, Prince Albert, Robert Burns, Sir John Moore, Lord Clyde, Thomas Campbell, Dr Thomas Graham, James Oswald, James Watt, William Gladstone and Sir Robert Peel.

614 GLASGOW, GREENBANK GARDEN   4H5

Flenders Road, Clarkston (6m S of city centre), off Mearns Road (B761) off A726. All year, daily 0930-sunset. Entrance charges. Group concessions. Shop and tearoom in season. (NTS) Tel: 041-639 3281.

Two and a half acres of walled garden and 13 acres of policies surround an elegant Georgian house (not open to the public) built in 1763 for a Glasgow merchant. The attractive garden shows the wide range of ornamental plants, annuals, perennials, shrubs and trees that can be grown in this area.

615 GLASGOW, HAGGS CASTLE   4H5
100 St Andrew's Drive. All year, Mon-Sat 1000-1700, Sun 1200-1800. Free. Tel: 041-427 2725.

Built in 1585 by John Maxwell of Pollok, the castle was acquired by the city in 1972, and, after restoration, was developed as a museum of history for children.

616 GLASGOW, HEATHERBANK MUSEUM OF SOCIAL WORK   4H5
163 Mugdock Road, Milngavie. Jan-Dec exc public holidays. Sun-Fri 1400-1700. Donations welcome. Car parking only. Gift shop. Refreshments. Sales area. Tel: 041-956 2687.

A 'hands-on' exhibition on juvenile justice and attitudes towards physical disability. Activities for children, videos, audio-visual, recordings including 'rap' songs about crime, library, picture library, educational resource material.

617 GLASGOW, HUNTERIAN ART GALLERY   4H5
University of Glasgow, Hillhead Street, 2m NW of city centre. Jan-Dec. (closed Glasgow Public Holidays), Mon-Sat 0930-1700. Mackintosh House closed 1230-1330. Free. Groups must book in advance. Sales point. University refectory nearby. Tel: 041-330 5431.

Unrivalled collections of work by Charles Rennie Mackintosh, including reconstructed interiors of the architect's house, and by J M Whistler. Works by Rembrandt, Chardin, Stubbs, Reynolds, Pissarro, Sisley, Rodin, plus Scottish painting from the 18th century to the present. Sculpture Courtyard. Varied programme of temporary exhibitions from 16th century to present. Alternative wheelchair entrance.

618 GLASGOW, HUNTERIAN MUSEUM   4H5
Glasgow University, 2m NW of city centre. Jan-Dec, Mon-Sat 0930-1700. Free. Parking available (Sat only). Bookstall, souvenir shop, coffee house. Tel: 041-330 4221.

Scotland's oldest museum, opened in 1807. The 'Earth . . . Life' exhibition in the refurbished main hall includes geological, archaeological and ethnographical material; coin gallery and exhibition on history of Glasgow University. Zoology museum nearby in grounds. The anatomical collection, and manuscripts and early printed books, can be seen on application. Major temporary exhibitions are mounted throughout the year. Alternative wheelchair entrance (via lift), please telephone.

619 GLASGOW, HUTCHESONS' HALL   4H5
158 Ingram Street, near SE corner of George Square. Jan-Dec, Mon-Fri 0900-1700, Sat 1000-1600. Subject to functions in hall. Shop. Free. (NTS) Tel: 041-552 8391.

Described as one of the most elegant buildings in Glasgow's city centre, Hutchesons' Hall was built in 1802-5 to a design by David Hamilton. It incorporates on its frontage the statues of the founders, George and Thomas Hutcheson, from an earlier building. A major reconstruction in 1876 by John Baird heightened the Hall to its present proportions and provided an impressive staircase. Category 'A' listed building. It is now used as a visitor centre, gift shop and the Trust's regional offices.

620 GLASGOW, KING'S THEATRE   4H5

Bath Street, Glasgow. Tel: 041-227 5511.

This 1,785 seat theatre dates back to 1904 and
preserves the style and elegance of the Edwardian
period. Now carefully modernised, it has become one
of the best equipped civic theatres in Scotland.

**621 GLASGOW, BARCLAY LENNIE
      FINE ART**   4H5

*Semi-basement, 203 Bath Street. Jan-Dec exc public holidays. Mon-Fri
1000-1700, Sat 1000-1300. Free. Tel: 041-226 5413.*

19th and 20th-century Scottish art. Paintings,
drawings, sculpture, decorative art. Usually four shows
by contemporary artists per year.

622 GLASGOW, McLELLAN GALLERIES   4H5

*Sauchiehall Street. Mon-Sat 1000-1700, Sun 1100-1700. Entrance charges
vary. Closed between exhibitions. Tel: 041-331 1854.*

The purpose-built 1854 exhibition galleries, completely
refurbished in time for Glasgow's celebrations as
Cultural Capital of Europe, now provide Glasgow
Museums with a major venue for large exhibitions.

623 GLASGOW, MERCHANTS' HOUSE   4H5

*W side of George Square. Open by appointment, please telephone. Free.
Tel: 041-221 8272.*

This handsome building occupies one of the best sites
in the city. Built in 1874 by John Burnet, it contains
the Glasgow Chamber of Commerce, the oldest in
Britain, the fine Merchants' Hall, with ancient relics,
portraits and good stained-glass windows, and the
House's own offices.

The Mitchell Library

624 GLASGOW, THE MITCHELL LIBRARY   4H5

*North Street, 1 mile W of city centre. Jan-Dec exc public holidays.
Mon-Fri 0930-2100, Sat 0930-1700. Free. Tearoom. Tel: 041-221 7030.*

Founded in 1874, this is the largest public reference
library in Europe, with stock of over one and a quarter
million volumes. Its many collections include probably
the largest on Robert Burns in the world, the
Glasgow Collection of local history and genealogical
resources. Resource unit for the visually impaired.

**625 GLASGOW, EWAN MUNDY
      FINE ART**   4H5

*48 West George Street, above Buchanan Street subway station entrance.
Jan-Dec exc public holidays. Mon-Sat 0930-1730. Free.
Tel: 041-331 2406.*

A fine art gallery specialising in paintings, drawings
and engravings by Scottish, English and French
20th-century artists.

**626   GLASGOW, MUSEUM OF
EDUCATION**   **4H5**

&   *Scotland Street School, 225 Scotland Street. Take first exit (East Kilbride)*
P   *off Kingston Bridge on S side. Jan-Dec exc public holidays. Mon-Sat*
T   *1000-1700, 1400-1700. Free. Parking available. Gift shop. Cafe.*
     Tel: 041-429 1202.

This magnificent building with its twin leaded towers
and Glasgow Style stone-carving was designed by
Charles Rennie Mackintosh in 1904. It now houses a
permanent exhibition on the History of Education.
There are Victorian, Second World War, 1950s and
1960s classrooms, a Drill Hall, an Edwardian Cookery
Room. Regularly changing temporary exhibitions
include subjects such as other cultures, Mackintosh,
art, craft, and exhibitions designed by and for children.
Activity sessions. The museum is run by Strathclyde
Region Department of Education.

Museum of Transport

627   GLASGOW, MUSEUM OF TRANSPORT   **4H5**

Kelvin Hall, 1 Bunhouse Road. Jan-Dec. Mon-Sat, 1000-1700,
Sun 1100-1700. Free. Cafe. Tel: 041-357 3929.

A new and considerably enlarged museum of the
history of transport, including a reproduction of a
typical 1938 Glasgow street. Other new features are a
larger display of the ship models and a walk-in Motor
Car Showroom with cars from the 1930s up to
modern times. Other displays include Glasgow trams
and buses, Scottish-built cars, fire engines, horse-drawn
vehicles, commerical vehicles, cycles and motorcycles,
railway locomotives and a Glasgow Subway station.
Run by Glasgow Museums.

628   GLASGOW, NECROPOLIS   **4H5**

Behind Glasgow Cathedral. Access restricted: contact Cemeteries &
Cremations, Port Dundas Place, Glasgow. Tel: 041-333 0800.

Remarkable and extensive burial ground laid out in
1833, with numerous elaborate tombs of 19th-century
illustrious Glaswegians and others; particularly the
Menteith Mausoleum of 1842.

629   GLASGOW, PEOPLE'S PALACE   **4H5**

In Glasgow Green. Jan-Dec. Mon-Sat 1000-1700, Sun 1100-1700. Free.
Shop. Wholefood snack bar/tearoom in Winter Gardens.
Tel: 041-554 0223.

Opened in 1898, contains important collections
relating to the tobacco and other industries, Glasgow
stained glass, ceramics, and political and social
movements including temperance, co-operation,
women's suffrage and socialism. Alternative
wheelchair entrance at west door (Winter Gardens).

630   GLASGOW, POLLOK HOUSE   4H5

2060 Pollokshaws Road (A736). Jan-Dec exc public holidays. Mon-Sat
1000-1700. Sun 1100-1700. Free. Parking available. Tearoom, gardens,
shop. Tel: 041-632 0274.

Built c 1750, with additions 1890-1908 designed by
Sir Robert Rowand Anderson. It houses the Stirling
Maxwell collection of Spanish and other European
paintings. Also displays of furniture, ceramics, glass
and silver (mostly 18th century). Alternative
wheelchair entrance to tearoom.

631   GLASGOW, PROVAN HALL   4H5

At Auchinlea Road (B806), Easterhouse, off M8, 4m E of city centre.
Parking available. Garden. (NTS) Tel: 041-552 8391.

Built in the 16th century, this is probably the most
perfect example of a pre-Reformation house in
Scotland. Now part of Auchinlea Park. The property
is leased to the City of Glasgow District Council and
while the old hall is closed at present, visitors may
view the surrounding garden and parkland.

632   GLASGOW, PROVAND'S LORDSHIP   4H5

Castle Street, opposite the Cathedral. Jan-Dec. Mon-Sat 1000-1700,
Sun 1100-1700. Free. Shop. Tel: 041-552 8819.

The only surviving medieval building in Glasgow
apart from the Cathedral. Built 1471 as the manse for
the chaplain of the Hospital of St Nicholas by Bishop
Andrew Muirhead. Period house displays, 1500-1900.

633   GLASGOW, QUEEN'S CROSS CHURCH   4H5

&
A
P

870 Garscube Road, ½ mile W of City centre. Jan-Dec. Tues, Thurs, Fri
1200-1730. Sun 1430-1700. Other times by arrangement with the
Director. Free. Parking available. Gift shop. Refreshments. Tel: 041-946
6600.

The only church (1897-1899) designed by Charles
Rennie Mackintosh, architect, artist and designer who
grew up and spent most of his professional life
practising in Glasgow. Restored by the Charles Rennie
Mackintosh society as its headquarters, the church has
a small exhibition area, reference library and specialised
shop.

634   GLASGOW, REGIMENTAL
HEADQUARTERS OF THE
ROYAL HIGHLAND FUSILIERS   4H5

518 Sauchiehall Street. Mon-Thu 0900-1630, Fri 0900-1600.
Parking available. Free. Tel: 041-332 0961.

The exhibits in this regimental museum include
medals, badges, uniforms and records which illustrate
the histories of The Royal Scots Fusiliers, The
Highland Light Infantry and the Royal Highland
Fusiliers, Princess Margaret's Own Glasgow and
Ayrshire Regiment.

635   GLASGOW, ROUKEN GLEN   4H5

Thornliebank. All reasonable times. Free. Tearoom.

One of Glasgow's most attractive parks with lovely
shaded walks and a waterfall. Children's playground,
boating pond, garden centre and butterfly farm.

636 GLASGOW ROYAL CONCERT HALL   4H5

& *2 Sauchiehall Street. From M8 westbound, exit at Junction 16; eastbound,*
P *Junction 17. Follow signs. Jan-Dec. Box office, daily, 1000-1800 (2100 on*
T *show nights). Shop, daily, 1000-1730 (and on selected show nights). Public*
tours Mon-Fri 1400. Other times by arrangement. Charge for tours and
performances. Parking available. Gift shop. Restaurant/tearoom/
refreshments. Induction loop. Tel: 041-332 6633.

The Glasgow Royal Concert Hall, opened in 1990,
provides a lasting tribute to Glasgow's reign as
Cultural Capital of Europe in that year. This world-
class multi-purpose venue with excellent acoustics
replaces the St Andrew Hall which was destroyed by
fire in 1964. The hall has hosted performances by
many major artistes and orchestras.

637 GLASGOW, ST DAVID'S 'RAMSHORN'
CHURCH   4H5

& *Ingram Street. All reasonable times. Access can be arranged with Director*
of Drama, University of Strathclyde. Free. Tel: 041-552 3489.

Impressive church built in 1824 with a graveyard
containing the graves of many notable citizens
including David Dale, creator of New Lanark.
Now University drama centre.

638 GLASGOW, ST MUNGO'S MUSEUM   4H5

Next to Cathedral, 1 mile NE of city centre. Jan-Dec. Mon-Sat
1000-1700, Sun 1100-1700. Free. Gift shop. Restaurant.
Tel: 041-553 2557.

Opened in April 1993, this museum explores the
universal themes of life, death and the hereafter,
through evocative art objects associated with different
religious faiths. Three galleries focus on art, religion
and world religions. Japanese Zen garden.

639 GLASGOW, ST VINCENT STREET
CHURCH   4H5

& *265 St Vincent Street. Service times, or by arrangement with Church*
A *Officer. Free. Induction loop. Tel: 041-221 1937.*

Church by Alexander 'Greek' Thomson of varied
styles high on a plinth — the only one of his churches
still in use.

640 GLASGOW SCHOOL OF ART   4H5

167 Renfrew Street. Jan-Dec. Mon-Fri 0930-1700, Sat 1000-1200.
Entrance to exhibitions free. Tours of building Mon-Fri 1100, 1400, Sat
1000. Additional tours in summer. Charge for tours. Mackintosh shop.
Refectory nearby. Tel: 041-332 9797.

Founded in 1844, Glasgow School of Art is one of the
oldest and largest art schools in Britain, and today
comprises schools of Design, Craft, Fine Art and
Architecture. Its reputation for quality and innovation
is complemented by its magnificent location — the
Mackintosh Building. Designed by architect, designer
and artist Charles Rennie Mackintosh, it is the first
important architectural monument to the modern
movement in Europe.

641 GLASGOW, SPRINGBURN MUSEUM   4H5
♿ *Atlas Square, Ayr Street, off A803 to City Centre. All year, Mon-Fri 1030-1700, Sat 1000-1630, Sun & Bank holidays 1400-1700. Free. Tel: 041-557 1405.*

The museum preserves the heritage of this typical Glaswegian community by recording the memories of the local people at work and at home. Springburn was once the largest centre of steam locomotive manufacture in the world. Winner of the British Museum of the Year award for Social and Industrial History 1989.

642 GLASGOW, STIRLING'S LIBRARY   4H5
♿ *111 Queen Street. Jan-Dec exc public holidays. Mon, Tues, Thurs*
A *0900-2000. Wed, Fri, Sat 0900-1700. Free. Tel: 041-221 1876.*

Formerly known as the Royal Exchange, and before that the Cunningham Mansion, the present building, used as a library, was designed in 1827 and has a particularly rich interior.

643 GLASGOW, THE INTERNATIONAL STOCK EXCHANGE   4H5
Nelson Mandela Place. All year, Mon-Fri 0900-1630. Free. Tel: 041-221 7060.

A 'French Venetian' building of 1877, with visitors' gallery.

644 GLASGOW, FORMER TEMPLETON'S CARPET FACTORY   4H5
Off Glasgow Green. View from outside only. Free.

Victorian factory built to copy the design of the Doge's Palace in Venice with ornate decoration of coloured glazed brick, battlements, arches and pointed windows.

645 GLASGOW, THE TENEMENT HOUSE   4H5
⛌ *145 Buccleuch Street, Garnethill, N of Charing Cross. Apr-Oct, daily 1400-1700; early Nov-Mar, Sat/Sun 1400-1600. Weekday morning visits arranged for educational and other groups by appointment only. Entrance charge. Group concessions. Publication sales. (NTS). Tel: 041-333 0183 (1000-1230 and 1400-1700).*

Built in 1892 when Garnethill was established as a superior residential district in Glasgow's West End, the Tenement House illustrates life in the city at the turn of the century, and the character given by the Victorian tenement buildings. The flat consists of two rooms, kitchen and bathroom and contains original box-beds, kitchen range, sink, coal bunker and many domestic items of the family who lived there for over 50 years. Ground-floor exhibition.

646 GLASGOW, THEATRE ROYAL   4H5
♿ *Hope Street. Booking office Mon-Sat 1000 to end of first interval (1800 on*
P *non-performance days). Group rates for parties of 10 or more. Bars and*
T *entertainment facilities. Induction loop. Tel: 041-332 9000.*

A fine Victorian theatre, elegantly restored as the home of Scottish Opera. Performances also by Scottish Ballet, national visiting companies and major concert artists. Induction loop.

647 GLASGOW, TRAMWAY 4H5

  P
  T

25 Albert Drive, Pollokshields. Jan-Dec. Exhibitions open Mon-Sun, 1100-1900. Box office 1200-1800. Performances 2000. Charges vary. Cafe open during exhibitions. Bar during performances. Tel: 041-422 2023.

Former tram depot, later Glasgow's Museum of Transport (1894). Now an international arts venue presenting innovative theatre, dance, music and visual arts from Britain, Europe and beyond.

648 GLASGOW, UNIVERSITY OF GLASGOW VISITOR CENTRE 4H5

  T

From Great Western Road (A82) turn into Byres Road at Botanic Gardens/Queen Margaret Drive junction. Go left at next lights into University Avenue. University on right at top of hill. Oct-Apr, Mon-Sat 0930-1700; May-Sept, Mon-Sat 0930-1700, Sun 1400-1700. Free. Tearoom. Tel: 041-330 5511.

Visitor centre has exhibits of the university at work, interactive slide/computer and video displays plus a 'hands-on' information system. Conducted tours of mid-Victorian Gilbert Scott Building and Campus available at a small charge. Grounds open.

649 GLASGOW VENNEL MUSEUM, IRVINE 4G6

Nos. 4 and 10 Glasgow Vennel, Irvine. Oct-May, Tues-Sat exc Wed 1000-1300, 1400-1700. June-Sept, Mon-Sat exc Wed 1000-1300, 1400-1700, Sun 1400-1700. Free. Car parking only. Tel: (0294) 75059.

Intimate gallery with varied exhibition programme. Exhibitions by local, national, international artists and groups. Also the heckling (flax dressing) shop where Robert Burns worked in 1781. Burns lodgings at No. 4 Glasgow Vennel.

650 GLASGOW, VICTORIA PARK AND FOSSIL GROVE 4H5

Victoria Park Drive North, facing Airthrey Avenue. Mon-Sat 0800-dusk; Sun 1000-dusk. Fossil Grove open by arrangement. Free. Tel: 041-959 9087.

Cornish elms, lime trees, formal flower garden and arboretum. Within the park is the famous Fossil Grove, with fossil stumps and roots of trees which grew here 330 million years ago.

651 GLASGOW, WILLOW TEAROOM 4H5

217 Sauchiehall Street, in precinct area above Henderson the Jeweller. Jan-Dec exc public holidays. Mon-Sat 0930-1630. Tel: 041-332 0521.

The Willow Tearoom is an original Charles Rennie Mackintosh building, designed for Miss Cranston 1904-1928. Re-opened in 1983, the tearoom still has original glass and mirror work and doors, and functions as a restaurant serving light meals, teas and coffees.

652 GLASGOW ZOO PARK 5A5

Uddingston, 6m SE of city centre on M74 (Glasgow/Carlisle) Signposted. Jan-Dec, daily 1000-1800 (1700 winter). Entrance charge. Parking available. Shop. Cafeteria. Tel: 041-771 1185.

A developing open plan collection, taking in 25 hectares, with another 25 more being developed. Many rare animals, most of them breeding. Speciality cats, reptiles; also education department. Long walks, picnic areas.

653 GLEN AFFRIC 2H9

*A831 to Cannich and to head of Loch Benevean car park. Jan-Dec.
Leaflets available from Forest Enterprise, Strathoich, Fort Augustus. (FE)*

The area is a Forest Nature Reserve, with a great
variety of wildlife at all points on walks and trails
through native pinewoods and other beautiful
woodland.

654 GLENAN BAY 4E5

*10 miles W of Tighnabruaich via B8000 and unclassified road from
Millhouse to Portavadie. All reasonable times. Free. Car parking only.
(FE)*

Glenan Bay is a secluded bay on the shore of Loch
Fyne, well away from traffic and disturbance. It lies on
the edge of Glenan Oakwood Forest Nature Reserve.
A path leads from the car park through the ancient
semi-natural woodland and returning to the car park.
Stout footwear is recommended.

655 GLENARN 4G4

&
P
T

*Glenarn Road, Rhu, 1 mile N of Helensburgh on A814. Late Mar-late
June. Daily, dawn-dusk. Entrance charge, honesty box. Leaflets, plant
stall. Tel: (0436) 820493.*

Woodland garden dating from 1840, developed and
planted from 1927 with rare rhododendrons,
magnolias and other exotic ericaceous plants. Many
bulbs and primulas in season. Currently undergoing
extensive renovation and replanting. Woodland walk
from gate leads up the glen, criss-crossing the burn, to
several viewpoints and the old orchard on the northern
boundary. Paths lead back to the rock garden and
daffodil lawn, returning through woodland to the
gate.

**656 GLENASHDALE FALLS AND
GIANTS' GRAVES** 4F7

*Whiting Bay, 9 miles S of Brodick on A841, Isle of Arran. Jan-Dec. All
reasonable times. Free. Parking available. Tearoom close to start of walk,
summer season. (FC) Tel: (0770) 2218.*

Forest trail commencing at Whiting Bay, following
the Glenashdale Burn and providing splendid
viewpoints overlooking the falls, a magnificent sight
when the burn is in full spate. On the south side of
the glen, a signposted path to the Giants' Graves gives
views over Whiting Bay and Holy Island. The cairns
are 'horned gallery graves' dating from the Neolithic
period. North of the falls are the remains of an Iron
Age fort. Glenashdale Falls walk, 2 hours. Giants'
Graves, a steep 1½ hours.

**657 GLENBARR ABBEY VISITOR CENTRE
(MACALISTER CLAN)** 4D7

&
P

*Glenbarr, on A83, 12 miles NW of Campbeltown. Easter-mid Oct.
Daily exc Tues, 1000-1800. Entrance charge. Parking available. Gift shop.
Tearoom. Tel: (058 32) 247.*

18th/19th century Gothic style house gives a glimpse
of family living, with antique toys, Spode and Sevres
china. Gloves worn by Mary, Queen of Scots are
among the exhibits in the museum. A large collection
of thimbles, owned by the present Mrs Macalister, is
on display. Lovely grounds, riverside and woodland
walks. Tours conducted by the Laird and Lady
Glenbarr (Mr and Mrs Macalister).

658 GLENCOE AND DALNESS   **4F1**

A82, 17 miles S of Fort William. Visitor Centre: April-late May, early Sept-mid Oct, daily 1000-1700; late May-early Sept, daily 0930-1800. Entrance charge. Parking available. Shop. Snack bar. (NTS) Tel: (085 52) 307.

The finest and perhaps the most famous glen in Scotland through which a main road runs. Scene of the Massacre of Glencoe, 1692, and centre for some of the best mountaineering in the country (not to be attempted by the unskilled). Noted for wildlife which includes red deer, wildcat, golden eagle, ptarmigan. NTS owns 14,200 acres of Glencoe and Dalness. Visitor centre gives information on walks and trails, audio-visual display. Ranger service guided walks in season.

659 GLENCOE AND NORTH LORN FOLK MUSEUM   **4F1**

In Glencoe village, off A82, on S shore of Loch Leven. Mid May-Sept, Mon-Sat 1000-1730. Entrance charge.

Glencoe Museum has four heather-thatched buildings. One is 'cruck' construction, where the bearing beams of the roof come down inside the walls. Costume, accessories and embroidery are displayed, along with models in 18th century Highland dress. Commemorative china, domestic bygones, weapons, dolls' houses, dolls and model soldiers, Jacobite and clan history. Books of old photographs. Outbuildings house natural history and agricultural exhibits, and a model of a slate worker and his tools. Model of the old railway station, and an illicit still.

660 GLENCOE CHAIRLIFT   **4G1**

Off A82 by Kingshouse. Jan-Apr, Thurs-Mon inclusive of Easter; Jun-Sept, daily 1000-1700. Charge for lift. Family tickets. Parking available. Tel: (085 56) 226.

Chairlift to 2,100 feet offers magnificent views of the areas around Glencoe and Rannoch Moor. Summer: access chairlift, snack bar, car park, toilets. Winter: two chairlifts and four tows for ski-ing, car park, toilets and snack bars.

661 GLENDRONACH DISTILLERY   **3F8**

On B9001, between Huntly and Inverurie. All year, Mon-Fri 1000 or 1400 (prior booking preferred). Free. Parking available. Shop. Tel: (046682) 202 (0830-1630).

Visitor Centre and guided tour around malt whisky distillery dating from 1826. Tasting.

662 GLENEAGLES CRYSTAL   **6D6**

37 Simpson Road, East Mains Industrial Estate, Broxburn. Jan-Dec exc Christmas and New Year. Mon-Sat 1000-1700, Sun 1200-1700. Free. Parking available. Shop. Coffee. Tel: (0506) 852566.

Factory where production of Gleneagles of Edinburgh hand-cut crystal can be seen from the viewing gallery. Factory shop with large selection of glass.

Glenelg Brochs

663 GLENELG BROCHS   2F10

Unclassified road from Eilanreach, 12m W of Shiel Bridge.
All reasonable times. Free. (HS) Tel: 031-244 3101.

Two Iron Age brochs, Dun Telve and Dun Troddan,
have walls still over 30 feet high.

664 GLENFARCLAS DISTILLERY   3D9

♿ P T

Off A95, 17m WSW of Keith and 17m NE of Grantown-on-Spey.
Jan-Dec exc Christmas and New Year. Oct-May, Mon-Fri 0900-1630.
June-Sept, also Sat 1000-1600, Sun 1300-1600. Other times by
arrangement. Groups by arrangement. Gift shop. Tel: (080 72) 257/245.

Malt whisky distillery with audio-visual, whisky
exhibition (4 languages), ship's room, cask filling
gallery, picnic area.

665 GLENFARG SILVER   6D3

♿

Folda, next to church in Glenfarg, Perthshire. Jan-Dec. 0900-1230,
1330-1700. Free. Car parking only. Shop. Tel: (0577) 830300.

Very small workshop where silversmith can be seen at
work. Display of finished work in silver and gold,
which can be purchased. All work is made in the
workshop and hallmarked in Edinburgh.

666 GLENFEOCHAN HOUSE GARDENS   4E2

♿ A P

Kilmore, 5m S of Oban, A816. Daily, Apr-Oct, 1000-1800.
Entrance charge. Parking available. Tel: (063 177) 273.

Glenfeochan House, built in 1875, is surrounded by
six acres of mature gardens. Many of the trees were
planted in the 1850s. A wide variety of rhododendrons
are on view, including a Loderi Collection. Walled
garden with herbaceous borders, vegetables and large
greenhouse containing peaches and nectarines, and
herb beds.

667 GLENFIDDICH DISTILLERY   3E8

♿ P T

1 mile N of Dufftown on A941, 16m S of Elgin. Jan-Dec exc Christmas
and New Year. Mon-Fri 0930-1630. Also Easter-mid Oct,
Sat 0930-1630, Sun 1200-1630. Free. Parking available. Gift shop.
Tel: (0340) 20373.

After an audio-visual programme available in six
languages, visitors are shown around the distillery and
bottling hall and then offered a complimentary dram
of the malt whisky. Picnic area.

668 GLENFINART DEER FARM   4G4

♿ P T

Barnacabber Farm, ½ mile N of Ardentinny. Easter-Oct, 1100-1700.
Nov-Easter, by appointment. Entrance charge. Parking available.
Gift shop. Full refreshment facilities in adjacent Glenfinart Hotel.
Tel: (036 981) 331.

Deer visitor centre with audio-visual display and
ranger-guided tours, set in scenic Glen Finart. The
former farm has been converted into tearoom,
restaurant and bar.

Glenfinnan Monument

669 GLENFINNAN MONUMENT   2F12

ASVA

A830, 18½m W of Fort William. Apr-late May, early Sept-mid Oct, daily 1000-1300, 1400-1700. Late May-early Sept, daily 0900-1800. Entrance charge. Parking available. Gift shop. Snack bar. (NTS) Tel: (039 783) 250.

The monument commemorates the raising of Prince Charles Edward Stuart's standard at Glenfinnan on 19 August 1745. The monument was erected by Alexander Macdonald of Glenaladale in 1815; a figure of a Highlander surmounts the tower. The Visitor Centre tells of the Prince's campaign from Glenfinnan to Derby and back to the final defeat at Culloden. Commentaries in four languages. Viewpoint.

670 GLENGOULANDIE DEER PARK   5A1

8 miles NW of Aberfeldy on B846 to Kinloch Rannoch. May-Oct. Daily, 0900 to 1 hour before sunset. Entrance charges. Group concessions. Parking available. Gift shop. Tel: (0887) 830261/830306.

Native animals housed in a natural environment. Many endangered species are kept, and there are fine herds of red deer and Highland cattle. Picnic area. Cars can drive through the park, or it can be explored on foot. No dogs, unless kept in car at all times.

671 GLENGOYNE DISTILLERY   4H4

P
T

On A81 Glasgow-Aberfoyle road, just S of junction with A875. Apr-Nov, conducted tours Mon-Fri, hourly from 1000-1600, Sat 1100 and 1500. July and Aug, also Tues and Thurs, 1900 and 2000. Easter-Oct, nosing sessions at 1930 (2 hors). Dec-Mar, by arrangement. Entrance charge for adults, children free. Parking available. Gift shop and Heritage Room. Whisky Bar in reception room. Tel: (036 050) 254.

Attractive, compact distillery, first licensed in 1833, nestles in Campsie Hills, and draws water from a 50-foot waterfall. Conducted tours in small groups show main processes of distilling a Highland malt whisky. Explanatory video. Heritage Room houses cooperage display, old artefacts and shop. Visitors taste a dram in reception room, overlooking dam, glen and waterfall.

672 GLEN GRANT DISTILLERY   3D8

P
T

Rothes. Late Apr-end Sep, Mon-Fri 1000-1600. Also Sats, July and Aug. Free. Tel: (034 03) 413 (during season)/(054 22) 8924 (during winter).

ASVA

Tours of distillery, with Reception Centre and whisky sample. Children under 8 not admitted to production areas but welcome in Reception Centre.

673 GLENKINCHIE DISTILLERY 6G7

From Pencaitland village, take Lempockwells road past farm, then right at crossroads. Distillery can be seen in glen. Jan-Dec exc Christmas and New Year. Mon-Fri 0930-1630. Parking available. Gift shop. Tel: (0875) 340451.

Set in a tiny valley, Glenkinchie, the only remaining malt whisky distillery close to Edinburgh, shows aspects of all the traditional distilling crafts, from malt storage to warehousing the whisky. The original floor maltings now house a collection of whisky artefacts, including a scale model of a malt distillery made for the British Empire Exhibition of 1924.

674 THE GLENLIVET DISTILLERY VISITOR CENTRE 3D9

    P
    T

B9008, 10m N of Tomintoul. Easter-end Oct, Mon-Sat 1000-1600 (July and Aug. 1900). Free. Coach parties by arrangement. Coffee shop. Gift shop. Tel: (080 73) 427 (during season)/(054 22) 6294 (during winter).

ASVA

Guided tours of distillery. Exhibits of ancient whisky tools and artefacts and life-size reproduction of Landseer's painting 'The Highland Whisky Still'. Free whisky sample. Children under 8 not admitted to production areas but welcome in Reception Centre. Video programme.

675 GLENLIVET ESTATE 3D10

    P
    T

Forest Office, Main Street, Tomintoul. Information Centre open July and Aug, 1000-1230, other times by arrangement depending on availability of Estate Ranger. Information also from Tomintoul Tourist Information Centre, The Square. Access to estate at all reasonable times. Free. Charge for Ranger-led Landrover tours. Tel: (080 74) 283 or TIC (080 74) 285.

Part of the Crown Estate, nearly 90 square miles of sheltered glens, forests and heather moors in the foothills of the NE Cairngorms. Over 40 miles of waymarked trails including the Speyside Way provide access for walking, mountain biking, pony trekking, Nordic skiing and other outdoor activities. An interpretative centre provides information about walks, history, wildlife and land use, and the Estate Ranger is available for advice on routes and places of interest. Landrover tours, slide talks, free Estate map and guide.

Glenluce Abbey

676 GLENLUCE ABBEY 4G10

Off A75, 2m N of Glenluce. Apr-Sept, opening standard. Oct-Mar, weekends only. Entrance charge. Group concessions. (HS) Tel: 031-244 3101.

Founded in 1192 by Roland, Earl of Galloway, for the Cistercian order. A fine vaulted chapter house is of architectural interest.

677 GLENMORE FOREST PARK   3C10

7m E of Aviemore, off B9152. Visitor centre. Open all year (exc 2 weeks in Nov). Parking available. (FE) Tel: (0479) 861220.

Over 5,000 acres of pine and spruce woods and mountainside on the north-west slopes of the Cairngorms, with Loch Morlich as its centre. Fine area for wildlife, including red deer, reindeer, wildcat, golden eagle, ptarmigan, capercailzie. Remnants of old Caledonian pinewoods. Well-equipped caravan and camping site and hostel open all year, canoeing, sailing, windsurfing, fishing, swimming, forest trails, hillwalking and wayfaring trail. Toilets, picnic areas, shop and cafe. Visitor Centre with audio visual display. Two small downhill ski tows, 37 kms of waymarked cross-country ski routes.

678 GLENMUICK AND LOCHNAGAR   3E11

9 miles S of Ballater along minor road off B976. Visitor Centre open Easter-Oct. Parking available. (SNH)

Superb mountain and loch scenery, including one of Scotland's best-known peaks. Upland plants and animals, including red deer. Well-developed network of walks give access to remote mountain scenery — around the loch and, for more experienced walkers, on the surrounding hills.

Glen Nant Forest Nature Reserve

679 GLEN NANT FOREST NATURE RESERVE   4F2

   A
   P
2 miles S of Taynuilt on B845. All reasonable times. Car parking only. (FE) Tel: (0631) 66155.

A site which combines historical interest with high nature conservation value. A 2½ mile walk through the reserve gives an insight into the management of native woodland for charcoal and tannin production. Rich flora and fauna, especially lichens and ants. Disabled visitor trail.

680 GLEN ORD DISTILLERY   3A8

On the outskirts of Muir of Ord, just off A832, 15 miles W of Inverness. Jan-Dec exc Christmas and New Year. Mon-Fri 0930-1200. Parking available. Gift shop. Tel: (0463) 870421.

Licensed in 1838, Glen Ord is in an area with an ancient tradition of distilling — last survivor of no less than nine distilleries which operated around Muir of Ord in Victorian days. Guided tours show the main processes of distilling, and visitors can taste the Glen Ord single malt whisky produced in the distillery's six stills.

681   GLENSHEE CHAIRLIFT   **3D12**

&   *Off A93, 10m S of Braemar. Christmas-mid Oct. Daily, 0900-1700.*
T   *Charge for chairlift. Parking available. Licensed restaurant and cafeteria.*
Shop. Tel: (033 97) 41320.

Ascends the Cairnwell mountain (3,059 feet) from the
summit of the highest main road pass in Britain (2,199
feet).

---

682   GLENTRESS FOREST   **5D6**

3 miles E of Peebles on A72. Jan-Dec. All reasonable times. Forest Drive
open weekends only, summer season. Parking available, charge. Tel: (0721)
20448.

One of the oldest forests in southern Scotland, with
several stands of 70-year-old conifers. Over 15 miles
of forest walks, with many more informal walks.
14 miles of bike trails — mountain bikes can be hired
locally. Short forest drive leads to several picnic places
and car parks. Pony trekking through forest from
nearby stables. Wayfaring course provides orienteering
for beginners and families.

---

683   GLENTURRET DISTILLERY   **6A2**

&   *From Crieff take A85 to Comrie for 1m, then turn right at crossroads*
P   *for ¼m. Mar-Dec, Mon-Sat 0930-1630, Sun 1200-1630. Jan, Feb,*
T   *Mon-Fri 1130-1430. Entrance charge. Group concessions (booking*
preferred for large parties). Parking available. Smugglers Restaurant,
Pagoda Room restaurant, whisky tasting bar. Whisky/souvenir shop.
Tel: (0764) 2424.

One of Scotland's oldest distilleries, guided tours, free
taste, award-winning visitors heritage centre, audio-
ASVA   visual presentation, 3-D exhibition 'The Spirit of the
Glen'.

---

684   GLENWHAN GARDENS   **4G10**

&   *Signposted, 1 mile off A75 at Dunragit, between Glenluce and Stranraer.*
P   *Apr-Sept. Daily exc Mon, 1200-1700. Other times by arrangement.*
T   *Entrance charge. Group concessions. Parking available. Gift shop.*
Tearoom. Tel: (058 14) 222.

This young garden was started in 1979, hewn from
a hillside covered in bracken and gorse. Now rhododendrons and azaleas, shrubs and shrub roses and
many unusual plants grow together around two small
lochans which were made by damming up the boggy
areas. A water garden creates a natural habitat for the
bog-loving genera, and the rocky outcrops are home
for alpines and scree plants, heathers and conifers.
Extensive nursery and plant centre.

---

685   GLOBE INN   **5B9**

&   *Off High Street, Dumfries. Jan-Dec. Mon-Sat 1100-2300,*
Sun 1230-2300. Restaurant. Tel: (0387) 52335.

Burns' favourite howff (pub) where his chair, inscribed
window pane and other relics can still be seen and
enjoyed in a convivial atmosphere.

---

686   GOATFELL   **4F6**

3½m NNW of Brodick, Arran. (NTS)

At 2,866 feet this is the highest peak on Arran. NTS
property includes Glen Rosa and Cir Mhor, with
grand walking and climbing. The golden eagle may
occasionally be seen, along with hawks, harriers, etc.

687 GOSFORD HOUSE 6F6

1 mile E of Longniddry. Jun and Jul, Wed, Sat & Sun 1400-1700.
Entrance charge. Group concessions. Parking available.
Tel: (087 57) 201.

In fine setting on the Firth of Forth. Central part of
the house by Robert Adam, 1800, north and south
wings by William Young, 1890. South wing contains
celebrated marble hall. Ornamental waters with
wildlife including (since 1983) nesting wild geese.
Prior notice preferred for disabled visitors.

688 GRACEFIELD ARTS CENTRE 5B9

1 mile N of Dumfries town centre on A701. Jan-Dec. Closed Mon in
Summer, Mon and Sun in winter. Please check details of opening times.
Car parking only. Cafe/bar. Tel: (0387) 62084.

Gallery, studios and pottery situated in beautiful
grounds overlooking the River Nith. Gracefield
houses a collection of over 400 Scottish paintings,
which are on show at regular intervals throughout the
year, and shows regular exhibitions of contemporary
art. Potter-in-residence at work, with products for
sale. Studios, darkroom, printroom.

689 HEATHER GRAHAM CRAFTS 2B7

Borve Cottage, Scarista, Isle of Harris. 13 miles W of Tarbert on A859.
Jan-Dec. 0900-1800. Free. Car parking only. Gift shop.
Tel: (085 985) 202.

Craft workshop and gift shop, specialising in Harris
and Shetland wool.

690 GRAIN EARTH HOUSES 1B11

Hatson, Kirkwall, Orkney. All reasonable times. Keykeeper. Free. (HS)
Tel: 031-244 3101.

An Iron Age souterrain; an entrance stair leads to an
underground passage and chamber.

691 GRAMPIAN TRANSPORT MUSEUM 3F10

At Alford, 25m W of Aberdeen on A944. Apr-Nov, daily 1000-1700.
Entrance charge. Group concessions. Parking available. Gift shop.
Tel: (097 55) 62292.

ASVA

An extensive collection of historic road vehicles housed
in purpose-built exhibition hall. Climb-aboard exhibits
for children include giant Mac snowplough, vintage
road roller and adventure playground. Also driving
simulator, video bus featuring motorsport and road
transport history and dance organ recitals. Summer
events programme. (See No 48).

692 GRANGEMOUTH MUSEUM 6B6

Victoria Library, Bo'ness Road, Grangemouth. Jan-Dec. Mon-Sat
1400-1700. Free. Parking available. Museum shop.
Tel: (0324) 483291/(0324) 24911, ext 2472.

Display relating to growth of Grangemouth from
sealock to a Victorian town. Exhibits on canals,
shipping and shipbuilding. The world's first practical
steamship, the *Charlotte Dundas* and local industries.

693 GRASSIC GIBBON CENTRE 3G11

   T

Arbuthnott, Laurencekirk. On B967, 10 miles S of Stonehaven. Easter-Oct. Daily, 1000-1630. Other times (groups) by arrangement. Entrance charge. Group concessions. Parking available. Gift shop. Coffee shop. Tel: (0561) 61668.

Visitor centre dedicated to the life and times of Lewis Grassic Gibbon (James Leslie Mitchell), featuring an exhibition with audio-visual display. Children's play area outside. Disabled access and toilet.

---

694 GREAT GLEN CYCLE ROUTE 2G12

Forest roads from Fort William to Inverness. Jan-Dec. All reasonable times. Parking available. (FE)

A cycle route in sections along the most scenic parts of the Great Glen, with spectacular views of the Lochs Ness, Oich and Lochy. A leaflet is available at Forest Enterprise offices in Lochaber and Fort Augustus. Many excellent forest walks in this area.

---

695 GREENHILL COVENANTERS' HOUSE 5B6

   P

In Biggar on A702, 26m from Edinburgh, A74 (South) 12m. Easter-early Oct, daily 1400-1700. Entrance charge. Group concessions. Gift shop. Parking available. Tel: (0899) 21050.

Farmhouse, rescued in ruinous condition and rebuilt at Biggar, ten miles from the original site. Exhibits include relics of local Covenanters, Donald Cargill's bed (1681), 17th-century furnishings, costume dolls, rare breeds of animals and poultry.
(See No 598).

---

696 GREENKNOWE TOWER 5E6

½m W of Gordon on A6089, 9m NW of Kelso. Open all reasonable times. Keykeeper. Free. Tel: (HS) 031-244 3101.

A fine turreted tower house of 1581, still retaining its iron yett (gate).

Gretna Green Smithies: see No 1013.

---

697 GREENOCK ARTS GUILD THEATRE 4G5

   A
   P

Campbell Street, Greenock. Jan-Dec. Charges for performances vary. Car parking only. Tearoom. Inductive loop. Tel: (0475) 23038.

Greenock Arts Guild was formed in 1945 as a venue for music, drama and the visual arts. A varied programme is offered throughout the year, embracing professional and amateur acts. Exhibitions in the gallery change monthly.

---

698 GREENOCK CUSTOM HOUSE MUSEUM 4G5

Customhouse Quay, Brenner Street, Greenock. Jan-Dec. Mon-Fri. 1000-1230, 1330-1600. Tel: (0475) 26331.

This fine building has been in continuous use as a Customs Offrice since it was completed in 1819. Now restored, it houses some excise departments as well as the museum, which gives an insight into the activities of Customs and Excisemen through the ages. Apart from features on Robert Burns and other well-known past members of the Department, there are items showing the modern technology used in the battle against illegal drugs. Other items include examples of endangered species which have been seized at importation, and a computer game which tests the visitor's skill at 'rummaging' a ship.

699 GREY CAIRNS OF CAMSTER 3D4

6m N of Lybster on Watten Road, off A9. All reasonable times.
Free. (HS) Tel: 031-244 3101.

Two megalithic cairns: a round cairn and a long cairn
containing chambers, probably 4th millennium BC.

Grey Mare's Tail

700 GREY MARE'S TAIL 5C7

Off A708, 10m NE of Moffat. (NTS) Tel: 041-552 8391.

A spectacular 200-feet waterfall formed by the Tail
Burn dropping from Loch Skene. The area is rich in
wild flowers and there is a herd of wild goats.
NB. Visitors should keep to the path to the foot of the
falls: there have been serious accidents to people
scrambling up and care should be exercised.

701 GROAM HOUSE MUSEUM AND PICTISH CENTRE 3B8

High Street, Rosemarkie. May-Oct, Mon-Sat 1100-1700, Sun 1430-1630.
Also weekends in winter, or by arrangement. Entrance charge.
Group concessions. Gift shop. Tel: (0381) 20961.

A remarkable collection of Pictish stones, carved with
rods, discs and crescents, birds and beasts. Wall
hangings by artist Marianna Lines. Visitors can play
a Pictish-style harp, and make rubbings from casts.
Videos and displays explain the history of the Painted
People.

702 GROGPORT ORGANIC TANNERY 4E6

Grogport Old Manse, 4 miles N of Carradale on E coast of Kintyre.
Jan-Dec. All reasonable times. Free. Car parking only. Tannery shop.
Tel: (058 33) 255.

Small, unusual organic tannery. Sheepskins, deerskins
and other skins can be seen in the process of being
tanned by the ancient methods, using tree bark, which
are centuries-old and said to produce the best leather.

703 GUILDHALL   6A5

*St John Street, Stirling. By arrangement. Free. Tel: (0786)
462373/479000.*

The Guildhall, or Cowane's Hospital, was built
between 1634 and 1649 as an almshouse for elderly
members of the Guild of Merchants. It contains
portraits of former Deans of Guild, and weights and
measures.

**704 NEIL M GUNN MEMORIAL
VIEWPOINT**   3A8

*Heights of Brae, Strathpeffer. All reasonable times. Free. Parking
available.*

Memorial viewpoint for the author Neil M Gunn
who lived nearby.

705 GURNESS BROCH   1B10

*Off A966 at Aikerness, about 4m NW of Kirkwall, Orkney. Apr-Sept,
opening standard. Oct-Mar, closed. Entrance charge. Group concessions.
Parking available. (HS) Tel: 031-244 3101.*

ASVA

An Iron Age broch still over 10 feet high, surrounded
by stone huts and a deep ditch. Later inhabited in
Dark Age and Viking times.

706 RUSSELL GURNEY WEAVERS   3F8

*Braecroft, Muiresk. 2½ miles from Turriff, off B9024. Jan-Dec. Mon-Sat
0930-1730. Free. Car parking only. Shop. Tel: (0888) 63544.*

Small business involved in handweaving clothing
fabrics in natural fibres, plus a range of made-up
articles such as ties, scarves, stoles and shawls. The
production processes can be demonstrated to visitors.
Handweaving courses.

707 GYLEN CASTLE   4E2

*On the island Kerrera, 1m W of Oban. Passenger ferry 2m S of Oban,
2m walk from ferry terminal. All reasonable times. Free.
Tel: (0631) 63122. (Oban TIC)*

The castle, dating from c 1582 and once a MacDougall
stronghold, is now in ruins.

708 HADDO COUNTRY PARK   3G9

*B999 Aberdeen-Pitmedden road, signposted to right between Pitmedden
and Tarves. All year. Discovery Room open daily, 1100-1800 during
summer season and at various other times. Free. Parking available.
Tel: (0651) 851489.*

180 acres, including woodland walks, lake, ponds, bird
hides, picnic areas, adventure playground and
Discovery Room. Ranger service.

709 HADDO HOUSE   3G9

*Off B999, 4m N of Pitmedden, 19m N of Aberdeen. May-Sept, daily
1400-1800. June-Aug, daily 1100-1800. Apr and Oct, weekends
1400-1700. Grounds open all year, 0930-sunset. Entrance charges. Group
concessions. Parking available. Trust shop. Restaurant. (NTS)
Tel: (065 15) 440.*

Designed in 1731 by William Adam, a pupil of Sir
William Bruce and father of the Adam brothers, for
William, second Earl of Aberdeen, Haddo House
replaced the old House of Kellie, home of the Gordons
of Methlick for centuries. Much of the interior is
'Adam Revival' carried out about 1880 for John,
seventh Earl and first Marquess of Aberdeen and his
Countess, Ishbel. Garden, James Giles Exhibition.
Walks, picnic area and adventure playground.

Hailes Castle

710   HAILES CASTLE   6H6

Off A1, 5m E of Haddington. Keykeeper monument.
Parking available. (HS) Tel: 031-244 3101.

These extensive ruins date from the 13th/15th
centuries. There is a fine 16th-century chapel. Here
Bothwell brought Mary, Queen of Scots on their
flight from Borthwick Castle in 1567.

711   HALLIWELL'S HOUSE MUSEUM
AND ROBSON GALLERY   5E7

Off main square, town centre, Selkirk. Apr-Oct, Mon-Sat 1000-1700,
Sun 1400-1600; Jul & Aug, open daily until 1800; Nov-Dec, daily
1400-1600. Free. Parking available. Gift shop. Tel: (0750) 20096.

Set in a row of 19th-century cottages, the house has
one of the best collections of domestic ironmongery in
the country. With local history forming the basis of
the museum displays, Halliwell's house traces the
growth of Selkirk from the nearby early Stone Age
settlement through to its role as an important textile
producing centre.

712   HAMILTON DISTRICT MUSEUM   5A6

¹⁄₂m SW of M74 at A723 interchange. Jan-Dec. Mon-Sat 1000-1700.
Closed 1200-1300 on Wed and Sat. Free. Parking available. Gift shop.
Tel: (0698) 283981.

Local history museum housed in a 17th-century
coaching inn, the Hamilton Arms, built by the Duke
and Duchess of Hamilton in 1696. London
stagecoaches stopped here daily. Past visitors include
William and Dorothy Wordsworth, Samuel Johnson,
Thomas Telford. The 18th-century Assembly Room,
with original plasterwork and musicians' gallery, still
survives. Horsedrawn vehicles and agricultural items in
former stable. Displays of art, archaeology, history,
costume, ceramics. Victorian Kitchen, Transport
Gallery. Temporary exhibitions.

713   HAMILTON OLD PARISH CHURCH   5A6

♿
T

All year, weekdays 1000-1500; Sat 1000-1200; Sunday Worship 1045 (tour 1230). Free. Group visits by arrangement. Coffee Bar, Sat a.m. and Sun after worship. Parking available. Inductive loop. Tel: (0698) 420002.

Present building (1734) is the only church designed by William Adam, the leading Scottish architect of his day. It is the oldest building in Hamilton still used for its original purpose and contains the pre-Norman Netherton Cross and the Covenanters 'Heads' Memorial. Also embroideries by Hannah Frew Paterson.

Hamilton Mausoleum: see No 1202.

714   HANDA ISLAND NATURE RESERVE   2G4

3m NW of Scourie. Small open ferry from Tarbet, or boat trips, Easter-Sept, by Scourie Boats, contact Ken Nash, Rangoon, Scourie. Tel: (0971) 502011. Charges for boats and for entrance to Handa Island Visitor Centre (open April-early Sept). (SNH)

Offshore island seabird sanctuary with spectacular seacliffs, home to one of the largest seabird colonies in north-west Europe. Puffins, guillemots, razor bills, skuas, fulmars, shags, gulls, kittiwakes. Guided trail around island includes stretches of boardwalk.

715   HANSEATIC BOOTH   1G4

♿
P

Symbister, Whalsay, Shetland. Jan-Dec. Open by arrangement, all reasonable times. Keykeeper in house next door. Entrance charge. Parking available. Tel: (Keykeeper) (080 66) 484.

The only restored Hanseatic Booth in Shetland, commemorating a trade which was carried on between the islands and the Hansa ports, mostly German.

716   HARBOUR COTTAGE GALLERY   5A11

Kirkcudbright. Mar-Dec, Mon-Sat 1030-1230, 1400-1700, certain Suns 1400-1700. Entrance charge.

Exhibitions of paintings and sometimes crafts in a picturesque whitewashed building beside the River Dee.

717   KEIR HARDIE STATUE   4H7

Cumnock town centre. All times. Free. Parking available.

Bust outside the Town Hall to commemorate James Keir Hardie (1856-1915), an early socialist leader, and founder of the Independent Labour Party in 1893.

718   HARESTANES COUNTRYSIDE VISITOR CENTRE   5E7

♿
T

Harestanes, by Ancrum, 3 miles N of Jedburgh. Easter-Oct. Daily, 1000-1700. Free. Parking available. Gift shop. Book shop. Tearoom. Tel: (083 53) 306.

Harestanes Countryside Visitor Centre is a group of converted farm buildings which house a variety of facilities designed to introduce the visitor to the Borders countryside. As well as interior displays, there are Ranger-led walks and other Ranger activities in the grounds of the estate. Games room, new play area adjacent.

719   HAUGHTON COUNTRY PARK   **3F10**

26m W of Aberdeen on A944, ½m N of the village of Alford. All year. Free. Parking available. Tel: (09755) 62453 or 62107.

Country Park with visitor centre and caravan site. 98 acres of woodland and parkland, with riverside, nature trails and twin track.

**720   HAWICK MUSEUM AND
            ART GALLERY**   **5E7**

In Wilton Lodge Park, on western outskirts of Hawick. Apr-Sep, Mon-Sat 1000-1200 and 1300-1700, Sun 1400-1700; Oct-Mar, Mon-Fri 1300-1600, closed Sat, Sun 1400-1600. Entrance charges. Group concessions. Parking available. Cafe. Tel: (0450) 73457.

In the ancestral home of the Langlands of that Ilk, an unrivalled collection of local and Scottish Border relics, natural history, with an art gallery. Situated in 107-acre Wilton Lodge Park, open at all times: riverside walks, gardens, greenhouses, recreations and playing fields. Scented garden.

721   THE HAYLIE CHAMBERED TOMB   **4G5**

Off A78 and through Douglas Park, Largs. All times. Free.

Chambered tomb of Clyde-Solway group once covered by large cairn.

722   THE HERITAGE OF GOLF   **6G5**

West Links Road, Gullane, 14m ENE of Edinburgh. Open by appointment. Free. Parking available. Items for sale. Tel: (087 57) 277.

The exhibition shows how the game of golf developed after it arrived in Scotland from Holland in the 15th century. The visitor can see the simple origins, the natural materials and the skill of the early makers; and the development of golf from early days to the present.

**723   HERMANESS NATIONAL NATURE
            RESERVE**   **1H1**

N end of Unst. A968, then B9086 to car park. Reserve open Jan-Dec. Visitor Centre, May-Sept. Free. Car parking, limited coach parking. (SNH) Tel: (095 781) 278 (May-Sept) or SNH Lerwick (0595) 3345.

Large seabird colonies with gannets, kittiwakes, guillemots and puffins. Moorland has one of the largest bonxie (great skua) colonies in Shetland. Fine coastal scenery and views to Muckle Flugga, northernmost tip of the United Kingdom.

724   THE HERMITAGE   **5B1**

Off A9, 2m W of Dunkeld. All reasonable times. Car park charge. (NTS)

A picturesque folly, built in 1758, restored in 1952, and again in 1986. It is set above the wooded gorge of the River Braan. There are nature trails in the area and a full programme of Ranger-led walks in summer and autumn. Details from Dunkeld Tourist Information Centre, or the NTS Ell Shop.

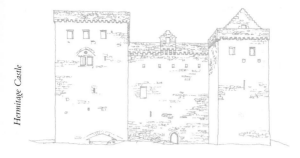

Hermitage Castle

725 **HERMITAGE CASTLE** **5E8**

In Liddesdale, 5½m NE of Newcastleton. April-Sept, opening standard. Oct-Mar, weekends only. Entrance charge. Group concessions. Parking available. (HS) Tel: 031-244 3101.

This grim 13th-century castle was a stronghold of the de Soulis family and, after 1341, of the Douglases. It has had a vivid, sometimes cruel history; to here Mary Queen of Scots made her exhausting ride from Jedburgh in 1566 to meet Bothwell, a journey which almost cost her her life. The building consists of four towers and connecting walls, outwardly almost perfect.

726 **HIDDEN HILLS** **3B6**

At Kintradwell, 2 miles N of Brora, and Borrobol, 13 miles W of Helmsdale. May-Aug. Charge for tours, including lunch. Car parking only. Tel: (043 13) 264 (Borrobol) or (0408) 621422 (Kintradwell). Bookings also through Helmsdale TIC (043 12) 640.

Two private estates offering a fascinating and complex environment for birdlife, flora and fauna. Three different guided wildlife tours are led by a local expert who introduces mammals, birds and land use in places far from public highways. Historic monuments dating back three centuries are also explained. Red deer are approached and seen in large parties. Extensive botany. Springtime bird list runs to around 130 species. Walks can be energetic or less demanding, depending on tour.

727 **HIGHBANK PORCELAIN POTTERY, LOCHGILPHEAD** **4E4**

On A816 on the W outskirts of Lochgilphead. Jan-Dec. Pottery tours, Mon-Fri 1030 & 1400. Shop open Mon-Fri 0900-1700, Sat 1000-1700, Sun 1100-1700. Charge for tour: children free. Parking available. Shop. Tel: (0546) 602044.

Pottery producing slip cases, hand-decorated porcelain model animals and vases.

728 **HIGHLAND AND RARE BREEDS FARM** **2G5**

Avalon, Elphin, 14 miles N of Ullapool on A835. May-Sep. Daily, 1000-1700. Entrance charge. Group concessions. Parking available. Theme shop. Refreshments. Tel: (085 486) 204.

The Scottish Farm Animal Centre has 40 breeds, ancient and modern, in 15 acres of farmland, river and mountain scenery. Highland cattle, Soay and Hebridean sheep, goats and outdoor pigs, poultry and rabbits live on this croft, adapted for education and conservation. This working organic farm also has an exhibition of farm tools, some farmwork demonstrations, guided tours and information sheets.

729 HIGHLAND FINE CHEESES 3B7

Blarliath, Tain, down shore road. Jan-Dec. 0830-1630. Free.
Parking available. Tel: (0862) 892034.

Visitors can watch fresh cheese-making according to
ancient Highland and Island traditions, without
rennet, artificial flavourings or colourings — but with
modern hygiene. Original recipes are used. Most of
the products have a long pedigree dating back to
Viking times. Some are local cottage cheeses, some
cream cheeses of the Western Isles, some contain local
wild garlic. Conducted tours and tasting.

Highland Folk Museum

730 HIGHLAND FOLK MUSEUM 3B11

Kingussie, 12m SW of Aviemore. Apr-Oct, Mon-Sat 1000-1800,
Sun 1400-1800; Nov-Mar, Mon-Fri 1000-1500. Closed Christmas and
New Year. Entrance charge. Group concessions. Parking available. Gift shop.
Tel: (0540) 661307.

ASVA

The open air museum, partly housed in an 18th-
century shooting lodge, features a 'Black House' from
Lewis, a Clack Mill and exhibits of farming equipment.
Indoors, the farming museum has fine displays of a
barn, dairy, stable and an exhibition of Highland
tinkers; and there are special features on weapons,
costume, musical instruments and Highland furniture.
Picnic garden. Special events Easter-September.

731 HIGHLAND LINE CRAFT CENTRE 2G8

Centre of Achnasheen, beside railway station. Apr-Oct. Daily 0900-1730.
Generally open Mon-Fri in winter, please telephone first. Free.
Parking available. Gift shop. Tel: (044 588) 227.

Craft centre incorporating jewellery/silversmithing
workshop. Viewing window allows visitors to watch
work going on, although demonstrations are not
given. Silver and gold jewellery, small silverware made
in the workshop on sale, together with other craft items.

732 HIGHLAND MARY'S MONUMENT 4H7

At Failford, on B743 3m W of Mauchline. All times. Free.
Tel: (0292) 282109.

The monument commemorates the place where, it is
said, Robert Burns parted from his 'Highland Mary',
Mary Campbell. They exchanged vows, but she died
the following autumn.

733   HIGHLAND MARY'S STATUE   4F5

Dunoon, near pier. All times. Free. Parking available.

The statue of Burns' 'Highland Mary' at the foot of
the Castle Hill. Mary Campbell was born on a farm in
Dunoon, and consented to become Burns' wife before
he married Jean Armour.

**734   HIGHLAND MUSEUM OF
        CHILDHOOD**   3A8

*The Old Station, Strathpeffer. Mar-May, Mon-Sat 1000-1600,
Sun 1300-1600. Jun-Sep, Mon-Fri 0900-1700, Sat 1000-1700,
Sun 1300-1600. Oct-Dec, Tue-Sun 1300-1600. Closed 24 Dec-end Feb.
Some evening openings in summer, telephone Curator for details. Entrance
charge. Family ticket. Parking available. Gift shop. Tearoom in station.
Tel: (0997) 421031.*

Within the converted Old Station, which has craft and
gift shops, coffee shop and other facilities, the Highland
Museum brings to life the story of childhood in the
Highlands. There are quizzes for children and a
regular programme of events and activities. Attractive
garden and picnic area.

735   HIGHLAND PARK DISTILLERY   1B11

*Kirkwall, Orkney. From the Cathedral, up Palace Road onto Dundas
Crescent, turn onto Holm Road. Highland Park Distillery is on the A961,
¼m on left-hand side. Easter-Oct, Mon-Fri 1000-1600. Tours every 30
mins. Also Sat, Jun-Aug. Nov-Easter, Mon-Fri, tour at 1430. Free.
Parking available. Gift shop. Tel: (0856) 4619 or 3107.*

Famous Orkney distillery, with traditional floor
maltings, which produces malt whisky with a particular
'peaty' taste. Video and audio-visual displays.

736   HIGHLAND STONEWARE   2G6

*Mill Street, Ullapool and Baddidarroch, Lochinver. Jan-Dec.
Mon-Fri 0900-1800. Sat opening, May-Oct. Other times by appointment.
Free. Parking available. Gift shops.
Tel: (057 14) 376 (Ullapool), (0854) 2980 (Lochinver).*

Ceramic factory/workshops in two locations, producing
hand-made and decorated giftware and tableware.
Visitors are welcome to see all processes in operation.
Guided tours at Lochinver only, by appointment.

737   HIGHLAND THEATRE   4E2

*George Street, Oban, Argyll. Summer: 0930-2200. Winter: 1700-2200.
Tel: (0631) 62444.*

An audio-visual experience and Highland exhibition.
Theatre and cinema open for shows and movies.

738   HIGHLAND WILDLIFE PARK   3B10

*Off A9 (B9152), 7m S of Aviemore. Open daily 1000-1600 (June-Aug,
1700); closed winter season. Entrance charge. Shop. Restaurant.
Tel: (0540) 651270.*

Highland Wildlife Park features breeding groups of
Scottish mammals and birds of the past and the
present, in a beautiful natural setting. Drive through
reserve with red deer, bison, Highland cattle, etc.
Walk around area displaying capercaillie, eagles, wolves
and wildcats, and many other species. Exhibition on
'Man and Fauna in the Highlands', in Centre with
cafeteria, shop and picnic areas. Owned and managed
by the Royal Zoological Society of Scotland.

739 HIGHLAND WINERIES 3A8

Moniack Castle, Kirkhill, 7 miles from Inverness on A862.
Jan-Dec. Mon-Sat 1000-1700. Free tours and tasting. Parking available.
Shop. Restaurant. Tel: (0463 83) 283.

Production of country wines, liqueurs and preserves.

The Hill House

740 THE HILL HOUSE 4G4

Upper Colquhoun Street, Helensburgh. Between A82 and A814, off
B832. Apr-late Dec. Daily 1300-1700. Entrance charges.
Group concessions. Parking available. Gift shop. Tearoom. (NTS)
Tel: (0436) 73900.

ASVA

High above the River Clyde at Helensburgh, this is
undoubtedly Charles Rennie Mackintosh's finest
domestic creation. The commission of Walter Blackie,
the Glasgow publisher, included furniture, fittings and
decorative schemes. Mackintosh's wife, Margaret
MacDonald, contributed fabric designs and a unique
gesso panel. The timeless rooms seem as modern today
as they must have done in 1904 when the Blackie
family moved in. Gardens reflect Mackintosh's designs.
Information room interprets the relationship between
Mackintosh and Blackie, the Glasgow Style, and some
of Mackintosh's most dazzling designs.

741 HILL OF TARVIT 6F3

A916, 2m S of Cupar. House: open weekends during Easter weekend and
April. Sat & Sun 1400-1800; May-Sept, daily 1400-1800
(last admission 1730). Garden: grounds open all year, 1000-sunset.
Entrance charges. Group concessions. Parking available. Tearoom. (NTS)
Tel: (0334) 53127.

ASVA

An Edwardian country house designed by Sir Robert
Lorimer for Mr Frederick Boner Sharp, an art collector
of note. Fine collection of furniture, paintings,
tapestries, Chinese porcelain and bronzes. Lovely
gardens, woodland walk to hilltop viewpoint.

742 THE HIRSEL, HOMESTEAD MUSEUM, CRAFT CENTRE AND GROUNDS 5F6

On A697, immediately W of Coldstream. All reasonable daylight hours
every day of the year. Parking available (small charge).
Tel: (0890) 882834.

Museum housed in old farmstead buildings with
history of estate, old tools, natural history. Craft
house, furniture, leatherwork, pottery and weaving
workshops. Walks in Leet Valley, round the grounds
of Hirsel House (not open to the public). Famous
rhododendron wood. Tearoom (groups by
arrangement). Picnic areas. Toilets.

743 JAMES HOGG MONUMENT 5D7

By Ettrick 1m W of B7009. All times. Free. Parking available.

A monument on the site of the birthplace of James Hogg (1770-1835), known as 'The Ettrick Shepherd', friend of Scott. His grave is in the nearby church. (See No 1124).

744 HOLMISDALE HOUSE TOY MUSEUM 2C9

& *Glendale, 8 miles W of Dunvegan on Glendale visitor route, Isle of Skye.*
A *Jan-Dec. Mon-Sat 1000-1800. Other times by arrangement. Entrance charge. Group concessions. Parking available. Gift shop. Tel: (047 081) 240.*

An opportunity to play with some of the toys of yesteryear in this museum. Visitors are encouraged to touch and even operate some of the games, toys and dolls.

745 HOLY LOCH FARM PARK AND HIGHLAND CATTLE CENTRE 4F4

& *Dalinlongart, Sandbank, 4 miles from Dunoon on A815. Apr-Oct. Daily*
P *1000-1800. Entrance charge. Group concessions. Parking available.*
T *Craft shop. Tearoom. Tel: (0369) 6429.*

Small working farm on the edge of the western Highlands, with a variety of domestic and rare breeds of animals — sheep, cattle, goats, pigs, poultry, ponies, donkeys, a Clydesdale horse. Childrens pets' corner with rabbits, guinea pigs and lambs. Sheep and goats can be fed, lambs bottle-fed in spring and early summer. Highland cattle are particularly featured.

746 HOLY TRINITY CHURCH 6A4

& *Keir Street, Bridge of Allan, close to Stirling University. Jun-Sep. Sat 1000-1600. Free. Parking available. Gift shop. Inductive loop. Tel: (0786) 832093.*

An attractive small church with fine stained glass windows. An important feature is the chancel furnishings which were designed in 1904 by Charles Rennie Mackintosh, and include pulpit carvings, communion table, organ screen and chancel rail.

Hopetoun House

747 HOPETOUN HOUSE 6D6

& *W of South Queensferry, Easter-Sept, daily 1000-1700 (last admission 1645).*
P *Entrance charges. Group concessions. Parking available. Gift shop.*
T *Licensed restaurant. Tel: 031-331 2451 (0900-1700).*

ASVA

This great Adam mansion is the home of the Hope family, Earls of Hopetoun and later Marquesses of Linlithgow. Started in 1699 to the designs of Sir William Bruce, it was enlarged between 1721-54 by William Adam and his son, John. Notable paintings by Gainsborough, Raeburn and Canaletto among others. Fine furniture, Meissen ceramics, tapestries, rugs, magnificent rococo ceilings. The magnificent grounds include deer parks with fallow and red deer, woodland walks, a walled garden and nature trails. Exhibitions include 'Horse and Man in Lowland Scotland', William Adam (building techniques), family museum and wildlife centre, rooftop viewing platform with panoramic views over Forth Bridges. Special arrangements for blind and disabled people with prior notice, and for school parties.

748   HORNEL ART GALLERY AND LIBRARY   5A11

♿ A

Broughton House, High Street, Kirkcudbright. Easter-Oct. Daily exc Tues 1100-1300, 1400-1700 (Sun 1400-1700 only). Entrance charges. Group concessions. Car parking only, coaches in town centre. Gift shop. Tel: (0557) 30437.

Home, studio and gallery of the artist E. A. Hornel (1864-1933), one of the group of artists known as the 'Glasgow Boys'. House contains collection of paintings by Hornel and other associated artists, fine furniture and oriental curios. The gallery is adorned with a replica of the Elgin marbles. Beautiful town garden with Japanese features.

The House of the Binns

749   THE HOUSE OF THE BINNS   6D6

Off A904, 4m E of Linlithgow. Reopening 1993 after essential restoration. Once completed, opening times will run: Easter weekend, May-Sep, daily except Fri, 1400-1700. Last tour 1630. Entrance charges. Group concessions. Guided tours only. Parking available. (NTS) Tel: (050 683) 4255.

Occupied for more than 350 years, The Binns dates largely from the time of General Tam Dalyell, 1615-1685, and his father, and reflects the early 17th-century transition in Scottish architecture from fortified stronghold to gracious mansion. There are magnificent plaster ceilings, fine views across the Forth and a visitor trail. Braille bats available.

750   HOUSE OF DUN   3F12

♿

On A935 4m W of Montrose. Grounds and courtyard buildings open Easter weekend, May-Oct, daily 1100-1730. Entrance charges. Group concessions. Parking available. (NTS) Tel: (067 481) 264.

ASVA

Palladian house overlooking the Montrose Basin, built in 1730 for David Erskine, Lord Dun, to designs by William Adam. Exuberant plasterwork in the saloon. Courtyard buildings include a potting shed and gamekeeper's room, and Angus Weavers giving displays of weaving linen tableware on traditional looms. Woodland walks.

751   ANNE HUGHES POTTERY   5A9

♿ A

Auchreoch, Balmaclellan, 2 miles E of New Galloway on A712. Easter-Sep. Daily 1000-1800. Free. Car parking only. Pottery shop. Tel: (064 42) 205.

A wide range of pottery work which is unusual, colourful and varied, with pierced flower plates a speciality, all made on the premises.

752   HUNTERSTON POWER STATION   4G5

♿ P T

By A78, 5 miles S of Largs. Mar-Nov, daily 0930-1630. Dec-Feb, tours by arrangement only. Tours last 1hr for Visitor Centre, 1hr for Power Station. Free. Parking available. Freephone: 0800 838 557.

This is a nuclear power station of advanced gas-cooled reactor (AGR) type. Parties of around 40 people are taken on guided tours and shown a video presentation about the generation of nuclear power. Visitor Centre has interactive videos and models.

Huntingtower Castle

753   HUNTINGTOWER CASTLE   6C2

Off A85, 3m WNW of Perth. Opening standard except Oct-Mar, closed Thurs pm and all day Fri. Entrance charge. Group concessions. (HS) Tel: 031-244 3101.

A 15th-century castellated mansion until 1600 known as Ruthven Castle. This was the scene of the Raid of Ruthven in 1582; James VI, then 16, accepted an invitation from the Earl of Gowrie to his hunting seat and found himself in the hands of nobles who demanded the dismissal of the royal favourites. When the king tried to escape, his way was barred by the Master of Glamis. The Ruthven conspirators held power for some months, but the Earl was beheaded in 1584. There are fine painted ceilings.

754   HUNTLY BRANDER MUSEUM   3F9

In the Library, Main Square. Jan-Dec. Tues-Sat 1000-1200, 1400-1600. Free. Tel: (0779) 77778.

Permanent local history exhibitions and temporary thematic exhibitions twice a year.

755   HUNTLY CASTLE   3F9

Castle Street, Huntly. Opening standard except Oct-Mar, closed Thurs pm and all day Fri. Entrance charge. Group concessions. Parking available. (HS) Tel: 031-244 3101.

An imposing ruin which replaced medieval Strathbogie Castle which, until 1544, was the seat of the Gordons, the Marquesses of Huntly, the most powerful family in the north until the mid-16th century. There are elaborate heraldic adornments on the castle walls. The castle, now in a wooded park, was destroyed by Moray in 1452, rebuilt, then rebuilt again in 1551-54, burned 40 years later and again rebuilt in 1602.

756   HUNTLY NORDIC SKI CENTRE   3F9

♿ T

Hill of Haugh, Huntly. Jan-Dec. Mon-Fri 1200-1800, Sat & Sun 1200-1700. Entrance free, charge for ski hire. Car parking only. Refreshments and snack bar. Tel: (0466) 794428.

New ski lodge with many amenities, plus artificial ski track where the basic techniques of cross-country skiing can be learned, and more experienced skiers can practise. Equipment for hire.

757   HYDRO-ELECTRIC VISITOR CENTRE   5B1

& P T

Pitlochry Power Station, on River Tummel at Pitlochry. Apr-Oct, daily 0940-1730. Entrance charge. Family tickets. Car parking only. Gift shop. Tel: (0796) 473152.

Exhibition describing HydroElectric as a generator, transmitter and distributor of electricity. Displays, videos, computer interactive displays and one touch-screen educational game. Salmon ladder with viewing chamber. Viewing gallery for power station interior. Dam.

Inchcolm Abbey

758   INCHCOLM ABBEY   6D5

On Inchcolm Island in the Firth of Forth; check South Queensferry for boat trips or hire. Apr-Sep, opening standard. Oct-Mar, closed. Entrance charge. Group concessions. Parking available. (HS) Tel: 031-244 3101.

ASVA

The monastic buildings, which include a fine 13th century octagonal chapter house, are the best preserved in Scotland. (See No 912).

759   INCHMAHOME PRIORY   4H4

On an island in the Lake of Menteith, A81, 4m E of Aberfoyle. Access by boat from lakeside, Port of Menteith. Apr-Sep, opening standard. Oct-Mar, closed. Entrance charge. Parking available. (HS) Tel: 031-244 3101.

The ruins of an Augustinian house, founded in 1238, where the infant Mary Queen of Scots was sent for refuge in 1547.

760   INCHNACARDOCH WALKS   2H10

Strathoich, 1 mile out of Fort Augustus on the Auchterawe/Jenkins Park road. Jan-Dec. All reasonable times. Free. Car parking only. (FE) Tel: (0320) 6322.

A variety of walks, mainly woodland, with riverside paths, picnic sites and parking at both ends. A leaflet is available at the Forest Office, Strathoich.

761   INNERPEFFRAY LIBRARY   6B2

B8062, 4m SE of Crieff. Apr-Sep. Mon-Sat 1000-1245, 1400-1645, Sun 1400-1600. Oct-Mar 1000-1245, 1400-1600, Sun 1400-1600. Closed all day Thurs. Entrance charge. Parking available. Tel: (0764) 2819.

One of the oldest libraries still in existence in Scotland, founded 1691, housed in a late 18th-century building. The nearby church was built in 1508.

762   INSHRIACH NURSERY   3C10

&

4 miles S of Aviemore on B970. Jan-Dec. Mon-Fri 0900-1700, Sat 0900-1230. Free. Car parking only. Tel: (0540) 651287.

Show garden and alpine plant nursery, growing a wide range of alpines, heathers, dwarf shrubs and dwarf rhododendrons.

763 **INTERNATIONAL LEAGUE FOR THE**
PROTECTION OF HORSES 4F10
♿ *Belwade Farm, between Kincardine O'Neil and Aboyne on A93.*
A *Jan-Dec. Wed, Sat, Sun 1400-1600. Free, donations welcome. Parking*
T *available. Gift shop. Tel: (033 98) 87186.*

Scottish rest and rehabilitation centre for the
International League for the Protection of Horses,
which is the largest equine welfare organisation in the
world.

764 **INVERARAY BELL TOWER** 4F3
♿ *The Avenue, Inveraray. Mid-May-Sept, Mon-Sat 1000-1300, 1400-1700;*
P *Sun 1400-1700. Charge to ascend the tower. Exhibition free.*
Tel: (0499) 2259.

The 126-feet high granite tower houses Scotland's
finest ring of bells and the world's second-heaviest
ring of ten bells. Excellent views, pleasant grounds.
Opportunities to see bells and ringers in action.
Recordings always available when tower open. Easy
staircase to top viewing gallery in bell chamber.

Inveraray Castle and Gardens

765 **INVERARAY CASTLE AND GARDENS** 4F3
½m N of Inveraray. Early Apr-Jun, Sep-mid Oct, Mon-Sat (not Fri)
1000-1200, 1400-1700, Sun 1300-1700; Jul-Aug, Mon-Sat 1000-1700,
Sun 1300-1700. (Closing times indicate last admission.) Entrance charges.
Family tickets. Group concessions. Parking available. Tel: (0499) 2203.

ASVA

Inveraray has been the seat of the chiefs of Clan
Campbell, Dukes of Argyll, for centuries. The present
castle was started in 1743 when the third Duke
engaged Roger Morris to build it. Subsequently the
Adam family, father and sons, were also involved. The
magnificent interior decoration was commissioned by
the fifth Duke from Robert Mylne. In addition to
many historic relics, there are portraits by
Gainsborough, Ramsay and Raeburn. Gardens open
by appointment.

766 **INVERARAY JAIL** 4F3
Church Square, Inveraray. Jan-Dec, exc Christmas and New Year,
0930-1800 (last admission 1700). Entrance charge. Family tickets. Group
concessions. Parking available. Gift shop. Tel: (0499) 2381.

ASVA
A living 19th-century prison. Uniformed guides,
lifelike figures, imaginative exhibitions, sounds, smells
and trials in progress all bring the 1820 courtroom and
former county prison back to life.

767   **INVERAWE SMOKERY**   4F2

&   *2 miles off A85 Oban-Glasgow road at Bridge of Awe, by Taynuilt.*
T   *Daily 0900-1800. Entrance charge. Car parking only. Gift shop.*
    Tearoom. Tel: (086 62) 446.

A detailed exhibition of how fish is cured and smoked
in the traditional fashion, using smoke boxes. Viewing
window to factory, showing all processes. Good walks,
children's play area.

768   **INVERESK LODGE GARDEN**   6F6

*S of Musselburgh, A6124, 7m E of Edinburgh. All year, Mon-Fri
1000-1630, Sun 1400-1700. Entrance charge. (NTS) Tel: 031-226 5922.*

This garden of a 17th-century house (not open to the
public) displays a range of plants suitable for the small
garden. Good shrub rose border and selection of
climbing roses.

769   **INVEREWE GARDEN**   2F7

&   *On A832 at Poolewe, 6m NE of Gairloch. Gardens: All year, daily
P   0930-sunset. Visitor Centre and Shop: Apr-late May, early Sept-mid Oct.
T   Mon-Sat 1000-1730, Sun 1400-1730. Late May-early Sept, Mon-Sat
    0930-1730, Sun 1200-1730. Restaurant closes 1630. Entrance charges.
    Group concessions. Parking available. Trust shop. Restaurant.
    Tel: (044 586) 200.*

ASVA

Plants from many countries flourish in this garden
created by Osgood Mackenzie over 120 years ago,
giving an almost continuous display of colour
throughout the year. Eucalyptus, rhododendron, and
many Chilean and South American plants are
represented in great variety, together with Himalayan
lilies and giant forget-me-nots from the South Pacific.
Garden for disabled, shop, restaurant, caravan and
camp site (1 Apr-30 Sep), petrol, plant sales. Disabled
visitors welcome. Guided walks with gardener.

770   **INVERKEITHING MUSEUM**   6D5

*The Friary, Inverkeithing. Jan-Dec. Wed-Sun 1100-1700. Free.
Tel: (0383) 413344.*

Small museum relating to the history of Inverkeithing
and Rosyth Dockyard. Of particular interest are items
belonging to Admiral Greig, believed to have founded
the Russian Navy.

771   **INVERNESS MUSEUM AND**
        ART GALLERY   3B8

&   *Castle Wynd, Inverness. Mon-Sat 0900-1700; Jul & Aug, Sun
    1400-1700. Free. Museum shop. Coffee shop. Tel: (0463) 237114.*

The museum interprets the social and natural history,
archaeology and culture of the Highlands, with fine
collections of Highland silver, bagpipes, and Jacobite
relics. Special exhibitions, performances and talks.

772   **INVERPOLLY NATIONAL NATURE**
        RESERVE   2G6

*Information Centre at Knockan Cliff, off A835, 12m NNE of Ullapool
May-Sept, Mon-Fri 1000-1730. Free. (SNH) Tel: (085 484) 254.*

A remote, almost uninhabited area of moorland,
woodland, bog, cliffs and summits. Nature and
geological trails, wildlife interest.

Iona

773 IONA 4B3

Off the SW tip of Mull; take A849 to Fionnphort, then ferry. (NTS) Tel: 041-552 8391.

ASVA

In 563 St Columba with 12 followers founded a monastery here. The monastery, often attacked by Norse raiders, was replaced in 1203 but, along with the Cathedral, fell into decay. Restoration started early this century. This monastery is the home of the Iona Community, (founded by Dr George Macleod in 1938) who have done much restoration of the Cathedral, which has a beautiful interior and interesting carvings. For centuries Iona was the burial place of Scottish kings and chiefs. The oldest surviving building is St Oran's Chapel, c 1080 (restored). The remains of the 13th-century nunnery can be seen and outside the Cathedral is 10th-century St Martin's Cross, 14 feet high and elaborately carved.

774 ISLE OF ARRAN HERITAGE MUSEUM 4F7

Rosaburn, Brodick, Isle of Arran. Early May to end Sept, Mon-Sat 1000-1300 and 1400-1700. Entrance charge. Group concessions. Tearoom. Tel: (0770) 2636.

A group of old buildings which were originally an 18th-century croft farm on the edge of the village. Smiddy, cottage furnished in late 19th-century style, stable block with displays of local history, archaeology and geology. Demonstrations of spinning and other hand crafts arranged periodically. Picnic area.

775 ISLE OF MAY 6H4

Access by boat from Anstruther. Contact Lynn or Jim Raeper, Anstruther Pleasure Trips, 30 Dreelside, Anstruther, Fife. May-Sept. Daily, weather permitting. Kiosk at Anstruther Harbour open 30 mins before sailing times. Charge for trip. Parking on pier. Tel: (0333) 310103.

The Isle of May is a nature reserve with a colony of grey seals and thousands of breeding birds including puffins, razorbills, kittiwakes, guillemots, eider ducks, shags and terns, as well as the remains of a 12th-century chapel. Anstruther Pleasure Trips also take coastal and fishing trips.

776 ISLE OF MULL WINE COMPANY 4C3

Old Town Smokehouse, Bunessan, Isle of Mull. Behind Argyll Arms. Jan-Dec. Mon-Fri 1000-1700, Sat 1000-lunchtime. Free. Car parking only. Gift shop. Tel: (068 17) 403.

Guided tours available at this small factory producing three 'Isle of Mull Vermouths'. The dry variety is blended with gin to make a 'Dry Mulltini'. The medium is blended with vodka and natural bitters to produce the 'Mull Riveter'.

159

777 **ITALIAN CHAPEL** 1B12

Lambholm, Orkney. All reasonable times. Free.

Using a Nissen hut, Italian prisoners-of-war in 1943 created this beautiful little chapel out of scrap metal, concrete and other materials.

778 **JACOBITE CRUISES** 3B8

   ♿ *On A82, 1¼ miles from Inverness town centre. Courtesy bus from TIC.*
   A   *Easter-Oct. Cruises at 1000, 1400, and 1830. Charges vary with cruise times. Group concessions. Parking available. Bar and refreshments on board. Tel: (0463) 233999.*

Cruises on the Caledonian Canal and Loch Ness, viewing scenery from deck or from covered, heated saloon.

Jail Museum: see Nos 766 and 781.

779 **JARLSHOF** 1G6

Sumburgh Head, approx 22m S of Lerwick, Shetland. Apr-Sept, opening standard. Oct-Mar, closed. Entrance charge. Group concessions. Parking available. (HS) Tel: 031-244 3101.

One of the most remarkable archaeological sites in Europe with the remains of three extensive village settlements occupied from Bronze Age to Viking times, together with a medieval farmstead and the 16th-century house of the Earls Robert and Patrick Stewart.

780 **JEDBURGH ABBEY AND VISITOR
CENTRE** 5E7

High Street, Jedburgh. Opening standard. Entrance charge. Group concessions. Parking available. (HS) Tel: 031-244 3101.

ASVA

Perhaps the most impressive of the four great Border Abbeys founded by David I, dating from c 1118. The noble remains are extensive, the west front has a fine rose window, known as St Catherine's Wheel, and there is a richly carved Norman doorway. Remains of other domestic buildings have been recovered recently. The visitor centre gives an interesting insight into the lives of the monks who inhabited the Abbey.

781 **JEDBURGH CASTLE JAIL AND
MUSEUM** 5E7

Castlegate, Jedburgh. Mon-Sat 1000-1700, Sun 1300-1700. Entrance charges. Group concessions. Parking available. Tel: (0835) 63254 or (0450) 73457.

On the site of Jedburgh Castle, a 'modern' reform jail was built in 1825. Rooms have been interestingly reconstructed to create the 'reformed' system of the early 19th century. A history of the Royal Burgh is interpreted. The jail is set in a grassy area, suitable for picnics, and forms part of the Jedburgh Town Trail.

782 **JEDFOREST DEER AND FARM PARK**   5E7

Mervinslaw Estate, Camptown, 5 miles S of Jedburgh on A68. Signposted. May-Oct. Daily 1000-1700 (May-Sept), 1100-1630 (Sept & Oct). Entrance charge. Group concessions. Parking available. Gift shop. Tearoom. Tel: (083 54) 364.

ASVA

Borders working farm with sheep, suckler cows, corn and red deer. Large display of rare breeds, including sheep, cattle, pigs, goats, poultry and waterfowl. Old and new breeds are compared. Emphasis on physical contact with animals and involvement with farm activities. Display boards with written, pictorial and hand-phone information. Daily bulletin board, coded walks, adventure land, conservation and wet areas. Tractor rides with commentary can be booked. Horse riding, educational resource material, guide book.

783 **JOHN PAUL JONES BIRTHPLACE MUSEUM**   5B10

Arbigland, Kirkbean, off A710 14 miles S of Dumfries. Apr-Sept. Mon-Sat 1000-1300, 1400-1700. Sun 1400-1700. Entrance charge. Parking available. Gift shop.

The Birthplace Museum is based around the cottage in which John Paul Jones, Father of the American Navy, spent the first thirteen years before taking up an apprenticeship in the merchant navy. The original building has been restored to the style of a gardener's cottage of the 1840s, with period furnishings. Information on headsets, slide tape audio visual, a replica of the cabin on the *Bonhomme Richard*, and a room containing a model of John Paul Jones and one of the cannons he is known to have used. The cottage gardens have been laid out in period style. Interpretative display and shop are in a former kennels block. (See No 62).

784 **JURA HOUSE WALLED GARDEN AND GROUNDS**   4C5

Isle of Jura. 5 miles from ferry connecting with Port Askaig, Isle of Islay. Jan-Dec. Mon-Sat 0900-1700. Entrance charge. Group concessions. Parking available. Tel: (049 682) 213.

Interesting woodland and cliff walks with points of local historical interest and, for keen natural historians, abundant wildlife and flowers. The organic garden offers a wide variety of unusual plants and shrubs suited to the protected West Coast climate, including a large Australasian collection. The house is not open to visitors.

785 **KAILZIE GARDENS**   5D6

2m E of Peebles on B7062. Early Mar-Oct. Daily 1100-1730. Entrance charge. Group concessions. Parking available. Gift shop. Tearoom. Plant centre. Tel: (0721) 20007.

A garden of 17 acres in the beautiful Tweed valley. The walled garden of 1812 is semi-formal, with fine herbaceous borders and old-fashioned roses. Formal rose garden, extensive greenhouses, woodland and burnside walks with primulas and meconopsis, rhododendrons in season. Duck pond. Children's play area. Art gallery. Picnic area.

786 KEATHBANK MILL 6D1

Balmoral Road, Blairgowrie, ½ mile N of town on A93. Apr-Oct. Daily 1000-1800. Entrance charge. Group concessions. Parking available. Gift shop. Coffee shop. Tel: (0250) 872025.

Built in 1864 on the bank of the River Ericht, the mill boasts Scotland's second largest working water wheel, an 1862 steam engine and 1937 diesel model. Heraldic workshops are now housed in the mill. These can be viewed, as well as a display of coats of arms, clan crests and shields. Outside, half a mile of model railway.

787 KELBURN COUNTRY CENTRE 4G6

A78 between Largs and Fairlie. Free minibus from Largs Station, weekends and bank holidays from May, daily July and Aug. Easter-mid Oct, daily 1000-1800. (Grounds and Riding School open in winter, 1100-1700. Café open Sun.) Entrance charge. Group concessions. Gift shop. Restaurant, café, ice-cream shop. Tel: (0475) 568685.

ASVA

The historic estate of the Earls of Glasgow, famous for rare trees and the Kelburn Glen. Also waterfalls, gardens, nature trails, exhibitions, adventure course, Marine assault course, children's stockade, pets' corner and pony-trekking. The central, 18th-century farm buildings have been converted to form a village square with craft shop, workshops, display rooms and licensed café. Ranger Service. Picnic tables and Commando Assault Course.

Kellie Castle and Gardens

788 KELLIE CASTLE AND GARDENS 6G3

On B9171, 3m NNW of Pittenweem, 10m S of St Andrews. Castle: Weekends in April 1400-1800. Easter, May-Sept, daily 1400-1800. Oct, daily 1400-1700 (last tour 1615). Garden and grounds, daily 1000-sunset. Entrance charges. Group concessions. Parking available. Tearoom. (NTS) Tel: (033 38) 271.

Fine domestic architecture of the 16th/17th centuries, though the oldest part dates from c 1360. Owned by the Oliphants for over 250 years, then by the Earls of Mar and Kellie, it was restored nearly a century ago by Professor James Lorimer. Notable plaster work and painted panelling. Four acres of gardens. Induction loop for the hard of hearing.

789 KELSO ABBEY 5F6

Bridge Street, Kelso. Open all reasonable times. Free. (HS) Tel: 031-244 3101.

This was the largest of the Border abbeys. One of the earliest completed by David I, it was founded in 1128. When the Earl of Hertford entered Kelso in 1545 the abbey was garrisoned as a fortress and was taken only at the point of the sword; the garrison of 100 men, including twelve monks, was slaughtered, and the building was almost entirely razed. The tower is part of the original building.

790 KELSO MUSEUM 5F6

*Turret House, Abbey Court, off Bridge Street. Apr-Oct.
Entrance charge. Group concessions. Parking available.
Tel: (0573) 225470 or (0450) 73457.*

Located in one of Kelso's oldest and most attractive
buildings, owned by the National Trust for Scotland,
the Museum interprets Kelso's history as a market
town, concentrating on the skinning and tanning
industry. Access to ground floor only for wheelchair
visitors.

791 KEMPOCK STONE 4G5

Castle Mansions of Gourock. All reasonable times. Free.

Granny Kempock's stone, of grey schist six feet high,
was probably significant in prehistoric times. In past
centuries it was used by fishermen in rites to ensure
fair weather. Couples intending to wed used to
encircle the stone to get Granny's blessing.

792 M.V. 'KENILWORTH' CRUISES 4G4

*Car and coach park at Helensburgh Pier. May-Sept, Mon-Sat,
cruises from 1040. Charge for cruises. Group concessions. Refreshments on
board. Tel: (0475) 21281.*

Attractive 1930s vintage well-maintained passenger
vessel. Other sailings to Dunoon, Rothesay, Millport, etc.

793 KERR'S MINIATURE RAILWAY 5E1

*In Arbroath, on the seafront 600yds from parking beside Hotel Seaforth
on A92. Apr-Sept, Sat and Sun 1400-1700. July and first half of Aug,
daily 1400-1700. Charge for trip. Group concessions. Tel: (0241) 79249.*

Steam and petrol-hauled trains (six locos) established
1935. Runs for 400yds alongside BR Edinburgh to
Aberdeen main line. Tunnel, footbridge and platforms,
turntable and loco shed. Miniature bus and fire engine
give trips for children along promenade.

794 KILBERRY SCULPTURED STONES 4D5

*Off B8024, 20m SSW of Lochgilphead. All reasonable times. Free. (HS)
Tel: 031-244 3101.*

A fine collection of late medieval sculptured stones.

795 KILCHURN CASTLE 4F2

*N tip of Loch Awe, 21m E of Oban. Open all reasonable times. (HS)
Tel: 031-244 3101.*

The keep was built in 1440 by Sir Colin Campbell of
Glenorchy, founder of the Breadalbane family. The
north and south sides of the building were erected in
1693 by Ian, Earl of Breadalbane, whose arms and
those of his wife are over the gateway. Occupied by
the Breadalbanes until 1740, in 1746 it was taken by
Hanoverian troops. A gale in 1879 toppled one of its
towers.

796 KILDALTON CROSS 4C6

*7m NE of Port Ellen, Isle of Islay. All reasonable times. Free. (HS)
Tel: 031-244 3101.*

Perhaps the finest Celtic cross in Scotland, and
sculptured slabs, are in Kildalton churchyard.

797 KILDRUMMY CASTLE 3E10

A97, 10m W of Alford. Apr-Sept, opening standard. Oct-Mar, weekends only. Entrance charge. Group concessions. Parking available. (HS)
Tel: 031-244 3101.

The most extensive example in Scotland of a 13th-century castle. The four round towers, hall and chapel remains belong in substance to the original. The great gatehouse and other work is later, to the 16th century. It was the seat of the Earls of Mar, and played an important part in Scottish history until 1715 when it was dismantled.

798 KILDRUMMY CASTLE GARDENS 3E10

&
A
T

A97, off A944, 10m W of Alford. Aberdeenshire. Apr-Oct, daily 1000-1700. Entrance charge. Children must be accompanied. Coach parties by arrangement. Parking available. Plant sales.
Tel: (097 55) 71277 or 71203.

The shrub and alpine garden in the ancient quarry are of interest to botanists for their great variety. The water gardens lie below the ruined castle. Specimen trees are planted below it in the Back Den. Play area, video room, woodland walk. Interesting old stones displayed. Museum opens on request. Dogs must be kept on leash.

Killiecrankie: see No 1040.

Kilmartin Sculptured Stones

799 KILMARTIN SCULPTURED STONES 4E4

A816, 7½m N of Lochgilphead. All reasonable times. Free. (HS)
Tel: 031-244 3101.

In this typical West Highland churchyard are preserved a number of grave slabs and fragments of at least two crosses, one showing Christ crucified on the front and Christ in Majesty on the back. The cross dates from the 16th century.
The area north of the Crinan Canal (No 312) to Kilmartin has many reminders of both prehistoric and medieval times. These include: Bronze Age cup-and-ring engravings at Ballygowan; Bronze Age and earlier burial cairns at Dunchraigaig, Nether Largie, Ri Cruin and Kilmartin Glebe; two stone circles at Temple Wood.

800 KILMORY CAIRNS 4F7

At S end of Arran, off A841. All times. Free.
Cairn Baan, 3½m NE of Kilmory village, is a notable Neolithic long cairn. Half a mile SW of A841 at the Lagg Hotel is Torrylin Cairn, a Neolithic chambered cairn. There are many other cairns in this area.

801 KILMORY CASTLE GARDENS 4E4

Off A83 road to Inveraray, on outskirts of Lochgilphead.
Parking available. Tel: (0546) 602127.

The garden was started in the 1770s and included
around 100 varieties of rhododendron, supplied plants
for Kew Garden and contained a collection of hardy
ferns and alpines. The gardens are being restored with
woodland walks and a nature trail. There are also
footpaths and a herbaceous border.

802 KILMORY WORKSHOP 4F7

Isle of Arran. ¾ mile from main A841, turn off at Torralyn Creamery.
Signposted. Above Kilmory Church. Jan-Dec. Tues-Fri 1000-1730 or
when flag is flying. Free. Car parking only. Tel: (077 087) 310.

Woodwork and pottery workshops and display
showroom. Woodwork made from local hard and soft
woods including turned work, furniture and toys.
Pottery is handthrown, high-fired stoneware,
functional and decorative.

803 KILMUN ARBORETUM 4F4

By Forest Office on A880, 1m E of junction with A815. 5m N of
Dunoon. All year. Daily, all day. Free. Parking available. (FC)
Tel: (036 984) 666.

A fascinating collection of tree species on a hillside to
the north-east of Holy Loch within the Argyll Forest
Park. (See No 81).

804 KILORAN GARDENS 4C4

Kiloran, Isle of Colonsay. Jan-Dec. Daily, all reasonable times. Free.
Car parking only. Tel: (095 12) 312.

Kiloran Rhododendron Woods, in the policies of
Colonsay House (not open to the public), create a
natural woodland garden with a stream, where native
trees and rare rhododendrons, bluebells and meconopsis
flourish. Shelter, and a mild climate, enable rare shrubs
from all parts of the world to grow happily, including
mimosa, eucalyptus, embothriums and magnolias.
Self-catering accommodation.

805 KILRAVOCK CASTLE 3B8

2 miles fom Croy, 6 miles W of Nairn off the B9091. End Apr-Sept.
Castle: Wed 1100-1700. Garden and grounds: Mon-Sat 0900-1700.
Entrance charge. Parking available. Sales point. Tearoom (Wed).
Lunches by prior arrangement. Tel: (066 78) 258.

The extensive grounds and garden of this 15th-century
castle are noted for a large variety of beautiful trees,
some centuries old. The tree garden, nature trails and
river host an abundance of wildlife. A plan location of
trees is available on request. Guided tours of the castle
and afternoon tea are available on Wednesdays.

806 KILT ROCK 2D8

Off A855, 17m N of Portree, Skye. Seen from the road. Parking
available. Care should be taken not to go too near the edge of the cliff.

The top rock is composed of columnar basalt, the
lower portion of horizontal beds, giving the
impression of the pleats in a kilt. There is also a
waterfall nearby.

807 KILWINNING ABBEY   **4G6**

Kilwinning, Ayrshire. All times. Free. Can be viewed from outside only.
(HS) Tel: 031-244 3101.

The ruins of a Tironensian-Benedictine Abbey. Most
of the surviving buildings date from the 13th century.

808 KINDROCHIT CASTLE   **3D11**

Balnellan Road, Braemar. Free. All reasonable times. Parking available.

Ruins of ancient important fortification. Legend
indicates that Malcolm Canmore built the first castle
of Kindrochit in the 11th century. The existing
remains stand above the Clunie and consist of walls
and grass-grown embankments.

809 KINGFISHER CRUISES   **4E3**

Ardfern Yacht Centre, between Oban and Lochgilphead, take B8002 off
A816. Jan-Dec. All times, weather permitting. Charge for cruises.
Car parking only. Tel: (085 25) 662.

Various cruises, from 1½ hours viewing seals, seabirds
and scenery in sheltered Loch Craignish, ¾-hour
cruises visiting nearby islands such as Jura, Scarba,
Luing and Shuna, to 5-8 hours visiting the
McCormaig Islands or the Garvellachs. Walkers 'ferry'
service to Jura.

810 KINGSPARK LLAMA FARM   **3C5**

Berriedale, on A9 N of Helmsdale. Jan-Dec. Daily, dawn-dusk. Entrance
charge. Parking available. Gift shop. Tel: (059 35) 202.

A breeding llama farm where visitors can mix freely
with geldings, females (some with babies), and the
stud male 'T.C.'. A llama walk along Dunbeath Strath
can be booked. Within the park, raccoons, goats,
pheasants, peacocks, a variety of birds, and chipmunks.

811 KING'S CAVE   **4E7**

On shore, 2m N of Blackwaterfoot on the west coast of Arran. All times.
Free.

A two-mile walk along the shore from the golf course
at Blackwaterfoot leads to a series of caves, the largest
being the King's Cave. Said to have been occupied by
Finn MacCoul and later by Robert the Bruce, this is
one of the possible settings for the 'Bruce and the
spider' legend. Carvings of figures are on the walls.

812 KINKELL CHURCH   **3G10**

On the E bank of the Don, 2m S of Inverurie, off B993. All reasonable
times. Free. (HS) Tel: 031-244 3101.

The ruins of an early 16th-century parish church with
some ornate details including a rich sacrament house
of unusual design, dated 1524.

Kinloch Castle

813   KINLOCH CASTLE   2D11

Isle of Rum, access by boat from Mallaig. Mar-Oct, as a hotel and hostel.
Tours by arrangement with the Castle staff. Reserve and trail guides
available from the Warden, White House, Kinloch, Rum. (SNH)
Tel: (0687) 2026.

Extraordinary and magnificent residence built at the
turn of the century for Sir George Bullough, still
containing many of its sumptuous fittings. The island
itself is a mountainous nature reserve, owned by
Scottish Natural Heritage, where experiments in deer
and woodland management have been conducted for
over 30 years.

814   KINLOCHLAICH HOUSE GARDENS   4F1
&
A   *Midway between Oban and Fort William on A828. Entry by police*
P   *station. Apr-mid Oct. Mon-Sat 0930-1730, Sun 1030-1730.*
T   *Mid Oct-Mar, Mon-Sat only. Donation to Scotland's Gardens Scheme.*
       Tel: (063 173) 342.

Walled garden, incorporating West Highland's largest
nursery garden centre. There are display beds of
primulas, alpines, rhododendrons, heathers as well as
fruiting and flowering shrubs and trees.

815   KINNEFF OLD CHURCH   3G12

Off unclassified road, E of A92, 2m N of Inverbervie. All reasonable
times. Free. Parking available. (Kinneff Old Church Preservation Trust)

Part of this historic church formed the original
building in which the Crown Jewels of Scotland were
hidden for nine years after being smuggled from
Dunnottar Castle (see No 424) through Cromwell's
besieging army in 1651. In the present church, which
dates from 1738, are the recently restored memorials
to the parish minister, Rev James Grainger, who
concealed the regalia under the flagstones of the
church; and to the governor of the castle, Sir George
Ogilvy of Barras.

**816   KINNEIL MUSEUM AND
         ROMAN FORTLET**   6C6

In Bo'ness, 16m WNW of Edinburgh on A904 (adjacent to Kinneil
House). Apr-Sep, Mon-Sat 1000-1700, Sun (Jun, Jul, Aug only)
1000-1700. Oct-Apr, Sat only 1000-1700. Free. Museum shop.
Tel: (0324) 24911, ext 2472.

Converted 17th century stables, with displays of
Bo'ness Pottery and cast iron work. An exhibition
entitled '2000 years of history' provides an insight into
the estate's colourful history and provides guidance for
viewing the remaining monuments, including a
consolidated Roman fortlet, medieval house, church &
village remains, and James Watt's cottage. History
tours of the estate by costumed interpreters is available
by calling (0506) 824318.

817   KINTAIL   2G10
&
N of A87 between Lochs Cluanie and Duich, 16m E of Kyle of
Lochalsh. Jan-Dec. Countryside Centre at Morvich (unmanned) open
May-late Sept, Mon-Sat 1000-1700, Sun 1400-1700. Entrance charge,
honesty box. Car parking only. (NTS) Tel: (059 981) 219.

Magnificent Highland scenery including the Falls of
Glomach and the Five Sisters of Kintail (four of them
over 3,000 feet). Red deer and wild goats. Visitor
Centre at Morvich gives best access to mountains. Site
of Battle of Glen Shiel, 5 miles east of village beside
road. Ranger-led walks in season.

818 KIRK YETHOLM   5F7

Off B6352, 8m SE of Kelso.

Attractive village, with Town Yetholm, once famous
as the home of the Scottish gypsies, now the northern
end of the Pennine Way.

**819 KIRKCALDY ART GALLERY
        AND MUSEUM**   6E5

& *By railway station. Jan-Dec exc public holidays. Mon-Sat 1100-1700,*
A *Sun 1400-1700. Parking available. Gift shop. Tearoom. Free.*
T *Tel: (0592) 260732.*

Award-winning art gallery, museum and exhibition
centre with a fine collection of Scottish painting,
displays tracing Fife's industrial heritage of mining,
linen and linoleum, and exhibitions of contemporary
art, craft and photography.

820 KIRKCALDY ICE RINK   6E5

& *Rosslyn Street, Kirkcaldy. Signposted. Jan-Dec. 0900-2400. Entrance*
A *charges. Parking available. Gift shop. Restaurant, refreshments.*
T *Tel: (0592) 52151.*

Ice rink, established 1938, home of Scottish Curling
Championships. Multi-purpose facility used for
concerts, shows and other events.

821 KIRKCALDY SWIMMING POOL   6E5

& *Esplanade, near town centre. Jan-Dec. Mon & Tue 0800-1830,*
T *Wed & Thurs 0800-2000, Fri 0800-1900, Sat & Sun 0800-1600.*
   Fitness room and Sauna suite open to 2000, Mon-Fri. Entrance charges.
   Car parking only. Cafe. Tel: (0592) 265366.

Opened in 1971, this building is a popular activity
centre offering casual and competitive swimming,
sauna, sunbeds, fitness room. Kirkcaldy residents used
to swim in the harbour before the pool opened.

**822 KIRKMAIDEN INFORMATION
        CENTRE**   4G11

& *Take A77 S from Stranraer, continue S on A716 (not turning off to*
   Portpatrick). Late May-mid Sept, Mon-Sat 1000-1600, Sun 1330-1600.
   Free. Parking available.

Visitor and information centre about the parish, places
to visit and surrounding area, history, genealogy.
Exhibition area.

Kirkwynd Cottages: see No 58.

Kirriemuir R.A.F. Museum

823 KIRRIEMUIR R.A.F. MUSEUM   5D1

& *Bellies Brae, Kirriemuir, 5 miles NE of Glamis Castle. Apr-Sept.*
A *Mon-Thurs, Sat 1000-1700, Fri & Sun 1100-1700. Donations accepted.*
   Parking available. Tel: (0575) 73233.

Wartime Royal Air Force memorabilia, including war
relics, uniforms, diaries and books, ejection seats,
medals and instruments, flying suits.

824 KISIMUL CASTLE   2A11

*On a tiny island in the bay by Castlebay, Isle of Barra. May-Sep, Wed
and Sat afternoons only. Charge for boatman and admission to the castle.
Tel: (08714) 336.*

For many generations Kisimul was the home and
stronghold of the Macneils of Barra, widely noted for
their lawlessness and piracy, and led by chiefs like
Ruari the Turbulent, 35th chief, who did not fear to
seize ships of subjects of Queen Elizabeth I of
England. The main tower dates from about 1120.
Restoration was commenced in 1938 by the 45th clan
chief, an American architect, and completed in 1970.

825 KITTIWAKE GALLERY   5F5

*Entrance to St Abbs village at Head Start Visitor Centre. Easter-Sept,
daily 1100-1730. Oct-Easter, Sat & Sun 1200-1600. Free. Parking
available. Gallery shop. Tearoom. Tel: (089 07) 71504 or 71588.*

Privately-owned gallery, displaying paintings and
limited edition prints, greetings cards by Frederick J.
Watson, the gallery proprietor. From Easter to
September, demonstrations of landscape and wildlife
painting of local subjects.

826 KNAP OF HOWAR   1B9

*W side of island of Papa Westray, 800 metres W of Holland House,
Orkney. All reasonable times. Free. (HS) Tel: 031-244 3101.*

Only recently recognised as one of the oldest sites in
Europe, these two 5000-year-old dwellings have also
yielded many unusual artefacts—whalebone mallets
and a spatula and unique stone borers and grinders.

Knockan Cliff: see No 772

Knockhill Racing Circuit

827 KNOCKHILL RACING CIRCUIT   6C4

*By Dunfermline, 5 miles N of M90 on A823. Jan-Dec. Entrance charges.
Parking available. Restaurant, cafe. Tel: (0383) 723337 or 622090.*

Racing track featuring motor and motorcycle events
almost every Sunday from April to mid-October. High
speed racing action, trackside parking, adventure
playground, music.

828 KYLE HOUSE   2E10

*½m from jetty at Kyleakin. Open May-Aug. All reasonable times.
Free (charity donation box). Car parking only. Tel: (0599) 4517.*

Situated by Loch Alsh the garden is protected in
winter by the Gulf Stream. This allows many tender
plants to attain quite large sizes. Most of the garden
was planted around 30 years ago by the late Colin
Mackenzie. It covers about three acres. Also a kitchen
garden and viewpoint from which can be seen the
Cuillin Hills on the Isle of Skye, the Isle of Raasay and
many other small islands.

Kylerhea Otter Haven

829   **KYLERHEA OTTER HAVEN**   2F10

♿ A

N of Kylerhea, Isle of Skye. Jan-Dec. Daily, dawn-dusk. Free. Car parking only. (FE)

An attractive viewing hide above the beach, where otters can be seen in their natural habitat. A wide range of other wildlife can also be seen, including golden and sea eagles, seals, wading birds, deer, and other sea birds. Visitors are recommended to bring binoculars, and may have to wait before animals are seen. The hide is around ¾ mile walk from car park.

830   **KYLES OF BUTE**   4F5

Narrow arm of the Firth of Clyde, between Isle of Bute and Argyll. Parking available.

A 16-mile stretch of water which presents a constantly changing view of great beauty. It can perhaps be best appreciated from the A8003, Tighnabruaich to Glendaruel road, where there are two view indicators. The western one (Scottish Civic Trust) looks over the West Kyle and identifies many features. The east indicator (NTS) looks over Loch Ridden and the East Kyle.

Lady Gifford Statue: see No. 595

831   **LADYKIRK**   5F6

♿

4 miles E of Swinton and ½ mile from Norham off B6470. All reasonable times. Parking available.

Ladykirk was built in 1500 by James IV, in memory of 'Our Lady' who had saved him from drowning. As the Border was only 300 yards away and in constant dispute, he ordered it built to withstand fire and flood — hence the all-stone construction of the kirk with no wooden rafters and, until this century, stone pews. The Wardens of the East March met regularly in the parish to resolve disputes between Scotland and England. In 1560, a copy of the last peace treaty between them was signed in Ladykirk, marking the end of sporadic warfare.

832 THE LADY MARGARET RESTAURANT BOAT 5A5

Forth and Clyde Canal, near the Stables Bar on A803 Bishopbriggs/ Kirkintilloch road. All year. Dinner cruises Thurs, Fri, Sat. Sunday lunch cruises. Group bookings at any time. Prices on application. Parking available. Tel: 041-776 6996 or (0236) 723523.

Restaurant boat on the Forth and Clyde Canal, providing quality lunch and dinner cruises for groups and individuals. Member of Taste of Scotland scheme. Floodlighting illuminates passing scenery at night.

833 LADY ROWENA, STEAM LAUNCH 4F2

Sails from BR Station Pier at Lochawe Village on A85. May-Sept 1030-1600, 7 days a week, hourly from 1000. Charge for cruises. Tearoom on pier. Tel: 041-334 2529 or (083 82) 440/449.

Restored Edwardian launch with genuine steam engine and peat-fired boiler. Cushioned seating and enclosed cabin. Variety of cruises (50 mins to 3 hrs) to places of interest on Loch Awe. Comfortable Pullman Carriage Tearoom on the pier with superb views of Kilchurn Castle. Ferry to castle. Also on Loch Awe, M.V. *Flower of Scotland*.

834 LAGAVULIN DISTILLERY 4C6

Port Ellen, Isle of Islay. Ferry from Kennacraig on West Loch Tarbert to Port Ellen or Port Askaig, or from Oban on Wed in summer. Jan-Dec exc Christmas & New Year. Mon-Fri, by appointment only. Parking available. Shop. Tel: (0496) 2400.

Lagavulin is one of the most distinctive of the peaty Islay malt whiskies. The distillery, home of the famous White Horse blend, was one of the first on the island, established legally in 1816. It stands by the sea on the site of a former illegal distillery and beside the ruins of Dun Naomhaig Castle, ancient stronghold of the Lords of the Isles. Tours and tastings.

835 LAGOON LEISURE COMPLEX 4H5

Paisley, off Mill Street. Jan-Dec. Mon-Fri 1000-2200. Sat, Sun, public holidays, 0930-1700. Charges vary. Parking available. Restaurant and bar. Tel: 041-889 4000.

Modern swimming pool complex with sauna, steam room, slides and jacuzzi. New full-size ice rink with disco light, curling and ice hockey facilities.

836 LAING MUSEUM 6E2

High Street, Newburgh, Fife. Apr-Sep, weekdays 1100-1800. Sat-Sun 1400-1700; Oct-Mar, Wed, Thurs 1200-1600, Sun 1400-1700. Free. Tel: (0334) 53722, ext. 141.

Museum with displays on the theme of Victorian Scotland—self-help, emigration, the antiquarian movement, geology and recreated Victorian study. Temporary exhibitions and historical reference library.

837 WILLIAM LAMB MEMORIAL STUDIO 5E1

24 Market Street, Montrose. Jul, Aug, Sat 1400-1700. Free. Car parking only. Gift shop. Tel: (0674) 73232.

Studio of William Lamb, ARSA (1893-1951), noted Montrose sculptor and etcher, containing a selection of his works including heads of HM Queen Elizabeth and HRH Princess Margaret as girls, and HM The Queen Mother as Duchess of York. His workrooms with tools, and living room with his own designs of furniture, are also featured.

838 LAND O' BURNS CENTRE   4G7

Opposite Alloway Kirk, 2m S of Ayr. All year, daily, 1000-1700 (exc July & Aug, 1730). Admission free; small charge for audio-visual display. Parking available. Tel: (0292) 443700.

ASVA

This Visitor Centre has an exhibition area and an audio-visual display on the life and times of Robert Burns. Landscaped gardens and tea room.

839 LANDMARK VISITOR CENTRE   3C10

♿
P
T

Carrbridge, 6m N of Aviemore on old A9. Jan-Dec. Apr-Jun, Sept-Oct, daily 0930-1800. Jul & Aug 0930-2000. Nov-Mar 0930-1700. Entrance charges. Group rates on request. Parking available. Scottish craft and bookshop. Restaurant, bar, snack bar, picnic area. Tel: (047 984) 613.

ASVA

The Landmark Visitor Centre was the first of its kind in Europe. The main events of the turbulent Highland history are presented in a three screen audio visual show and in a dramatic permanent exhibition. Outdoor attractions include tree top trail, pine forest nature centre and trails, woodland maze and adventure playground with giant slide and aerial net walkways. The Scottish Forestry Heritage Park tells the story of the timber industry from early times. Exhibits include the steam-powered sawmill and 65-ft viewing tower. Forestry skills demonstrations take place throughout the summer.

840 LAPHROAIG DISTILLERY   4C6

Port Ellen, Isle of Islay. 1½m along road to Ardbeg from Port Ellen. Tours by prior arrangement. Tel: (0496) 2418/2393.

Malting, distilling and warehousing of malt whisky.

841 LARGS MUSEUM   4G5

♿
A

Kirkgate House, Manse Court, Largs. Jun-Sep, Mon-Sat 1400-1700. Open at other times by arrangement. Donation box. Tel: (0475) 687081.

The museum holds a small collection of local bygones, with a library of local history books and numerous photographs, put together by the local historical society.

842 LAUDER FOREST WALKS   4F4

3 miles S of Strachur on A815, turn right, signposted Glenbranter. All reasonable times. Free. Parking available. (FE) Tel: (036 984) 666.

Glenbranter Estate, formerly owned by Sir Harry Lauder, was leased to the Forestry Commission in 1921. The village was later built on the site of a former World War II prisoner-of-war camp. The forest walks go through a mixed coniferous and broadleaved woodland, with a rhododendron collection established in 1925, and dramatic waterfalls. Half a mile away on the Dunoon road are the Lauder memorials. Sir Harry Lauder erected an obelisk here in memory of his only son John, killed in World War I, and a Celtic cross to commemorate Lady Lauder who died in 1927. The forest car park is on the site of the former Glenbranter House. (See No 81).

843 LAXFORD CRUISES   2G4

Fanagmore, 3 miles N of Scourie. Signposted. Easter-mid Sept. 1000-1600. Charge for cruises. Parking available. Tel: (0971) 502409.

Pleasure cruises around Loch Laxford, seeing many different species of birds; also seals, occasional sightings of otters, dolphins, porpoises and whales.

Leadhills Library: see No 1073.

844 LECHT SKI CENTRE   3D10

Off A939, 7m SE of Tomintoul. Jan-Dec. Daily 0830-1730. Charge. Concessions on application. Parking available. Licensed cafeteria. Tel: (097 56) 51440.

Ski tows operating to slopes on both sides of the Lecht Road, famous for its snowfalls. Ski hire, ski school. Dry ski slope.

845 LECKMELM SHRUBBERY
AND ARBORETUM   2G6

3 miles S of Ullapool on A835. Apr-Sept, daily 1000-1800. Honesty box. Parking available. Tel: (0854) 612356.

Delightful 10-acre arboretum and 2½ acre walled garden on the shores of Loch Broom, laid out in the 1870s and under restoration since 1985. Some rare and unusual trees and a wide range of rhododendrons and azaleas.

846 LEIGHTON LIBRARY   6A4

& *The Cross, Dunblane, 6 miles N of Stirling on M9.*
A   *May-Oct. Mon-Fri 1030-1230, 1430-1630. Free. Parking available.*

The Leighton Library is said to be the oldest private library in Scotland. Built in 1684, it contains 4,500 books from 1500 onwards, in around 50 languages. The collection covers a very wide range of subjects, now used as an international working library. The building and its contents were almost forgotten for 150 years until restoration in 1989-90, and full opening to the public in 1991.

847 LEITH HALL 3F9

    B9002, 7m S of Huntly. House: May-Sept, daily 1400-1800;
P *Oct, Sat and Sun 1400-1700. Grounds: All year 0930-sunset. Entrance*
T *charges for house. Group concessions. Gardens and grounds by donation.*
Parking available. Tearoom. (NTS). Tel: (046 43) 216.

ASVA

The mansion house of Leith Hall is at the centre of a
286-acre estate which was the home of the head of the
Leith family from 1650. The house contains personal
possessions of successive Lairds, most of whom followed
a tradition of military service. Exhibition entitled 'For
Crown and Country: The Military Lairds of Leith
Hall'. The grounds contain varied farm and
woodlands. There are two ponds, a bird observation
hide and three countryside walks, one leading to a
hilltop viewpoint. Unique 18th-century stables, Soay
sheep, Highland cattle, ice house. Extensive and
interesting informal garden of borders, shrubs and
rock garden. Trail beside pond suitable for wheelchairs.

Lennoxlove House

848 LENNOXLOVE HOUSE 6G6

    On B6369, 1m S of Haddington. Easter Weekend and May-Sept, Wed,
A *Sat, Sun 1400-1700. Entrance charges. Group concessions.*
P *Parking available. Gift shop. Tearoom. Gardens.*
T *Tel: (062 082) 3720.*

ASVA

Originally named Lethington, it was owned for
centuries by the Maitlands, one of whom was
Secretary to Mary, Queen of Scots. In 1672 the
Duchess of Lennox (La Belle Stewart, who was the the
model for Britannia on the coinage), bought and
bequeathed it to Lord Blantyre, stipulating that it be
renamed Lennoxlove in memory of her devotion to her
husband. House has a threefold interest: its historic
architecture; the association of the proprietors with
the Royal House of Stewart; and the Hamilton Palace
collection of portraits, furniture and porcelain.

849 LETHAM GLEN 6F4

    Leven, off A915. Glen open all year, daily, dawn-dusk. Nature Centre,
A *Jan-Dec exc Christmas & New Year. Mon-Fri 1200-1500. Summer, Sat*
1400-1600, Sun 1400-1630. Winter, Sat 1300-1500, Sun 1300-1530.
Free. Car parking in summer. Tel: (0333) 429231.

This picturesque glen has a variety of educational and
recreational facilities for visitors. Rustic bridges, a
doocot, putting green and pets' corner. In the heart of
the glen is the Alpine-style Nature Centre where
exhibitions are staged throughout the year, and where
students demonstrate crafts in summer. (Easy access
for disabled visitors.) Mile-long nature trail from the
centre to the far end of the Glen. Information booklets
available.

Leuchars Parish Church

850 LEUCHARS PARISH CHURCH 6G2

  ♿ *Main Street, Leuchars, 5 miles from St Andrews on A919 to Dundee.*
A T *Mar-Oct. Daylight hours up to 1900. Visitors are also welcome to join services. Other times by arrangement. Free, donations welcome. Parking available. Tours and tearoom on Tuesdays. Teas, coffees by arrangement on other days. Tel: (Church officer's house) (0334) 838884.*

Leuchars Parish Church comprises an ancient Norman chancel and apse, richly ornamented, with a fine 17th-century bell tower. The rest of the church is Victorian. Many and varied stone carvings inside and outside, with masons' marks. Handbook available.

851 LEVENMOUTH SWIMMING POOL
AND SPORTS CENTRE 6F4

  ♿ *Promenade, Leven. Jan-Dec exc Christmas & New Year. Mon, Wed, Fri*
T *0800-2200. Tues, Thurs 0700-2200. Sat, Sun 0800-2100. Charges for activities. Parking available. Sports shop. Cafeteria. Tel: (0333) 429866.*

Centre has leisure pool with wave-making machine, water cannons, flume, whirlpool spa, water jets and geysers. Four-court gameshall, fitness room, sunbeds, sauna and other facilities.

852 LEWIS BLACK HOUSE 2C4

At Arnol, 15m NW of Stornoway, Isle of Lewis. Opening standard, except closed Sun. Entrance charge. Group concessions. Parking available. (HS) Tel: 031-244 3101.

A good example of a traditional type of Hebridean dwelling, built without mortar and roofed with thatch on a timber framework and without eaves. Characteristic features are the central peat fire in the kitchen, the absence of any chimney and the byre under the same roof. The house retains many of its original furnishings.

853 LEYDEN OBELISK AND TABLET 5E7

Denholm on A698 NE of Hawick. All times. Free.

The village was the birthplace of John Leyden (1776-1811), poet, orientalist and friend of Sir Walter Scott. An obelisk was set up in 1861 and a tablet on a thatched cottage records his birth there. Another famous son of Denholm was Sir James Murray, editor of the *Oxford English Dictionary* whose birth is commemorated on a tablet on a house in Main Street.

854   LHAIDHAY CROFT MUSEUM   3D4

& *On A9, 1m N of Dunbeath. Easter-mid Oct, daily 1000-1800. Entrance*
T   *charge. Group concessions. Parking available. Tearoom. Picnic area. Tel:*
    (059 33) 244.

An early 18th-century croft complex with stable,
dwelling house and byre under one thatched roof with
adjoining barn. Completely furnished in the fashion of
its time, the barn is of cruck-construction. Blind
people may handle items.

855   LILLIE ART GALLERY   4H5

& *Station Road, Milngavie, off A81, 8m N of Glasgow. Jan-Dec. Mon-Fri*
    1000-1700, Sat and Sun 1400-1700. Free. Parking available.
    Tel: 041-943 3247.

A modern purpose-built art gallery with a permanent
collection of 20th-century Scottish paintings, sculpture
and ceramics, and temporary exhibitions of
contemporary art. Alternative entrance with ramp.

856   LINCLUDEN COLLEGIATE CHURCH   5B9

Off A76, 1m N of Dumfries. All reasonable times. Key keeper.
Entrance charge. (HS) Tel: 031-244 3101.

A 15th-century Collegiate Church and Provost's
House remarkable for heraldic adornment and for the
tomb of Princess Margaret, daughter of Robert III.
There is a motte in the grounds.

**857   LINLITHGOW HERITAGE TRUST
        MUSEUM**   6C6

Annet House, 139 High Street, Linlithgow. Apr-Sept.
Mon-Sat 1000-1600, Sun 1300-1600. Parking available. Gift shop.
Refreshments. Tel: (0506) 670677.

Historical and industrial museum relating to
Linlithgow.

Linlithgow Palace

858   LINLITHGOW PALACE   6C6

S shore of loch, Linlithgow. Opening standard. Entrance charge.
Group concessions. Parking available. (HS) Tel: 031-244 3101.

The splendid ruined Palace overlooking the loch is the
successor to an older building which was burned
down in 1424. The Chapel and Great Hall are late
15th-century and the fine quadrangle has a richly-
carved 16th-century fountain. In 1542 Mary, Queen of
Scots was born here while her father, James V, lay
dying at Falkland Palace. In 1746 the palace was
burned, probably by accident, when occupied by
General Hawley's troops. George V held a court in the
Lyon Chamber here in 1914.

859 LINLITHGOW UNION CANAL SOCIETY MUSEUM AND BOAT TRIPS 6C6

   P
   T
Manse Road Basin, Union Canal, Linlithgow. Easter-Sept, Sat & Sun, 1400-1700. Museum free, charge for cruises. Group concessions during the week. Parking available. Tearoom. Boats for hire. Tel: (0506) 842575.

The museum, housed in former canal stables, built around 1822, when the canal opened, has photographs, records, audio-visual display and relics of the history and wildlife of the Union Canal. Nearby, the canal boat *Victoria* is a replica of a Victorian steam packet offering half-hour pleasure cruises on the canal. Disabled visitors must be able to get out of wheelchairs.

860 "LITTLE WHEELS" 4F11

   T
Portpatrick. Easter and main holiday season. 1100-1600, extended as necessary during July and Aug. Phone for latest times (Ansaphone service). Entrance charge. Group rates for parties over 20. Limited parking available. Gift and collectors' shop. Refreshments. Tel: (077 681) 536.

Model railway (over 100 metres of track), toys, dolls and miniature transport exhibition. Children can usually 'drive' some of the trains. New displays each year.

861 LIVINGSTON ARENA 6C7

5 Almondvale West, centre of Livingston, West Lothian. Aug-Apr. Daily 1000-2200. Entrance charges. Group concessions. Parking available. Cafeteria. Lounge bar/restaurant. Tel: (0506) 462222.

Olympic-size ice pad for curling, skating, and ice hockey, one of Scotland's most modern ice sports facilities, with 800 pairs of skates for hire. Host for national and international events.

David Livingstone Centre

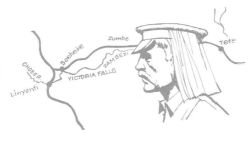

862 DAVID LIVINGSTONE CENTRE 5A6

At Blantyre, A724, 3m NW of Hamilton. All year, Mon-Sat 1000-1700, Sun 1300-1700. (Last entry) Entrance charge. Family ticket. Group concessions. Parking available. Shop. Tearoom. Tel: (0698) 823140.

Shuttle Row is an 18th-century block of mill tenements where David Livingstone, the famous explorer/missionary, was born in 1813, went to school and worked while studying to become a doctor. The David Livingstone Centre, which illustrates his life and contains many interesting relics of the Industrial Revolution and of Africa, is in this building, now surrounded by parkland.

863 LOANHEAD STONE CIRCLE 3G9

¼m NW of Daviot, 5m NW of Inverurie, off B9001. All reasonable times. Free. (HS) Tel: 031-244 3101.

The best known example of a widespread group of recumbent stone circles in east Scotland.

864   LOCH AN EILEIN POTTERY   3C10

&   *2½ miles SW of Aviemore, just off B970 on road to Loch an Eilein.*
P   *Jan-Dec. Daily, 1000-1800 in summer, mornings only in winter. Free.*
     Car parking only. Pottery shop. Tel: (0479) 810837.

Small rural craft pottery workshop with display area of
pots for sale. Pottery is red earthenware, domestic and
functional, specialising in jugs of all sizes, and garden
pots. Thursday is 'throw-your-own' day, when visitors
can try their hand at making a pot which will be
glazed, fired and posted on to them.

865   LOCH AN EILEIN VISITOR CENTRE   3C10

&   *Rothiemurchus Estate, 2½ miles S of Aviemore on B970 — Feshiebridge*
P   *turn-off on right. Jan-Dec exc Christmas Day. Daily, 0930-1630. Charge*
     for car park. Coaches by arrangement. Gift shop, ice cream, drinks,
     confectionery for sale (Easter-Oct). Tel: (0479) 810858.

A cottage beside this attractive small loch contains an
exhibition showing the management and conservation
of the native Scots pine forest.

866   LOCHBROOM MUSEUM   2G6

Quay Street, Ullapool. Jun-Aug, Mon-Sat 0900-2200. Sept-May,
Mon-Sat 0900-1800. Tel: (0854) 612356.

A tiny museum of character, established for 50 years,
and telling the story of Ullapool and the Loch Broom
area. Fine rock collection illustrates the land formation
of the area. Artefacts from ancient times to World
War II, and relics associated with famous people from
the Duke of Wellington to Sir Harry Lauder.

867   LOCH DOON CASTLE   4H8

From A713, 10m S of Dalmellington, take road to Loch Doon.
All reasonable times. Free. (HS) Tel: 031-244 3101.

This early 14th-century castle was devised to fit the
island on which it was originally built. When the
waters of the loch were raised in connection with a
hydro-electric scheme the castle was dismantled and re-
erected on the shores of the loch. The walls of this
massive building, once known as Castle Balliol, vary
from 7-9 feet thick and stand about 26 feet high.

**868   LOCH DRUIDIBEG NATIONAL NATURE
        RESERVE**   2A9

In the N part of South Uist, Outer Hebrides. All year, daily. Please call at
Warden's Office for full details of access. Free. (SNH) Tel: (087 05) 206.

One of the two remaining native populations of
greylag geese in Britain breeds here, in a typical
example of the Outer Hebrides environment, machair,
fresh and brackish lochs.

869   LOCH ETIVE CRUISES   4F2

&   *Taynuilt, 12 miles E of Oban on A85, follow signs on reaching village.*
A   *May-Sept, cruises Mon-Fri at 1030 & 1400, Sat & Sun 1400. Easter-end*
     Apr, Oct, cruises daily at 1400 only. Duration 3 hours. Charge for cruise.
     Group concessions. Parking available. Free transport from Taynuilt village
     to vessel for foot passengers. Refreshments. Tel: (086 62) 430.

Cruises on lovely Loch Etive, inaccessible except by
boat, take in 20 miles of sheltered water from Connel
Bridge to the mountains of Glencoe. Seals may be
visible on the rocks, golden eagle on Ben Starav, deer
on crags, the ancient home of Deirdre of the Sorrows,
fine mountain scenery.

870 LOCH GARTEN NATURE RESERVE   3C10

Off B970, 8m NE of Aviemore. If ospreys present, daily mid Apr-Aug 1000-2000 along signposted track to Observation Post. Other access into bird sanctuary strictly forbidden Apr-Aug but elsewhere on the reserve access unrestricted throughout the year. Entry charge to Osprey Viewing Hide for non-members. Parking available. Shop. (RSPB) Tel: (0479) 83694 or 031-557 3136.

Ospreys, extinct in Scotland for many years, returned here to breed in 1959. Their treetop eyrie may be viewed through fixed binoculars from the Observation Hut. The surrounding area, owned by the RSPB, includes extensive stretches of old Caledonian Pine forest with rich and varied wildlife. Closed-circuit TV on osprey nest for live and recorded pictures.

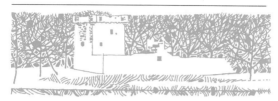

Loch Leven Castle

871 LOCH LEVEN CASTLE   6D4

On an island on Loch Leven, Kinross. Access by boat from Kinross. Apr-Sept, opening standard. Oct-Mar, closed. Entrance charge. Parking available. (HS) Tel: 031-244 3101.

The tower is late 14th or early 15th-century. Mary, Queen of Scots was imprisoned here in 1567 and from it escaped eleven months later.

Loch Leven Nature Reserve: see No 1272.

872 LOCH LOMOND   4H4

Cruises available from a number of operators, including: MacFarlane & Son, Balmaha. Tel: (036 087) 214. Sweeney's Boatyard, Balloch. Tel: (0389) 52376. Loch Lomond Sailings, Balloch. Tel: (0389) 51481. Lomond Lady, Luss. Tel: (043 686) 257.

Loch Lomond, largest stretch of inland water in Britain, and framed by lovely mountain scenery, is a popular centre for all watersports. Cruises around the banks and attractive small islands are available.

873 LOCH MORAR   2E11

SE of Mallaig. Parking available.

Said to be the deepest fresh water loch in Britain and the home of Morag, a monster with a strong resemblance to the Loch Ness Monster.

874 LOCH NAN UAMH CAIRN   2E12

Off A830, S of Arisaig. Parking available.

The loch is famous for its association with Bonnie Prince Charlie. The memorial cairn on the shore marks the spot from which Prince Charles Edward Stuart sailed for France on 20 September 1746 after having wandered round the Highlands as a fugitive with a price of £30,000 on his head.

875 LOCH NESS 3A9

SW of Inverness

This striking 24-mile-long loch in the Great Glen forms part of the Caledonian Canal which links Inverness with Fort William. Up to 700 feet deep, the loch contains the largest volume of fresh water of any lake in the British Isles. Famous world wide for its mysterious inhabitant, the Loch Ness Monster, it is also ideal for cruising and sailing. (See also Nos 1012, 1026 and 1270).

Loch Ness Lodge Visitor Centre

876 LOCH NESS LODGE VISITOR CENTRE 3A9

A82 S from Inverness to Drumnadrochit, turn onto A831 to Cannich 50 metres on right. All year 0900-1800, June-Sept 0900-2100. Adult £2.00, child: £1.00, OAP: £1.75, family: £5.00 (2 adults and up to 5 children). Group rates: £1.75 for parties over 10. Parking available. (Loch Ness Lodge Hotel Co. Ltd.) Tel: (04562) 342.

Large screen cinema on Loch Ness, its history and myth. Pictorial display of local culture and items of interest. Gift shop. Coffee shop specialising in home baking. Loch Ness sonar scanning cruises.

877 LOCH NESS VIDEO SHOW 3A9

Kiltmaker, 4/9 Huntly Street, Inverness. Jun-mid Sept, Mon-Sat 0900-2100, Sun 0900-1700. Oct-May, Mon-Sat 0900-1600. Entrance charge. Parking available. Tel: (0463) 222781.

A 40-45 minute video show on the art of kiltmaking, and the Loch Ness Monster search. Preview of the Loch Ness Monster Exhibition at Drumnadrochit.

878 LOCH OF KINNORDY NATURE RESERVE 5D1

On B951, 1m W of Kirriemuir, Angus. Open daily throughout the year except Sat in Sept and Oct. Parking available. (RSPB) Tel: 031-557 3136.

Fresh water marsh with large numbers of nesting water birds. Small car park and three observation hides.

879 LOCH OF THE LOWES 5B1

Off A923, 2m NE of Dunkeld. Visitor Centre open Apr-Sept. Observation Hide is open permanently. Free. Parking available. (SWT) Tel: (0350) 727337.

Loch with woodland fringe, waterfowl and ospreys. Observation hide and Visitor Centre with wildlife display and slide programme.

880 LOCH TAY POTTERY 5A1

Loch Tay, Fearnan, 3 miles W of Kenmore. Jan-Dec. Daily, 0900-1800. (Occasionally closed for holidays, Oct-Mar: please telephone.) Free. Car parking only. Pottery shop. Tel: (0887) 830 251.

The pottery and showroom occupy an original croft house overlooking Loch Tay. An individual and wide-ranging selection of pottery, all hand-thrown, decorated with the owners' own glazes — some including ash from their own fires. Ovenware and tableware, plus customers' own commissions. All pottery sold solely on these premises.

881 LOCHALSH WOODLAND GARDEN 2F9

*Balmacara Estate, off A87, 3m E of Kyle of Lochalsh.
Garden: Jan-Dec, daily 0900-sunset. Information kiosk and Coach House:
May-late Sept, Mon-Sat 1000-1700, Sun 1400-1700. Entrance charge.
Parking available. (NTS) Tel: (059 986) 207.*

Set in the 5,616 acre Balmacara Estate, Lochalsh
Woodland Garden provides pleasant sheltered walks by
the loch. A wide variety of native trees and shrubs and
more exotic plants from Tasmania, New Zealand, the
Himalayas, Chile, Japan and China grow in the
grounds of Lochalsh House (not open to the public).
Information and coach house display, ranger-led walks
in the summer.

882 LOCHINDORB 3C9

Unclassified road off A939, 10m NW of Grantown-on-Spey.

On an island in this lonely loch stand the ruins of a
13th-century castle, once a seat of the Comyns. It was
occupied in person by Edward I in 1303 and greatly
strengthened. In 1336 Edward III raised the siege in
which the Countess of Atholl was beleaguered by the
Regent Moray's troops. In 1371 the castle became the
stronghold of the 'Wolf of Badenoch', the vicious Earl
of Buchan who terrorised the area. It was dismantled
in 1456.

Lochmaben Castle

883 LOCHMABEN CASTLE 5C9

*Off B7020 on S shore of Castle Loch, by Lochmaben, 9m ENE of
Dumfries. All reasonable times. Free. (HS) Tel: 031-244 3101.*

This castle was captured and recaptured twelve times
and also withstood six attacks and sieges. James IV
was a frequent visitor, and Mary, Queen of Scots was
here in 1565. Now a ruin, this early 14th-century
castle is on the site of a castle of the de Brus family,
ancestors of Robert the Bruce who is said to have been
born here.

884 LOCHORE MEADOWS COUNTRY PARK 6D4

*Between Lochgelly and Ballingry on B920. Country Park: At all times.
Park Centre: Summer 0900-2100, winter 0900-1700. Fishery: 15 Mar-6 Oct.
Charge for some Country Park facilities: concessions available.
Parking available. Cafeteria. Groups welcome—please book in advance.
Tel: (0592) 860086.*

Green, pleasant countryside around large loch reclaimed
from coal mining waste in the 1960s. Reclamation
makes fascinating story told in slide show, displays and
ranger-guided walks. Plenty of scope for birdwatching,
wildlife study, walks, picnics. Many ancient historical
remains. Cafe and information in park centre.
Activities include boat and bank fishing, sailing,
windsurfing, canoeing, golf, horse riding, trim trail,
wayfaring, self-guided trails, picnic areas. Wide range
of provisions for visitors with special needs. Children's
adventure play area.

885 LOCHRANZA CASTLE 4E6

On N coast of Isle of Arran. Open all reasonable times. Free. Apply custodian. (HS) Tel: 031-244 3101.

A picturesque ruin of a castle erected in the 13th/14th centuries and enlarged in the 16th. Robert the Bruce is said to have landed here on his return in 1307 from Rathlin in Ireland at the start of his campaign for Scottish independence.

886 LOCHWINNOCH NATURE RESERVE 4G6

Largs Road, Lochwinnoch, 9m SW of Paisley. All year, daily 1000-1715. Entrance charge. School parties by arrangement. Parking available. Shop. Weekend tearoom. (RSPB) Tel: (0505) 842663/031-557 3136.

Purpose-built Nature Centre with observation tower, displays and shop. Three observation hides overlooking marsh reached by walk through woods and along boardwalk.

Logan Botanic Garden

887 LOGAN BOTANIC GARDEN 4F11

& P T

Off B7065, 14m S of Stranraer. Mid Mar-Oct. Daily, 1000-1800. Entrance charge. Group concessions. Parking available. Shop. Restaurant (in season). Tel: (0776) 86231.

Part of the Royal Botanic Garden, Edinburgh. A profusion of plants from the warm and temperate regions of the world flourish in some of the mildest conditions in Scotland. There are cabbage palms, tree ferns and many other Southern Hemisphere species.

888 LOGAN FISH POND 4F11

Off B7065, 14m S of Stranraer. Easter-Sept, daily 1200-2000. Entrance charge. Tel: (0292) 268181.

This tidal pool in the rocks, 30 feet deep and 53 feet round, was completed in 1800 as a fresh-fish larder for Logan House. Damaged by a mine in 1942, it was reopened in 1955. It holds around thirty fish, mainly cod, so tame that they come to be fed by hand.

889 LOSSIEMOUTH FISHERIES AND COMMUNITY MUSEUM 3D7

& P T

Situated at the harbour, East Basin, Lossiemouth. Apr-Sept, Mon-Sat 1100-1700. Entrance charges. Parking available. Tel: (0343) 813772.

Permanent features include Memorial Room for local people lost or drowned, killed in active service, fishermen and study of the late J Ramsay McDonald, Prime Minister.

890 LOUDOUN HALL   4G7

*Boat Vennel, off Cross in Ayr town centre. Jul-end Aug, Mon-Sat
1000-1700 or by arrangement. Free, but donation box available. Group
visits if booked can have guided walk of Ayr (approx 1 hour) with light
refreshments. Parking available. Tel: (0292) 282109/611290/79077.*

A late 15th-century/early 16th-century town house
built for a rich merchant, one of the oldest surviving
examples of burgh architecture to remain in Scotland.
For a period it was the town house of the Campbells,
Earls of Loudoun, and the Moore family; both families
played prominent parts in the life of Ayr. Local history
publications for sale.

891 LOVAT MINERAL WATER   3A1

*Fanellan, just S of Beauly off A831 Cannich road. Apr-Oct.
Mon-Fri 0930-1630. Free. Parking available. Gift shop. Coffee shop/
restaurant. Tel: (0463) 74620.*

Built in 1991/92, this is one of Europe's most modern
mineral water bottling plants. The Visitor Centre
incorporates a viewing gallery of production areas,
scale models of catchment area, production lines and
boreholes. Video, staff on hand to explain processes.

892 LUFFNESS   6G5

*1m E of Aberlady on A198. By arrangement. Free. Parking available.
(Luffness Ltd) Tel: (087 57) 218.*

A 16th-century castle with a 13th-century keep built
on the site of a Norse camp. There are extensive old
fortifications, an old moat and gardens.

893 LUNDERSTON BAY   4G5

*On coast road, A770, from Gourock to Inverkip. Jan-Dec.
Daily, 0900-1600 in winter, 0900-2030 summer. Free. Parking available.
Tel: (0475) 521129.*

Part of Clyde Muirshiel Regional Park, Lunderston
Bay is a coastal site with a large grassed area, picnic
sites and toilets. The shoreline contains rocky outcrops,
pools and two sandy beach areas, looking out towards
the Cowal peninsula. A path runs along the head of
the shore for approximately ¾ mile. Ranger-led walks
available.

894 LYTH ARTS CENTRE   3D3

*Signposted 4 miles off A9 between Wick and John o' Groats.
Jul-Aug, daily 1000-1800. Entrance charge, free for children, students,
OAP, unemployed. Parking available. Snack bar.
Tel: (095 584) 270 (Apr-Sept)./031-226 6424 (Oct-Mar).*

Up to ten new exhibitions of contemporary fine art
shown simultaneously each season, ranging from local
landscape to the work of established British and
foreign artists. Regular performances by touring
drama, music and dance companies.

895 McCAIG'S TOWER   4E2

On a hill overlooking Oban. All times. Free.

McCaig was a local banker who tried to curb
unemployment by using local craftsmen to build this
tower from 1897-1900 as a memorial to his family. Its
walls are two feet thick and from 30-47 feet high. The
courtyard within is landscaped and the tower is
floodlit at night in summer. An observation platform
on the seaward side was added in 1983.

**896 HUGH MACDIARMID MEMORIAL
SCULPTURE**   **5D9**

*At Whita Hill Yett, approx 2m NE of Langholm on the Langholm to
Newcastleton road. At any time.*

Steel and bronze sculpture by Jake Harvey to
commemorate the literary achievements of the
Langholm-born poet and Scots Revivalist. Nearby is
Malcolm Monument.

---

897 FLORA MACDONALD'S BIRTHPLACE   **2A10**

*W of A865, 200 yds up farm track ½m N of Gearraidh Bhailteas
(Milton), Isle of South Uist. All times. Free.*

A cairn inside the ruins of an old thatched house marks
the spot where Flora Macdonald was born in 1722.
Parking at Kildonan Museum close by.

---

898 FLORA MACDONALD'S MONUMENT   **3B8**

Inverness Castle. All times. Free.

Monument to Flora Macdonald (1722-1790) on the
esplanade of the Victorian castle. Flora Macdonald is
famed for the help she gave to the Young Pretender in
June 1746, enabling him to escape from Benbecula to
Portree.

**899 SIR HECTOR MacDONALD'S
MEMORIAL**   **3A8**

Mitchell Hill, Dingwall. All times. Free.

An impressive monument erected to the memory of
General Sir Hector MacDonald, who was born near
Dingwall in the parish of Ferintosh in 1853.

---

900 McEWAN GALLERY   **3E11**
 ♿
 A

*On A939, 1m W of Ballater. Jan-Dec exc Christmas & New Year.
Daily 1000-1800. Free. Parking available. Tel: (033 97) 55429.*

An unusual house built by the Swiss artist Rudolphe
Christen in 1902, containing works of art, mainly of
the Scottish school. Also history, natural history,
sporting books, bronzes and ceramics. Occasional
special exhibitions are held. Full advisory and
restoration services.

---

901 RODERICK MACKENZIE MEMORIAL   **2H10**

1m E of Ceannacroc on A887, 13m W of Invermoriston. All times. Free.

A cairn on the south of the road commemorates
Roderick Mackenzie, who in 1746 pretended to be
Prince Charles Edward Stuart and was killed by
soldiers searching for the Prince after Culloden.

**902 MACLAURIN GALLERY AND ROZELLE
HOUSE**   **4G7**

*1½m S of Ayr, off road to Burns Cottage at Alloway. Free.
Parking available. Tel: (0292) 45447.*

Set in extensive parkland the gallery was formerly
stables and servants' quarters attached to the mansion
house. A programme of temporary exhibitions operates
throughout the year covering Fine Art, Sculpture,
Photography and Crafts. The gallery shows many major
Arts Council exhibitions. Rozelle House operates a
programme of temporary exhibitions and also houses
the Maclaurin Contemporary Art Collection and the
District Collection's Henry Moore sculpture in the
gallery courtyard.

903 **McLEAN MUSEUM AND
ART GALLERY**   **4G5**

*15 Kelly Street, Greenock. Jan-Dec. Mon-Sat 1000-1200, 1300-1700.
Free. Parking available. Shop. Tel: (0475) 23741.*

A local museum with art collection, natural history,
shipping exhibits, ethnographic material and items
relating to James Watt, who was born in Greenock.
Wheelchair access at front of building.

MacLellan's Castle

904 **MacLELLAN'S CASTLE**   **5A11**

*Off High Street, Kirkcudbright. Apr-Sept, opening standard. Oct-Mar,
weekends only. Entrance charge. Group concessions. (HS) Tel: 031-244 3101.*

A handsome castellated mansion overlooking the
harbour, dating from 1577. Elaborately planned with
fine architectural details, it has been a ruin since 1752.
In Kircudbright also see the 16th/17th-century
Tolbooth and the Mercat Cross of 1610.

905 **MACPHERSON MONUMENT**   **3B10**

Off old A9 (A86), 3m NE of Kingussie. All times. Free.

Obelisk to James 'Ossian' Macpherson (1736-1796),
Scottish poet and 'translator' of the Ossianic poems.

906 **MacROBERT ARTS CENTRE**   **6A5**

*University of Stirling. Group rates. Parking available.
Tel: (0786) 61081 or 73171, ext 2543.*

A five-hundred seat theatre, art gallery and studio,
providing all year theatre, opera, dance, films, concerts,
conferences and exhibitions. Theatre bar. For details of
events, contact the box office. Induction loop system.

907 **MacTAGGART POOL**   **4C6**

*School Street, Bowmore, Isle of Islay. Jan-Dec. Tues-Fri 1230-2030, Sat &
Sun 1030-1730. Entrance charges. Group concessions. Parking available.
Shop. Refreshments. Tel: (049 681) 767.*

Swimming pool (25 metres) with sauna, conference
rooms, aerobic facility.

908 **MABIE RECREATION AREA**   **5B10**

*Mabie Forest, Ae Village, 3½ miles S of Dumfries on A710.
All reasonable times. Charge for car park (disabled drivers free).
Tel: (0387) 86247.*

Woodland recreational area with a variety of walks,
including two for less able walkers, four cycle routes,
children's play area with forest play structures, picnic
sites with toilets including some for disabled visitors,
forest nature reserve (birds and butterflies), barbecues.

909 MACHRIE MOOR STANDING STONES 4E7

1½ E of A841, along Moss Farm Road, S of Machrie on W coast of Arran. All reasonable times. Free. (HS) Tel: 031-244 3101.

These 15-feet high standing stones are the impressive remains of six Bronze Age stone circles. Some have now fallen.

910 MAES HOWE 1B11

Off A965, 9m W of Kirkwall, Orkney. Opening standard. Entrance charge. Group concessions. Parking available. (HS) Tel: 031-244 3101.

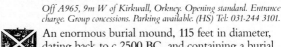

ASVA

An enormous burial mound, 115 feet in diameter, dating back to c 2500 BC, and containing a burial chamber which is unsurpassed in Western Europe. In the 12th century Viking marauders broke into it in search of treasures and Norse crusaders sheltered from a storm in the Howe. They engraved a rich collection of runic inscriptions upon the walls.

911 MAGNUM LEISURE CENTRE 4G6

& T

From Glasgow take the A736 to Irvine and follow signs for Harbourside (Magnum). Jan-Dec, daily 0900-2200. Entrance charges. Parking available. Shop. Bars, restaurant, fast food. Tel: (0294) 78381.

Leisure Centre attractions include new state-of-the art indoor water park, indoor bowling, sports hall, ice rink, theatre/cinema, soft play area, 'kiddies superbounce' area (May to August only), squash courts, sauna, fitness salon.

912 MAID OF THE FORTH 6D6

& A

Hawes Pier, South Queensferry, 7 miles W of Edinburgh. Easter-Sept. Daily. Sailing schedule on request. Charge for cruises. Group concessions. Parking available. Gift shop, tearoom and bar on board. Tel: 031-331 4857.

Boat trip under the Forth Bridge and downriver to Inchcolm Island to visit 12th-century Augustinian abbey. Bird sanctuary, seals may also be seen. Full commentary on the way. Cruise time 2½ hours, including 1½ hours on Inchcolm. (See No 758).

913 MAINSRIDDLE POTTERY 5B10

& A

The Tenements, Mainsriddle, 15 miles SW of Dumfries on A710. Jan-Dec. Daily 1000-1800 (Showroom only). Car parking only. Tel: (038 778) 633.

Small studio pottery, specialising in handmade stoneware and porcelain. Showroom displays a changing selection of colourful pots, all made on the premises.

914 MALLAIG MARINE WORLD 2E11

& T

The Harbour, Mallaig, 45 miles N of Fort William on A830. Jun-Sept, daily, 0900-2100, Oct-May 0900-1700. Entrance charges. Family tickets. Group concessions. Parking available. Gift shop. Tel: (0687) 2292.

Marine aquarium and exhibition featuring local marine species. Fishing displays on the work of the Mallaig fishing fleet. Video illustrating boats at work at different fishings and in all weathers, including the work of the lifeboat. Pond garden, indoor and outdoor seating, marine scientist on hand.

915 MALLENY HOUSE GARDENS 6D7

In Balerno, off A70, 7½m SW of Edinburgh. Gardens: open all year, daily 1000-sunset. Entrance charge. Parking available. (NTS) Tel: 031-226 5922.

Adjoining a 17th-century house (not open) is a garden with many interesting plants including a good collection of shrub roses. The National Bonsai Collection for Scotland is housed here. No dogs please.

Manderston

916 MANDERSTON   5F5

Off A6105, 2m E of Duns. Mid May-Sep, Thu & Sun 1400-1730.
Entrance charges for house and grounds. Group concessions by
arrangement. Shop. Tearoom. Tel: (0361) 83450.

One of the finest Edwardian country houses in
Scotland, with extensive estate buildings and gardens
particularly noted for their rhododendrons. The house
contains a silver staircase, thought to be unique.
Gardens, stables and marble dairy.

917 MARINER LEISURE CENTRE   6B6

On A803 1m W of Falkirk's High Street and 24m from Glasgow and
Edinburgh. All year, daily. Cafeteria. Parking available.
Tel: (0324) 22083.

Lagoon-shaped pool with wave machine, games hall,
squash courts, sauna and solarium, fitness room, creche
or general purpose room.

918 MARJORIBANKS MONUMENT   5F6

At E entrance to Coldstream. All times. Free.

Obelisk with a stone figure of Charles Marjoribanks,
elected the First Member of Parliament for Berwickshire
after the passing of the Reform Act of 1832.

919 MARNOCH OLD CHURCH   3F8

Situated off the A97 Banff-Huntly Road. Free. Parking available.
Access obtainable by telephoning Aberchirder (04665) 885/276.

The forced induction of an unwanted minister here in
1841 was a flashpoint leading to the Disruption of the
Kirk in 1843 and the formation of the Free Church.
Erected 1792. Standing stone nearby.

Mar's Wark

920 MAR'S WARK   6A5

At the top of Castle Wynd, Stirling. All reasonable times. Free. (HS)
Tel: 031-244 3101.

Mar's Wark is one of a number of fine old buildings on
the approach to Stirling Castle. Built c 1570 by the first
Earl of Mar, Regent of Scotland, it was a residence of
the Earls of Mar until the 6th Earl had to flee the
country after leading the 1715 Jacobite Rebellion.

921 MARTELLO TOWER 1B12

Hackness, Island of Hoy, Orkney. All times. Can be viewed from the outside only. (HS) Tel: 031-244 3101.

An impressive tower built during the Napoleonic and American wars at the beginning of the 19th century. The tower was renovated in 1866 and used again in the First World War.

922 MARTYRS' MONUMENT 4H10

Near Wigtown, A714, 7m S of Newton Stewart. All reasonable times. Free. Tel: (0671) 2431.

A monument on the hill and a pillar on the shore of Wigtown Bay where in 1685 two women, aged 18 and 63, were tied to stakes and drowned for their religious beliefs during the persecution of the Covenanters in 'the Killing Times'. Their graves may be seen in the churchyard.

Marwick Head Nature Reserve

923 MARWICK HEAD NATURE RESERVE 1A11

Access along path N from Marwick Bay, Orkney. Any time. Free. Parking available. (RSPB)
Tel: (0856) 850176/031-557 3136.

Seabird cliffs with huge and spectacular colonies of seabirds. Best time April-July. Also the clifftop memorial to Lord Kitchener, close by the point where the cruiser *HMS Hampshire*, taking Kitchener to Russia, was sunk in 1916.

924 MARY, QUEEN OF SCOTS HOUSE 5E7

Queen Street, Jedburgh. Easter-mid Nov, daily 1000-1700. Entrance charge. Group concessions. Parking available.
Tel: (0835) 63331/(0450) 73457.

A 16th-century bastel house in which Mary, Queen of Scots is reputed to have stayed in 1566 when attending the Court of Justice. Now a new, thought-provoking visitor centre offering a fresh interpretation of the Mary theme.

925 MAXWELTON HOUSE 5B9

13m NW of Dumfries on B729, 3 miles W of Moniaive. House, Gardens, Chapel and Museum: Easter-Sept. Daily, 1030-1730. Parking available. Gift shop, antiques and crafts. Tearoom. Tel: (084 82) 385.

ASVA

The house dates back to the 14th-15th centuries. It was originally the stronghold of the Earls of Glencairn, later (1682) the birthplace of Annie Laurie, of the famous Scottish ballad. House totally restored by the late Hugh C Stenhouse, 1970. The Victorian chapel is still used for weddings and christenings; and the museum displays early domestic, farming and gardening tools.

926   MAYBOLE COLLEGIATE CHURCH   4G8

In Maybole, S of A77. Not open to the public—can be viewed from outside.
Free. (HS) Tel: 031-244 3101.

The roofless ruin of a 15th-century church, built for a
small college established in 1373 by the Kennedies of
Dunure.

927   MEADOWSWEET HERB GARDEN   4F10

Soulseat Loch, Castle Kennedy, Stranraer. Turn off A75 at Inch Church.
May-Aug. Daily exc Wed, 1200-1700. Entrance charge. Parking available.
Gift shop. Tel: (0776) 82288.

On the site of Soulseat Abbey, of which only a few
mounds remain, Meadowsweet Herb Gardens
occupies a 'tongue' in Soulseat Loch. Galloway's
original herb garden has over 120 herbs in individual
display beds. Fresh and dried herbs are sold, and herb
teas can be sampled.

928   MEFFAN INSTITUTE   5D1

&   *20 West High Street, Forfar. Jan-Dec. Mon-Sat 1000-1700. Free.*
P   *Gift shop. Tel: (0307) 68813 or 64123.*
T

Art gallery and museum has two exhibition galleries,
one exhibiting works from the permanent collection
of Angus District Council, and the other staging
touring exhibitions, which feature works by major
Scottish and international contemporary artists in a
wide-ranging programme. The museum is designed to
tell the story of Forfar.

929   MEGGINCH CASTLE GARDENS   6E2

&   *A85, 10m E of Perth. Apr-Jun and Sep, Wed only 1400-1700, Jul and*
A   *Aug, Mon-Fri 1400-1700. Entrance charge. Parking available.*
P   *Tel: (0821) 642222.*

The gardens around the 15th-century castle have
daffodils, rhododendrons and 1,000-year-old yews.
There is a double-walled kitchen garden, 16th-century
rose garden and 19th-century flower parterre as well as
the Gothic courtyard with pagoda-roofed dovecote.
There is also an interesting example of topiary,
including a golden yew crown. The 18th-century
physic garden contains a new astrological garden.

Meigle Museum

930   MEIGLE MUSEUM   5C1

In Meigle, on A94, 12m WSW of Forfar. Apr-Sept, opening standard.
Oct-Mar, closed. Entrance charge. (HS) Tel: 031-244 3101.

This magnificent collection of 25 sculptured
monuments of the Celtic Christian period, all found
at or near the old churchyard, forms one of the most
notable assemblages of Dark Age sculpture in Western
Europe.

931 MEIKLEOUR BEECH HEDGE 6D1

A93, just S of Meikleour, 12m NNE of Perth. Parking available.

Listed as the highest of its kind in the world, the
Beech Hedge was planted in 1746 and is now 580
yards long and 100 feet high. Information board.

Mellerstain House

932 MELLERSTAIN HOUSE 5E6

*Off A6089, 7m NW of Kelso. Easter; May-Sep, Sun-Fri 1230-1630.
Entrance charge. Group rates for parties over 20. Parking available.
Gift shop. Self-service tearoom. Tel: (057 381) 225.*

This is one of the most attractive mansions open to
the public in Scotland, with exceptionally beautiful
interior decoration and plaster work. Begun about
1725 by William Adam, it was completed between
1770 and 1778 by William's son Robert. There are
attractive terraced gardens and pleasant grounds with
fine views, a lake and thatched cottage.

933 MELROSE ABBEY 5E6

*Main Square, Melrose. Opening standard. Entrance charge. Group concessions.
Parking available. (HS) Tel: 031-244 3101.*

ASVA

This Cistercian Abbey, founded in 1136, is notable for
its fine traceried stonework. It suffered the usual
attacks of all the Border abbeys during English
invasions, but parts of the nave and choir dating from
a rebuilding of 1385 include some of the best and most
elaborate work of the period in Scotland. In addition
to the flamboyant stonework, note on the roof the
figure of a pig playing the bagpipes. There is an
interesting museum in the Commendator's House, at
the entrance.

934 MELROSE MOTOR MUSEUM 5E6

*200 yards from Melrose Abbey, towards Newstead. Mid May-mid Oct,
daily 1030-1730 or by arrangement. Part-time from Easter to mid May.
Entrance charges. Group concessions. Parking available.
Tel: (089 682) 2624 or (0835) 22356.*

Private collection with vehicles on loan, mainly vintage
from 1909 to the late 1960s. Excellent motorcycles and
bicycles with a quantity of old signs and memorabilia.
Display cases of toy cars, cigarette cards, etc.

935 MELVILLE MONUMENT 6A2

*1m N of Comrie, 6m W of Crieff. Access by footpath from parking place
on Glen Lednock road. All times. Free. Parking available.*

The obelisk in memory of Lord Melville (1742-1811)
stands on Dunmore, a hill of 840 feet, with delightful
views of the surrounding country. The access path is
linked to the scenic 4 mile Glen Lednock Circular
Walk, running from Comrie and back through varied
woodland (signposted).

Menstrie Castle

936　MENSTRIE CASTLE　　6B4

In Menstrie, A91, 5m E of Stirling. Exhibition Rooms: Opening by
arrangement with NTS Perth office. Tel: (0738) 31296.

The 16th-century restored castle was the birthplace of
Sir William Alexander, James VI's Lieutenant for the
Plantation of Nova Scotia. A Nova Scotia Exhibition
Room (NTS) displays the coats of arms of 109 Nova
Scotia Baronetcies.

937　MERTOUN GARDENS　　5E7

St Boswells. Apr-Sept, Sat, Sun & Mon Public Holidays 1400-1800
(last entry 1730). Entrance charge. Group concessions. Parking available.
Tel: (0835) 23236.

20 acres of beautiful grounds with delightful walks
and river views. Fine trees, herbaceous borders and
flowering shrubs. Walled garden and well preserved
circular dovecote thought to be the oldest in the
county. No dogs please.

938　MIDHOWE BROCH AND CAIRNS　　1B10

On the W coast of the island of Rousay, Orkney. All reasonable times.
Free. (HS) Tel: 031-244 3101.

An Iron Age broch and walled enclosure situated on a
promontory cut off by a deep rock-cut ditch. Adjacent
is Midhowe Stalled Cairn 'an elongated ship of death'.
The island of Rousay has many other chambered
tombs.

939　MILL OF TOWIE　　3E8

Auchindachy, 3 miles SW of Keith on B9014. Mill: Easter-Christmas,
Mon-Sat 1000, Sun 1100-1600. Grain Store: May-Oct. Mon-Sat exc
Tues, 1030-1700. Sun 1030-1830. Entrance charges. Parking available.
Craft shop. Restaurant/tearoom. Tel: (054 281) 307.

On the edge of the Drummuir Castle estate (see No
372), the Mill of Towie is a restored 19th-century
water mill, now working to produce stone-ground
oatmeal in the traditional manner. Visitors can follow
the process around three floors of machinery, all
powered by nature. The Craft Shop on the ground
floor of the mill sells local crafts, hand-painted silk
scarves and hangings produced by resident artist May
Dempster, and oatmeal products from the mill.
Restaurant in nearby Grain Store building. Play area,
Shetland ponies, picnic tables.

940 MILL ON THE FLEET 5A10

High Street, Gatehouse of Fleet. Mar-Oct (all year for booked parties). Daily, 1000-1730 (last admission to exhibition 1630). Nov-late Dec, weekends only 1130-1600. Entrance charge. Disabled parking on site. Gift shop. Tearoom. Tel: (0557) 814099.

The Mill on the Fleet Heritage Centre, based in a restored 18th-century cotton mill, recalls the industrial history of the town. Exhibition with sound, two audio-visual programmes illustrating Galloway landscape and history, plus further temporary and permanent exhibits. Special feature about water and water power. Tearoom gives access to riverside terrace.

941 MILLBUIES LOCHS 3D8

Longmorn, 5 miles S of Elgin on A941 to Rothes. Jan-Dec (fishing Mar-Oct). Daily. Free. Parking available. Tel: (0343) 86234.

The lochs are in a wooded setting with numerous walks where wildlife and flora can be seen. Four boats are available for anglers.

Hugh Miller

942 HUGH MILLER'S COTTAGE 3B7

Church Street, Cromarty, 22m NE of Inverness via Kessock Bridge. Apr-Sept, Mon-Sat 1000-1300, 1400-1700; Sun 1400-1700. Entrance charges. (NTS) Tel: (038 17) 245.

The birthplace of Hugh Miller (1802-56), stonemason, who became an eminent geologist, theologian and writer. The furnished thatched cottage, built c 1711 by Miller's great-grandfather, contains an exhibition and video programme on his life and work. Cottage garden.

943 MILNHOLM CROSS 5E9

1 mile S of Newcastleton beside B6357. All times. Parking available.

Erected around 1320, and owned by the Clan Armstrong Trust, Milnholm Cross is a memorial to Alexander Armstrong who was murdered in Hermitage Castle some four miles away. It faces the ruin of Mangerton Castle, seat of the Armstrong chiefs for three hundred years. Nearby, in Newcastleton, is the Janet Armstrong House, museum and clan information centre of the Armstrongs, open from Easter to September.

944 MINARD CASTLE 4F4

Off A83, 14m S of Inveraray. May-Oct, Mon-Fri 1100-1600. Viewing by appointment only. Tel: (0546) 86272.

The castle is originally 16th-century with subsequent extensions and contains paintings of the Franco-Scottish Royal House.

945 MOAT PARK HERITAGE CENTRE 5B6

    Biggar town centre. Easter-Oct, Mon-Sat 1000-1700, Sun 1400-1700.
    Entrance charge. Parking available. Gift shop. Tel: (0899) 21050.

This former church has been adapted to display the
history of the Upper Clyde and Tweed Valleys, from
the days of the volcano and the glacier right up to
yesterday's newspapers. Fine collection of embroidery
including the largest known patchwork cover,
containing over eighty figures from the 1850s.

946 MOFFAT MUSEUM 5C8

    The Neuk, off High Street, Moffat. Easter week, Whit-Sept, Mon-Sat
    exc Wed 1030-1300, 1430-1700, Sun 1430-1700. Entrance charge.
    Family tickets. Tel: (0683) 20868.

Situated in an old bakehouse in the oldest part of the
town. The Scotch oven is a feature of the ground
floor. The museum tells the story of Moffat and its
people, including Border raids, Covenanters,
education, sports and pastimes, famous people
associated with the town.

947 MOFFAT POTTERY 5C8

    20 High Street, Moffat. Jan-Dec. Mon-Sat 0900-1700. Free.
    Tel: (0683) 20793.

Studio pottery known as the home of Moffat's
'Singing Potter', Gerard Lyons. Pots, tapes and
paintings of the potter, also metal sculptures by John
McPhail and jewellery by Irene McPhail.

948 MONIKIE COUNTRY PARK 5D1

    Off B962, 1m N of Newbigging, 10m N of Dundee. Signposted. All
    year exc Christmas & New Year, 1000-dusk. Parking available. Souvenirs.
    Tearoom (May-Sept). Tel: (082 623) 202.

Country park situated on a reservoir complex of three
areas of water, constructed by the Dundee Water
Company over a span of 20 years from 1845. Ground
consists of parkland, conifer and mixed woodlands,
and covers 185 acres. Countryside Ranger Service,
woodland walks, watersports including canoeing,
sailing and windsurfing courses. Children's play area,
rowing, sailing and windsurf hire, picnic areas with
barbecue sites.

**949 MONTROSE MUSEUM AND ART
GALLERY** 5E1

    Panmure Place. Jan-Dec. Mon-Sat 1000-1700. Free. Car parking only.
    Gift shop. Tel: (0674) 73232.

Museum exhibits tell the story of Montrose from prehistoric times, including Pictish stones from Inchbrayock
and Farnell, the maritime history of the port, local
geology and wildlife. Montrose silver, pottery, whaling
and Napoleonic artefacts are of particular interest. The
art gallery features many local artists including George
Paul Chambers. Temporary exhibitions feature
contemporary Scottish artists.

950 MONUMENT HILL 4F2

    2m SW of Dalmally, off the old road to Inveraray. All times. Free.

Monument to Duncan Ban Macintyre (1724-1812),
the 'Burns of the Highlands', who was born near
Inveroran.

951   MONYMUSK ARTS CENTRE   3G10
&
T
Monymusk, 18 miles W of Aberdeen on A944 Alford road. May-Sept (crafts), Sept-Feb (music). Daily 1000-1600. Charge for performances. Parking available. Gift shop. Tearoom.

Musical recitals, arts and crafts exhibitions, a museum of local history and topography all have a place in this building, originally an 18th-century lapidary mill. In 1801 the Episcopal congregation at Blairdaff moved to Monymusk and converted the mill into a church. During World War II the church was boarded up and used to store furniture for the next fifty years, but has now been restored by the Monymusk Arts Trust. The church organ is the subject of a restoration project.

952   MONYMUSK WALLED GARDEN   3G10
&
Home Farm, Monymusk, 20 miles from Aberdeen on B993. Mar-Oct: Tues-Sat 1000-1700, Sun 1400-1700. Nov-Mar: Tues, Thurs, Sat 1000-1500. Also open most Mons in Apr, May, Sept, Oct. Parking available. Tel: (046 77) 543.

In 1796, Monymusk Walled Garden was 'a gloire to the parrish and delighte to the beholder'. Currently under restoration, it is now a nursery garden specialising in herbaceous plants and including unusual varieties. Trees, shrubs, climbers, seeds and bulbs available. Walks, gardening courses throughout the year. Period plants and display borders.

953   MORAY MOTOR MUSEUM   3D8
&
T
Bridge Street, Elgin. ½ mile off main Inverness-Aberdeen road. April-Oct. Daily, 1100-1700. Entrance charge. Parking available. Small shop. Restaurant. Tel: (0343) 542660.

Over forty exhibits of cars and motor bikes from 1904 to 1968, including Jaguar, Rolls Royce, Bentley, Bristol.

954   MORTLACH CHURCH   3E8
&
A
Dufftown. Easter-Oct, daily 1000-1600 (except during services). Donations appreciated. Tel: (0340) 20380.

Founded c 566 AD by St Moluag. Part of present building dates from 11th/12th centuries. In 1016 it was lengthened by 3 spears' length on the command of King Malcolm after his victory over the Danes. Believed to be one of the oldest churches in continual use for public worship. Sculptured stones in vestibule and very fine stained glass. Battle stone in churchyard; old watch tower.

955   MORTON CASTLE   5B8
A702, 17m NNW of Dumfries. Closed to the public but may be viewed from the outside. (HS) Tel: 031-244 3101.

Beside a small loch, this castle was occupied by Randolph, first Earl of Moray, as Regent for David II. It afterwards passed to the Douglases and is now a well-preserved ruin.

956   MOSSBURN ANIMAL CENTRE   5C9
Hightae, 6 miles W of Lockerbie on B7020. Jan-Dec exc Christmas. Daily, 1030-1600. Donations appreciated. Parking available. Tel: (0387) 811288.

Horse and pony rescue centre with other animals and reptiles which visitors may handle while learning about their habits and needs. Picnic area with barbecue, woodland walks.

957 MOTTE OF MARK   5E7

Off A710, 5m S of Dalbeattie. All reasonable times. Free.

An ancient hill fort on the estuary of the River Urr at
Rockliffe, overlooking Rough Island, an NTS bird
sanctuary. This motte is one of the best preserved
examples in Scotland. Good views of Cumbrian hills.

958 MOTTE OF URR   5B10

Off B794, 5m NE of Castle Douglas. All reasonable times. Free.

The most extensive motte & bailey castle in Scotland,
dating from the 12th century A.D., though the bailey
may have been an earlier earthwork of hillfort type.

959 MOUSA BROCH   1G5

*On the island of Mousa, accessible by boat from Sandwick, Shetland.
Daily bus service between Lerwick and Sandwick. Boat for hire; May-Sep
afternoons; also Sat and Sun mornings, and some evenings.
Open at all reasonble times. Free. (HS) Tel: 031-244 3101.*

The best preserved example of the remarkable Iron Age
broch towers peculiar to Scotland. The tower stands
over 40 feet high. Its outer and inner walls contain a
rough staircase which can be climbed to the parapet.

960 MUGDOCK COUNTRY PARK   4H5

*3 miles N of Milngavie, 3 miles S of Strathblane on A81. Jan-Dec. Daily.
Visitor Centre 1300-1630. Free. Car parking only. Gift shop. Tearoom.
Tel: 041-956 6100.*

Woodlands, marshes, lochs, pastures and the remains
of Mugdock and Craigend Castles. Information and
exhibition centre, picnic areas, barbecue site, adventure
play areas, footpaths (most suitable for wheelchairs),
viewpoints, bridleway and orienteering course.
Programme of guided walks, talks and educational
facilities.

961 JOHN MUIR COUNTRY PARK   6H5

*W side of Dunbar, East Lothian. Jan-Dec. All times. Free. Parking available.
Tel: (0368) 63886.*

Country park, established 1976 and named after John
Muir who lived in Dunbar before emigrating to
America. He was in the forefront of the movement to
establish the National Parks in America — Yosemite,
Sequoia and General Grant National Parks. The
country park extends for 8½ miles from Dunbar
Castle, with a variety of natural habitats to explore
including cliffs, dunes, saltmarsh and woodlands.
Clifftop trail gives access to the coastline.

962 JOHN MUIR HOUSE   6H5

*126-128 High St, Dunbar. Jun-Sept or by arrangement with Dunbar
TIC. Free. Parking available. Tel: (0368) 63353. (TIC)*

Birthplace of John Muir, famous American
conservationist and author (See 961 above). The top
flat has been restored to the period (1838).

963 MUIRSHIEL COUNTRY PARK   4G6

*Off B786, N of Lochwinnoch, 9m SW of Paisley. Jan-Dec, daily
1000-1600 (winter), 1000-1800 (summer). Free. Parking available.
Tel: (0505) 842803.*

Attractive countryside featuring trails and walks on an
old shooting estate at the head of the Calder Valley,
with picnic sites and an information centre. Ranger-
led walks.

964 MULL MUSEUM
             4C1

♿ *Main Street, Tobermory, Isle of Mull. Easter-mid Oct, Mon-Fri 1030-1630, Sat 1030-1330. Entrance charge.*

Local history museum situated on Main Street.

965 MULL RAILWAY
             4D2

♿
T
*Old Pier Station, Craignure, Isle of Mull. Easter-mid Oct. Mon-Sat. Sunday operates only when Caledonian-MacBrayne are running a Sunday service. Single/return fares. Family tickets. Souvenirs. Tearoom at Torosay Castle. Trains can be chartered by prior arrangement and group booking and charters must be made direct with the company.
(Mull & West Highland Narrow Gauge Railway Co Ltd, Smiddy House, Aros, Isle of Mull.)
Tel: (068 02) 494 (station) or (0680) 300389 (out of season).*

10¼″ gauge railway operating a scheduled service to Torosay Castle and Gardens (see No 1297) from Craignure (Old Pier) Station. Steam and diesel-hauled trains, superb sea and mountain panorama and woodland journey. Distance 1¼ miles, journey time 20 minutes. The first passenger railway on a Scottish island. Limited accommodation on trains for disabled passengers in wheelchairs.

966 MULL LITTLE THEATRE
             4C1

*Dervaig, Isle of Mull. Open Spring-Autumn.
Tel: (068 84) 250/(0688) 2062.*

World famous as Britain's smallest professional theatre. It holds 43 seats in a converted cow byre. Continuous repertory of four varied plays featuring two or more actors, with some other shows out of season.

967 MUNESS CASTLE
             1H2

SE corner of Isle of Unst, Shetland. Open at all reasonable times. Free. Apply keykeeper. (HS) Tel: 031-244 3101.

A late 16th-century building, rubble-built with fine architectural detail.

Murray's Monument: see No 589.

968 MUSEUM NAN EILEAN
             2D4

Francis Street, Stornoway. Jun-Aug, Tues-Sat 1000-1230, 1400-1730, Sep-May Tues-Sat 1400-1700. Free. Tel: (0851) 3773.

The museum contains displays illustrating aspects of the history of Lewis and the daily life and work of its people with sections on archaeology, agriculture and working life, domestic life, and fishing and the sea. A further gallery is devoted to a changing programme of temporary and travelling exhibitions.

969 MUSEUM OF BORDER ARMS AND ARMOUR
             5D8

9m S of Hawick on A7 at Teviothead. All year, daily 0900-1900. Entrance charge. Parking available. Tel: (045 085) 237.

Former smithy with craft gallery. The museum houses a display of weapons and equipment from the 16th century.

970 MUSEUM OF THE CUMBRAES
             4G6

♿
A
T
*Garrison House, Millport, Isle of Cumbrae. Jun-Sept, Mon-Sat 1100-1300, 1330-1700. Other times by arrangement. Free. Parking available.
Tel: (0475) 530741.*

A fine local museum showing the island way of life includes photographs, memorabilia and local objects. New temporary exhibitions each summer. Gardens.

971 MUSEUM OF FLIGHT   6H5

& *By East Fortune Airfield, off B1347, 4½m S of North Berwick.*
T *Apr-Sept, daily 1030-1630, and several open days. Entrance charge.*
Parking available. Shop. Tearoom. (NMS) Tel: (062 088) 308.

Aircraft on display at this World War II former RAF
airfield range from a supersonic Lightning fighter to
the last Comet 4 which was in airline service. The
varied collection also includes a Spitfire and a 1930
Puss Moth. Special exhibitions relate to the
development of fighter aircraft from 1914 to 1940 and
to the airship R34 which flew from East Fortune to
New York in 1919. Toilets, picnic area.

972 MUSEUM OF ISLAY LIFE   4B6

& *Port Charlotte, Isle of Islay. Easter-Oct, Mon-Sat 1000-1700, Sun*
T *1400-1700. Nov-Mar, Mon-Wed 1000-1300. Other times by arrangement.*
Entrance charges. Parking available. Gift shop. Tel: (049 685) 358 or 393.

Award-winning museum with changing displays of
pre-history, traditional craft work and tools, a
maritime section, domestic bygones, children's corner
and quizzes for all ages. An important collection of
carved stones, from the 6th to the 16th century, can be
seen in the lapidarium below the museum.

973 MUSEUM OF LEAD MINING   5B8

& *Wanlockhead, 6 miles from M74 Abington, 6 miles from A76 Mennock.*
T *End Mar-Nov, daily, 1100-1630 (last tour 1600). Nov-Mar, by*
appointment only. Entrance charge. Parking available. Gift shop.
Restaurant, tearoom. Tel: (065 974) 387.

At Wanlockhead, one of Scotland's highest villages,
guides take visitors through the dark underground
world of Lochnell lead mine. Life in a miner's home,
over two centuries, is also shown. Visitor centre
houses a fine collection of rare minerals extracted
locally. There are hands-on displays, mineral collecting
areas and an open-air visitor trail.

974 MUSEUM SGOIL LIONACLEIT   2A9

& *On island of Benbecula, 4m S of Baile a'Mhanaich (Balivanich) on the B892.*
T *All year. Free. Parking available. Cafeteria. Tel: (0870) 602211, ext 137.*

The museum organises exhibitions and other events
designed to illustrate aspects of the history and culture
of the Uists and Barra, and also provides a forum for
travelling exhibitions.

975 MUTHILL CHURCH AND TOWER   6B3

At Muthill, A822, 3m S of Crieff. All reasonable times. Free. (HS)
Tel: 031-244 3101.

Ruins of an important church of the 15th-century,
incorporating a 12th-century tower.

976 MUTHILL MUSEUM   6B3

In centre of Muthill beside Muthill Church and Tower. Easter and
June-Sept, Tues, Thurs, Sat and Sun 1430-1700. Free.

Small folk museum/heritage centre in attractive
conservation village.

977 MYRETON MOTOR MUSEUM 6G5

Off A198, 17m from Edinburgh and 6m SW of North Berwick. May-Oct, daily 1000-1800; Nov-Apr, daily 1000-1700. Entrance charges. Parking available. Tel: (087 57) 288.

A varied collection of road transport from 1897, including motor cars, cycles, motorcycles, commercials, World War II military vehicles and automobilia. Catalogue and children's quiz book.

978 NAIRN FISHERTOWN MUSEUM 3C8

Laing Hall, King Street. May-Sept, Mon-Sat 1430-1630; Mon, Wed & Fri 1830-2030. Entrance charge. Groups by donation. Limited car parking. Tel: (0667) 53331.

The museum tells the story of the fisherfolk, the fishertown and the fishing industry; and how the decline in the herring fishing changed people's lives. Pictures, photographs, model boats, lines, herring nets, creels and a varied assortment of exhibits illustrate a way of life which disappeared with the outbreak of World War II.

979 NAIRN LEISURE PARK 3C8

Marine Road, Nairn. Swimming, steam room, adventure park: Jan-Dec, Mon-Fri 0800-2100, Sat & Sun 0900-1700. Outdoor games complex open Easter-Sept, daily 1100-1800 (2100 in July & Aug). Activity charges. Parking available. Refreshments. Tel: (0667) 53061.

Set beside the town beach, on the Moray Firth, Nairn Leisure Park has indoor and outdoor sporting and games facilities, including swimming pool and steam room with picnic patio, aerial runway, adventure play trails, trim trail, adventure fort, outdoor board games, woodland suspension bridge, toddlers' playground and more.

980 NAIRN LITERARY INSTITUTE MUSEUM 3C8

Viewfield House, Nairn. June-Sept. Mon-Sat 1430-1630. Free, donations welcome. Parking available.

The museum is housed in a three-storey building dating from around 1803, and has a collection of ethnographic material, natural history and artefacts illustrating social and local history. The museum was founded in 1858 by a local doctor, Dr Grigor, and remains, with the Institute, a private charitable trust.

981 NATIONAL BURNS MEMORIAL TOWER 4H7

Lies on A76 Dumfries-Kilmarnock Road in Mauchline. Easter-Sept, daily, hours vary. Oct-Easter, Mon-Fri 0915-1300, 1400-1700. Free. Roadside parking. Tel: (0290) 51916.

ASVA

Opened in 1898 as a memorial to Robert Burns. Tourist Information Office on ground floor. There is an interpretation centre on the first and second floors and viewing area at the top of the tower.

National Wallace Monument

982 NATIONAL WALLACE MONUMENT 6A4

Abbey Craig, off A807 Hillfoots Road, 1½ miles NNE of Stirling. Apr-Oct, daily 1000-1700 (1800 in July & Aug). Entrance charges. Gift shop. Coffee house. Tel: (0786) 475019.

ASVA

The National Wallace Monument takes visitors back in time almost 700 years, to the days of Scotland's first struggle for independence. The story of William Wallace, freedom fighter and national hero, is told along with the background and events that shaped this period of history. The tower, 220 feet high, gives superb views. Not suitable for wheelchair access.

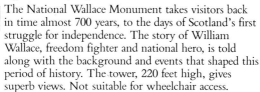

Neidpath Castle

983 NEIDPATH CASTLE 5C6

A72, 1m W of Peebles. Thurs before Easter until Sept 30, Mon-Sat 1100-1700, Sun 1300-1700. Oct, Tues only 1100-1600. Groups at other times by arrangement. Entrance charges. Group concessions. Parking available. Gift shop. Tel: (0721) 720333.

In a beautiful valley among wooded hills, Neidpath Castle is dramatically situated high above the River Tweed. This medieval castle, with walls nearly 12 feet thick, contains a rock-hewn well and pit prison, and two of the three original vaults. It is also an interesting example of how such a fortress could be adapted to the more civilised living conditions of the 17th century. There are fine views from many levels, right up to the roof. Also small museum and tartan display.

984 NELSON TOWER 3C8

Grant Park, Forres. May-Sept. Tues-Sun 1400-1600. Free. Parking available. Sales point. Tel: (0309) 673701).

The tower has displays on the life of Admiral Nelson, the Forres Trafalgar Club, and views of old Forres. Viewpoint looks over the Moray Firth.

985 NEPTUNE'S STAIRCASE 2G12

3m NW of Fort William off A830 at Banavie. Parking available.

A series of 8 locks, built between 1805 and 1822, which raises Telford's Caledonian Canal 64 feet. (See No 214).

986 NESS HISTORICAL SOCIETY 2D3
(Comunn Eachdraidh Nis)

Old School, Lionel, Ness, Isle of Lewis. Open all Summer. Annual ticket. Entrance charge. Tel: 0851 81 576.

A permanent display of photographs and documents relating to local history with artefacts from domestic life, croft work and fishing. Videos and slides can be viewed on request.

987 NESS OF BURGI 1G6

On the coast at the tip of Scatness, about 1m SW of Jarlshof, S end of mainland Shetland. All reasonable times. Free. (HS) Tel: 031-244 3101.

A defensive stone-built structure of Iron Age date, which is related in certain features to the brochs.

988 NEVIS RANGE 2G12

Torlundy. New access road signposted Aonach Mor, 6 miles N of Fort William on A82. Jan-Apr, daily 0900-1630. May-Oct, daily 1000-1700 (and evenings, July & Aug). Charge for gondola trip. Family tickets. Group concessions. Parking available. Gift shop. Restaurant, bar, cafeteria. Tel: (0397) 705825.

Ski area and summer visitor attraction in the heart of the western Highlands on Aonach Mor (4,006 feet) beside Ben Nevis. A ride in one of eighty enclosed gondolas gives spectacular views. Restaurant and bar at 2,150 feet, shop and mountain walks at top gondola station. At base, cafe, forestry walks and mountain bike hire. In winter, extensive skiing with eight ski lifts, ski school and ski hire.

989 NEW ABBEY CORN MILL 5B10

New Abbey, 6m S of Dumfries on A710. Opening standard, except Oct-Mar closed Thurs pm and all day Friday. Entrance charge. Group concessions. (HS) Tel: 031-244 3101.

ASVA

A late 18th-century water powered corn mill, still in working order and demonstrated regularly to visitors.

New Lanark Visitor Centre

990 NEW LANARK VISITOR CENTRE 5B6

   1m S of Lanark. Jan-Dec, daily exc Christmas & New Year, 1100-1700. Entrance charge. Group concessions. Parking available. Gift shop. Tearoom. Tel: (0555) 661345.

The best example in Scotland of an industrial village, the product of the Industrial Revolution in the late 18th and early 19th centuries, now the subject of a major conservation programme. Founded in 1785 by David Dale and Richard Arkwright, it was the scene of early experiments in the paternalistic management and care for the workers, particularly by Robert Owen (1771-1858), Dale's son-in-law. Imaginative new Visitor Centre with exhibitions, working machinery, coffee and gift shop (See also No 547).

Newark Castle, Port Glasgow

991 NEWARK CASTLE, PORT GLASGOW   4G5

Off A8, through shipyard at E side of Port Glasgow. Apr-Sept, opening standard. Oct-Mar, closed. Entrance charge. Group concessions. Parking available. (HS) Tel: 031-244 3101.

A large, fine-turreted mansion house of the Maxwells, overlooking the River Clyde, still almost entire and in a remarkably good state of preservation, with a 15th-century tower, a courtyard and hall, the latter dated 1597.

992 NEWTON STEWART MUSEUM   4H10

York Road, Newton Stewart. Apr-Sept. Mon-Sat 1400-1700. July, Aug, Sept, also Sun 1400-1700. July, Aug, also Mon-Sat 1000-1230. Entrance charges. Parking available. Gift shop.

This former church, which is a listed building, has displays covering local history and Scottish life, both domestic and agricultural.

993 NICOLSON LEWIS SPORTS CENTRE   2D4

Sandwick Road, Stornoway, Isle of Lewis. Jan-Dec. During school term, Mon-Fri evenings, all day Sat. During holidays, Mon-Sat, all day. Entrance charge. Car parking only. Tel: (0851) 702603.

The Nicolson Lewis Sports Centre has a 25-metre swimming pool and multi-use sports hall. Football, badminton, aquafit.

994 NORTHLANDS VIKING CENTRE   3E3

The Old School, Auchingill, Caithness. On A9 between Wick and John O'Groats. June-Sep daily 1000-1600. Admission charge. Parking, shop, picnic area, toilets.

The displays explore the chambered cairns, brochs, and Picts of pre-Viking Caithness through to the late Norse period and the excavations of the settlements at Freswick; also features the archaeological contribution made by John Nicholson. Broch nearby.

995 NIDDRY CASTLE   6D6

10m W of Edinburgh, turn off A89 1m W of Newbridge. May-Sept, Sun only 1400-1630. At other times by arrangement for groups. Donations. Tel: (0506) 890 753.

Late 15th-century Scottish castle, a refuge for Mary Queen of Scots, now restored from a crumbling ruin to its former splendour. Tours include access to Great Hall, guardhouse and dungeon, also Queen Mary's apartment if not occupied, and tea in Laird's Hall. Accommodation available.

996 NOLTLAND CASTLE 1B9

Isle of Westray, Orkney. All reasonable times. Free. (HS)
Tel: 031-244 3101.

Extensive ruins of a castle originally built in 1420 by
Thomas de Tulloch, then the Governor. Later besieged
by Sir William Sinclair of Warsetter, it fell into the
hands of Gilbert Balfour of Westray, from whose time,
around the mid 16th century, much of the building
appears to date. It was partly destroyed in 1746. The
stately hall, vaulted kitchen and fine winding staircase
are impressive.

997 NORTH AYRSHIRE MUSEUM 4G6

Manse Street, Kirkgate, Saltcoats. June-Sept, Mon-Sat exc Wed,
1000-1300, 1400-1700. Oct-May, Tues-Sat exc Wed, 1000-1300,
1400-1700. Free. Car parking only. Tel: (0294) 64174.

Local museum housed in mid 18th-century church,
covering North Ayrshire area. Exhibitions change
regularly, themed exhibitions on local topics staged
two to three times a year. Good collections of local
photographs, Ayrshire whitework and local memorabilia.

998 NORTH BERWICK LAW 6H5

S of North Berwick, off B1347. All times. Free.

The 613-ft volcanic rock is a fine viewpoint and is
crowned by a watch tower dating from Napoleonic
times, and an archway made from the jawbone of a
whale.

999 NORTH BERWICK MUSEUM 6H5

School Road. Easter-end May, Sat and Mon 1000-1300, 1400-1700, Fri
and Sun 1400-1700. Jun-mid Sept, Mon-Sat 1000-1300, 1400-1700, Sun
1400-1700. Mid Sept-late Oct, Sat & Mon 1000-1300, 1400-1700, Fri
& Sun 1400-1700. Free. Tel: (0620) 3470.

Local museum with displays of natural history, including
a new exhibition about the Bass Rock; local history,
with finds from Tantallon Castle and North Berwick
Priory; old golf clubs and memorabilia; domestic life,
costume and decorative arts. 'Hands-on' activities for
children.

1000 NORTH BERWICK OUTDOOR POOL 6H5

Near harbour, North Berwick. June, late Aug, daily 1400-1800. July-mid
Aug, daily 1100-1800. Entrance charges. Season tickets. Refreshments.

Large swimming pool and smaller teaching pool, both
filled with heated sea water. Two chutes, floats, diving
board, hot showers.

1001   NORTH CARR LIGHTSHIP   6H3

Anstruther Harbour. Easter-Oct. Daily, 1100-1700. Also evening tours with hospitality, nostalgic 'Radio Days' events — please contact for details. Entrance charge. Parking available. Sales point. Tel: (0333) 310589.

The lightship, stationed off Fife Ness from 1933-75, is now a floating museum and the only one of its kind in the world. All the interior fitments have been refurbished to give an impression of life on board. Permanent exhibition 'Lightships of the World' tells of vessels around the world; small exhibition tells the story of the lightship during World War II. Interpretation boards on history of North Carr.

1002   NORTH EAST FALCONRY VISITOR CENTRE   3F9

    T

Broadland, Cairnie, 3 miles from Huntly. Signposted off A96 and A920. Apr-Oct, daily, 1000-1800. Nov-Mar, Sat & Sun 1000-dusk. Entrance charges. Group concessions. Parking available. Gift shop. Tearoom. Tel: (0466) 87344.

Almost 40 birds of prey on permanent display, including eagles, owls and falcons. Flying demonstrations, described by the falconers, take place regularly throughout the day.

1003   NORTH EAST OF SCOTLAND AGRICULTURAL HERITAGE CENTRE (ADEN COUNTRY PARK)   3H8

    A
    P
    T

On A950 between Old Deer and Mintlaw, 30m N of Aberdeen. May-Sept, daily 1100-1700. Apr, Oct, Sat & Sun 1200-1700. Parking available. Gift shop. Tearoom. Tel: (0771) 22857.

ASVA

Housed in the carefully restored Aden Home Farm, the Centre imaginatively interprets 20th-century estate life with audio-visual programme, horseman's house and costume guide. Additionally, North-East farming innovation over 200 years is highlighted in the award-winning 'Weel Vrocht Grun' (Well-Worked Ground) exhibition by use of special dioramas, atmospheric soundtrack and video film. Farming in the 1950s is re-created at the reconstructed 20-acre Hareshowe Farm. (See No 41).

1004   NORTH GLEN GALLERY   5B10

Palnackie, 5 miles SE of Castle Douglas, 4 miles SW of Dalbeattie off A711. Jan-Dec. Daily, 1000-1800. (Please telephone if travelling far.) Entrance charge, refunded against purchases. Parking available. Studio shop. Tel: (055 660) 200.

Home and studio gallery featuring the work of international glass artist Ed Iglehart and lighting design by Tom Iglehart. Glassblowing, sculpture and decorative work often in progress. Advice on local walks and natural history, situated in beautiful surroundings overlooking the Urr estuary.

1005   NORTH HOY NATURE RESERVE   1A11

Reached by boat from Stromness, Orkney. Access at all times. Free. (RSPB). Tel: (0856) 79298 or 031-557 3136.

Extensive area of mountain and moorland with huge seacliffs including Old Man of Hoy (see No 1019). Moorland birds and large numbers of seabirds.

1006 NORTHFIELD FARM MUSEUM   3G7

10m W of Fraserburgh. From A98 follow signs for New Aberdour. From B9031 follow New Pitsligo signs. June-Sept. Daily, 1100-1730. Entrance charge. Parking available. Tel: (077 17) 504.

A large collection of farm equipment including tractors, implements, stationary engines, household bric-a-brac from the 1870s. Vintage motor bikes. Smithy, line shafting workshop operating at weekends. Llamas and aviary.

1007 NOSS NATURE RESERVE   1G5

Isle of Noss, 5m E of Lerwick, Shetland. Access by inflatable boat each day (1000-1700) except Mon & Thu. Island open from mid-May until end of Aug; see local SNH staff or Shetland Tourist Board. Entrance charge. (SNH) Tel: (0595) 3345.

Spectacular island with 600-feet cliffs and vast colonies of breeding auks, gulls and gannets. Modest display on natural history and restored Pony Pund (Shetland Pony Stud Farm) open to visitors.

Nova Scotia Room: see No 936.

1008 OATMEAL MILL   3F10

Montgarrie Mills, 1 mile N of Alford. Apr-Oct. By arrangement only, Tues & Thurs at 1400 and 1530. Entrance charge. Group concessions. Parking available. Tel: (097 55) 62209.

A family-owned working watermill which has been in continuous production since at least the 1870s, milling oatmeal in the traditional way. Visitors are accommodated while work is in progress, and must prebook.

1009 OBAN DISTILLERY   4E2

Stafford Street. Jan-Dec exc Christmas & New Year, Mon-Fri, 0930-1700. Gift shop. Tel: (0631) 64262.

ASVA

The distillery, founded in 1794, is famous for its Classic Malt whisky. Reception centre exhibition tells the story of the Stevenson family who developed Oban from a fishing village into a resort with light industry. Tours, tastings.

1010 OBAN EXPERIENCE   4E2

Heritage Wharf, Railway Pier. Jan-Dec, dawn-dusk. Free. Parking available. Gift shop. Tearoom. Tel: (0631) 66969.

Visitor centre depicting Oban in Victorian times with audio-visuals and exhibits.

1011 OBAN GLASS   4E2

Heritage Wharf, Railway Pier. Free. Factory Shop: May-Oct, Mon-Sat 0900-2100, Sun 1100-1700. Nov-Apr, Mon-Sat 0900-1730. Factory viewing: Mon-Fri 0900-1700 (all year). Parking available. Tel: (0631) 63386.

Paperweight-making from the raw materials stage through all the processes to the finished article. Factory shop with an extensive range of glassware.

1012 OFFICIAL LOCH NESS MONSTER EXHIBITION   3A9

   ♿
   T

Drumnadrochit, 15 miles S of Inverness. Jan-Dec exc Christmas & Boxing Day. Peak opening: daily, 0930-2130. Mid-season: daily, 0930-1730. Winter: daily, 1000-1600. Entrance charges. Group concessions. Parking available. Shops. Restaurant, bar, coffee shop, hotel on site. Tel: (045 62) 573 or 218.

Forty-minute audio-visual presentation and exhibition which displays much of the equipment used in the exploration of Loch Ness. The centre also houses a number of shops — woollen shop, glass blowers, jewellery with craft demonstration. Garden includes life-size 'Nessie' on an outdoor lochan.

Old Blacksmith's Shop Centre

1013 OLD BLACKSMITH'S SHOP CENTRE   5D10

   ♿
   T

Gretna Green, just off A74 at Scottish/English border. Daily, all year. Entrance charge. Parking available. Gift shops. Self-service restaurant. Tel: (0461) 38441 or 38224.

The old Blacksmith's Shop, famous for runaway marriages, has a museum with anvil marriage room and coach house. Gretna Green was once a haven for runaway couples seeking to take advantage of Scotland's then laxer marriage laws, when couples could be married by a declaration before witnesses; this was made illegal in 1940. Elopers can still, however, take advantage of Scottish law permitting marriage without parental consent at 16. Among places where marriages took place were the Old Toll Bar (now bypassed) when the road opened in 1830, and the Smithy. Arts centre with Border Fine Arts Gallery, pottery, flower shop, woodturner and tourist information centre.

1014 OLD BRIDGE HOUSE   5B9

   ♿
   A
   P

Mill Road, Dumfries, at Devorgilla's Bridge. Apr-Sept, Mon-Sat 1000-1300, 1400-1700; Sun 1400-1700. Free. Parking available. Tel: (0387) 56904.

The house, built in 1660, now has rooms furnished in period style to illustrate life in Dumfries over the centuries. Rooms include kitchens of 1850 and 1900, a Victorian nursery and a dental laboratory dating from 1900. Devorgilla's Bridge was originally built by Lady Devorgilla Balliol, who endowed Balliol College, Oxford.

1015 THE OLD BYRE 4C1

& A

Dervaig, Isle of Mull, 1m along Torloisk road. Easter-Oct, daily, 1030-1830. Entrance charge. Group concessions. Parking available. Craft/gift shop. Licensed tearoom. Tel: (068 84) 229.

An audio-visual museum and visitor centre with displays of the bird and animal life of Mull, supported by audio-visual shows at ½-hourly intervals. New video 'Mull through the Ages' uses detailed models to tell the island's story from the first settlers, 8,000 years ago, to the Clearances.

1016 OLD GALA HOUSE AND CHRISTOPHER BOYD GALLERY 5E6

& P T

Scott Crescent, Galashiels. On A7 northbound; fork left at St Peter's Church School. Southbound: follow signs from War Memorial. Easter-Nov. Easter-Sept 1000-1600 (Sun 1400-1600); Oct 1200-1600 (Sun 1400-1600). Parking available. Sales point. Tearoom. Tel: (0750) 20096.

Dating from 1583, Old Gala House is the former home of the Lairds of Gala. Reopened in 1988 as an interpretation centre exploring the early history of the burgh. Especially interesting painted ceiling (1635). Gardens, art galleries. with changing programme of exhibitions and events.

1017 OLD HAA MUSEUM 1G3

& P

Burravoe, Yell, Shetland Islands. Open Apr-Sep Tues, Wed, Thurs, Sat, Sun 1000-1600. Groups and other times by arrangement. Free. Parking available. Tearoom. Craft shop. Tel: (095 782) 339 or (0957) 2127.

The Old Haa of Burravoe is the oldest building on Yell. Facilities include exhibition areas for the display of local flora and fauna, arts and craft as well as themes of local historic interest; photographic collection, video and tape recordings of local musicians and storytellers; genealogical information may be available for inspection by arrangement. Craft shop and art gallery. Recording studio facilities available. Garden.

1018 OLD INVERLOCHY CASTLE 2G12

2m NE of Fort William. Limited access due to work in progress—may be viewed from outside. (HS) Tel: 031-244 3101.

A ruined 13th-century square building, with round corner towers.

Old Man of Hoy

1019 OLD MAN OF HOY 1A12

NW coast of Isle of Hoy, Orkney.

A 450-feet-high isolated stack (pillar) standing off the magnificent cliffs of NW Hoy. It can also be well seen from the Scrabster-Stromness ferry. A challenge to experienced climbers. (See also No 1005).

1020 OLD MILLS 3D8

W end of Elgin off the A96. April-Sep. Tue-Sun 0900-1700. Entrance charge. Group concessions. Parking available. Sales point. Tel: (0309) 673701.

The oldest and only remaining meal mill on the River Lossie. Its history can be traced back to a Royal Charter of 1230 granting its rights to the monks of Pluscarden Priory. Visitor Centre, ladeside trail, outdoor exhibits and picnic area.

1021 OLD PLACE OF MOCHRUM 4G10

Off B7005, 11m W of Wigtown. Not open to the public; can be seen from the road.

Known also as Drumwalt Castle, this is mainly 15th and 16th century with two picturesque towers.

1022 OLD SEMEIL HERB GARDEN 3E10

&
A
T

Strathdon, just off the A944. Alternatively, 1 mile along side road off A977 from Dinnet to Huntly. Easter-Sept. April, weekends only. May-Aug, daily exc Thurs. Sept, Mon-Sat exc Thurs. 1000-1700. Free. Parking available. Gift shop, plant sales. Conservatory tearoom. Tel: (097 56) 51343.

Situated at 1,000 feet in the foothills of the Grampian Mountains, in a sheltered spot at the edge of a conifer forest. The garden contains about 150 different growing herbs labelled and landscaped in formal beds. Catalogue, advice on planting and growing herbs. Plants for sale from the nursery and greenhouse.

1023 OLD SKYE CROFTER'S HOUSE 2E10

Luib, 7m NW of Broadford, Isle of Skye. Daily 0900-1800. Entrance charge. Group concessions. Parking available. Tel: (047 022) 296.

Thatched traditional dwelling house furnished in keeping with the early 20th century, including agricultural implements.

1024 ORCADIAN STONE COMPANY 3B6

Main Street, Golspie, Sutherland. Jan-Dec, Mon-Sat 0900-1800. Also Sun, Apr-Oct. Adults charged for museum entrance, children, OAP, students free. Parking available. Gift shop. Tel: (0408) 633483.

Exhibition of local geology with interpretative panels and scale model of Assynt area; fine mineral specimens from all over the world. In the workshop, articles are made from natural stone—mostly local—such as clocks, lamps, pens, tables, hearthstones, house names, business signs. Gift shop specialises in mineral specimens, stone giftware, semi-precious stone jewellery, geological books and maps.

Orchardton Tower

1025 ORCHARDTON TOWER 5B10

Off A711, 6m SE of Castle Douglas. Open all reasonable times. Free. Apply custodian at nearby cottage. (HS) Tel: 031-244 3101.

An example, unique in Scotland, of a circular tower house, built by John Cairns about the middle of the 15th century.

1026 ORIGINAL LOCH NESS VISITOR CENTRE
3A9

    Drumnadrochit, 14 miles W of Inverness on A82. June-Oct, daily,
T *0800-2130. Oct-May, daily, 0900-1700. Entrance charges. Family tickets. Group concessions. Parking available. Woollen shop, bookshop, kitchen and whisky shop, Celtic craft shop, 2 gift shops. Licensed all day coffee house, ice cream kiosk, hotel on site. Tel: (045 62) 342.*

Visitor centre specialising in foreign language service, with simultaneous translations of its film, which focuses on the history, mystery and latest developments on Loch Ness. Boat cruises on loch with commentary by local skipper, and on-board sonar for monster-spotting. Eight acres of woodland to explore, garden with seating. Entertainment and all facilities at hotel.

1027 ORKNEY FARM AND FOLK MUSEUM
1A10/ 1B11

    Kirbister, Birsay and Corrigall, Harray. Mar-Oct. Mon-Sat 1030-1300,
A *1400-1700. Sun 1400-1700. Entrance charge. Parking available. Gift shop. Tel: (0856) 77268 (Kirbister) or 77411 (Corrigall).*

Farm and folk museum in two locations. Buildings, crafts and implements which illustrate traditional island life and the changes which have taken place, up to the end of the 19th century.

1028 ORKNEY FARM PARK
1B11

    Nearhouse, Harray. Take the A986 out of Finstown and follow the signs.
A *Third week in May-first week in Sept. Daily exc Mon and a.m. Fri,*
P *1000-1800. Entrance charge. Group concessions. Parking available. Gift shop. Tel: (085 676) 243.*

A private collection of rare and minority breed farm animals, with cows, pigs, sheep, ducks and poultry living in natural surroundings—along with llamas and pot-bellied pigs. Wide walkways allow visitors to wander among the animals. Information panels. Nursery with young animals to hold; goats, ponies, large duck pond.

1029 ORKNEY WIRELESS MUSEUM
1B12

Church Road, St Margaret's Hope, South Ronaldsay, 11m S of Kirkwall. Apr-Sept, daily 1000-1900. Entrance charge. Parking available.

Museum of wartime communications at Scapa Flow, with many of the instruments used by the thousands of service men and women posted here to protect the Home Fleet, shown in their proper context. Also many handsome wireless sets of the 1930s.
(See also No 1139).

1030 ORMISTON MARKET CROSS
6F6

At Ormiston, B6371, 2m S of Tranent. (HS) Tel: 031-244 3101.

A 15th-century cross in the main street.

1031 ORPHIR CHURCH
1B11

By A964, 8m WSW of Kirkwall. All reasonable times. Free. (HS) Tel: 031-244 3101.

The remains of Scotland's only circular medieval church, built in the first half of the 12th century and dedicated to St Nicholas. Nearby is the site of the Earl's Bu, a great hall of the Earls of Orkney.

Ospreys: see No 870 and 874.

1032 OUR LADY OF THE ISLES   2A9

N of South Uist, Western Isles. All reasonable times. Free.

On Reuval Hill—the Hill of Miracles—is the statue of the Madonna and Child, erected in 1957 by the Catholic community with contributions from all over the world. The work of Hew Lorimer, it is 30 feet high.

1033 OUSDALE WEAVING   3C5

♿
T

Ousdale, Berriedale, 7 miles N of Helmsdale on A9. Easter-Oct, daily, 0900-1700. Nov-Easter, Mon-Fri 0900-1700. Free. Parking available. Gift shop. Tearoom. Tel: (043 12) 371.

Fabrics, shawls, serapes being produced for sale in the mill shop and for export all over the world. Explanatory boards describe the processes of weaving in a number of languages.

Paisley Abbey

1034 PAISLEY ABBEY   4H5

♿
A
P

In Paisley, 7m W of Glasgow. Outwith the hours of divine worship. Open all year, Mon-Sat 1000-1530. Free. Group visits by arrangement. Gift shop. Tearoom. Tel: 041-889 7654.

A fine Cluniac Abbey Church founded in 1163. Almost completely destroyed by order of Edward I of England in 1307. Rebuilt and restored after Bannockburn and in the century following. Choir in ruins from 16th to 19th century, but now fully restored. The choir contains a fine stone-vaulted roof, stained glass and the tombs of Princess Marjory Bruce and King Robert III. See the St Mirin Chapel with St Mirin carvings (1499). Note outside the Norman doorway, cloisters and Place of Paisley. The Barochan Cross, a weathered Celtic cross, 11 feet high and attributed to the 10th century, is also in the Abbey.

1035 PAISLEY MUSEUM AND ART GALLERIES   4H5

♿
A
T

High Street, Paisley. Jan-Dec exc public holidays. Mon-Sat 1000-1700. Free. Car parking, coaches by arrangement. Gift shop. Tel: 041-889 3151.

The late 19th-century museum and art galleries house the world-famous collection of Paisley shawls. Displays trace the history of the Paisley pattern; the development of weaving techniques is demonstrated and the social aspects of what was a close-knit weaving community are explored. Exhibitions from the fine collections of local history, natural history. 19th century Scottish painting, and modern studio ceramics. Access to the adjacent Coats Observatory (see No 278).

1036 PALACE THEATRE 4H6

Kilmarnock town centre. Variable opening and ticket prices depending on shows. Group rates by arrangement. Phone for details. Parking available. Tel: (0563) 23590.

The Palace Theatre was formerly a music hall, the venue being popular throughout the Victorian and Edwardian eras. It has now been fully refurbished. Licensed. Bar/Cafe.

1037 PALACERIGG COUNTRY PARK 6A6

  P T *Unclassified road, 2½m SE of Cumbernauld. Jan-Dec. Park: dawn to dusk. Visitor Centre: winter 1000-1630, summer 1000-1800 (closed Tues). No dogs. Free. Booking required for parties over 6. Charge for pony-trekking. Parking available. Coffee shop from 1100 in summer, weekends in winter. Tel: (0236) 720047.*

ASVA

Wildlife includes roe deer, badger, fox and stoat. Bison, wildcat, lynx and mouflon in paddocks. Deer park, 18-hole golf course and pony-trekking. Children's farm and nature trails. Picnic sites and barbecues; ranger service.

1038 PALGOWAN OPEN FARM 4H10

By Glentrool, Newton Stewart. From 1400 each day. Parties anytime by arrangement. Easter week, then mid May, Jun, Sep, Oct, Tue, Wed & Thu. Jul-Aug Mon-Fri. Adult: £1.50, Child: £1.00. Tea & biscuits provided in price. Tel: 0671 84 227.

Highland and Galloway cattle, sheep, sheep dogs. Demonstrations in stane dyking, stick making, skin curing. Special career opportunity demonstrations and talk for schools. Picnic areas. Information on cassette.

1039 PARALLEL ROADS 2H11

Glen Roy, unclassified road off A86, 18m NE of Fort William.

These 'parallel roads' are hillside terraces marking levels of lakes dammed by glaciers during the Ice Age.

1040 PASS OF KILLIECRANKIE 3C12

  T *Off A9, 3m N of Pitlochry. NTS Visitor Centre: Apr-Oct, daily 1000-1700. Jun-Aug, daily 0930-1800. Site open all day. Entrance charge for adults. Children free. Parking available. Trust shop. Snack bar. (NTS) Tel: (0796) 473233.*

A famous wooded gorge where in 1689 the Government troops were routed by Jacobite forces led by 'Bonnie Dundee'. Soldier's Leap. NTS centre features the battle, natural history and ranger services. The Pass is on the network of Garry-Tummel walks, which extend for 20 miles in the area. Disabled access to Visitor Centre.

1041 PAXTON HOUSE 5F5

  T *5 miles W of Berwick upon Tweed on B6461. Easter-Oct. Daily. First tour 1200, last tour 1615. Entrance charge. Group concessions. Parking available. Gift shop. Licensed tearoom, daily in season 1000-1700. Tel: (0289) 86291.*

ASVA

Paxton House is a Georgian, Palladian country mansion set in 70 acres of gardens, parkland and woodland. The house was built for the Homes of Wedderburn, designed by the Adam family and furnished by Chippendale. The restored Regency picture gallery is an outstation of the National Galleries of Scotland. Tearoom has facilities for coach parties. Adventure playground.

1042 PEASE DEAN 5F5

Near Cockburnspath, signposted off A1. Car park on road by entrance to caravan site. Free. All reasonable times. (SNH)

Mixed gorge woodland with resident and migrant birds, wild flowers, terns and mosses. Circular walk forming part of the Southern Upland Way.

1043 PEEL RING OF LUMPHANAN 3F10

A980, 11m NW of Banchory. All reasonable times. Free. (HS) Tel: 031-244 3101.

A major early medieval earthwork 120 feet in diameter and 18 feet high. There are links with Shakespeare's *Macbeth*.

1044 PERTH ART GALLERY AND MUSEUM 6D2

  A *George Street. All year, Mon-Sat 1000-1700. Free. Tel: (0738) 32488.*
  T

Collections of local history, fine and applied art, natural history and archaeology. Changing programme of temporary exhibitions.

1045 PERTH LEISURE POOL 6D2

Glasgow Road, signposted from town centre. Jan-Dec exc 2 weeks before Christmas. Daily 1000-2200. Entrance charges. Group concessions. Parking available. Sales point at reception. Cafeteria, bistro, ice cream bar. Tel: (0738) 30535 (recorded information) or (0738) 35454.

ASVA

This award-winning centre, which aims to offer a family day at the seaside — indoors — welcomed its 3 millionth visitor in February 1993. It has four pools: multi-activity leisure pool with flumes, whirlpools, wild water channel, bubble beds, fan spray, water cannons and 'kiddies' lagoon; 25-metre training pool; toddlers' pool; all-year outdoor lagoon. Luxury health suite with sauna, steam room, jacuzzi, sun beds, fitness and relaxation areas. Disabled access to all areas.

1046 PERTH REPERTORY THEATRE 6D2

High Street, Perth. Group concessions available, but variable. Tel: (0738) 21031.

An intimate Victorian theatre, built in 1900 in the centre of Perth, offering a variety of plays, musicals, etc. Induction loop for hard of hearing. Coffee bar and restaurant open during day and for performances.

1047 PIER ARTS CENTRE 1A11

Victoria Street, Stromness, Orkney. All year, Tues-Sat 1030-1230 and 1330-1700. Free. Parking available. Tel: (0856) 850209.

Former merchant's house (c 1800) adjoining buildings (Pier Gallery) former coal store and fishermen's sheds which have been converted into a gallery, housing a permanent collection of 20th-century paintings and sculpture as well as changing exhibitions.

1048 PIEROWALL CHURCH 1B9

At Pierowall, Island of Westray, Orkney. All reasonable times. Free. Parking available. (HS). Tel: 031-244 3101.

A ruin consisting of nave and chancel, the latter canted out of alignment. There are some finely lettered tombstones.

1049 THE PIPING CENTRE, BORRERAIG   2C9

Dunvegan, Isle of Skye. Easter-mid Oct. Admission charge. Parking available. Tel: (047 081) 369.

Old school and schoolhouse now museum of the Highland Bagpipe and the family MacCrimmon, pipers to the chiefs of the clan MacLeod from circa 1500 to 1800. Famous pipers, teachers and composers of piobaireachd.

Pitlochry Festival Theatre

1050 PITLOCHRY FESTIVAL THEATRE   5B1

P
T
Off A9 bypass at Pitlochry local access. May-Oct, open all day for refreshments and art exhibitions. Box Office. Parking available. Catering and bar facilities. Coffee shop from 1000. Lunch 1200-1400. Dinner 1830. Inductive loop. Tel: (0796) 2680.

Scotland's 'Theatre in the Hills' is housed in a magnificent building by the River Tummel. A repertoire of seven different plays is presented each season, with concerts on many Sundays. Magnificent view from foyer and restaurant.

1051 PITMEDDEN GARDEN   3G9

T
1 mile W of Pitmedden village on A920, 14m N of Aberdeen. May-Sept, daily 1000-1800. Last tour 1715. Entrance charges. Group concessions. Parking available. Tearoom. (NTS) Tel: (0651) 842352.

The highlight is the 17th-century Great Garden originally laid out by Sir Alexander Seton, with elaborate floral designs, pavilions, fountains and sundials. The 'thunder houses' at either end of the west belvedere are rare in Scotland. The Museum of Farming Life contains a collection of agricultural and domestic implements. On the 100-acre estate is a woodland and farmland walk. Visitor Centre, herb garden, picnic area.

1052 PITSLIGO CASTLE   3G7

By Rosehearty, 3m W of Fraserburgh. All times. Free.

Ruined castle dating from 1424 which passed through various families to the 4th and last Lord Pitsligo who is remembered for his generosity to the poor and for his successful attempts to evade arrest after the '45 Jacobite Rebellion.

1053 PITTENCRIEFF HOUSE MUSEUM   6D5

A
Pittencrieff Park, Dunfermline. May-Oct, daily except Tues 1100-1700. Free. Parking available. Small shop. Tel: (0383) 722935 (May-Oct) or 721814.

The house, standing in a fine park, was built in 1610 for the Lairds of Pittencrieff, and was briefly owned by Andrew Carnegie in 1902. There are displays of local, social and natural history, archaeology and costumes. The top floor is an art gallery showing international exhibitions.

1054 PLUSCARDEN ABBEY 3D8

*From B9010 at Elgin take unclassified road to Pluscarden, 6m SW.
All year, daily 0500-2030. Free. Parking available. Gift shop.
Tel: (034 389) 257/388 (0900-1100 and 1430-1700).*

Originally a Valliscaulian house, the monastery was
founded in 1230. In 1390 the Church was burned,
probably by the Wolf of Badenoch who burned Elgin
about the same time. It became a dependent priory of
the Benedictine Abbey of Dunfermline in 1454 until
the suppression of monastic life in Scotland in 1560.
Thereafter the buildings fell into ruins until 1948 when
a group of Benedictine monks from Prinknash Abbey,
Gloucester, returned to restore it. Monastic church
services open to the public. Visitor Centre, retreats.

1055 POLKEMMET COUNTRY PARK 6C7

*From Whitburn take B7066 W for 2m. Signposted on right-hand side.
All year. Facilities vary according to season and weather. Park free, charge
for activities. Restaurant, bar. Parking available. Tel: (0501) 43905.*

Former private estate of a prominent local family, the
Baillies of Polkemmet, whose mausoleum is in the
park. Now equipped with golf course and driving
range, information centre, bowling green, putting,
restaurant and bar. Children's play area, country walks,
Ranger service.

1056 PRESTON MARKET CROSS 6F6

*½m S of Prestonpans, 8m E of Edinburgh. All times. Free. (HS)
Tel: 031-244 3101.*

An outstanding Scottish market cross, the only one that
still stands where and as it was built. The tall shaft,
surmounted by a unicorn, stands on a circular structure
with niches and a parapet. It was probably erected by
the Hamiltons of Preston after they obtained the right
to hold a fair in 1617.

Preston Mill and Phantassie Doocot

1057 PRESTON MILL AND PHANTASSIE DOOCOT 6H5

*Off A1 at East Linton, 6m W of Dunbar. Apr-Sept, Mon-Sat
1100-1300, 1400-1700; Sun 1400-1700; Oct, Sat 1100-1300, 1400-1630,
Sun, 1400-1600 (last tour 20 mins before closing). Entrance charges.
Group concessions. Parking available. (NTS) Tel: (0620) 860426.*

A picturesque water-mill, possibly the only one of its
kind still in working condition in Scotland. Nearby is
Phantassie Doocot (dovecot), originally containing 500
birds, and the Rennie Memorial, which contains a part
of John Rennie's Waterloo Bridge. (See No 1081).

1058 PRESTON TOWER AND GARDENS 6F6

Prestonpans, 8 miles E of Edinburgh on B1361. Tower: by arrangement, all year. Gardens open daily, dawn-dusk, all year. Car parking only. Tel: (0875) 810232 (Mon-Fri) for access to tower.

An imposing 15th-century tower house with a two-storey 17th-century addition. The original three-storeys consist of basements (with dungeon), hall and bedrooms. The upper storeys contain more living accommodation. New stairs exist between the basement and first floor, where once there was only a sealable trap door. The gardens have been restored with elements of Scottish 17th and 18th-century gardens, including a laburnum arch, topiary, old-fashioned roses beside seating alcoves, a herb garden and a docot.

1059 PRESTONPANS BATTLE CAIRN 6F6

E of Prestonpans on A198. All times. Free. Parking available.

The cairn commemorates the victory of Prince Charles Edward over General Cope at the Battle of Prestonpans in 1745.

1060 JAMES PRINGLE WEAVERS OF INVERNESS 3B8

Holm Woollen Mills, Dores Road. Signposted (Holm Mills) on B862. Jan-Dec. Mill: Mon-Fri 0900-1700. Visitor facilities: summer, daily, 0900-1730; winter, Mon-Sat 0930-1700. Free. Parking available. Gift shop. Restaurant. Tel: (0463) 223311.

James Pringle Weavers of Inverness offers tours round a fully-operational weaving mill which dates back to 1790. Self-guided tours with information in six languages. Clan tartan centre where ancestral roots can be researched. Mill shop, weaving mill and restaurant have wide aisles and no steps for wheelchairs.

1061 PRIORWOOD GARDENS 5E6

In Melrose, by Abbey, on B6361. Open 2-30 Apr and 1 May-24 Dec, Mon-Sat 1000-1730; May-Oct, Mon-Sat 1000-1730, Sun 1330-1730. Admission by donation. Trust shop. (NTS) Tel: (089 682) 2555.

A garden which specialises in flowers suitable for drying. There is an NTS Visitor Centre. Picnic tables, orchard walk, dry flower garden.

1062 BEATRIX POTTER GARDEN AND EXHIBITION 6C1

Birnam Institute, Station Road, Birnam. 12 miles N of Perth off A9. Exhibition: June-Sept. Mon-Sat 1000-1200, 1400-1600, Sun 1400-1600. Gardens open all year. Free, donations accepted.

Beatrix Potter drew much of the inspiration for her renowned children's books from the area around Dunkeld, where she spent many family holidays. The garden includes animal figures based on Potter's characters, and a children's rabbit warren, while the exhibition tells the story of her visits to Perthshire.

1063 PUCK'S GLEN 4F5

In Argyll Forest Park, 5 miles W of Dunoon on A815. All reasonable times. Free. Car parking only.

One of the most famous walks on the Cowal peninsula. The path runs through the narrow gorge of the Eas Mor, which is lined by magnificent Douglas firs, some of which are 120 feet high. This spectacular walk is not suitable for disabled visitors; however, a wheelchair access route following an abandoned public road gives views of the lower parts of the glen.(See No 81

**1064   QUEEN ELIZABETH FOREST PARK
VISITOR CENTRE**   **4H3**

*Off A821, 1m N of Aberfoyle. Easter-Oct, daily 1000-1800. Free.
Parking available. Shop. Cafeteria. (FC) Tel: (087 72) 258.*

ASVA

An ideal place to begin a visit to the Queen Elizabeth
Forest Park and the Trossachs, this centre offers
information about all the activities available in the
park: walks, fishing, the Achray Forest Drive (see No
39), picnic sites, camping, wayfaring, cycle trails and
more. On site there is a shop, cafeteria, toilets, picnic
area, and audio-visual showing forest life through the
seasons. All centre facilities are accessible to disabled
people. Within the park there are miles of waymarked
forest walks (three forest trails begin at the centre),
graded for their degree of difficulty.

**1065   QUEEN'S OWN HIGHLANDERS
REGIMENTAL MUSEUM**   **3B8**

P

*Fort George, near Ardersier, 14 miles E of Inverness. Apr-Sept, Mon-Fri
1000-1800, Sun 1400-1800. Oct-Mar, Mon-Fri 1000-1600. Free.
Parking available. Tel: (0463) 224380.*

Regimental museum with collections of medals,
uniforms and other items showing the history of the
Queen's Own Highlanders, Seaforth Highlanders, The
Queen's Own Cameron Highlanders and Lovat
Scouts. (See No 574).

1066   QUEEN'S VIEW, LOCH LOMOND   **4H4**

Off A809, 12m NNW of Glasgow.

From the west side of the road a path leads to a
viewpoint where in 1879, Queen Victoria had her first
view of Loch Lomond.

**1067   QUEEN'S VIEW CENTRE,
LOCH TUMMEL**   **5A1**

*6 miles NW of Pitlochry on B8019. April-Oct. Daily 1000-1730. Free.
parking available (charge). Gift shop. Tearoom. (FE) Tel: (0796) 473123.*

ASVA

Forestry exhibition about Tay Forest Park, with
information, audio visual, shop, tearoom. Picnic tables.
Guided walks through ancient woodland or
magnificent mature forests. Forest walks, paths and
cycle routes. Views along Loch Tummel to the peak of
Schiehallion; Queen Victoria visited the spot in 1866.

Queensberry Aisle: See No 431.

1068   QUEENSFERRY MUSEUM   **6D6**

*Burgh Chambers, High Street, South Queensferry. Jan-Dec. Mon, Thurs,
Fri, Sat 1000-1300, 1415-1700, Sun 1200-1700. Free. Parking available.
Tel: 031-331 1590.*

Queensferry Museum tells the story of the town,
known as the 'Queen's Ferry' in honour of the saintly
Queen Margaret (d. 1093) who encouraged pilgrims
to use the ferry crossing to travel to the shrine of St
Andrew in Fife. The development of the Queensferry
Passage, the growth of the former Royal Burgh, the
building of the Forth Bridges are described. Life, work
and pastimes, including life-size model of the 'Burry
Man' and the annual Ferry Fair.

1069 QUIRANG   2D7

Off unclassified Staffin-Uig road, 19m N of Portree, Isle of Skye. Limited car parking.

An extraordinary mass of towers and pinnacles into which cattle were driven during forays. A very rough track (not suitable for elderly or infirm) zigzags up to The Needle, an imposing obelisk 120 feet high, beyond which, in a large amphitheatre, stands The Table, a huge grass-covered rock-mass. Impressive views.

1070 QUOYNESS CHAMBERED TOMB   1C10

E side of Els Ness, S coast of island of Sanday, Orkney. All reasonable times. Free. (HS) Tel: 031-244 3101.

A spectacular tomb with a main chamber standing to a height of about 13 feet. Analysis suggests that the tomb was in use about 2900 BC.

1071 RAIDERS ROAD   5A10

6 miles W of New Galloway on A712 or 3 miles S of New Galloway on A762. Apr-Sept. Daily, 0900-1800 (2100 in summer). Charge for drive. Cars only. (FE) Tel: (0556) 3626.

Ten-mile forest drive through spectacular Galloway scenery. Two-way traffic, three car parks and picnic places (including one with toilet facilities for able and less able people). Four forest walks, including one for less able. Opportunities to see all aspects of forest life close at hand—mountains, lochs, wildlife. Famous bronze otter sculpted by local artist Penny Wheatley. (See No 589).

1072 RAINBOW SLIDES LEISURE CENTRE   6A5

Goosecroft Road, central Stirling. Opening times vary with activities. Swimming: Mon, Wed, Fri 0900-2100, Tues 0900-1700, Thurs 0900-1800, Sat 0900-1600, Sun 0830-1600. Parking available. Restaurant. Tel: (0786) 62521

Exciting water fun centre, with two swimming pools, three water slides, fully-equipped gymnasium, professional sports injury clinic, sauna suite. Holiday play sessions with inflatables for children.

1073 ALLAN RAMSAY LIBRARY   5B7

On B797 at Leadhills. Wed, Sat, Sun 1400-1600 or by arrangement. Entrance charge. Tel: (0659) 74326/74216.

Lead miners' subscription library, founded in 1741, with rare books, detailed 18th-century mining documents and local records.

1074 RANDOLPH'S LEAP   3C8

Off B9007, 7m SW of Forres. Parking available.

The River Findhorn winds through a deep gorge in the sandstone, and from a path above are impressive views of the clear brown water swirling over rocks or in still dark pools. Randolph's Leap is the most striking part of this valley.

1075 RAVENSCRAIG CASTLE AND PARK   6E4

On a rocky promontory between Dysart and Kirkcaldy. Daily, Oct-Apr 1000-1500, May-Sept 1000-1900. Accessible from shore at all reasonable times. Tel: (0592) 642090.

Imposing ruin of a castle founded by James II in 1460. Later it passed into the hands of the Sinclair Earls of Orkney. It is perhaps the first British castle to be symmetrically designed for defence by firearms. Public park adjacent.

1076 RED CASTLE 5E1

Off A92, 7m S of Montrose. All times. Free.

This red stone tower on a steep mound beside the sandhills of Lunan Bay probably dates from the 15th century when it replaced an earlier fort built for William the Lion by Walter de Berkely. Robert the Bruce gave it to Hugh, 6th Earl of Ross, in 1328.

1077 RED DEER RANGE 4H9

8 miles W of New Galloway on A712, car park signposted. Late June-early Sept. Tues, Thurs 1100 and 1400, Sun 1500. Charge for tour of range. (FE)

Native Galloway red deer are seen close at hand in their natural habitat on a guided tour through the deer range, mingling with stags, hinds and calves. Tour lasts 1½ hours, guided by forest ranger. Stout footwear advisable and, if possible, a camera.

1078 REELIG GLEN 3A9

Moniack, 8 miles from Inverness. 1 mile S of A862 Inverness-Beauly. All times. Free. Car parking only. (FE)

Two woodland walks with viewpoint and picnic place. A feature is the number of specimen trees on the walk, with some of the tallest trees in Britain. Leaflet available from Forest Enterprise, Fort Augustus.

1079 'REMAINS TO BE SEEN' 3G9

   ♿
A
P
T

Quilquox Croft. From Ellon take B9005 to Methlick until Quilquox sign on right. Cross river and bear left up hill. Croft on left, approx 1½m. Apr-Oct, daily 1000-1900; Nov-Mar 1100-1600. Parking available. Complimentary tea and coffee. Tel: (035 87) 229.

An exhibition of period clothes and accessories, lace and jewellery and a porcelain room. Gardens planted by ornithologist to attract birds. Children's play area.

1080 RENNIBISTER EARTH HOUSE 1B11

About 4½m WNW of Kirkwall on the Finstown road (A965), Orkney. All reasonable times. Free. (HS) Tel: 031-244 3101.

An excellent example of the Orkney type of Iron Age souterrain or earth-house, consisting of a passage and underground chamber with supporting roof-pillars.

1081 RENNIE'S BRIDGE 5F6

Kelso. All times. Free. (Borders Regional Council).

A fine 5-arched bridge built over the River Tweed in 1803 by Rennie to replace one destroyed by the floods of 1797. On the bridge are two lamp posts from the demolished Old Waterloo Bridge in London, which Rennie built in 1811. There is also a fine view to Floors Castle (No 567).

1082 RESTENNETH PRIORY 5D1

Off B9113, 1½m ENE of Forfar. All reasonable times. Free. (HS) Tel: 031-244 3101.

A house of Augustinian canons, probably founded by David I on the site of an earlier church, in an attractive setting. A feature of the ruins is the tall square tower, with its shapely broach spire, and an early doorway at its base.

Ring of Brogar

1083 RING OF BROGAR   !B11

Between Loch of Harray and Loch of Stenness, 5m NE of Stromness,
Mainland, Orkney. All reasonable times. Free. (HS) Tel: 031-244 3101.

Magnificent stone circle of 36 stones (originally 60)
surrounded by a deep ditch cut into solid bedrock.
Nearby are large mounds and other standing stones,
notably the Comet Stone. (See No 1193).

1084 ROB ROY AND TROSSACHS
VISITOR CENTRE   5A3

& *Ancaster Square, Callander. Mar-May and Oct-Dec, daily 1000-1700;*
T *June & Sept, daily 0930-1800; July & Aug, daily 0900-2200; (last*
admission 30 mins before closing). Entrance charge. Group concessions.
Parking available. Themed souvenir shop, bookshop. Tel: (0877) 30342.

ASVA

Exciting new visitor attraction using modern
technology to take the visitor back three centuries to
rediscover the daring adventures of Scotland's most
colourful folk hero, Rob Roy Macgregor, in the heart
of his wildly beautiful homelands, the Trossachs.
Tourist information centre.

1085 ROB ROY'S GRAVE   4H2

W end of Balquhidder Churchyard, off A84, 14m NNW of Callander.
All reasonable times. Free.

Three flat gravestones enclosed by railings are the graves
of Rob Roy, his wife and two of his sons. The church
itself contains St Angus' Stone (8th century), a 17th-
century bell from the old church and old Gaelic Bibles.
(See No 203).

1086 ROB ROY'S STATUE   3G10

W end of Peterculter by A93. All times. Free.

Statue of Rob Roy standing above the Leuchar Burn
can be seen from the bridge on the main road.

1087 ROMAN BATH HOUSE   4H5

Roman Road, Bearsden, 5m NW of Glasgow. All reasonable times.
Free. (HS) Tel: 031-244 3101.

A Roman bath house built in the 140s AD for the use
of the soldiers stationed in the adjacent Antonine Wall
fort. The best surviving visible Roman building in
Scotland. (See No 60).

Rosslyn Chapel

1088 ROSSLYN CHAPEL   6E7

At Roslin, off A703, 7½m S of Edinburgh. Apr-Oct, Mon-Sat 1000-1700, Sun 1200-1645. Entrance charge. Group concessions. Coffee shop. Crafts. Tel: 031-440 2159.

This 15th-century chapel is one of Scotland's loveliest and most historic churches, renowned for its magnificent sculpture and Prentice Pillar.

1089 ROTHESAY CASTLE   4F5

At Rothesay, Isle of Bute. Opening standard, except Oct-Mar closed Thurs am and Fri. Entrance charge. Group concessions. (HS) Tel: 031-244 3101.

One of the most important medieval castles in Scotland. Rothesay was stormed by Norsemen in 1240; their breach can still be detected. The walls, heightened and provided with four round towers in the late 13th century, enclose a circular courtyard unique in Scotland.

1090 ROTHIEMURCHUS ESTATE VISITOR CENTRE   3C10

♿
T

1m from Aviemore. All year, 0900-1700. Parking available. Shops. Tearoom (Easter-Oct). Buffet and barbecue lunches by arrangement. Tel: (0479) 810858.

ASVA

Estate tours, farm tours by tractor and trailer (Easter-Oct), Landrover safari tours, guided walks. Guided walks in Cairngorms National Nature Reserve, Highland cattle, red deer, Caledonian pine forest. Trout farm (fish can be fed), fresh and smoked trout and venison for sale, fishing lochs and Spey river beats. Designer knitwear and craft shop. Clay pigeon shooting, off-road driving, falconry, Loch an Eilein (see No 865), corporate hospitality.

1091 ROUGH CASTLE   6A6

Off B816, 6m W of Falkirk. All reasonable times. Free. (HS) Tel: 031-244 3101.

The best preserved of the forts of the Antonine Wall, with ramparts and ditches easily seen.
(See also Nos 60 and 1087).

1092 ROXBURGH CASTLE   5F7

Off A699, 1m SW of Kelso. All times. Free.

The earthworks are all that remain of the once mighty castle, destroyed by the Scots in the 15th century, and the walled Royal Burgh which gave its name to the county. The present village of Roxburgh dates from a later period.

Royal Museum of Scotland: see Nos 487 and 501.

1093 ROYAL LOCHNAGAR DISTILLERY VISITOR CENTRE 3D11

Just off B976. Turn off A93 at Crathie, nr Ballater. Jan-Dec exc Christmas & New Year. Mon-Fri 1000-1700. Also Sat 1100-1600 (Easter-Oct). Parking available. Gift shop. Coffee shop. Tel: (033 97) 42273.

ASVA

The distillery, which was granted a Royal Warrant of Appointment by Queen Victoria in 1848, is set in beautiful scenery close to Balmoral Castle. New visitor centre features the distillery's associations with Queen Victoria. Tours and tasting. Home of Royal Lochnagar Special Reserve Single Malt Whisky.

1094 RUMBLING BRIDGE 6C4

A823 at Rumbling Bridge. Free. All reasonable times. Parking available.

The River Devon is spanned here by two bridges, the lower one dating from 1713, the upper one from 1816. A footpath from the north side gives good access to spectacular and picturesque gorges and falls, one of which is known as the Devil's Mill. Another, Cauldron Linn, is a mile downstream, whilst Vicar's Bridge is a beauty spot a mile beyond this.

1095 RUTHERGLEN MUSEUM 4H5

King Street. Mon-Sat 1000-1700; Sun 1100-1700. Small shop. Tel: 041-647 0837.

A museum of the history of the former royal burgh of Rutherglen, with regularly changing displays and temporary exhibitions.

Ruthven Barracks

1096 RUTHVEN BARRACKS 3B11

On B970, ½m S of Kingussie. All reasonable times. Free. (HS) Tel: 031-244 3101.

Considerable ruins, on a site once occupied by a fortress of the Wolf of Badenoch, of barracks built 1716-18 to keep the Highlanders in check, and added to by General Wade in 1734. After the disaster of Culloden, 1746, Prince Charles' Highlanders assembled at Ruthven hoping he might take the field again. When they realised the cause was hopeless, they blew up the barracks.

Ruthven Castle: see No 753.

1097 RUTHWELL CROSS 5C10

In Ruthwell Church, B724, 8½m SE of Dumfries. All reasonable times. Free. (HS) Tel: 031-244 3101.

This preaching cross, which is 18 feet high, is carved with Runic characters. It dates back to the 8th century and is a major monument of Dark Age Europe.

1098 ST ANDREWS CASTLE 6G2

Shore at St Andrews. Opening standard. Entrance charge.
Group concessions. (HS) Tel: 031-244 3101.

ASVA

The ruined castle, overlooking the sea, was founded in
1200 and rebuilt at several periods. Here Cardinal
Beaton was murdered in 1546, and the first round of
the Reformation struggle was fought out in the siege
that followed.

1099 ST ANDREW'S CATHEDRAL, INVERNESS 3B8

♿
A

Ness Walk, Ardross Street, below Ness Bridge. Jan-Dec. Daily
0830-1800, later opening May-Sept. Donations requested. Parking
available. Gift shop and tearoom (May-Sept). Tel: (0463) 233535.

Cathedral Church in Gothic style built, 1866-69, by
local architect Alexander Ross. It was the first cathedral
to be built in this style since the Reformation.
Monolithic pillars of polished Peterhead granite,
stained glass, sculpture, carved reredos. Angel font
after Thorvaldsen (Copenhagen), Founder's Memorial,
ikons presented by Tsar of Russia, ten bells. Fine choir
sings at Sunday services.

St Andrews Cathedral, St Andrews

1100 ST ANDREWS CATHEDRAL, ST ANDREWS 6G2

In St Andrews. Charge for Museum and St Rule's (Regulus') Tower.
Opening standard. Entrance charge. Group concessions. (HS)
Tel: 031-244 3101.

ASVA

The cathedral was once the largest church in the
country. The remains include parts of the east and west
gables, the south wall of the nave, and portions of the
choir and south transept, mostly built in the 12th and
13th centuries.

1101 ST ANDREWS MUSEUM 6G2

♿
T

Kinburn Park, Doubledykes, St Andrews. Apr-Sept, daily 1100-1800;
Oct-Mar, Mon-Fri 1100-1600. Sat & Sun 1400-1700. Free. Car parking
only. Gift shop. Tearoom. Tel: (0334) 77706.

Display—with sounds and smells— of the history of
the town of St Andrews from medieval to modern
times. Temporary exhibitions programme; children's
activity room; children's events during school holidays.
Gallery talks and other events for adults.

1102 ST ANDREWS PRESERVATION TRUST MUSEUM 6G2

  ♿ A *12 North Street, St Andrews. Easter weekend, mid Jun-mid Sept, daily 1400-1630. Also 30 Nov (St Andrew's Day). Donations. Gift shop. Tel: (0334) 77629.*

Converted fishermen's houses. Collection comprises items of interest from St Andrews including displays from a well-known grocer's shop and also a chemist, fishing equipment and photographs. Features work of the Trust in conservation and renovation.

1103 ST ANDREWS SEA LIFE CENTRE 6G2

The Scores, St Andrews. All year, daily 1000-1800 (2100 in July & Aug). Entrance charges. Group concessions. Gift shop. Restaurant. Tel: (0334) 74786.

St Andrews Sea Life Centre reveals some of the secrets beneath the sea. Creatures from shrimps and starfish to stingrays, sharks, conger eel and octopus feature in dramatic displays which re-create their natural habitats. Resident Common Seals Batman, Laurel and Hardy share spacious outdoor pools. Daily talks and demonstrations.

St Andrews University

1104 ST ANDREWS UNIVERSITY 6G2

  ♿ A P *St Andrews town centre. Tel: (0334) 76161, ext 258/488.*

The oldest university in Scotland, founded in 1411. See the 15th-century Church of St Salvator, now the chapel for the united colleges of St Salvator (1450) and St Leonard (1511); St Mary's College (1537) with its quadrangle; and the 16th-century St Leonard's Chapel. Also in the town are St Mary's House built in 1523 and now St Leonard's School Library, and Holy Trinity Church with a 16th-century tower and interesting interior features. Guided tours operate twice daily (6 days a week) in July and August.

1105 ST BEAN'S CHURCH 6B2

  ♿ A *At Fowlis Wester, off A85, 5m NE of Crieff. All year, daylight hours. Free. Tel: (0764) 83205.*

An attractive 13th-century church, restored in 1927, containing a finely carved Pictish stone cross and a 'leper's squint'. Opposite is Fowlis Wester Sculptured Stone, an 8th century Pictish stone with remarkably clear carvings, standing in the square of this attractive little village. Above the church, a Pictish stone circle.

1106 ST BLANE'S CHAPEL 4F6

8½m S of Rothesay, Isle of Bute. All reasonable times. Free. (HS) Tel: 031-244 3101.

Ruins of a chapel built c 1100. Nearby are the foundations of a monastery founded by St Blane in the 6th century.

1107 ST BRIDE'S CHURCH   5A7

Douglas, 12m SSW of Lanark. Open all reasonable times. Free. Apply keykeeper. (HS) Tel: 031-244 3101.

The restored chancel of this ancient church contains the tomb of the 'Bell the Cat' Earl of Angus (died 1514). The nearby tower (1618) has a clock of 1565 said to have been gifted by Mary, Queen of Scots.

1108 ST BRIDGET'S KIRK   6D5

Dalgety Bay, off A92, 2m SW of Aberdour. Open all reasonable times. (HS) Free. Tel: 031-244 3101.

Ruins of an ancient church dedicated to St Bridget in 1244.

1109 ST CLEMENT'S CHURCH   2B7

At Rodel, S end of Harris, Western Isles. All reasonable times. Free. (HS) Tel: 031-244 3101.

A cruciform church of c 1500 with rich decoration and sculptured slabs.

1110 ST COLUMBA'S CAVE   4E5

1m N of Ellary on W shore of Loch Killisport (Caolisport), 10m SW of Ardrishaig. All times. Free.

Traditionally associated with St Columba's arrival in Scotland, the cave contains a rock-shelf with an altar, above which are carved crosses. A large basin, perhaps a Stone Age mortar, may have been used as a font. The cave was occupied from the Middle Stone Age. In front are traces of houses and the ruins of a chapel (possibly 13th century) and another cave is nearby.

1111 ST CORMAC'S CHAPEL   4D5

Isle of Eilean Mor, E of Jura. All reasonable times. Free. Access: private launch to Eilean Mor (tel: Ormsary (088 03) 239 evenings, Mr Rodgers). (HS) Tel: 031-244 3101.

This medieval chapel is 15 feet by 8 feet with an upper chamber only accessible by ladder. It contains a sculpture of a priest.

St Cyrus National Nature Reserve

1112 ST CYRUS NATIONAL NATURE RESERVE   3G12

Old Lifeboat Station, Nether Warburton. From Montrose take A92 north: after crossing North Esk River take first right for ½m. From St Cyrus take A92 for 1m, turn left before crossing North Esk bridge and proceed for ½m. May-Sept, Tues-Sun 0930-1730. Free. Parking available. (SNH) Tel: (067 48) 3736.

The reserve has many botanical and ornithological interests while the visitor centre houses displays on local history, natural history, salmon fishing and wildlife. There are children's games, a salt water aquarium and an audio visual. Guide dogs not allowed.

1113 ST DUTHUS CHAPEL AND COLLEGIATE CHURCH 3B7

Tain. Chapel: All reasonable times. Free. Church: Open daily, enquire locally. Free. Museum: Easter-Sept 1000-1630. Entrance charge. Tel: (0862) 892140 or 893422.

The chapel was built between 1065 and 1256. St Duthus died in 1065 and was buried in Ireland, but 200 years later his remains were transferred to Tain. The chapel was destroyed by fire in 1427. St Duthus Church was built c 1360 by William, Earl and Bishop of Ross, in Decorated style, and became a notable place of pilgrimage. Tain and District Museum and Clan Ross Centre in grounds, is a developing heritage centre with displays of old documents including a Papal Bull, telling the story of the area, of medieval pilgrims and of the Pictish people of the area.

1114 ST FILLAN'S CAVE 6G4

Cove Wynd, Pittenweem, near harbour, 9m SSE of St Andrews. All year, 1000-1700. Charge for adults only.

St Fillan's Cave gave Pittenweem (Pictish for *The Place of the Cave*) its name. In the 12th century, Augustinian monks from the Isle of May established the Priory, the Great House and the Prior's Lodging above the cave, cutting through the rock from the garden to the holy cave-shrine below. Restored and rededicated in 1935 by St John's Episcopal Church.

1115 ST JOHN'S KIRK 6D2

&⟨T⟩ *St John Street, Perth. Daily, exc Thurs pm. Holy Communion, Sun 0930. Tel: (0738) 21755/23358.*

Consecrated in 1242, this fine cruciform church largely dates from the 15th century, and was restored 1923-28 as a war memorial. Here John Knox in 1559 preached his momentous sermon urging the 'purging of the churches from idolatry'. The 'Town Kirk' of Perth, St John's is a venue for musical and dramatic productions from time to time. Wheelchair access via south door.

St Kilda

1116 ST KILDA Map 2 Inset

110m W of Scottish mainland. Access difficult: NTS organises work parties. (NTS/SNH) Tel: 031-226 5922.

This remote and spectacular group of islands was evacuated in 1930. The cliffs at Conachair, 1397 feet, are the highest in Britain. The wildlife, some of which (Soay sheep, St Kilda mouse and wren) is unique, includes the world's biggest gannetry and myriads of fulmars and puffins. Remains of the primitive dwellings; working parties to maintain these visit in summer. In 1986 St Kilda was designated Scotland's first World Heritage Site.

St Magnus Cathedral

1117 ST MAGNUS CATHEDRAL   1B11

♿   *Kirkwall, Orkney. May-Aug, Mon-Sat 0900-1700. Sept-Apr, Mon-Sat 0900-1300, 1400-1700. Graveyard open all reasonable times. Closed Sun (except for services). Free. Inductive loop. Tel: (0856) 874894.*

Founded by Jarl Rognvald in 1137 and dedicated to his uncle St Magnus. The remains of both men are in the massive central piers. The original building dates from 1137 to 1200 but additional work went on for a further 300 years. It is still in regular use as a church, and contains some of the finest examples of Norman architecture in Scotland, with small additions in transitional styles and very early Gothic.

1118 ST MAGNUS CHURCH   1B10

Isle of Egilsay, Orkney. All reasonable times. Free. (HS) Tel: 031-244 3101.

An impressive church, probably 12th-century, with a remarkable round tower of the Irish type, which still stands to a height of nearly 50 feet.

1119 ST MARY'S CHAPEL, BUTE   4F5

A845, ½m S of Rothesay. All reasonable times. Free. (HS) Tel: 031-244 3101.

The remains of the late medieval Church of St Mary, including two fine recessed and canopied tombs containing effigies of a knight in full armour, and a lady and child.

1120 ST MARY'S CHAPEL, CROSSKIRK   3C2

Off A836, 6m W of Thurso. All reasonable times. Free. (HS) Tel: 031-244 3101.

A rudely-constructed chapel with very low doors narrowing at the top in Irish style. Probably 12th century.

St Mary's Chapel, Wyre: see No 325.

1121 ST MARY'S CHURCH, AUCHINDOIR   3E9

3m N of Kildrummy. All reasonable times. Free. (HS) Tel: 031-244 3101.

Ruins of one of the finest medieval parish churches remaining in Scotland.

1122 ST MARY'S CHURCH, GRANDTULLY   5B1

At Pitcairn Farm, 3m ENE of Aberfeldy, off A827. All times. Free. (HS) Tel: 031-244 3101.

A 16th-century church, with a remarkable 17th-century painted wooden ceiling of heraldic and symbolic subjects.

1123 ST MARY'S COLLEGIATE CHURCH 6G6

& *Sidegate, Haddington. Apr-Sept, Mon-Sat 1000-1600, Sun 1300-1600.*
T *Donations accepted. Parking available. Gift shop. Tearoom.*
Tel: (062 082) 5111.

14th-century medieval church, built on the scale of a
cathedral. Choir and transepts badly damaged at siege
of Haddington, completely restored (1971-73).
Features include fibreglass ceiling, Burne Jones and Sax
Shaw windows, East Lothian tapestries, Lauderdale
Aisle. The home church of Scots Reformer, John Knox.
Nearby, St Mary's Pleasance.

St Mary's Loch

1124 ST MARY'S LOCH 5D7

Off A708, 14m ESE of Selkirk. Parking available.

Beautifully set among smooth green hills, this three-
mile-long loch is used for sailing and fishing. On the
neck of land separating it from Loch of the Lowes at
the south end stands Tibbie Shiel's Inn, long kept by
Tibbie Shiel (Elizabeth Richardson, 1783-1878) from
1823, and a meeting-place for many 19th-century
writers. Beside the road towards the north end of the
loch is a seated statue of James Hogg, the 'Ettrick
Shepherd', author of the *Confessions of a Justified Sinner*
and a friend of Scott, who farmed in this district.
(See No 743). On the route of the Southern Upland
Way.

1125 ST MARY'S PARISH CHURCH,
MONYMUSK 3G10

& *Village Square, Monymusk, 18 miles from Aberdeen. Apr-Oct.*
Daylight hours. Free. Parking available.

The only Norman church in north-east Scotland, St
Mary's has been in constant use since it was built in
the 12th century. The site was visited by St Columba.
Modern church music was introduced to Scotland here
in the 17th century, and John Wesley preached here twice.

1126 ST MICHAEL'S PARISH CHURCH 6C6

& *Beside Linlithgow Palace, on S shore of the loch, Linlithgow. Oct-May,*
A *Mon-Fri 1000-1200, 1400-1600. Jun-Sep, daily 1000-1200, 1400-1600.*
Free. Car parking only. Gift shop. Tel: (0506) 842188.

Medieval parish church, consecrated in 1242 on the site
of an earlier church. Associated with the royal house
of Stewart, as Mary, Queen of Scots, born in the palace
nearby, was baptised in the church. There is a
contemporary aluminium crown, designed by Geoffrey
Clarke, replacing the medieval crown which was
removed in 1820, in danger of collapsing.

St Monan's Church

1127 ST MONAN'S CHURCH 6G4

In St Monans, A917, 12m S of St Andrews. All reasonable times. Free.

Possibly a Ninianic foundation, c 400 AD. A place of
healing from early times. David I was reputedly cured
of an arrow wound here. It became a Royal Votive
Chapel perhaps at that time. Alexander III initiated new
building work c 1265. David II repaired and remodelled
the Choir area in 1362 as a thanksgiving for deliverance
from a storm at sea. James III gifted it to the
Dominicans c 1460 and it became the Parish Church
in 1646.

1128 ST NINIAN'S CHAPEL, ISLE OF WHITHORN 4H11

At Isle of Whithorn, 3m SE of Whithorn. All reasonable times. Free. (HS)
Tel: 031-244 3101.

Ruins of a 13th-century chapel on a site traditionally
associated with St Ninian. On the shore by Kidsdale,
2m W, is St Ninian's Cave, with early Christian crosses
carved on the rock.

1129 ST NINIAN'S CHAPEL, TYNET 3E8

Tynet, 3m E of Fochabers on A98. All year, dawn-dusk. Free. Parking
available. The Church is in use weekly and is open daily. Visitors are
requested to respect its character as a place of worship. The access road is
single-track and is unsuitable for coaches. Tel: (0452) 32196.

Built about 1755 by the Laird of Tynet, ostensibly for
his own use as a sheepcote but in reality as a Mass
centre for the Catholics of the neighbourhood. It has
undergone many extensions and alterations since, the
latest being in the 1950s under the direction of Ian G
Lindsay, RSA. St Ninian's has the distinction of being
the oldest post-Reformation Catholic church still in use.
Mass 1730 Saturday, all year.

1130 ST NINIAN'S ISLE 1F5

By B9122 off W coast of Mainland, Shetland. All times. Free.

Holy Well, foundations of chapel c 12th century and
pre-Norse church where a hoard of Celtic silver was
discovered (now in the Museum of Antiquities, Queen
Street, Edinburgh). (See No 487).

1131 ST PETER'S CHURCH 3C3

Near the Harbour at Thurso. All reasonable times. Free.
Parking available.

Ruins situated in the attractively restored old part of
Thurso. Of medieval or earlier origin; much of the
present church dates from the 17th century.

1132 ST RONAN'S WELLS INTERPRETATIVE CENTRE 5D6

    Wells Brae, Innerleithen. Easter-Oct. Daily 1400-1700. Parking available. Gift shop. Tearoom. Tel: (0721) 20123.

History of the site and building told in display of objects, photographs and documents relating to the well, made famous in Sir Walter Scott's novel of the same name. Herb garden, tearoom and the original well.

1133 ST VIGEAN'S MUSEUM 5E1

½m N of Arbroath. Open all reasonable times. (HS) Tel: 031-244 3101.

A cottage museum containing Pictish gravestones which are among the most important groups of early Christian sculpture in Scotland. Attractive St Vigean's Church nearby.

1134 SADDELL ABBEY 4E1

B842, 9m NNW of Campbeltown. All reasonable times. Free.

The abbey was built in the 12th century by Somerled, Lord of the Isles, or his son Reginald. Only the walls of the original building are left, with sculptured carved tombstones.

1135 SANQUHAR POST OFFICE 5A8

39-41 High Street, Sanquhar. Jan-Dec. Mon-Sat (half-day Thurs & Sat). Parking available. Tel: (0659) 50201.

Dating from 1738, the Post Office at Sanquhar is the world's oldest working post office. Displays telling of the evolution of the postal service, philately, and Robert Burns' connection with the town are planned for 1994.

1136 SAVINGS BANKS MUSEUM 5C10

In Ruthwell, 6½m W of Annan. All year (except Sun and Mon in winter) 1000-1300, 1400-1700. Free (pre-booking for large parties). Parking available. Sales point. Tel: (0387) 87640.

The first Savings Bank, founded by Rev Dr Henry Duncan in 1810. This room is a mine of information on the early days of the Savings bank movement and the restoration of the Ruthwell Cross. (See No 1097).

Scalloway Castle

1137 SCALLOWAY CASTLE 1G5

6m W of Lerwick, Shetland. All reasonable times. Free. (HS) Tel: 031-244 3101.

Built in 1600 by Earl Patrick Stewart, in medieval style. When the Earl, a notoriously cruel character, was executed in 1615, the castle fell into disuse.

1138   SCALLOWAY MUSEUM   1G5

Main Street, Scalloway, Shetland. May-Oct, Tue, Wed & Thur,
1400-1700. Sat 1000-1300, 1400-1700. Sun 1400-1700.
Tel: (059 588) 256/675.

The museum is located in a converted shop in Main
Street. It is run by volunteers of the Scalloway History
Group and contains displays of local artefacts. Main
display recalls some of the exploits of the Norwegian
Resistance fighters who created the legendary
"Shetland Bus" of the last war. There is also an
extensive display of photographs of old Scalloway.

1139   SCAPA FLOW   1B12

Sea area, enclosed by the mainland of Orkney and the islands of Burray,
South Ronaldsay, Flotta and Hoy.

Major naval anchorage in both wars and the scene of
the surrender of the German "High Seas" Fleet in
1919. Today a centre of marine activity as Flotta is a
pipeline landfall and tanker terminal for North Sea Oil.
Interpretation Centre at Lyness, Hoy in old pumphouse,
used to feed fuel to ships.
(See No 1029).

Scone Palace

1140   SCONE PALACE   6D1

ASVA

Off A93 Braemar Road, 2m NE of Perth. Easter-mid Oct, Mon-Sat
0930-1700; Sun 1330-1700 (Jul & Aug 1000-1700), other times by
arrangement. House, grounds and pinetum: Entrance charges. Group
concessions. Parking available. Produce and gift shop. Restaurant, coffee
shop, banqueting facilities. Tel: (0738) 52300.

The present castellated palace, enlarged and embellished
in 1803, incorporates the 16th-century and earlier
palaces. It has notable grounds and a pinetum and is still
the family home of the Earl of Mansfield. The Moot
Hill at Scone, known in the 8th century and earlier,
was the site of the famous coronation Stone of Scone,
brought there in the 9th century by Kenneth MacAlpine,
King of Scots. In 1296 the Stone was seized by the
English and taken to Westminster Abbey. The ancient
Abbey of Scone was destroyed by followers of John
Knox. Magnificent collection of porcelain, furniture,
ivories, 18th-century clocks and 16th-century
needlework. Parties of disabled visitors welcome.

1141 SCOTS DYKE 5D9

Off A7, 7m S of Langholm. All reasonable times. Access is not easily identified. Free.

The remains of a wall made of clods of earth and stones, which marked part of the border between England and Scotland.

1142 SCOTSTARVIT TOWER 6F3

Off A916, 3m S of Cupar. All reasonable times. Free. (HS)
Tel: 031-244 3101.

A fine tower known to have been in existence in 1579.

1143 CAPTAIN SCOTT AND DR WILSON CAIRN 3E12

In Glen Prosen on unclassified road NW of Dykehead. All times. Free.

The cairn replaces the original fountain which was erected in memory of the Antarctic explorers, Captain Scott and Dr Wilson. Early planning for the expedition took place at Dr Wilson's home in the glen.

1144 SCOTTISH CENTRE FOR FALCONRY 6D4

& T *Turfhills, Kinross, next to Granada service station on Junction 6 on M90. Mar-Dec. Daily, 1000-1730 (last entry 1700). Entrance charges. Group concessions. Parking available. Gift shop. Restaurant. Tel: (0577) 862010.*

Display on the history of falconry and conservation relating to birds of prey. Aviary birds, weathering area with unrestricted views where visitors can take photographs of birds. Flying displays at regular intervals during the day. In spring and early summer, breeding birds rearing their young can be watched with the aid of closed circuit television.

1145 SCOTTISH DEER CENTRE 6D3

On A91, 3m W of Cupar, 12m W of St Andrews. All year except Christmas and New Year. Apr-Oct 1000-1700. Later in summer. Special tours by arrangement, all year. Entrance charge. Group discount. Parking available. Craft shop. Winery selling Scottish wines and foods. Tel: (033781) 391.

ASVA

The centre offers a unique opportunity to see many species of deer: feed, stroke and photograph during a ranger-led tour. Falconry demonstrations every day. Audio-visual show and walk through multi-media exhibition. Giant outdoor adventureland, treetop canopy walk and maze. Farm walk and picnic sites.

Scottish Fisheries Museum

1146 SCOTTISH FISHERIES MUSEUM 6H3

& T *At Anstruther harbour, 10m SSE of St Andrews. Apr-Oct, Mon-Sat 1000-1730, Sun 1100-1700. Nov-Mar, Mon-Sat 1000-1630. Sun 1400-1630. Entrance charges. Group concessions. Parking available. Gift shop. Tearoom. Tel: (0333) 310628.*

16th to 19th-century buildings housing marine aquarium, fishing and ships' gear, model and actual fishing boats (including 'Fifie' and 'Zulu' in harbour), fisher-home interiors, reference library.

1147 THE SCOTTISH HORSE MUSEUM 5B1

&. T *The Cross, Dunkeld. Easter to Sept, daily exc Tues & Wed, 1000-1200, 1400-1700.*
Entrance charge (children free). Parking available.
Tel: (035 02) 296.

Exhibits, uniforms, photographs, maps and rolls of all
those who served in this Yeomanry Regiment.

1148 SCOTTISH INDUSTRIAL RAILWAY CENTRE 4H8

At Minnivey Colliery, Dalmellington, take the A713 S from Ayr, turn
left to Burnton just before Dalmellington Village, left again at 'T' junction,
follow road right up to the Centre. June-Sept, every Sat. Also Steam Days,
check dates. Entrance charge. Group concessions. Parking available. Gift
shop. Tearoom. Tel: (0292) 313579 or 531144.

8 steam locomotives (including one fireless), 12 diesels
and a large collection of rolling stock. Museum, loco
shed, brake van rides. (See No 361).

1149 SCOTTISH MARITIME MUSEUM 4G6

&. P *Harbourside, Irvine. Apr-Oct. Entrance charges. Family tickets.*
Parking available. Gift shop. Tearoom. Tel: (0294) 78283.

ASVA Boatshed exhibition. Historic vessels at pontoon
moorings, including a Scottish puffer, lifeboat and tug.
Wharf and harbour, ferry, restored Edwardian shipyard
worker's flat. Boatshed suitable for disabled visitors.

1150 SCOTTISH MINING MUSEUM, NEWTONGRANGE 6F7

&. T *Lady Victoria Colliery, Newtongrange, 10 miles SE of Edinburgh o.. A7.*
Apr-Sept. Daily, 1100-1600. (Last tour 1500.) Entrance charge. Group
concessions. Parking available. Gift shop. Tearoom. Tel: 031-663 7519.

ASVA Recently renovated Victorian colliery. A Grant Ritchie
steam winding engine is one of many attractions on
the pithead tour. The Visitor Centre contains a life-like
display introducing a Victorian pit village through the
eyes of a typical miner. A self-drive Coal Heritage Trail
links Lady Victoria Colliery to the Museum's other
site at Prestongrange.

1151 SCOTTISH MINING MUSEUM, PRESTONGRANGE 6F6

Prestongrange, on B1348 between Musselburgh and Prestonpans.
Apr-Sept. Daily, 1100-1600. (Last tour 1500.) Entrance charges.
Group concessions. Parking available. Gift shop. Refreshments.
Tel: 031-663 7519.

Exhibitions: 'The Miner's Skills' and 'Cutting the
Coal', on mechanical coal extraction. Cornish beam
pumping engine house. Self-drive Coal Heritage Trail
to Lady Victoria Colliery. Also on view are steam
locomotives, a steam crane, a colliery winding engine
and remains of a Hoffman kiln. Special 'Steam Days'
on first Sunday of each month, April to October.

1152 SCOTTISH MUSEUM OF WOOLLEN TEXTILES 5D6

&. *Tweedvale Mill. On main road (A72) at Walkerburn, 9m ESE of Peebles.*
Apr-Oct, Mon-Sat 0900-1700. Free. Parking available. Large mill shop.
Coffee shop. Tel: (089 687) 619.

This display features the growth of the Scottish textile
trade, with many interesting exhibits. Group bookings
by arrangement.

1153 SCOTTISH SCULPTURE WORKSHOP AND SCULPTURE WALK   3E9

&
T

Main Street, Lumsden, between Alford and Huntly. Jan-Dec. Mon-Fri 1000-1600 or by arrangement. Free. Parking available. Tel: (046 46) 372.

Founded in 1979, and led since then by Frederick Bushe, a sculptor of international standing, the workshop is a fusion of local culture and international influences, bringing sculptors from all over the world to work in wood, ceramic, constructed and cast metal, granite and other stone. The workshop aims to place sculpture in the community, and the results are to be seen all over Scotland.

1154 SCOTTISH TARTANS MUSEUM   6A2

Drummond Street Comrie, 6m W of Crieff. Apr-Oct, Mon-Sat 1000-1800, Sun 1100-1700. Nov-Mar, check times with office. Family Ticket. Entrance charge. Group rates for parties of over 20 persons. Tel: (0764) 670779.

The Scottish Tartans Society is the custodian of the largest collection in existence of material relating to tartans and Highland dress. The Tartan Room (over 450 tartans on display), Exhibition of the History of Highland Dress. A reconstructed weaver's cottage. Dye weaving plant, garden, shop. Children's corner. Clan history certificates.

1155 SCOTTISH WOOL CENTRE   4H3

&
T

Off main street, Aberfoyle. Jan-Dec exc Christmas & New Year. Daily, 1000-1800. Entrance charge. Group concessions. Parking available. Large retail area. Restaurant, tearoom. Tel: (087 72) 850.

ASVA

Opened in 1992, the Scottish Wool Centre is a custom-built all-weather visitor centre presenting the 'Story of Scottish Wool' from the sheep to the shops. 'Sheep Spectacular' presented daily in 170-seat amphitheatre; craft area features carding, spinning and weaving as well as traditional Shetland knitting; 'Kid's Farm' tells the story of cashmere, along with cashmere kids and baby lambs.

SS "Sir Walter Scott"

1156 SS "SIR WALTER SCOTT"   4H3

&
A
T

From Trossachs Pier, E end of Loch Katrine, 9m W of Callander. Apr-Sept, Sun-Fri 1100, 1345 and 1515; Sat 1400, 1530. Fares vary with sailings. Charter available. Parking available. Shop. Cafeteria. Tel: 041-355 5333.

Regular sailings in summer from the pier to Stronachlachar in this fine old steamer. Views include Ben Lomond. Visitor Centre.

1157 SIR WALTER SCOTT'S COURTROOM   5E7

♿ A

Market Place, Selkirk. Jul-Aug. Daily 1400-1600, other times by arrangement with Museums Officer, Ettrick and Lauderdale District Council, Municipal Buildings, High Street, Selkirk. Free. Parking available. Tel: (0750) 20096.

The bench and chair from which Sir Walter Scott, as Sheriff of Selkirk, administered justice here for thirty years, are on display, with portraits of Scott, James Hogg, Mungo Park and Robert Burns, with ancient charters. Also displayed are watercolours by Tom Scott, RSA.

1158 SCOTT'S VIEW   5E6

B6356, 4 miles E of Melrose.

A view over the Tweed to the Eildon Hills, beloved by Scott; here the horses taking his remains to Dryburgh for burial stopped as they had so often before for Sir Walter to enjoy this panorama.

1159 DUNS SCOTUS STATUE   5F5

At Duns, in public park. All times. Free.

Duns was the birthplace of John Duns Scotus (1266-1308), a Franciscan who became a leading divine and one of the greatest medieval philosophers. It is said the word 'dunce' came into the English language as a result of criticism of his work after his death. (See No 1257).

1160 SEA LIFE CENTRE, OBAN   4E2

♿ A T

Barcaldine, on A828, 10 miles N of Oban. Mid Feb-Nov, daily, 0900-1800. (1900 in July & Aug). Dec-mid Feb, weekends only. Entrance charges. Group concessions. Parking available. Gift shop. Restaurant. Tel: (0631) 72386.

ASVA

A display of native marine life, from sinister British sharks to lovable seals, in a lochside setting second to none. New seal pup nursery and seashore nature trails.

1161 SEAMEN'S MEMORIAL   3E7

Buckie. Key at 6 New Street. Free. Parking available. Tel: (0542) 32426.

A small chapel with beautiful stained glass windows dedicated to local fishermen who lost their lives at sea since 1946. Opened by HM The Queen in 1982.

1162 M.V. 'THE SECOND SNARK'   4G5

♿

Princes Pier, Greenock. May-Sept. Variable fares according to length of cruise. Group concessions. Parking available. Bar and refreshments on board. Tel: (0475) 21281.

Attractive Denny-built motor vessel in original appearance. Departures from Greenock (Princes Pier) to Helensburgh, Kilcreggan, Dunoon and Loch Goil, Rothesay and Tighnabruaich, Kyles, Loch Riddon, Millport, Largs and round the Cumbraes.

1163 SELKIRK GLASS   5E7

Off A7 N of Selkirk. All year, Mon-Fri 0900-1700, Sat 1000-1630, Sun 1200-1600. Glass making: Mon-Fri 0900-1630. Free. Coffee shop. Tel: (0750) 20954.

Visitors are welcome at factory and showroom to see a range of paperweights and watch craftsmen at work.

1164 SETON COLLEGIATE CHURCH   6F6

Off A198, 13m E of Edinburgh. Apr-Sept, opening standard. Oct-Mar, closed. Entrance charge. (HS) Tel: 031-244 3101.

An important ecclesiastical monument of the late 15th century, with a fine vaulted chancel and apse.

1165 SHAMBELLIE HOUSE MUSEUM OF COSTUME 5B10

New Abbey, 6m S of Dumfries on A710. May-Sept, Thu-Sat, Mon & Tues 1100-1700, Sun 1200-1700. Entrance charge. (NMS) Tel: 031-225 7534.

A mid-Victorian small country house designed by David Bryce. Each year there is a new display of material from the National Costume Collection.

1166 SHAWBOST SCHOOL MUSEUM 2C4

A858, 19m NW of Stornoway, Isle of Lewis. Apr-Nov, Mon-Sat, 1000-1800. Donation box. Tel: (0851) 71 213.

Created under the Highland Village Competition 1970, the museum illustrates the old way of life in Lewis.

1167 SHETLAND CROFT HOUSE MUSEUM 1G6

Voe, Dunrossness, on unclassified road E of A970, 25m S of Lerwick. May-Sept. Daily, 1000-1300, 1400-1700. Entrance charge. Parking available. Tel: (0595) 5057.

Typical mid-19th century thatched Shetland croft house, complete with all outbuildings and working water mill. Furnished in period style, c 1890. Attendant in charge at all times.

1168 SHETLAND MUSEUM 1G4

Lower Hillhead, Lerwick. All year, Mon, Wed & Fri 1000-1900, Tue, Thu & Sat 1000-1700. Free. Tel: (0595) 5057.

The collection in this museum is entirely local in character but international in interest. The theme is the history of man in Shetland from pre-history to the present day. Four continuous galleries are devoted to archaeology, art and textiles, folk life and shipping.

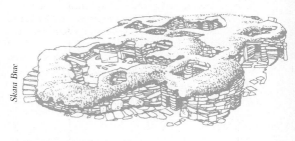

1169 SKARA BRAE 1A11

19m NW of Kirkwall, Mainland, Orkney. Opening standard. Entrance charges. Group concessions. (HS) Tel: 031-244 3101.

ASVA

A Neolithic village occupied from about 3000 BC to perhaps 2700 BC. The main period of settlement included eight or so houses joined by covered passages. Stone beds, fire places, cupboards and dressers survive. The inhabitants were farmers and herds who buried their dead in tombs like Quoyness (see No 1070). The amazing preservation of the village is due to its inundation by sand which buried it for 4500 years until it was revealed by a storm in 1850.

1170 SKELMORLIE AISLE 4G5

Bellman's Close, off main street, Largs. Apr-Sept, opening standard. Oct-Mar, closed. Entrance charge. (HS) Tel: 031-244 3101.

A splendid mausoleum of 1636, with painted roof, interesting tombs and monuments.

1171 SKIPNESS CASTLE AND CHAPEL   **4E6**

Skipness, B8001, 10m S of Tarbert, Loch Fyne. Closed to the public but may be viewed from outside. (HS) Tel: 031-244 3101.

The remains of the ancient chapel and the large 13th-century castle overlook the bay.

1172 SKYE ENVIRONMENTAL CENTRE   **2E10**

   ё
T   *Harrapool, Broadford, Isle of Skye. Jan-Dec. Daily, 0900-1700. Free. Car parking only. Gift shop. Tel: (047 12) 487.*

Environmental museum and data base situated on the Isle of Skye. Displays relate the island's complex geology to the natural environment, its wildlife and fauna. The centre, a registered charity, works in the fields of environmental education and wildlife conservation.

1173 SKYE HERITAGE CENTRE   **2D9**

   ё
P
T   *Viewfield Road, Portree, Isle of Skye. Mar-June, Oct-Dec, daily 0900-1800. July-Sept 0900-2100. Other times by arrangement. Forest walks all year. Entrance charges. Group concessions. Parking available. Gift shop. Restaurant. Tel: (0478) 3649.*

An introduction to events in Skye's history from 1700 to the present, told from the point of view of the ordinary people rather than clan chiefs and landlords. Approximately 45 minutes. Tours available using infra-red headsets which pick up information in different areas. Suitable for all ages, disabled and hard of hearing. Forest walks.

1174 SKYE MUSEUM OF ISLAND LIFE   **2D8**

   ё
T   *Hungladder, Kilmuir, 20m NNW of Portree, Isle of Skye. Apr-Oct, Mon-Sat 0900-1730. Entrance charge. Tel: (047 052) 279.*

Seven thatched cottages portraying life in a crofting township in the mid-19th century. Exhibits include a wall bed, farming and domestic implements, hand loom and a collection of old photographs and historical papers. Nearby at Kilmuir are Flora MacDonald's grave and memorial.

1175 SKYE SERPENTARIUM   **2E10**

   ё
T   *The Old Mill, Harrapool, Broadford, Isle of Skye. On A850 to Portree. Easter-Sept, Mon-Sat 1000-1700. Also Suns, July & Aug. Other times by arrangement. Entrance charge. Family tickets. Group concessions. Parking available. Gift shop. Tel: (0471) 822209.*

Reptile exhibition, the only one of its kind in Scotland, and shop, housed in a converted watermill. On show are snakes, lizards, frogs and tortoises from all over the world, living in simulated habitats. Visitors can handle a number of the animals, under supervision. Breeding of the animals also takes place on the premises. Member of staff always on hand to answer questions.

1176 SLAINS CASTLE   **3H9**

Off A975, 7m SSW of Peterhead. All reasonable times. Free. Parking available.

Extensive cliff-top ruins of a castle of 1597 which was extended and remodelled in the gothic style in the 19th century. Once the home of the Earls of Erroll, it inspired Bram Stoker for the setting of Dracula and featured in a number of his other stories. (Care should be taken on the cliff-tops.)

1177 SMA' SHOT COTTAGES   4H5

    11/17 George Place, Paisley. Apr-Sept, Wed & Sat 1300-1700, or parties by arrangement. Free. Tearoom. Tel: 041-889 1708 or 041-889 0530.

19th-century millworkers' two-storey houses. Traditionally Scottish, with back of house iron staircase. Two exhibition rooms with displays of linen, lace, Paisley shawls. There is also an 18th-century weaver's cottage which has recently been restored. Garden.

1178 SMAILHOLM TOWER   5E7

Off B6404, 6m NW of Kelso. Apr-Sept, opening standard. Oct-Mar, closed. (HS) Tel: 031-244 3101.

ASVA

An outstanding example of a 16th-century Border peel tower built to give surveillance over a wide expanse of country. It is 57 feet high, in a good state of preservation and houses an exhibition of dolls and tapestries on the theme of Sir Walter Scott's 'Minstrelsy of the Scottish Border'. At nearby Sandyknowe Farm, Scott spent some childhood years.

1179 ROBERT SMAIL'S PRINTING WORKS   5D6

7/9 High Street, Innerleithen, 30m S of Edinburgh. Shop only: May-midsummer daily, except Tues & Sun. Restored Printing Works and Shop: midsummer-Oct, Mon-Sat 1000-1300 and 1400-1700, Sun 1400-1700. Entrance charges. Group concessions. Groups by arrangement only. Parking available. Trust Shop. (NTS) Tel: (0896) 830206.

ASVA

These buildings contain an office, a paper store with reconstructed water wheel, composing and press rooms. Visitors may view the printer at work. Victorian office contains many historic items.

1180 SMITH ART GALLERY AND MUSEUM   6A5

Dumbarton Road, Stirling. Open all year. Free. Cafe. Tel: (0786) 471917 for programme details and opening hours. Parking available.

A lively award-winning museum and art gallery near the King's Park, below the dramatic skyline of Stirling Castle and old town. There is a wide-ranging programme of exhibitions and events offering opportunities for seeing, joining in and finding out about art, history, craft and design. Small shop stocks local interest books, postcards and souvenirs.

1181 ADAM SMITH THEATRE   6E5

Bennochy Road, Kirkcaldy. Tel: (0592) 260498.

Theatre with performances all year, named after Adam Smith, the economist who was born in Kirkcaldy in 1723.

1182 SMOLLETT MONUMENT   4H5

On A82 N of Dumbarton at Renton. All times. Free.

A monument to Tobias Smollett (1721-1771), novelist and surgeon. Dr Johnson wrote the Latin epitaph to him in 1773.

Smoo Cave

1183 SMOO CAVE   2H3

A838, 1½m E of Durness. All reasonable times. Free.
Tel: (0971) 511259.

Three vast caves at the end of a deep cleft in the
limestone cliffs with waterfall. The entrance to the first
resembles a Gothic arch. The second cavern is viewable
from platform. Access by steep path, or boat trips to
second and third cavern. Contact Durness Tourist
Information Centre.

1184 SORN CASTLE   4H7

   ♿
A *3 miles E of Mauchline on B743. Grounds open Apr-Oct. House, 2 weeks*
in July and 2 weeks in Aug, daily 1400-1700. Entrance charge.
Parking available. Tel: (0290) 51555.

The Castle stands on a cliff overlooking the River Ayr.
It dates from 1380, with the main building from 1764.
Essentially a family home, it contains many fine
paintings, mainly by Scottish artists. The grounds are
laid out along the river bank, with fine trees and shrubs.

1185 SOUTER JOHNNIE'S COTTAGE   4G8

   ♿
T *At Kirkoswald, on A77, 4m W of Maybole. Apr-Oct, daily 1200-1700,*
or by arrangement. Entrance charge. Group concessions. (NTS)
Tel: (065 56) 274.

This thatched cottage was the home of the village
cobbler (Souter) John Davidson at the end of the 18th
century. Davidson and his friend Douglas Graham of
Shanter Farm, known to Robert Burns in his youth in
Kirkoswald, were later immortalised in 'Tam o' Shanter'.
The cottage contains Burnsiana and contemporary tools
of the cobbler's craft. Life-sized stone figures of the
Souter, Tam, the innkeeper and his wife are in the
restored ale-house in the cottage garden.

1186 SOUTH BANK FARM PARK   4F7

   ♿
P
T *East Bennan, 12 miles from Brodick, Isle of Arran. Easter-Oct.*
Daily, 1000-1800 (last admission 1700). Entrance charge. Group
concessions. Parking available. Small gift shop. Tearoom. Tel: (077 082) 221.

Working farm over 60 scenic acres, with rare breeds
including sheep, pigs, cattle, goats, 35 to 40 breeds of
poultry, ponies and rabbits. Visit includes housed
animals and a farm trail to see animals in their natural
surroundings. Red deer enclosure. Visitors are
encouraged to handle and feed animals whenever
possible.

1187 SPEYSIDE COOPERAGE VISITOR CENTRE
3D8

  Dufftown Road, Craigellachie. Jan-Dec exc Christmas & New Year.
  Easter-mid Oct, Mon-Sat 0930-1630. Mid Oct-Easter, Mon-Fri 0930-1630.
  Entrance charge. Group concessions. Parking available. Gift shop.
  Tel: (0340) 871108.

ASVA

The only working cooperage with a visitor centre in
Britain. 'Acorn to Cask' exhibition tells of the history
and development of the cooperage industry;
reconstructed Victorian cooperage has life-sized models
which speak in the local dialect. In the workshop,
skilled coopers and apprentices repair casks for the
whisky industry. Static displays illustrate the art of
making new casks. Picnic area, Highland cattle.

1188 SPEYSIDE HEATHER GARDEN CENTRE
3C9

  Skye of Curr, Dulnain Bridge. From Aviemore take B9152 (old A9) approx
  4½ miles N, turn R onto A95 Elgin/Grantown-on-Spey road. Continue
  on A95 for approx 4m. Watch for 'Thistle' signs to Heather Centre. Turn
  left on Skye of Curr road. Heather Centre is 200yds up on right-hand side.
  Closed Jan, except by appointment. Mar-Oct, Mon-Sat 0900-1700/1800
  (Sun 1000-1700/1800); Nov-Feb, Mon-Sat 0900-1700 (closed Sun).
  Garden and Craft Shop, free. Heritage Centre, entrance charge. Group
  concessions. Parking available. Heather Craft Shop. Gift shop, plant sales.
  'Clootie Dumpling' tearoom. Boutique. Tel: (047 985) 359.

ASVA

Centre consists of Heather Heritage Centre which
houses an exhibition on historical uses of heather, eg
thatching, weaving ropes, doormats, baskets; its uses in
medicine, drinks, dyeing wool, etc. Ornamental garden
and landscaped show garden displaying approx 300
varieties of heathers.

1189 STAFFA
4C2

  W of Mull, Argyll, 6m NE of Iona. Access by local boats, including
  Gordon Grant Marine (Staffa Ferries), Isle of Iona. Tel: (068 17) 338.
  (Apr-Oct); David R Kirkpatrick, Isle of Iona. Tel: (068 17) 373; Iain
  Morrison, Penmore Mill, Dervaig. Tel: (068 84) 242.

This romantic and uninhabited small island is famous
for its basaltic formations and remarkable caves, the best
known of which is Fingal's Cave. Immortalised by
Mendelssohn in his celebrated 'Hebrides' overture, its
cluster columns and man-made-looking symmetry gives
the cave a cathedral-like majesty. Other famous visitors
to the cave have included Queen Victoria and Prince
Albert, the artist J M W Turner, and poets and writers
Keats, Wordsworth, Tennyson and Sir Walter Scott.
Improved landing stage with handrail.

1190 STAINED GLASS STUDIO 5C9

&

Dalton, 5 miles S of Lochmaben. Signposted on A75 from Dumfries. Jan-Dec. Mon 1200-1700, Tues-Sat 1100-1700. Free. Shop. Coffee room. Tel: (038 784) 688.

Small studio of character—a former Victorian soup kitchen—in picturesque setting. Displays of stained glassware, painting demonstrated in the studio. Small groups welcome.

1191 STATESMAN CRUISES 2G4

&
A

Kylesku Bridge, A894 over Loch a' Cairn Bhan. March-Oct. Daily, 1100 & 1400. Charge for cruise. Parking available. Tel: (057 14) 446.

Boat cruises up Loch Glencoul to Eas Coul Aulin, Britain's highest waterfall, most of which can be seen from the boat. During the cruise, in sheltered waters, seals may be seen, also golden eagles, herons, ravens, guillemot, peregrine falcon, red and black throated divers, greylag geese, terns and shag. (See No 439).

1192 STEINACLEIT CAIRN AND STONE CIRCLE 2D4

S end of Loch an Duin, Shader, 12m N of Stornoway, Lewis. All reasonable times. Free. (HS) Tel: 031-244 3101.

A mysterious stone grouping, oval in layout, dating from 3rd or 2nd millennium BC. Other standing stones nearby.

1193 STENNESS STANDING STONES 1B11

Between Loch of Harray and Loch of Stenness, 5m NE of Stromness, Mainland Orkney. All times. Free. (HS) Tel: 031-244 3101.

Four large upright stones are the dramatic remains of a stone circle, c 3000 BC, encircled by a ditch and bank. The area around Stenness is particularly rich in such remains. (See also Ring of Brogar, No 1083).

1194 STEVENSON HOUSE 6G6

&
A
P

2 miles E of Haddington, signposted from A1. House: 6-week open period, July-mid Aug: Thurs, Sat, Sun 1400-1730. Other times by arrangement, Apr-Oct. Guided tour takes minimum 1 hour. Charge. Under-7s free, must be accompanied. Garden: open all year. Honesty box. Parking available. Self-service tea and coffee. Tel: (062 082) 3376.

Stevenson, originally Stevenstoun, features in a charter granted to the Cistercian Nunnery at Haddington in 1359, and was later gifted to William Douglas of Straboc. The present house dates from the 16th century and was acquired in 1624 by the Sinclairs of Longformacus. The 3rd Baronet put in hand the alterations which gave the house its late-Restoration/early Georgian character. On the death of the 9th Baronet without issue, the estate was broken up, only the mansion house, garden and policies being retained. Restored again after Army occupation from 1940-45, the house is still lived in as a family home.

1195 STEWARTRY MUSEUM 5A11

&

St Mary Street, Kirkcudbright. Mar-Oct, Mon-Sat 1100-1600; later openings and Suns in summer. Nov-Easter, Sat only. Entrance charge. Parking available. Gift shop. Tel: (0557) 31643.

A museum depicting the life of the area with prehistoric articles, relics of domestic life and crafts of earlier days. Works of local artists are featured, especially Jessie M King (1875-1949). John Paul Jones, a founder of the American Navy who was born in the Stewartry and had varied associations with Kirkcudbright, is also the subject of a special display.

1196 STIRLING BRIDGE 6A5

By A9 off Stirling town centre. All times. Free. (HS)

The Old Bridge built c 1400, was for centuries of great strategic importance as the 'gateway to the north' and the lowest bridging point of the River Forth. Near site of Battle of Stirling Bridge, where William Wallace defeated the English Army in 1297.

Stirling Castle

1197 STIRLING CASTLE 6A5

In central Stirling. Apr-Sept, daily 0930-1715 (last entry). Oct-Mar, daily 0930-1615 (last entry). Castle closes 45 mins after last entry. Entrance charge. Group concessions. Parking available. (HS) Tel: 031-244 3101.

ASVA

Stirling Castle on its 250-feet great rock has dominated much of Scotland's vivid history. Wallace recaptured it from the English in 1297; Edward I retook it in 1304, until Bruce won at nearby Bannockburn in 1314. Later it was a favourite Royal residence: James II was born here in 1430 and Mary, Queen of Scots and James VI both spent some years here. Long used as a barracks, and frequently rebuilt, the old towers built by James IV remain, as do the fine 16th-century hall, the splendid Renaissance palace of James V, the Chapel Royal of 1594 and other buildings. On Castle Hill there is a Visitor Centre which has an audio-visual display as an introduction to the castle.

1198 STORR 2D8

2m from A855, 8m N of Portree, Isle of Skye. Parking available.

A series of pinnacles and crags rising to 2,360-feet. No access, but may be seen from road. The Old Man of Storr, at the east end of the mountain, is a black obelisk, 160 feet high, first climbed in 1955. Visitors can see Storr from the main road; due to erosion it is now closed to walkers.

1199 STORYBOOK GLEN 3G10

  T
Maryculter, 5 miles W of Aberdeen on B9077. Mar-Oct, daily, 1000-1800. Nov-Feb, Sat & Sun 1100-1600. Entrance charge. Group concessions. Parking available. Gift shop. Restaurant. Tel: (0224) 732941.

In 22 landscaped acres, over 100 nursery rhymes are depicted in fibreglass models, including the Old Woman and her Shoe and the Three Bears' House. Elsewhere, the Glen has waterfalls, seating areas and restaurant.

1200 STRANRAER MUSEUM 4F10

  T
Old Town Hall, George Street, Stranraer. All year, Mon-Sat 1000-1700. Free. Gift shop. Tel: (0776) 5088.

Local museum with permanent displays of archaeology, farming and polar exploration. Temporary exhibition programme. Activity sheets for children. Holiday events programme, photographic service, education service. Information point with details of town trail.

1201 STRATHAVEN CASTLE   5A6

Kirk Street/Stonehouse Road, Strathaven, 14m W of Lanark.
All reasonable times. View from outside only.

Also known as Avondale Castle, this ruin dates from
the 15th century.

1202 STRATHCLYDE COUNTRY PARK   5A6

&♿
P
T

On both sides of M74 between Hamilton and Bothwell interchanges (A723
and A725). All year. Tours start: Easter-Sept, daily at 1500, also Sat and
Sun at 1900 during July-August; winter Sat and Sun at 1400 (groups by
arrangement). Free (charges for facilities). Group rates on request. Parking
available. Cafeteria (Easter-Oct). Tel: (0698) 66155.

A countryside park with man-made loch, nature trails,
fun park, sandy beaches and a wide variety of sporting
facilities including an international rowing centre.
Within the park is Hamilton Mausoleum, created in
the 1840s by the 10th Duke of Hamilton, which has a
remarkable echo and huge bronze doors.

1203 STRATHISLA DISTILLERY   3E8

&♿
P
T

Keith. Easter-Sept, Mon-Fri 0900-1630. Free. Tel: (054 22) 7471.

A typical small old-fashioned distillery, one of the
oldest established in Scotland, dating from 1786.
Reception Centre with video presentation.

ASVA

1204 STRATHNAVER MUSEUM   3B3

&♿

Beside A836 at Bettyhill. Apr-Oct, Mon-Sat 1000-1700. Entrance charge. Parking
available. Tel: (064 12) 421.

A local museum depicting past life in the Highlands,
with particular reference to the Clearances and to Clan
MacKay. Also houses the late Pictish Farr Stone.

1205 STRATHSPEY STEAM RAILWAY   3C10

&♿
A
P
T

Aviemore to Boat of Garten. Access at Aviemore: cars take B970 then
Dalfaber Road, pedestrians take underpass from Main Road at Bank of
Scotland. Boat of Garten: Station beside Boat Hotel. Open daily, July &
Aug. Daily exc Sat, June & Sept. Other dates: timetables available locally.
Stations open 0930-1800. 1st and 3rd class single and return fares, children
half fare, under 5 free. Parking available. Buffet car. Coffee service.
Tel: (0479) 810725.

The railway is part of the former main line between
Perth and Inverness. Closed in 1965, this railway was
reopened in 1978 by the independent Strathspey
Railway Company. Passenger services and restoration
are carried out by a mainly volunteer workforce. The
station buildings at Aviemore Speyside are from
Dalnaspidal, the footbridge from Longmorn and the
turntable from Kyle of Lochalsh. At Boat of Garten a
small relic museum and rolling stock are on display.

1206 STUART CRYSTAL STRATHEARN
GLASS WORKS   6B2

&♿

Muthill Road, Crieff. Jan-Dec exc Christmas & New Year, daily 0900-1900.
Free. Parking available. Coffee shop. Crystal shop. Tel: (0764) 4004.

Manufacturer of Scottish crystal. Visitors to the factory
can see the traditional skills involved in the decoration
of full lead crystal. Video on glass making, picnic area,
museum display. Shop sells first and second quality glass.

1207 JOHN McDOUALL STUART MUSEUM 6E4

Rectory Lane, Dysart, 2m N of Kirkcaldy. Jun-Aug, daily exc public holidays 1400-1700. Free. Tel: (0592) 260732.

A 17th-century building restored by the National Trust for Scotland as part of their 'little houses' scheme. Birthplace of the explorer John McDouall Stuart (1815-1866) who crossed Australia's desert heart in 1861. Permanent display relating to the explorer. Nearby are other NTS 'little houses' and the picturesque harbour.

1208 STUDIO GALLERY 2A10

Askernish, 5 miles N of Lochboisdale, Isle of South Uist. Signposted. Apr-Sept, Mon-Sat 1000-1800. Winter: please telephone. Free. Car parking only. Tel: (087 84) 237.

Studio gallery showing paintings by local landscape and wildlife artist, William Neill. Work mainly in watercolour with a selection of limited edition reproductions for sale. Information on wildlife available (the artist is local representative of the Scottish Wildlife Trust), current Western Isles Bird Reports for sale. Panoramic views over croftlands of South Uist and the distant Isle of Barra.

1209 SUENO'S STONE 3C8

At E end of Forres. All times. Free. (HS) Tel: 031-244 3101.

One of the most remarkable early sculptured monuments in Scotland, 20 feet high with elaborate carving.

1210 SUMMER ISLES 2F6

Off Achiltibuie, Ullapool, Wester Ross. Cruises from Ullapool: Mackenzie Marine, tel (0854) 2008. From Achiltibuie, tel (0854) 82200. Enquire at Post Office.

An attractive group of islands, the largest of which is Tanera Mhor. Pleasure cruises give views of seals, birdlife and extraordinary rock formations, occasionally landing on one of the islands. Suitable for fully-equipped campers, canoeing, yachting.

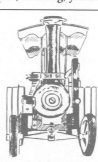

Summerlee Heritage Trust

1211 SUMMERLEE HERITAGE TRUST 5A5

West Canal Street, Coatbridge. Jan-Dec exc Christmas & New Year. Daily, 1000-1700. Free. Parking available. Gift shop. Tearoom. Tel: (0236) 431261.

ASVA

Summerlee interprets the social and industrial history of communities in the west of Scotland in the 19th and early 20th centuries. Large exhibition hall features historic machinery in operation daily, plus social history displays with recreated period shop interiors. Outside, excavation of 1835 Summerlee Ironworks, and rides on Scotland's only working electric tramway. Miners' row, dating from 1840, underground coalmine. Temporary exhibitions, special events.

1212 SUNTRAP 6D6

   ♿
   T

At Gogarbank, between A8 and A71, 6m W of Edinburgh. Garden all year, daily 0930-dusk. Advice centre all year, Mon-Fri 0930-1630; except when staff member is on holiday. Apr-Sept, also Sat and Sun 1430-1700. Entrance charge. NTS members free. Parking available. Tel: 031-339 7283.

Three-acre site with several gardens in one: Italian, rock, rose, peat and woodland gardens. Started in 1957 by philanthropist and keen amateur gardener George Boyd Anderson, bequeathed 1972 to National Trust for Scotland and Lothian Region as a centre for gardening advice and horticultural education. Now run by Oatridge Agricultural College, with excellent demonstration facilities. Special sections for disabled gardeners.

1213 SUTHERLAND POTTERY 3A5

   ♿

Shinness, 4½ miles N of Lairg. Apr-Oct, daily 0800-2200. Free. Parking available. Pottery shop. Tearoom. Tel: (0549) 2223.

Hand-thrown and decorated pottery. Visitors can participate in pot-making, buy pots from the adjoining showroom, walk around the croft, which is still active, and see artefacts and implements preserved from the days of the present owner's parents, and earlier.

Sweetheart Abbey

1214 SWEETHEART ABBEY 5B10

At New Abbey, A710, 7½m S of Dumfries. Opening standard except Oct-Mar, closed Thurs pm and all day Fri. Entrance charge. Group concessions. (HS) Tel: 031-244 3101.

Founded in 1273 by Devorgilla in memory of her husband, John Balliol (she also founded Balliol College, Oxford), this beautiful ruin has a precinct wall built of enormous boulders. (See also No 1014).

1215 SWILKEN GOLF VISITOR CENTRE 6G2

Argyll Business Park, Largo Road, 1 mile from centre of St Andrews. Jan-Dec. Mon-Fri 0900-1700, Sat 1000-1600 (shop only). Free. Parking available. Shop. Tel. (0334) 72266.

Specialised golf visitor centre with showroom and computerised club fitting bay. Craftsmen in the factory produce quality golf clubs from traditional hickory-shafted putters to the latest boron metal woods. Resident professional. Computerised swing analysis.

1216 SWINTON KIRK   5F6

♿
A
Swinton, 6 miles from Coldstream, 6 miles from Duns on A6112.
All reasonable times. Free. Parking available.

Although Swinton Kirk has been much altered, the
south and east walls are 1,000 years old. It was
originally a long, narrow building, with the altar at
the east end, and the Aumbry which can still be seen.
The bell is dated 1499 and was rung as a death knell
after Flodden (1513). Behind the communion table is
an effigy of Alan Swinton from 1200, while the oldest
coat of arms in Britain (of the Swinton family) is
above the gallery door. A copy of one of the longest
recorded family trees in Britain (Swinton) is in the kirk.

1217 TALISKER DISTILLERY   2D9

Carbost, Isle of Skye. Turn off A850 at Sligachan on to A863, then B8009.
Jan-Dec exc Christmas & New Year. Mon-Fri 0900-1630. Car parking only.
Shop. Tel: (047 842) 203.

ASVA

The only distillery on Skye, founded in 1830 by two
sons of a doctor from Eigg. Until the 1960s, puffers
brought supplies and took whisky from the distillery's
own pier. Their story is told in the visitor centre,
along with tales of island life and the distillery up to
the present day. Tours and tasting.

1218 TAMDHU DISTILLERY   3D9

⚙
Off B9102 8m W of Craigellachie at Knockando. Apr-Oct,
Mon-Fri 1000-1600. Also Sat, June-Sept. Free. Parking available.
Tel: (034 06) 486.

ASVA

Guided tour with large graphic display and views of
distilling plant from viewing gallery. Visitor centre,
tasting.

1219 THE TAMNAVULIN-GLENLIVET DISTILLERY, OLD MILL VISITOR CENTRE   3D9

♿
P
T
Tomnavoulin, 3½m NNE of Tomintoul on B9008. Mar-Oct,
Mon-Fri 0930-1630; also Sat, Apr-Sept. Free. Parking available. Shop.
Tel: (080 73) 442.

An old carding mill on the River Livet has been
converted into an attractive visitor centre complete
with authentic water wheel. Audio-visual on making
of whisky, guided tour, followed by tasting of the malt
whisky or Glayva liqueur. The distillery name comes
from the Gaelic for 'mill on the hill'. The picnic area is
in a level secluded area by the Livet, close to walks.

1220 TANKERNESS HOUSE   1B11

♿
Broad Street, Kirkwall, Orkney. All year, Mon-Sat 1030-1230, 1330-1700;
also May-Sep, Sun 1400-1700. Entrance charge. Oct-Mar, free.
Tel: (0856) 873191.

Dating from 1574, this is a fine example of an Orkney
merchant-laird's mansion, with courtyard and gardens.
Now a museum of life in Orkney through 5,000 years,
with additional special exhibitions. A fine garden with
lawns, flowerbeds and shrubbery, gravel paths.

Tantallon Castle

1221 TANTALLON CASTLE 6H5

A198, 3m E of North Berwick. Opening standard, except Oct-Mar closed Thurs pm and all day Fri. Entrance charge. Group concessions. Parking available. (HS) Tel: 031-244 3101.

ASVA

Extensive red ruins of a 14th-century stronghold of the Douglases, in magnificent clifftop setting. Although the castle withstood a regular siege by James V in 1528, it was eventually destroyed by General Monk in 1651.

1222 TARVES MEDIEVAL TOMB 3G9

4m NE of Oldmeldrum, in the kirkyard of Tarves. All reasonable times. Free. (HS) Tel: 031-244 3101.

A fine altar-tomb of William Forbes, the laird who enlarged Tolquhon Castle. It shows an interesting mixture of Gothic and Renaissance styles. (See also No 1238).

1223 TAY FOREST PARK 5A1

Tay and Tummel valleys—Forest Enterprise area near Dunkeld, Kenmore, Pitlochry, Tummel Bridge and Rannoch. All times. Free. Parking available. Gift shop. Tearoom. (FE) Tel: (0350) 727284.

Spectacular forests with superb views from six waymarked forest walks with a choice of route, two waymarked mountain bike trails and several peaceful picnic sites. Forest campsite. Guided walks can be arranged at Queen's View Centre (see No 1067) in the heart of the park; forest exhibition, shop and tearoom.

1224 TEALING EARTH HOUSE AND DOVECOT 6F1

Off A929, 5m N of Dundee, ½m on unclassified road to Tealing and Auchterhouse. All reasonable times. Free. (HS) Tel: 031-244 3101.

A well-preserved example of an Iron Age souterrain or earth-house comprising a passage and long curved gallery and small inner chambers. Nearby is a fine dovecote built in 1595.

1225 TEDDY MELROSE, SCOTLAND'S TEDDY BEAR MUSEUM 5E6

The Wynd, Melrose. Jan-Dec, daily 1000-1700. Entrance charge, children free, must be accompanied by an adult. Parking available. Gift shop. Tearoom and tea garden. Tel: (089 682) 2464.

Scotland's Teddy Bear museum informs and entertains visitors with its individual presentation of famous character bears, accompanied by the history of great British bear manufacturers. Combined displays offer the most comprehensive collection of British bears in the world—including Rupert, Paddington, Winnie and Bully Bears. Access for disabled visitors through the Wynd. Braille panels accompany the displays.

245

1226 TELFORD MEMORIAL 5D9

At Westerkirk, B709, 6m NW of Langholm. All times. Free.
Tel: (038 73) 80976.

Memorial to Thomas Telford (1757-1834), the engineer
who was born in the valley of the Meggat Water near
Westerkirk. There are several reminders of him nearby
at Langholm. Access for wheelchair users (next to road).

Thirlestane Castle

1227 THIRLESTANE CASTLE 5E6

&

A
P
T

Lauder, 28m S of Edinburgh on A68. Easter. May, Jun & Sept,
Wed, Thu & Sun only; Jul & Aug, every day except Sat, 1400-1700.
Last admission 1630. Grounds: same dates, 1200-1800. Entrance charges.
Family tickets. Group concessions. Parking available. Gift shop. Tearoom.
Tel: (0578) 722430.

ASVA

Thirlestane Castle was rebuilt in the 16th century as
the home of the Maitland family. It became the seat of
the Earls of Lauderdale and was enlarged in the 17th
century by the Duke of Lauderdale, who commissioned
the magnificent plasterwork ceilings in the state rooms.
Still a family home, Thirlestane houses a large collection
of early toys in the nursery wing, and the Border
Country Life Exhibition. The old servants' hall today
serves as the tearoom, and there are picnic tables in the
woodland walk.

1228 THISTLE BAGPIPE WORKS 4G4

&

Luss, Loch Lomond, 8 miles N of Balloch on A82. Jan-Dec. Daily,
0900-1700. (Open later, May-Sept.) Free. Car parking only. Gift shop.
Tel: (043 686) 250.

Bagpipe making, complete Highland dress outfitters,
kiltmaker. Exhibition of antiques.

1229 ANN R THOMAS GALLERY 4E5

&
P
T

Harbour Street, Tarbert, Loch Fyne. Just off A83 Glasgow-Campbeltown,
facing fish quay. Jan-Dec exc Christmas & New Year. Summer, Mon-Sat
0900-1830, Winter 1000-1730. Early closing Wed, open Sun for shorter
period. Free. Gift shop. Tel: (0880) 820390.

Art gallery featuring paintings and prints by Ann
Thomas, books, crafts, gifts, stationery, art materials.

Threave Castle

1230 THREAVE CASTLE   **5A10**

N of A75, 3m W of Castle Douglas. Apr-Sept, opening standard.
Oct-Mar, closed. (HS) Parking available. Tel: 031-244 3101.

Early stronghold of the Black Douglases, on an island
in the Dee. The four-storeyed tower was built between
1639 and 1690 by Archibald the Grim, Lord of
Galloway. In 1455 it was the last Douglas stronghold to
surrender to James II.

1231 THREAVE GARDEN   **5A10**

& *S of A75, 1m W of Castle Douglas. Gardens: all year, daily 0900-sunset.*
T *Visitor Centre: Apr-Oct. Daily 0900-1700. Entrance charge. Parking*
available. Trust shop. Plant sales. Restaurant. (NTS) Tel: (0556) 2575.

ASVA

The extensive garden provides interest all year, with
colour always in evidence—in particular, the magnificent
springtime display of nearly 200 varieties of daffodil.
The Victorian house (not open to the public) is the
Trust's School of Horticulture. Visitor centre with
exhibitions, video programme, publications.

1232 THURSO HERITAGE MUSEUM   **3C3**

& *Town Hall, High Street, Thurso. Jun-Sept, Mon-Sat 1000-1300, 1400-1700.*
A *Entrance charge. Parking available.*

Exhibition of agricultural and domestic life, geology,
local trades and crafts with a room of an old Caithness
cottage. Photographic display of Thurso, old and new.

1233 THE TIME CAPSULE, MONKLANDS   **5A5**

& *Buchanan Street, Coatbridge, off M8 at Junction 8. Jan-Dec exc*
T *Christmas Day & New Year's Day. 1000-2200. Entrance charges.*
Group concessions. Parking available. Gift shop. Restaurant, bars.
Tel: (0236) 449572.

Themed ice and water complex. Leisure pool area
features a 'journey through time', and includes waves,
flumes, rubber ring ride, slides, 'kiddies' harbour',
bubblers, whirlpool, rapids, cavemen, dinosaurs, space
ships and sound and light effects. The free form ice
rink has a giant video wall, disco lighting and sound,
snow and a giant woolly mammoth.

1234 TIMESPAN HERITAGE CENTRE 3C5

Dunrobin Street, Helmsdale. 70 miles N of Inverness on A9 to John o'Groats. Easter-Oct. Mon-Sat 1000-1700, Sun 1400-1700 (1800 in July & Aug). Entrance charge. Parking available. Gift shop. Tel: (043 12) 327.

ASVA

Award-winning Timespan features the dramatic story of the Highlands, from Picts and Vikings, murder at Helmsdale Castle, the last burning of a witch, the Highland Clearances, the Church, the 19th-century sporting scene, the Kildonan Goldrush, through the crofting and fishing past to the present day and the North Sea oilfields. Scenes from the past are re-created with life-size sets and sound effects. Audio visual. Herb garden, beside Telford's bridge over the River Helmsdale.

1235 TINGWALL AGRICULTURAL MUSEUM 1G4

At Veensgarth off A971, 5m NW of Lerwick, Shetland. July & Aug, daily 1400-1700. Other times by arrangement. Entrance charge. Group concessions. Parking available. Tel: (059 584) 344.

A private collection of tools and equipment used by the Shetland crofter, housed in a mid 18th-century granary, stables, bothy and smithy. Blacksmith's, wheelwright's, cooper's tools. The crofter, Jeanie Sandison, guides visitors.

1236 TOBERMORY DISTILLERY VISITOR CENTRE 4C1

End of Main Street, Tobermory harbour front, Isle of Mull. Apr-Oct. Mon-Fri 1000-1600. Entrance charge. Parking available. Gift shop. Tel: (0688) 2119.

Guided tour of distillery, together with expert descriptions of the processes involved in making malt whisky.

1237 TOLBOOTH MUSEUM 3G11

Old Quay, The Harbour, Stonehaven. June-Sept, daily exc Tues, 1400-1700. Also Mon, Thurs, Fri & Sat 1000-1200. Free. Tel: (0779) 77778.

This 16th-century former storehouse of the Earls Marischal was later used as a prison. In 1748-49, Episcopal ministers lodged inside and baptised children through the windows. The museum displays local history, archaeology and, in particular, fishing.

1238 TOLQUHON CASTLE 3G9

Off B999, 7m ENE of Oldmeldrum. Apr-Sept, opening standard. Oct-Mar, weekends only. Entrance charge. Group concessions. (HS) Tel: 031-244 3101.

Once a seat of the Forbes family, an early 15th-century rectangular tower, with a large quadrangular mansion of 1584-89. Two round towers, a fine carved panel over the door, and the courtyard are features. (See No 1222).

1239 TOMATIN DISTILLERY 3B9

Off A9, 16m S of Inverness at Tomatin. Mar-Oct. Mon-Fri 0900-1630. Also Sat, Jun-Oct, 0930-1230. All other times by prior arrangement. Free. Parking available. Gift shop. Tel: (080 82) 234.

Scotland's largest malt whisky distillery. New reception centre (opened 1992) with video, static displays and full product range. Guided tour (approx 45 mins) is followed by a taste of 'The Tomatin'.

**1240 TOMB OF THE EAGLES AND BRONZE
AGE HOUSE** 1B12

  ♿
P
*Liddle, St Margaret's Hope, 22 miles SE of Kirkwall, Orkney. Jan-Dec.
Daily, 1000-2200 in summer, 1000-dusk in winter. Entrance charge.
Parking available. Publications for sale. Tel: (0856) 83339.*

A new approach to archaeology at this ancient site,
where visitors hear a talk in the small museum, and
can handle many Stone Age artefacts. On the way to
the Tomb of the Eagles, another talk is given at the
Bronze Age house.

**1241 TOMBUIE SMOKEHOUSE AND
NATURE TRAIL** 5A1

*2½ miles NE of Aberfeldy on Weem/Strathtay road. Apr-Oct. Daily,
1100-1800. Entrance charge, children free. Car parking only. Farm shop.
Tel: (0887) 820127..*

South-facing farm, overlooking the River Tay at
Aberfeldy. Picnic areas, nature trail. Large collection of
cheese presses, a three-horse mill gang, one of the few
remaining in Scotland, and a standing stone. The farm
shop sells products from the Smokehouse.

1242 TOMINTOUL MUSEUM 3D10

*The Square, Tomintoul. Apr, May, Oct, Mon-Sat 1000-1730,
Sun 1400-1730; June, Sept, Mon-Sat, 0930-1800, Sun 1400-1800; July,
Aug, Mon-Sat 0930-1900, Sun 1000-1300, 1400-1900. Free.
Tel: (0309) 673701,.*

Displays on local history, reconstructed farm kitchen
and blacksmith's shop, wildlife and the environment.

1243 TOMNAVERIE STONE CIRCLE 3E10

3m NW of Aboyne. All reasonable times. Free. (HS) Tel: 031-244 3101.

The remains of a recumbent stone circle probably
1800-1600 BC. Unexcavated.

1244 TONGLAND TOUR 5A11

*By A711, 2m N of Kirkcudbright. Early May-end Aug. Guided tours,
Mon-Sat 1000, 1130, 1400, 1530. Free. Free transport from
Kirkcudbright. To book Tel: (0557) 30114 (0294) 822311.*

Hydro-electric power station and dam. Video plus
displays.

1245 TORHOUSE STONE CIRCLE 4H10

*Off B733, 4m W of Wigtown. All reasonable times. Free. (HS)
Tel: 031-244 3101.*

A circle of 19 boulders standing on the edge of a low
mound. Probably Bronze Age.

1246 TORNESS POWER STATION 6H6

*By A1, 6m SE of Dunbar. May-Sept. Guided tours, weekdays and Sats,
between 1000 and 1600. Free. Refreshments available. Parking available.
Tel: (0368) 63500, ext. 3871/2.*

Nuclear Power Station. This plant, the most modern
power station in Britain, is operated by Scottish
Nuclear Ltd and produces a quarter of all the
electricity consumed in Scotland.

1247   TOROSAY CASTLE AND GARDENS   4D2

*A849, 1½m SSE of Craignure, Isle of Mull. Mid Apr-mid Oct, daily
1030-1730. Gardens open 0900-1900 in summer, daylight hours in winter.
Entrance charges. Group concessions. Parking available. Gift shop.
Tel: (068 02) 421.*

ASVA

The castle, designed by David Bryce, is a family home,
lived in and cared for by its owners. The furniture,
pictures and scrap books date from Victorian times.
Displays of travel in Antarctica and by wind-jammer,
of wartime escapes and hunts for the Loch Ness
Monster. The 12-acre garden comprises formal terraces
and the exceptional Italian Statue Walk, surrounded by
informal shrubbery, water garden, woodland and
eucalyptus walks. Splendid views over the sea to the
mountains of Appin and Lorn. (See No 965).

1248   TORPHICHEN PRECEPTORY   6C6

*B792, 5m SSW of Linlithgow. Apr-Sept, opening standard. Oct-Mar,
closed. Entrance charge. (HS) Tel: 031-244 3101.*

Once the principal Scottish seat of the Knights
Hospitallers of St John. An exhibition depicts the
history of the Knights in Scotland and overseas.

1249   TORR ACHILTY DAM FISH LIFT   3A8

*Torr Achilty Power Station, 2 miles W of Marybank on Strathconon road.
Near Muir of Ord. May-Oct exc public holidays. Mon-Fri 0900-1000,
1500-1600. Fish lift only. Free. Car parking, limited coach parking.
Tel: (099 73) 223.*

Borland fishlift, which includes a viewing window.

1250   TORRIDON   2F8

*Off A896, 9m SW of Kinlochewe. Estate open all year. Countryside
Centre, May-late Sept, Mon-Sat 1000-1700, Sun 1400-1700. Entrance
charge. Parking available. (NTS) Tel: (044 587) 221.*

About 16,000 acres of some of Scotland's finest
mountain scenery whose peaks rise over 3,000 ft. Of
major interest also to geologists: Liathach (3,456 ft)
and Beinn Alligin (2,232 ft) are of red sandstone, some
750 million years old. The NTS Visitor Centre at the
junction of A896 and Diabaig road has audio-visual
presentation of wild life. Deer museum (unmanned)
and deer park open all year. Ranger led walk in season.
Disabled access to visitor centre and deer museum
only.

1251 TOURIST ISLAND, THE HIGHLAND MOTOR HERITAGE CENTRE 6C1

Off A9 at Bankfoot, 6 miles N of Perth. Jan-Dec. Easter-Sept, daily, 0830-2030. Oct-Easter, Mon-Fri 1000-1800, weekends 0830-2030. (Exc weekends Nov-Feb, 0830-1800.) Entrance charges. Family tickets. Group concessions. Parking available. Gift shop. Licensed restaurant. Tel: (0738) 87696

A collection of classic and vintage cars, costumes and memorabilia is displayed using authentic period settings. Other attractions in the museum include a driving game, free slot car racing and motor heritage videos.

1252 TRAPRAIN LAW 6H6

Off A1, 5m W of Dunbar. All times. Free.

734 feet high whale-backed hill, with Iron Age fortified site, probably continuing in use as a defended Celtic township until 11th century. A treasure of 4th-century Christian and pagan silver excavated here in 1919 is now in the Museum of Antiquities, Queen Street, Edinburgh. (See No 487).

Traquair House

1253 TRAQUAIR HOUSE 5D6

B709, off A72, 8m ESE of Peebles. Easter week, May-Sept, daily 1330-1730 (1030-1730, July & Aug). Groups at other times by arrangement. Entrance charges. Family tickets. Group concessions. Parking available. Gift shop. Restaurant/tearoom. Tel: (0896) 830323.

Dating back to the 12th century, this is said to be the oldest continuously inhabited house in Scotland. Twenty-seven Scottish and English monarchs have visited it, including Mary, Queen of Scots, of whom there are relics. William the Lion held court here in 1175. The well-known Bear Gates were closed in 1745, not to be reopened until the Stuarts should ascend the throne. Ale is regularly produced at the 18th-century brewhouse. Exhibitions and special events are held during the summer months. Craft workshops, brewery, woodland and River Tweed walks and maze.

1254 TREASURES OF THE EARTH 2G12

Mallaig Road, Corpach, 4 miles outside Fort William on A830. Feb-Dec. Daily, 1000-1700 (2000 in July & Aug). Entrance charge—free entry to gift shop. Groups please book in advance. Parking available. Coach service from Fort William TIC. Gem and gift shop. Tel: (0397) 772283.

Award-winning attraction with superb collection of priceless gemstones, many weighing hundreds of pounds, beautiful crystals and exotic minerals from around the world. Display, covering 6,500 square feet, recreates the fascinating world beneath our feet with glistening rock cavities and caverns set among primeval scenes. Shop specialises in gemstone jewellery, ornaments from around the world and many local stone items.

1255 THE TREE SHOP   4G3

  ᕕ *Ardkinglas Estate Nurseries, Clachan Farm. At head of Loch Fyne near Cairndow on A83 Glasgow-Oban and Campbeltown. Apr-Sept, daily 0930-1900. Oct-Mar (exc Jan), daily, 0930-1700. Free. Parking available. Gift shop. Plant sales. Tel: (049 96) 263 or 261*

The Tree Shop at the head of Loch Fyne specialises in specimen trees, indigenous Highland trees, rhododendrons and azaleas, heathers and unusual shrubs. Much of the plant sales area is under cover, with a canopy designed to ensure the hardiness of the plants. Inside the Tree Shop, a range of quality woodwork, basketware and shepherds' crooks.

1256 TRIMONTIUM EXHIBITION   5E6

Ormiston Institute, The Square, Melrose. April-Oct. Daily 1030-1630. Entrance charge. Gift shop. Tel: (089 682) 2463.

The Trimontium Exhibition — 'A Roman Frontier Post and its People' — tells the story of the Celts and Romans at the 370-acre complex in the lee of the three Eildon Hills (Trimontium). Exhibition room has display panels and cases; video room, photographs, models of the Trimontium and Cappuck forts, and interesting finds. There is also a street corner with replica blacksmiths's and potter's workshops; huge stones from the Langlee temple; replica legionary helmet, sword and armour. Visitors can 'join' the garrison and become troopers.

1257 TRINITY TEMPLE (TEAMPULL NA TRIONAID)   2B8

Off A865, 8 miles Sw of Lochmaddy, Isle of North Uist. All reasonable times. Free.

Ruins of medieval college and monastery said to have been founded by Beathag, daughter of Somerled, in the early 13th century, and where Duns Scotus studied (see No 1159). Beside it is Teampull Clann A'Phiocair, the chapel of the MacVicars, teachers at the college. Also several ancient cup and ring marks, and the Field of Blood, site of a clan battle. Great care should be taken in the ruins of the temple.

1258 TUGNET ICE HOUSE   3E7

Spey Bay, 5m W of Buckie. May-Sep, daily 1000-1600. Free. Parking available. Sales point. Tel: (0309) 673701.

Permanent exhibition telling the story of the River Spey, its salmon fishing and wildlife, established in a historic ice house building, possibly the largest in Scotland, dated 1830. Picnic site.

1259 TULLIBARDINE CHAPEL   6B3

Off A823, 6m SE of Crieff. All reasonable times. Free. Apply adjacent farmhouse. (HS) Tel: 031-244 3101.

Founded in 1446, this is one of the few rural churches in Scotland which was entirely finished and still remains unaltered.

1260 TULLOCHVILLE FARM HEAVY HORSE CENTRE   5A1

5 miles W of Aberfeldy on B846. Easter-Oct, daily, 1000-1700. Entrance charge. Group concessions. Parking available. Refreshments. Tel: (0887) 830365

Display of farm implements used on a small hill farm (Tullochville), and once pulled by horses, with a collection of harness and memorabilia from the same period. Clydesdale horses, sometimes with foal. Smaller ponies used for pony trekking.

1261 TURNBERRY CASTLE   4G8

Off A719, 6m N of Girvan. All reasonable times. Free.

The scant remains of the castle where Robert the Bruce was probably born in 1274.

1262 TWEED BRIDGE   5F6

A698 at Coldstream, 9m ENE of Kelso.

The 300 feet long bridge was built in 1766 by Smeaton and in the past was a crossing into Scotland for eloping couples taking advantage of Scotland's then-easier marriage laws.

1263 TWEEDDALE MUSEUM AND PICTURE GALLERY   5C6

High Street, Peebles. Jan-Dec, Mon-Fri 1000-1300, 1400-1700. Also weekends, 1400-1700, Easter-Oct. Tel: (0721) 20123

Housed in the Chambers Institution, which was given to Peebles in 1859 by William Chambers the publisher, the museum presents regularly changing displays on various themes of Tweeddale's heritage and culture. Gallery showing contemporary art.

1264 TWEEDHOPE SHEEP DOGS   5C8

At Moffat Fisheries, A708 on outskirts of Moffat. Easter-Oct. Mon-Fri 1030-1630. Demonstrations 1100, 1500. Weekends and winter by appointment. Entrance charge. Parking available. Craft shop. Tearoom. Tel: (0683) 21471.

Border Collie visitor centre shows working sheep dogs using their skills in a natural hillside setting. Demonstrations twice daily, plus special attractions such as 'Baa Baa Black Sheep'.

1265 UGIE SALMON FISH HOUSE   3H8

At the mouth of the River Ugie across from the golf course in Peterhead. Mon-Fri 0900-1200, 1400-1700. Sat 0900-1200. Free. Parking available. Tel: (0779) 76209.

The oldest Salmon Fish House in Scotland dating from 1585. Built for George Keith, 5th Earl Marischal of Scotland. Fresh and smoked salmon always available.

1266 UI CHURCH/EAGLAIS NA H-AOIOHG   2D5

At Aiginis, off A866, 2m E of Stornoway, Isle of Lewis. All reasonable times. Free. Parking available.

Ruined church (pron. 'eye') containing some finely carved ancient tombs of the Macleods of Lewis.

1267 ULLAPOOL MUSEUM 2G6

 ♿
P
T

7 & 8 West Argyle Street, Ullapool. Late Mar-early Nov. Mon-Fri, 1000-1700 (also 1900-2100, June-Sept). Entrance charge. Group concessions. Gift shop.

The museum depicts the social and economic history of Ullapool since its foundation in 1788 as an area of employment, by the British Fisheries Society, to stem emigration following the break-up of the clan system and the Highland Clearances. The village follows a plan by Telford and the former church in which the museum is housed, is to his design and has original furnishings. Extensive photographic exhibition supplemented with archives, display of implements, and community art in a bicentenary tapestry and quilts.

Union Canal: see No 859

1268 UNION SUSPENSION BRIDGE 5G6

Across River Tweed, 2m S of Paxton on unclassified road.

This suspension bridge, the first of its type in Britain, was built by Samuel Brown in 1820 and links England and Scotland.

1269 UNSTAN CHAMBERED TOMB 1B11

3½m NNE of Stromness, Orkney. All reasonable times. Free. (HS) Tel: 031-244 3101.

A cairn containing a chambered tomb (over 6 feet high) divided by large stone slabs. The type of pottery discovered in the tomb is now known as Unstan Ware.

Urquhart Castle

1270 URQUHART CASTLE 3A9

2m SE of Drumnadrochit, on W shore of Loch Ness. Apr-Sept, daily 0930-1830. Oct-Mar, Mon-Sat 0930-1630, Sun 1130-1630. Entrance charge. Group concessions. Parking available. (HS) Tel: 031-244 3101.

Once one of the largest castles in Scotland, the castle is situated on a promontory on the banks of Loch Ness, from where sitings of the 'monster' are most frequently reported. The extensive ruins are on the site of a vitrified fort, rebuilt with stone in the 14th century. The castle was gifted by James IV, in 1509, to John Grant of Freuchie, whose family built much of the existing fabric and held the site for four centuries. The castle was blown up in 1692 to prevent its being occupied by Jacobites. (See also No 875).

1271   VALE OF LEVEN SWIMMING POOL   4H5

&   *North Main Street, Alexandria, Dunbartonshire. Jan-Dec. Mon-Fri*
T   *0900-2100, Sat & Sun 0900-1600. Entrance charge. Parking available.*
Tearoom. Tel: (0389) 56931.

25-metre main swimming pool and children's splash
pool. Sauna facilities, lounge suite with television and
refreshments, tanning sunbeds, fitness room with
computerised equipment.

Vane Farm Nature Reserve

1272   VANE FARM NATURE RESERVE   6D4

*On S shore of Loch Leven, on B9097, off M90 and B996, 4½m S of
Kinross. Apr-Oct, daily 1000-1700, Nov-Mar, daily 1000-1600, except
Christmas/New Year. Entrance charge; school parties by arrangement.
Parking available. RSPB shop. Tearoom (weekends). (RSPB)
Tel: (0577) 62355.*

The Nature Centre is a converted farm building
equipped with displays designed to interpret the
surrounding countryside and the loch. Between the
last week of September and April, the area is a
favourite feeding and resting place for vast numbers of
wild geese and duck; binoculars and closed circuit
television are provided for observation. Also
observation hide and nature trail. Picnic space. Path up
Vane Hill through birchwoods with impressive views.
Disabled access to car park, picnic area, observation
room, the mini nature trail, shop and toilets.

1273   VICTORIA FALLS   2F7

*Off A832, 12m NW of Kinlochewe, near Slattadale. All times. Free.
Parking available.*

Waterfall named after Queen Victoria who visited
Loch Maree and area in 1877.

1274   VILLAGE GLASS   6A4

&   *Queen's Lane, Bridge of Allan, 4 miles N of Stirling. Jan-Dec. Mon-
Thurs 0900-1700, Fri 0900-1600, Sat 0900-1200. Free. Parking
available. Gift shop. Tel: (0786) 832137.*

Craftsmen at work creating miniature bottles, fruit
and flowers, glass ships in bottles, decorative glassware.
Showroom and sales of items designed by Tom Young,
collector's pieces, special commissions.

1275   THE VILLAGE STORE   3D8

&   *96-98 High Street, Aberlour. 14 miles S of Elgin. Jan-Dec, Mon-Sat
T   1000-1800. Sun 1400-1730. Closed Christmas & New Year. Free.
Parking available. Tel: (0340) 871243.*

This old village general store had one owner from
1920 until he retired in 1978. It stayed closed for ten
years, and then disclosed a wealth of clothing,
hardware, haberdashery and the shop records from
1920. Boxes of hats, stockings, liberty bodices, corsets,
woollen knickers and underpants—enough to create a
'hands-on' museum. Many visitors have added to the
collection since opening.

Black Watch Memorial, Wade's Bridge

1276 WADE'S BRIDGE 5A1

On B846, north of Aberfeldy. All times. Free. Parking available.

The bridge across the River Tay was begun in 1733 by General Wade with William Adam as architect. It is considered to be the finest of all Wade's bridges. The Black Watch Memorial is a large cairn surmounted by a kilted soldier, erected close to the bridge in Queen Victoria's Jubilee Year (1887). Easy access across lawn to river bank.

1277 JOHN WALKER & SONS 4H6

Hill Street, Kilmarnock, Ayrshire. Tours: Mon-Thurs 0945 & 1345. Fri 0945 only. Each tour lasts approximately two hours. Parties of up to 40 by prior arrangement. Minimum age 5. Entrance charge. Parking available. Shop. Tel: (0563) 23401 (Visitor Centre).

Whisky blending and bottling plant with guided tours.

1278 WALTZING WATERS 3B11

Balavil Brae, Newtonmore. All year exc mid Jan-late Feb Daily, 1000-1700, shows on the hour, and at 2030. Entrance charges. Group concessions. Craft shops. Refreshments. Tel: (0540) 673752.

ASVA

Elaborate light, water and music spectacle, patterns of moving water synchronised with a wide variety of music. Spacious reception has craft area, children's play area and tourist information points. Wide-screen audio visual introduction to Scotland.

1279 WANLOCKHEAD BEAM ENGINE 5B8

Wanlockhead Village, Dumfries and Galloway. At all times. Free. Tel: (0659) 74387.

An early 19th-century wooden water-balance pump for lead mining with the track of a horse engine beside it. Nearby is the Museum of Scottish Lead Mining (See No 973).

1280 WATERFOWL AND COUNTRY PARK 3A8

The Croft, Drumsmittal, North Kessock. Just N of Inverness over Kessock Bridge. Jan-Dec. Daily, 1000-dusk. Entrance charge. Group concessions. Parking available. Tel: (046 373) 656.

Ornamental waterfowl, ducks, geese, swans, rare breeds, cattle, sheep, pigs, goats, rabbits, chickens, bantams, pheasant. Children's corner in farmyard area has ponds, chicks hatching most days in summer. Chambered cairn on site.

1281 WATERLOO MONUMENT   5E7

Off B6400, 5m N of Jedburgh. Easter-Oct. Free. No access to interior.
Tel: (083 53) 306.

This prominent landmark on the summit of
Penielheugh Hill (741 feet) was built in 1815 by the
Marquess of Lothian and his tenants. Can be seen from
a walk from Harestanes Countryside Visitor Centre.
(See No 718).

1282 P.S. 'WAVERLEY'   4H5

Rates and full details of departure points and times from
Waverley Excursions Ltd, Anderston Quay, Glasgow G3 8HA.
Parking available. Tel: 041-221 8152.

Historically one of the most interesting vessels still in
operation in the British Isles, the *Waverley* is the last
paddle steamer to be built for service on the Clyde,
and now the last sea-going paddle steamer in the
world. A variety of cruises from Glasgow and Ayr
along the Clyde Coast, with meals, bar and light
refreshments available.

1283 THE WEATHER CENTRE   5A10

Laurieston, 6 miles NW of Castle Douglas. Apr-Oct, Tues-Fri, Sun.
Tours at 1000, 1200, 1430. Nov-Mar, by arrangement. Groups please
book in advance. Entrance charge. Group concessions. Limited parking.
Sales point. Tel: (064 45) 264.

Fully functioning weather centre, where visitors can
see how weather forecasts are prepared, using
instruments and satellite equipment.

Weaver's Cottage

1284 WEAVER'S COTTAGE   4H5

Shuttle Street, Kilbarchan, off A737, 5m W of Paisley. Apr-May, Sep-Oct,
Tue, Thu, Sat and Sun 1300-1700; Jun-Aug, daily 1300-1700.
Entrance charge. Group concessions. (NTS) Tel: (050 57) 5588.

In the 18th century Kilbarchan was a thriving centre of
handloom weaving. The cottage is preserved as a
typical weaver's home of the period, with looms,
weaving equipment and domestic utensils. Attractive
cottage garden. Weaving demonstrations, video
programme.

1285 THE WEAVERS' COTTAGES MUSEUM   5A5

From Airdrie town centre, N up 5th Bridge Street, left onto High Street,
left onto Wellwynd. Museum 100yds down hill. Mon-Fri 1000-1700, Sat
1000-1300, 1400-1700, closed Wed & Sun. Free. Public car park nearby.
Tel: (0236) 47712.

The museum consists of two but-and-ben cottages
which were originally built in 1780. They have now
been restored and one is fitted out as a master weaver's
house giving a fascinating insight into the lives of the
local weavers. The other cottage is an exhibition area
for the display of local artefacts, temporary and
travelling exhibitions.

1286 WELL OF THE SEVEN HEADS   2H11
Off A82 on the W shore of Loch Oich. All times. Free. Parking available.

A curious monument inscribed in English, Gaelic, French and Latin and surmounted by seven men's heads, stands above a spring and recalls the grim story of the execution of seven brothers for the murder of the two sons of a 17th century chief of Keppoch.

1287 WEMYSS CAVES   6E5
East Wemyss, 5 miles E of Kirkcaldy on A955. Signposted. Jan-Dec. Open access to some caves, for others, request key in advance from Wemyss Environmental Education Centre, East Wemyss, weekdays 1000-1500 exc public holidays. Free. Parking available. Tel: (0592) 714479. (WEEC)

Several caves, cut into the sandstone cliffs by sea erosion during the last Ice Age, show evidence of prehistoric and recent occupation. They contain a fine set of wall inscriptions, some possibly showing Bronze Age influence, while others are attributable to the Picts and Norsemen. The more famous inscriptions include a Viking longship and the god Thor, as well as animal illustrations of horse, salmon and swan—the swan being incorporated in the coat of arms of the Earl of Wemyss to this day.

West Highland Museum

1288 WEST HIGHLAND MUSEUM   2G12
Cameron Square, Fort William. All year, Mon-Sat 1000-1300, 1400-1700, Jul and Aug, Mon-Fri 0930-1800, Sun 1400-1700. Closed Mon, Nov-Mar. Entrance charge. Group concessions. Gift shop. Tel: (0397) 702169.

Historical, natural history and folk exhibits, local interest and a tartan section. Jacobite relics including a secret portrait of Prince Charles Edward Stuart.

1289 THE WEST PORT   6G2
St Andrews, at W end of South Street. All times. Free. (HS) Tel: 031-244 3101.

One of the few surviving city gates in Scotland. Its building contract is dated 1589 although it was completely renovated in 1843. It now consists of a central archway protected from above by battlements between two semi-octagonal turrets with gun loops.

1290 WESTQUARTER DOVECOT   6B6
In Westquarter, 2m E of Falkirk, off A9. May be viewed from outside only. (HS) Tel: 031-244 3101.

A rectangular dovecot of considerable architectural merit. Over the entrance doorway there is a heraldic panel dated 1647 containing the arms of Sir William Livingstone of Westquarter.

1291 WESTSIDE CHURCH   1B9

Bay of Tuquoy, south coast of island of Westray, Orkney. All reasonable times. Free. (HS) Tel: 031-244 3101.

A 12th-century church, with nave and chancel, the former lengthened in the latter Middle Ages.

1292 WHITEKIRK   6H6

St. Mary's Parish Church: on A198 approach from A1 or from North Berwick. Free. Early morning-late evening. Sunday worship: 1130 (unless stated otherwise). Visitors welcome. Parking available. Printed guide available.

The history and architecture of the church date back to 6th century. Large red sandstone building with high square tower (Norman). Famed for pilgrimages in medieval times and a healing well. The tithe barn behind the church is one of the oldest still standing. Its history is linked to St. Baldred.

1293 THE WHITHORN DIG   4H11

45-47 George Street, Whithorn. 18 miles S of Newton Stewart, signposted. Apr-Oct. Daily, 1030-1700. (Last tour 1630.) Entrance charge. Group concessions. Parking available. Craft/souvenir shop. Tel: (098 85) 508.

An all-weather attraction which tells the archaeological story of excavation at Whithorn Priory, the site of Scotland's first recorded Christian community. Introductory audio-visual, interpretative displays, models, murals and up-to-date archaeological finds from 400 AD to the present. Tours visit the reinstated foundations of the Northumbrian Church and burial chapel (750 AD), and see archaeologists at work in summer. Picnic site on dig field.

Whithorn Priory and Museum

1294 WHITHORN PRIORY AND MUSEUM   4H11

Main Street, Whithorn, 10m S of Wigtown. Apr-Sept, opening standard. Oct-Mar, weekends only. Entrance charge. Group concessions. (HS) Tel: 031-244 3101.

Here St Ninian founded the first Christian Church in Scotland in 397. The present priory ruins date from the 12th century. Early Christian crosses, some carved in the rock, others now displayed in the museum attached to the priory, are notable.

1295 WICK HERITAGE CENTRE   3E3

Bank Row, Wick. Jun-Sep, Mon-Sat 1000-1700; or by arrangement for groups. Entrance charge. Tel: (0955) 3385.

Prize-winning exhibition of the herring fishing industry and domestic life. Gardens.

1296 WIDEFORD HILL CAIRN   1B11

2½m W of Kirkwall on W slope of Wideford Hill, Orkney. All reasonable times. Free. (HS) Tel: 031-244 3101.

A cairn with three concentric walls surrounding a passage and megalithic chamber.

1297 WIGTOWN MUSEUM   4H10

& *County Buildings, Wigtown. Summer months, Mon-Fri 1400-1600. Free.*
T *Sales and information point. Tel: (0776) 5088.*

Changing displays on local history and Wigtown area.
Information on town trail which can be followed by
wheelchair users. Disabled access.

1298 WILD WOOD TURNERY   3F8

& *Craigston Castle Estate, 2 miles from Turriff on A947 Banff road. Turn*
R onto B9105. Jan-Dec, daily. Free. Parking available. Shop.
Tel: (0888) 551246.

A woodturning workshop specialising in wet turning,
as well as kiln dried. All timber used is home grown
on the Craigston Estate. (See No 299).

1299 WINTON HOUSE   6F6

& *Pencaitland, East Lothian. B6355, 6m SW of Haddington. Open by*
A *prior arrangement to parties of 10 and over and exceptionally to others.*
Entrance charge. Tel: (0875) 340222 or 340357.

A gem of Scottish Renaissance architecture dating from
1620. Associations with Charles I and Sir Walter Scott.
Beautiful plaster ceilings, unique carved stone chimneys,
fine pictures and furniture. Terraced gardens, fine trees,
in springtime masses of daffodils.

1300 ALEXANDRA WOLFFE STUDIO GALLERY   5A10

& *The Toll House, High Street, Gatehouse of Fleet. Easter-Oct. Mon-Fri*
1000-1200, or by request at house next door. Free. Parking available.
Paintings and ceramics for sale. Tel: (0557) 814300.

Small gallery and ceramic workshop, where visitors are
welcome to watch the artist making one-off ceramic
models, such as portrait models of favourite pets,
champion stock, etc. Models and paintings displayed
and sold.

1301 THE JOHN WOOD COLLECTION   5F5

& *Fishers Brae, Coldingham. Apr-Oct, 0900-1800, Mon-Sat. Free.*
A *Car parking only. Tel: (089 07) 71259.*
P

A garage in this Berwickshire village is the unusual
setting for a remarkable collection of Victorian and
Edwardian photographs. In 1983, garage owner
Robert Thomson stumbled upon two boxes of glass
plate negatives; after cleaning them he was able to
make prints of ploughmen, soldiers, stonemasons and
early motor vehicles. The photographs were taken by
John Wood, providing a record of rural life in the late
19th and early 20th centuries.

1302 WOOD OF CREE NATURE RESERVE   4H10

On minor road from Minigaff, 4m NW of Newton Stewart. Can be
viewed at any time from road or paths through the wood. Car park. Donation.
(RSPB) Tel: (0671) 2861.

One of the finest areas of remaining native oak and
birch woodland in Scotland with woodland birds and
flowers.

1303 WOODEN EWE   3D2

& *Duncailleinn, Dunnet, Caithness. 8 miles E of Thurso on A836. Signposted*
from Dunnet Post Office. May-Sept, daily, 1030-2200. Winter, please
telephone. Free. Car parking only. Gift shop. Tel: (0847) 85765.

Studio and shop in a Caithness but-and-ben on working
croft, producing rustic items such as clocks, kitchenware,
lamps, mainly in the form of farmyard animals. Only
pre-harvested pine is used, with non-toxic paints, stains
and varnishes.

1304 WOODSIDE STUDIO GALLERY   5B10

&
A

William Street, Dalbeattie. All year, daily, 0930-1900. Free.
Parking available. Tel: (0556) 610517.

Exhibition of large selection of original paintings of
subjects including Galloway landscapes, for sale. Also
framing.

1305 WOOL STONE   6H6

In Stenton, B6370, 5m SW of Dunbar. All reasonable times. Free.
Parking available.

The medieval Wool Stone, used formerly for the
weighing of wool at Stenton Fair, stands on the green.
See also the 14th-century Rood Well, topped by a
cardinal's hat, and the old doocot.

1306 A WORLD IN MINIATURE   4E2

&
A

North Pier, Oban. Easter-Oct, Mon-Sat 1000-1700, Sun 1200-1730.
Entrance charges. Group concessions. Tel: (085 26) 272 or (0631) 66300.

ASVA

Remarkable exhibition of miniature rooms, furniture,
tools, musical instruments, paintings, all in 1/12 scale.

1307 YARROW   5E7

A708, W from Selkirk. Parking available.

A lovely valley praised by many writers including Scott,
Wordsworth and Hogg, who lived in this area. Little
Yarrow Kirk dates back to 1640, Scott's great-great-
grandfather was minister there. The nearby Deuchar
Bridge (not now in use) was built in the 17th-century.
On the hills around Yarrow are the remains of ancient
Border keeps.

1308 YESTER PARISH CHURCH   6G7

Gifford, B6369, 5m SSE of Haddington. All reasonable times. Free.

The Dutch-looking church dates from 1708, and in it is
preserved a late mediaeval bell, and also a 17th century
pulpit. A tablet near the church commemorates the Rev
John Witherspoon (1723-94), born at Gifford, principal
of Princeton University, USA, and the only cleric to
sign the American Declaration of Independence. No
guide dogs, please.

Younger Botanic Garden

1309 YOUNGER BOTANIC GARDEN   4F4

&
P
T

Benmore, on A815, 7m NNW of Dunoon. Mid Mar-Oct, daily 1000-1800.
Entrance charge. Group concessions. Parking available. Gift shop.
Specialist plant sales. Tearoom. Tel: (0369) 6261.

Extensive woodland gardens featuring conifers,
rhododendrons, azaleas, many other shrubs and a
magnificent avenue of Sierra redwoods. Part of the
Royal Botanic Garden, Edinburgh.

INDEX

Antiquities

Monuments and Memorials

Churches, Cathedrals, Abbeys and Chapels

Castles

Stately Homes and Mansions

Other Historic and/or Notable Buildings

Museums

Art Galleries, Arts Centres, etc.

Theatres

Visitor Centres and Specialty Attractions

Swimming Pools, Sports and Leisure Centres

Robert Burns and the Burns Heritage Trail

Bridges

See Scotland at Work

Gardens and Plant Nurseries

Scenic and Nature Interest, Cruises, etc.

Zoos, Farms, Animal Collections, etc.

For Children

ANTIQUITIES

33 Aberlemno Sculptured Stones	779 Jarlshof
34 Abernethy Round Tower	791 Kempock Stone
60 Antonine Wall	794 Kilberry Sculptured Stones
74 Ardestie and Carlungie Earth Houses	796 Kildalton Cross
124 Barsalloch Fort	799 Kilmartin Sculptured Stones
141 Blackhammer Cairn	800 Kilmory Cairns
173 Brechin Round Tower	826 Knap of Howar
178 Brough of Birsay	863 Loanhead Stone Circle
200 Burnswark Hill	909 Machrie Moor Standing Stones
209 Cairnpapple Hill	910 Maes Howe
215 Callanish Standing Stones	930 Meigle Museum
248 Castlelaw Fort	938 Midhowe Broch and Cairns
250 The Caterthuns	957 Motte of Mark
255 The Chesters Fort	958 Motte of Urr
269 Clava Cairns	959 Mousa Broch
271 Clickhimin Broch	987 Ness of Burgi
281 Columba's Footsteps	994 Northlands Viking Centre
289 Corrimony Cairn	1043 Peel Ring of Lumphanan
291 Coulter Motte	1070 Quoyness Chambered Tomb
328 Cullerlie Stone Circle	1080 Rennibister Earth House
331 Culsh Earth House	1083 Ring of Brodgar
335 Cuween Hill Cairn	1087 Roman Bath House
358 Dogton Stone	1091 Rough Castle
374 Drumtrodden	1097 Ruthwell Cross
386 Dun Carloway Broch	1114 St Fillan's Cave
387 Dun Donaigil Broch	1130 St Ninian's Isle
388 Dunadd Fort	1141 Scots Dyke
432 Dwarfie Stane	1169 Skara Brae
433 Dyce Symbol Stones	1192 Steinacleit Cairn and Stone Circle
434 Eagle Stone	1193 Stenness Standing Stones
440 Eassie Sculptured Stone	1209 Sueno's Stone
527 Edinshall Broch	1224 Tealing Earth House and Dovecote
656 Glenashdale Falls and Giants' Graves	1240 Tomb of the Eagles and Bronze Age House
663 Glenelg Brochs	1243 Tomnaverie Stone Circle
690 Grain Earth House	1245 Torhouse Stone Circle
699 Grey Cairns of Camster	1252 Trapain Law
705 Gurness Broch	1269 Unstan Chambered Tomb
721 Haylie Chambered Tomb	1287 Wemyss Caves
	1293 Whithorn Dig

1294 Whithorn Priory and Museum
1296 Wideford Hill Cairn
1305 Wool Stone

MONUMENTS AND MEMORIALS

  46 Alexander III Monument
  85 Johnie Armstrong of Gilnockie
     Memorial
 131 Bell Obelisk
 162 Boswell Museum and Mausoleum
 181 Bruce's Stone
 182 Bruce's Stone
 194 Burns Family Tombstones
     and Cairn
 197 Burns Mausoleum
 198 Burns Monument, Alloway
 199 Burns Monument
     and Museum, Kilmarnock
 279 Cobb Memorial
 285 Commando Memorial
 318 Cross of Lorraine
 323 Robinson Crusoe Statue
 472 Edinburgh, Greyfriars Bobby
 511 Edinburgh, Scott Monument
 560 Fettercairn Arch
 566 Flodden Monument
 583 Fyrish Monument
 669 Glenfinnan Monument
 704 Neil M. Gunn Memorial Viewpoint
 717 Keir Hardie Statue
 732 Highland Mary's Monument
 733 Highland Mary's Statue
 743 James Hogg Monument
 595 Lady Gifford Statue
 842 Lauder Memorials
 853 Leyden Obelisk and Tablet
 862 David Livingstone Centre
 874 Loch Nan Uamh Cairn
 896 Hugh MacDiarmid Memorial
     Sculpture
 897 Flora Macdonald's Birthplace
 898 Flora Macdonald's Monument
 899 Sir Hector MacDonald's Memorial
 901 Roderick Mackenzie's Memorial
 905 Macpherson Monument
 918 Marjoribanks Monument
 922 Martyrs' Monument
 895 McCaig's Tower
 935 Melville Monument
 943 Milnholm Cross
 950 Monument Hill
 981 National Burns Memorial Tower
 982 National Wallace Monument
 984 Nelson Tower
1030 Ormiston Market Cross
1032 Our Lady of the Isles
1056 Preston Market Cross
1059 Prestonpans Battle Cairn
1085 Rob Roy's Grave
1086 Rob Roy's Statue
1143 Captain Scott and Dr Wilson Cairn
1159 Duns Scotus Statue
1161 Seamen's Memorial
1182 Smollett Monument
1222 Tarves Medieval Tomb
1226 Telford Memorial
1281 Waterloo Monument
1286 Well of the Seven Heads

CHURCHES, CATHEDRALS, ABBEYS AND CHAPELS

   1 Abbey St Bathans
   4 Abercorn Church
  21 Aberdeen, Kirk of St Nicholas
  26 Aberdeen, St Machar's Cathedral
  27 Aderdeen, St Mary's Cathedral
  71 Achnaba Church
  49 Alloway Auld Kirk
  54 Amulree Parish Church
  63 Arbroath Abbey

  71 Ardchattan Priory
  72 Ardclach Bell Tower
  88 Athelstaneford Church
  93 Auld Kirk
  94 Auld Kirk Museum
 108 Balmerino Abbey
 110 Balnakeil Church
 127 Beauly Priory
 128 Bedrule Church
 137 Biggar Kirk
 160 Borthwick Church
 166 Bowmore Round Church
 173 Brechin Round Tower
 178 Brough of Birsay
 218 Cambuskenneth Abbey
 224 Carfin Grotto
 242 Castle Semple Collegiate Church
 253 Chapel Finian
 258 Church of the Holy Rude
 259 Cille Bharra
 305 Crathie Church
 313 Croick Parliamentary Church
 317 Cross Kirk
 319 Crossraguel Abbey
 321 Cruggelton Church
 327 Cullen Old Church
 330 Culross Abbey
 341 Dalmeny Kirk
 350 Deer Abbey
 353 Deskford Church
 362 Dornoch Cathedral
 375 Dryburgh Abbey
 392 Dunblane Cathedral
 400 Dundee, Cathedral Church of St Paul
 415 Dundrennan Abbey
 416 Dunfermline Abbey
 418 Dunglass Collegiate Church
 420 Dunkeld Cathedral
 431 Durisdeer Parish Church
 452 Edinburgh, Canongate Kirk
 457 Edinburgh, Corstorphine Old Parish
     Church
 473 Edinburgh, Kirk of the Greyfriars
 486 Edinburgh, Magdalen Chapel
 505 Edinburgh, St Cuthbert's Church
 506 Edinburgh, St Giles Cathedral
 507 Edinburgh, St John's Church
 508 Edinburgh, St Mary's Cathedral
 509 Edinburgh, St Triduana's Chapel
 529 Edrom Norman Arch
 535 Elgin Cathedral
 541 Eynhallow Church
 557 Fearn Abbey
 570 Fogo Kirk
 578 Fortrose Cathedral
 585 Fyvie Church
 605 Glasgow Cathedral
 633 Glasgow, Queen's Cross Church
 637 Glasgow, St David's 'Ramshorn'
     Church
 639 Glasgow, St Vincent Street Church
 676 Glenluce Abbey
 713 Hamilton Old Parish Church
 746 Holy Trinity Church
 758 Inchcolm Abbey
 759 Inchmahone Priory
 764 Inveraray Bell Tower
 773 Iona
 777 Italian Chapel
 780 Jedburgh Abbbey
 789 Kelso Abbey
 807 Kilwinning Abbey
 812 Kinkell Church
 815 Kinneff Old Church
 831 Ladykirk
 850 Leuchars Parish Church
 856 Lincluden Collegiate Church
 919 Marnoch Old Church
 926 Maybole Collegiate Church
 933 Melrose Abbey
 954 Mortlach Church
 975 Muthill Church and Tower
1031 Orphir Church
1034 Paisley Abbey
1048 Pierowall Church
1054 Pluscarden Abbey
 431 Queensberry Aisle

1082	Restenneth Priory
1088	Rosslyn Chapel
1099	St Andrew's Cathedral, Inverness
1100	At Andrews Cathedral
1105	St Bean's Church
1106	St Blane's Chapel
1107	St Bride's Church
1108	St Bridget's Kirk
1109	St Clememt's Church
1110	St Columba's Cave
1111	St Cormac's Chapel
1113	St Duthus Chapel and Collegiate Church
1115	St John's Kirk
1117	St Magnus Cathedral
1118	St Magnus Church
1119	St Mary's Chapel, Bute
1120	St Mary's Chapel, Crosskirk
325	St Mary's Chapel, Wyre
1121	St Mary's Church, Auchindoir
1122	St Mary's Church, Grandtully
1123	St Mary's Collegiate Church
1125	St Mary's Parish Church, Monymusk
1126	St Michael's Parish Church
1127	St Monan's Church
1128	St Ninian's Chapel, Isle of Whithorn
1129	St Ninian's Chapel, Tynet
1131	St Peter's Church
1133	St Vigean's Church
1134	Saddell Abbey
1164	Seton Collegiate Church
1170	Skelmorlie Aisle
1171	Skipness Chapel
1214	Sweetheart Abbey
1216	Swinton Kirk
1248	Torphichen Preceptory
1257	Trinity Temple
1259	Tullibardine Chapel
1266	Ui Church
1291	Westside Church
1292	Whitekirk
1307	Yarrow Kirk
1308	Yester Parish Church

CASTLES

11th Century
| 453 | Edinburgh Castle |

12th Century
77	Ardrossan Castle
225	Carleton Castle
241	Castle of St John
245	Castle Stuart
246	Castle Sween
325	Cubbie Row's Castle
351	Delgatie Castle
380	Duffus Castle
382	Dumbarton Castle
610	Glasgow, Crookston Castle
808	Kindrochit Castle
824	Kisimul Castle
1197	Stirling Castle
1261	Turnberry Castle

13th Century
140	Balhousie Castle
147	Blair Castle
163	Bothwell Castle
176	Brodick Castle and Gardens
205	Caerlaverock Castle
227	Carnasserie Castle
326	Culcreuch Castle
356	Dirleton Castle
367	Drum Castle
377	Duart Castle
429	Dunstaffnage Castle
430	Dunvegan Castle
532	Eilean Donan Castle
584	Fyvie Castle
710	Hailes Castle
725	Hermitage Castle
797	Kildrummy Castle
882	Lochindorb
885	Lochranza Castle

892	Luffness Castle
955	Morton Castle
983	Neidpath Castle
1018	Old Inverlochy Castle
1089	Rothesay Castle
1092	Roxburgh Castle
1098	St Andrews Castle
1171	Skipness Castle

14th Century
30	Aberdour Castle
105	Balgonie Castle
112	Balvenie Castle
247	Castle Tioram
252	Cawdor Castle
261	Clackmannan Tower
309	Crichton Castle
347	Dean Castle
424	Dunnottar Castle
427	Duns Castle
459	Edinburgh, Craigmillar Castle
555	Fast Castle
867	Loch Doon Castle
871	Loch Leven Castle
883	Lochmaben Castle
1221	Tantallon Castle
1270	Urquhart Castle

15th Century
80	Ardvreck Castle
90	Auchindoun Castle
142	Blackness Castle
160	Borthwick Castle
171	Breacachadh Castle
223	Cardoness Castle
236	Castle Campbell
284	Comlongon Castle
298	Craignethan Castle
364	Doune Castle
396	Dundee, Broughty Castle
428	Dunscaith Castle
604	Glasgow, Cathcart Castle
753	Huntingtower Castle
795	Kilchurn Castle
805	Kilravock Castle
995	Niddry Castle
996	Noltland Castle
1021	Old Place of Mochrum
1025	Orchardton Tower
1052	Pitsligo Castle
1058	Preston Tower
1075	Ravenscraig Castle
1076	Red Castle
1201	Strathaven Castle
1238	Tolquhon Castle

16th Century
69	Ardblair Castle
177	Brodie Castle
191	Burleigh Castle
232	Carsluith Castle
237	Castle Fraser
239	Castle Menzies
240	Castle of Park
244	Castle Stalker
249	Castles Girnigoe and Sinclair
286	Corgarff Castle
304	Crathes Castle
368	Drumcoltran Tower
376	Dryhope Tower
402	Dundee, Claypots Castle
437	Earlshall Castle
484	Edinburgh, Lauriston Castle
530	Edzell Castle and Garden
533	Elcho Castle
559	Ferniehirst Castle
596	Gilknockie Tower
615	Glasgow, Haggs Castle
696	Greenknowe Tower
707	Gylen Castle
755	Huntly Castle
788	Kellie Castle
904	MacLellan's Castle
936	Menstrie Castle
944	Minard Castle
967	Muness Castle
991	Newark Castle, Port Glasgow

1142 Scotstarvit Tower
1178 Smailholm Tower

17th Century
168 Braemar Castle
299 Craigston Castle
369 Drumlanrig Castle
599 Glamis Castle
1137 Scalloway Castle
1176 Slains Castle
1227 Thirlestane Castle
1230 Threave Castle

18th Century
332 Culzean Castle
567 Floors Castle
765 Inveraray Castle
1184 Sorn Castle

19th Century
263 Armadale Castle
98 Ayton Castle
109 Balmoral Castle
149 Blairquhan Castle
372 Drummuir Castle
426 Dunrobin Castle
813 Kinloch Castle
1247 Torosay Castle

STATELY HOMES AND MANSIONS

3 Abbotsford House
67 Arbuthnott House and Gardens
69 Ardblair Castle
104 Balcaskie House and Gardens
109 Balmoral Castle
147 Blair Castle
164 Bowhill
176 Brodick Castle and Gardens
177 Brodie Castle and Gardens
216 Callendar House
252 Cawdor Castle
296 Craigcleuch Castle Collection
304 Crathes Castle and Garden
332 Culzean Castle
340 Dalmeny House
351 Delgatie Castle
367 Drum Castle
369 Drumlanrig Castle
372 Drummuir Castle
377 Duart Castle
378 Duff House
426 Dunrobin Castle
430 Dunvegan Castle
437 Earlshall Castle and Gardens
484 Edinburgh, Lauriston Castle
495 Edinburgh, Palace of Holyroodhouse
532 Eilean Donan Castle
554 Fasque
565 Finlaystone
567 Floors Castle
584 Fyvie Castle
599 Glamis Castle
630 Glasgow, Pollok House
657 Glenbarr Abbey Visitor Centre (Macalister Clan)
687 Gosford House
709 Haddo House
740 The Hill House
741 Hill of Tarvit
747 Hopetoun House
749 House of the Binns
750 House of Dun
765 Inveraray Castle
788 Kellie Castle
813 Kinloch Castle
847 Leith Hall
848 Lennoxlove House
916 Manderston
925 Maxwelton House
932 Mellerstain House
936 Menstrie Castle
1041 Paxton House
1140 Scone Palace
1184 Sorn Castle
1194 Stevenson House
1227 Thirlestane Castle
1247 Torosay Castle
1253 Traquair House
1299 Winton House

OTHER HISTORIC AND/ OR NOTABLE BUILDINGS

20 Aberdeen, King's College
22 Aberdeen, Marischal College
25 Aberdeen, Provost Skene's House
83 Argyll's Lodging
122 Barrie's Birthplace
151 Boath Doocot
153 Bod of Gremista
183 Michael Bruce's Cottage
226 Carlyle's Birthplace
228 Carnegie Birthplace Museum
254 Chatelherault
261 Clackmannan Tower
270 Click Mill
272 Cloch Lighthouse
302 Crail Tolbooth
314 Cromarty Courthouse
330 Culross Palace
398 Dundee, Camperdown
406 Dundee, Howff Burial Ground
421 Dunkeld Little Houses
422 Dunmore Pineapple
435 Earl Patrick's Palace and Bishop's Palace
436 Earl's Palace, Birsay
438 Earthquake House
454 Edinburgh City Art Centre
460 Edinburgh, Cramond
462 Edinburgh, Dean Village
468 Edinburgh, Georgian House
469 Edinburgh, General Register House
470 Edinburgh, Gladstone's Land
474 Edinburgh, George Heriot's School
477 Edinburgh, Huntly House
481 Edinburgh, John Knox House
482 Edinburgh, Lady Stair's House
483 Edinburgh, Lamb's House
491 Edinburgh, National Library of Scotland
492 Edinburgh, New Town Conservation Centre
496 Edinburgh, Parliament House
504 Edinburgh, St Cecilia's Hall
523 Edinburgh, Usher Hall
525 Edinburgh, White Horse Close
546 Falkland Palace
572 Fort Augustus Abbey and Fort
573 Fort Charlotte
574 Fort George
581 Foulden Tithe Barn
593 Gearrannan Village
607 Glasgow, City Chambers
611 Glasgow, Custom House Quay
613 Glasgow, George Square
619 Glasgow, Hutchesons' Hall
623 Glasgow, Merchants' House
624 Glasgow, The Mitchell Library
628 Glasgow, Necropolis
631 Glasgow, Provan Hall
632 Glasgow, Provand's Lordship
636 Glasgow, Royal Concert Hall
640 Glasgow School of Art
642 Glasgow, Stirling's Library
643 Glasgow, The International Stock Exchange
644 Glasgow, Former Templeton's Carpet Factory
645 Glasgow, Tenement House
651 Glasgow, Willow Tearoom
695 Greenhill Covenanters' House
703 Guildhall
715 Hanseatic Booth
724 The Hermitage
761 Innerpeffray Library
766 Inveraray Jail
786 Keathbank Mill
837 William Lamb Memorial Studio
846 Leighton Library

852 Lewis Black House
858 Linlithgow Palace
890 Loudoun Hall
920 Mar's Wark
921 Martello Tower
924 Mary Queen of Scots House
942 Hugh Miller's Cottage
962 John Muir House
989 New Abbey Corn Mill
1013 Old Blacksmith's Shop Centre
1020 Old Mills
1023 Old Skye Crofter's House
1057 Preston Mill and Phantassie Doocot
1096 Ruthven Barracks
1104 St Andrews University
1135 Sanquhar Post Office
1157 Sir Walter Scott's Courtroom
1177 Sma' Shot Cottages
330 The Study
1220 Tankerness House
330 Town House, Culross
1258 Tugnet Ice House
1284 Weaver's Cottage
1285 The Weavers' Cottages Museum
1289 West Port
1290 Westquarter Dovecote

MUSEUMS

Clan and Tartan
262 Clan Cameron Museum
263 Clan Donald Centre
264 Clan Donnachaidh Museum
265 Clan Gunn Heritage Centre
    and Museum
657 Clan McAlister Centre
266 Clan Macpherson Museum
455 Edinburgh, Clan Tartan Centre
1154 Scottish Tartans Museum

Folk and Agriculture
47 Alford Heritage Centre
50 Almond Valley Heritage Centre
53 Alyth Museum
58 Angus Folk Museum
89 Atholl Country Collection
91 Auchindrain Old Highland Township
159 Borreraig Park Exhibition Croft
256 Choraidh Croft
280 Colbost Folk Museum
295 Craig Highland Farm
300 Craigston Museum
337 Dalgarven Mill –
    The Ayrshire Museum
    of Countryside and Costume
512 Edinburgh, Scottish Agricultural
    Museum
553 Farm Life Centre
562 Fife Folk Museum
568 Fochabers Folk Museum
659 Glencoe and North Lorn Folk
    Museum
695 Greenhill Covenanters' House
730 Highland Folk Museum
742 The Hirsel, Homestead Museum
852 Lewis Black House
854 Lhaidhay Caithness Croft Museum
976 Muthill Museum
1003 North East of Scotland
    Agricultural Heritage Centre
1006 Northfield Farm Museum
1015 The Old Byre
1023 Old Skye Crofter's House
1027 Orkney Farm and Folk Museum
1166 Shawbost School Museum
1167 Shetland Croft House Museum
1173 Skye Heritage Centre
1174 Skye Museum of Island Life
1235 Tingwall Agricultural Museum
1284 Weaver's Cottage
1285 The Weavers' Cottages Museum

General and Miscellaneous
13 Aberdeen, James Dun's House
22 Aberdeen, Marischal Museum
29 Aberdeen, University Zoology
    Museum

175 British Golf Museum
184 John Buchan Centre
203 Bygones Museum and Balquidder
    Visitor Centre
228 Andrew Carnegie Birthplace Museum
257 Christian Heritage Museum
267 Clapperton Daylight Photographic
    Studio
268 Jim Clark Memorial Trophy Room
296 Craigcleuch Castle Collection
308 Creetown Gem Rock Museum
310 Crichton Royal Museum
355 Dick Institute
365 Doune Motor Museum
383 Dumfries and Galloway Aviation
    Museum
395 Dundee, Barrackstreet Museum
408 Dundee, McManus Galleries
449 Edinburgh, Camera Obscura
482 Edinburgh, Lady Stair's House
487 Edinburgh, Museum of Antiquities
488 Edinburgh, Museum of Childhood
489 Edinburgh, Museum of Fire
501 Edinburgh, Royal Museum
    of Scotland, Chambers Street
504 Edinburgh, St Cecilia's Hall
516 Edinburgh Scout Museum
519 Edinburgh, Sir Jules Thorne
    Historical Museum
522 Edinburgh University Collection
    of Historical Musical Instruments
587 Galloway Deer Museum
594 Giant MacAskill Museum
600 Glasgow, Art Gallery and Museum
603 Glasgow, The Burrell Collection
615 Glasgow, Haggs Castle
616 Glasgow, Heatherbank Museum
    of Social Work
618 Glasgow, Hunterian Museum
633 Glasgow, C. R. Mackintosh Society
622 Glasgow, McLellan Galleries
626 Glasgow, Museum of Education
627 Glasgow, Museum of Transport
638 Glasgow, St Mungo's Museum
693 Grassic Gibbon Centre
698 Greenock Custom House Museum
701 Groam House Museum
    and Pictish Centre
720 Hawick Museum
722 The Heritage of Golf
734 Highland Museum of Childhood
744 Holmisdale House Toy Museum
771 Inverness Museum
781 Jedburgh Castle Jail and Museum
783 John Paul Jones Birthplace Museum
823 Kirriemuir RAF Museum
836 Laing Museum
862 David Livingstone Centre
930 Meigle Museum
934 Melrose Motor Museum
953 Moray Motor Museum
971 Museum of Flight
977 Myreton Motor Museum
980 Nairn Literary Institute Museum
1029 Orkney Wireless Museum
1044 Perth Museum
1079 'Remains to be Seen'
1136 Savings Banks Museum
1165 Shambellie House Museum of
    Costume
1168 Shetland Museum
1180 Smith Art Gallery and Museum
1207 John McDouall Stuart Museum
1225 Teddy Melrose
1251 Tourist Island, The Highland
    Motor Heritage Centre
1275 The Village Store
1306 A World in Miniature

Local History
2 Abbot House Heritage Centre
66 Arbuthnot Museum
94 Auld Kirk Museum
96 Avoch Heritage Association
102 Baird Institute Museum
113 Banchory Museum
114 Banff Museum

121 Barony Chambers Museum
135 Bennie Museum
152 Boathouse Visitor Centre
153 Bod of Gremista
169 Braemar Highland Heritage Centre
172 Brechin Museum
186 Buckhaven Museum
201 Burntisland Museum
202 Bute Museum
230 Carnegie Museum
277 Clydebank District Museum
301 Crail Museum and Heritage Centre
314 Cromarty Courthouse
360 Dollar Museum
379 Dufftown Museum
385 Dumfries Museum
391 Dunbeath Heritage Centre
396 Dundee, Broughty Castle Museum
408 Dundee, McManus Galleries
417 Dunfermline District Museum
477 Edinburgh, Huntly House
497 Edinburgh, The People's Story
     Museum
536 Elgin Museum
540 Eyemouth Museum
544 Falconer Museum
545 Falkirk Museum
564 Finlaggen Centre
580 Fossil Visitor Centre
586 Gairloch Heritage Museum
598 Gladstone Court Museum
629 Glasgow, People's Palace
641 Glasgow, Springburn Museum
701 Groam House Museum
711 Halliwell's House Museum
     and Robson Gallery
712 Hamilton District Museum
754 Huntly Brander Museum
770 Inverkeithing Museum
774 Isle of Arran Heritage Museum
790 Kelso Museum
841 Largs Museum
857 Linlithgow Heritage Trust Museum
866 Lochbroom Museum
903 McLean Museum and Art Gallery
928 Meffan Institute
945 Moat Park Heritage Centre
946 Moffat Museum
949 Montrose Museum
951 Monymusk Arts Centre
964 Mull Museum
968 Museum nan Eilean
970 Museum of the Cumbraes
972 Museum of Islay Life
974 Museum Sgoil Lionacleit
978 Nairn Fishertown Museum
986 Ness Historical Society
992 Newton Stewart Museum
997 North Ayrshire Museum
999 North Berwick Museum
994 Northlands Viking Centre
1010 Oban Experience
1014 Old Bridge House
1016 Old Gala House
1017 Old Haa Museum
1035 Paisley Museum
1049 The Piping Centre, Borreraig
1053 Pittencrieff House Museum
1068 Queensferry Museum
1095 Rutherglen Museum
1101 St Andrews Museum
1102 St Andrews Preservation Trust
     Museum
1132 St Ronan's Wells Interpretative
     Centre
1138 Scalloway Museum
1195 Stewartry Museum
1200 Stranraer Museum
1204 Strathnaver Museum
1220 Tankerness House
1232 Thurso Heritage Museum
1234 Timespan Heritage Centre
1237 Tolbooth Museum
1242 Tomintoul Museum
1256 Trimontium Exhibition
1263 Tweedale Museum
1267 Ullapool Museum

1288 West Highland Museum
1295 Wick Heritage Centre
1297 Wigtown Museum
1301 The John Wood Collection

Maritime
  24 Aberdeen Maritime Museum
 187 Buckie Maritime Museum
 214 Caledonian Canal
 283 PS 'Comet' Replica
 312 Crinan Canal
 352 Denny Ship Model Experimental Tank
 396 Dundee, Broughty Castle Museum
 403 Dundee, Discovery Point
 405 Dundee, Frigate 'Unicorn'
 575 Forth/Clyde Canal
 611 Glasgow, Custom House Quay
 692 Grangemouth Museum
 770 Inverkeithing Museum
 859 Linlithgow Union Canal Society
     Museum and Boat Trips
 889 Lossiemouth Fisheries
     and Community Museum
 978 Nairn Fishertown Museum
 985 Neptune's Staircase
1001 North Carr Lightship
1146 Scottish Fisheries Museum
1149 Scottish Maritime Museum
1168 Shetland Museum
1237 Tolbooth Museum
1258 Tugnet Icehouse
1265 Ugie Salmon Fish House
1282 PS 'Waverley'
1295 Wick Heritage Centre

Industrial
  48 Alford Valley Railway
  52 The Aluminium Story
  65 Arbroath Museum
  86 Arran and Argyll Transport Museum
 123 Barry Mill
 136 Biggar Gasworks Museum
 139 Birkhill Fireclay Mine
 155 Bonawe Iron Furnace
 156 Bo'ness and Kinneil Railway
 251 Cathcartston Visitor Centre
 270 Click Mill
 273 Clock Mill Heritage Centre
 287 The Cornice Museum
     of Ornamental Plasterwork
 336 Dalbeattie Museum
 361 Doon Valley Heritage
 366 Dounreay Exhibition Centre
 414 Dundee, Verdant Works
 479 Edinburgh, Kinloch Anderson Heritage
     Room
 510 Edinburgh, The Scotch Whisky
     Heritage Centre
 538 Errol Station Railway Heritage Centre
 571 Fordyce Joiner's Workshop
     and Visitor Centre
 641 Glasgow, Springburn Museum
 691 Grampian Transport Museum
 692 Grangemouth Museum
 816 Kinneil Museum and Roman Fortlet
 819 Kirkcaldy Museum
 857 Linlithgow Heritage Trust Museum
 940 Mill on the Fleet
 973 Museum of Lead Mining
 990 New Lanark
1073 Allan Ramsay Library
1148 Scottish Industrial Railway Centre
1150 Scottish Mining Museum
1151 Scottish Mining Museum
1152 Scottish Museum of Woollen Textiles
1179 Robert Smail's Printing Works
1205 Strathspey Railway
1211 Summerlee Heritage Trust
1279 Wanlockhead Beam Engine
1284 Weaver's Cottage

Regimental
  17 Aberdeen, Gordon Highlanders
     Regimental Museum
  84 Argyll and Sutherland
     Highlanders' Museum
 140 Black Watch Regimental Museum

219 Cameronians (Scottish Rifles)
Regimental Museum
282 Combined Operations Museum
634 Glasgow, Regimental Headquarters
of the Royal Highland Fusiliers
969 Museum of Border Arms and Armour
1065 Queen's Own Highlanders
Regimental Museum
1147 Scottish Horse Museum

ART GALLERIES, ARTS CENTRES, ETC.

6 Aberdeen Arts Centre Gallery
7 Aberdeen Art Gallery
23 Aberdeen, Peacock Printmakers
40 Kathryn Ade Designer Jewellry
45 Aldessan Gallery
55 An Lanntair Gallery
56 An Tuireann Arts Centre
64 Arbroath Art Gallery
179 Broughton Gallery
306 Crawford Arts Centre
355 Dick Institute
408 Dundee, McManus Galleries
417 Dunfermline, Small Gallery
447 Edinburgh, Calton Gallery
454 Edinburgh City Art Centre
456 Edinburgh, Collective Gallery
464 Edinburgh, Flying Colours Gallery
466 Edinburgh, Fruitmarket Gallery
467 Edinburgh Gallery
478 Edinburgh, Kingfisher Gallery
490 Edinburgh, National Gallery
of Scotland
492 Edinburgh, Netherbow Arts Centre
494 Edinburgh, Open Eye Gallery
503 Edinburgh, Royal Scottish Academy
514 Edinburgh, Scottish National Gallery
of Modern Art
515 Edinburgh, Scottish National Portrait
Gallery
517 Edinburgh, Stills
518 Edinburgh, Talbot Rice Gallery
520 Edinburgh, 369 Gallery
524 Edinburgh, West Register House
558 Fergusson Gallery
600 Glasgow Art Gallery and Museum
603 Glasgow, The Burrell Collection
608 Glasgow, Collins Gallery
609 Glasgow, Compass Gallery
612 Glasgow, Design Council Scotland
617 Glasgow, Hunterian Art Gallery
621 Glasgow, Barclay Lennie Fine Art
625 Glasgow, Ewan Mundy Fine Art
647 Glasgow, Tramway
688 Gracefield Arts Centre
689 Greenock Arts Guild Gallery
716 Harbour Cottage Gallery
720 Hawick Art Gallery
748 Hornel Art Gallery and Library
771 Inverness Museum and Art Gallery
819 Kirkcaldy Art Gallery
825 Kittiwake Gallery
837 William Lamb Memorial Studio
855 Lillie Art Gallery
894 Lyth Arts Centre
900 McEwan Gallery
902 Maclaurin Gallery
and Rozelle House
903 McLean Museum and Art Gallery
906 MacRobert Arts Centre
928 Meffan Institute
1004 North Glen Gallery
1016 Old Gala House
and Christopher Boyd Gallery
1035 Paisley Art Gallery
1044 Perth Art Gallery
66 Peterhead Arbuthnot Art Gallery
1047 Pier Arts Centre
1153 Scottish Sculpture Workshop
and Sculpture Walk
1180 Smith Art Gallery and Museum
1190 Stained Glass Studio
1208 Studio Gallery
1229 Ann R Thomas Gallery
1300 Alexandra Wolffe Studio Gallery
1304 Woodside Studio Gallery

THEATRES

18 Aberdeen, His Majesty's Theatre
138 Biggar Puppet Theatre
204 The Byre Theatre
333 Cumbernauld Theatre
442 Eden Court Theatre
480 Edinburgh, King's Theatre
500 Edinburgh, Royal Lyceum
521 Edinburgh, Traverse Theatre
606 Glasgow, Citizen's Theatre
620 Glasgow, King's Theatre
646 Glasgow, Theatre Royal
647 Glasgow, Tramway
697 Greenock Arts Guild Theatre
737 Highland Theatre
966 Mull Little Theatre
1036 Palace Theatre
1046 Perth Repertory Theatre
1050 Pitlochry Festival Theatre
1181 Adam Smith Theatre

VISITOR CENTRES AND SPECIALTY ATTRACTIONS

15 Aberdeen, Family History Shop
28 Aberdeen, Satrosphere,
The Discovery Place
115 Bannockburn Heritage Centre
126 Baxters Visitor Centre
167 Braeloine Centre
311 Crieff Visitors' Centre
329 Culloden Moor
344 Darnaway Farm Visitor Centre
445 Edinburgh Brass Rubbing Centre
463 Edinburgh Experience
648 Glasgow, University
of Glasgow Visitor Centre
693 Grassic Gibbon Centre
737 Highland Theatre
793 Kerr's Miniature Railway
822 Kirkmaiden Information Centre
839 Landmark Visitor Centre
860 'Little Wheels'
876 Loch Ness Lodge Visitor Centre
877 Loch Ness Video Show
1012 The Official Loch Ness Monster
Exhibition Centre
1013 Old Blacksmith's Shop Visitors' Centre
1026 Orignal Loch Ness Visitor Centre
1084 Rob Roy and the Trossachs Visitor
Centre
1254 Treasures of the Earth
1278 Waltzing Waters

SWIMMING POOLS, SPORT AND LEISURE CENTRES

5 Aberdeen Amusement park
8 Aberdeen, Beach Leisure Complex
61 Aquatec
95 Aviemore Mountain Resort
157 Bonnyrigg Leisure Centre
229 Carnegie Leisure Centre
292 Cowdenbeath Leisure Centre
324 Crystals Arena
334 Cupar Sports Centre
384 Dumfires Ice Bowl
390 Dunbar Leisure Pool
397 Dundee, Broughty Ferry Harbour
441 East Sands Leisure Centre
444 Edinburgh, Ainslie Park Leisure Centre
476 Edinburgh, Hillend Ski Centre
485 Edinburgh, Leith Waterworld
499 Edinburgh, Royal Commonwealth
Pool and Nautilus Flume Complex
756 Huntly Nordic Ski Centre
820 Kirkcaldy Ice Rink

821 Kirkcaldy Swimming Pool
827 Knockhill Racing Circuit
835 Lagoon Leisure Complex
844 Lecht Ski Centre
851 Levenmouth Swimming Pool
and Sports Centre
861 Livingston Arena
907 MacTaggart Pool
911 Magnum Leisure Centre
917 Mariner Leisure Centre
979 Nairn Leisure Park
993 Nicholson Lewis Sports Centre
1000 North Berwick Outdoor Pool
1045 Perth Leisure Pool
1072 Rainbow Slides Leisure Centre
1215 Swilken Golf Visitor Centre
1233 The Time Capsule, Monklands
1271 Vale of Leven Swimming Pool

BURNS AND THE BURNS HERITAGE TRAIL

49 Alloway Auld Kirk
93 Auld Kirk
99 Bachelors' Club
180 Brow Well
192 Robert Burns Centre
193 Burns Cottage and Museum
194 Burns Family Tombstones and Cairn
195 Burns House, Dumfries
196 Burns House Museum, Mauchline
197 Burns Mausoleum
198 Burns Monument, Alloway
199 Burns Monument and Museum,
Kilmarnock
347 Dean Castle and Country Park
482 Edinburgh, Lady Stair's House
537 Ellisland Farm
624 Glasgow, Mitchell Library
649 Glasgow Vennel Museum and
Heckling Shop
685 Globe Inn
732 Highland Mary's Monument
733 Highland Mary's Statue
838 Land o' Burns Centre
981 The National Burns Memorial Tower
1185 Souter Johnnie's Cottage

BRIDGES

9 Aberdeen, Bridge of Dee
10 Aberdeen, Brig o' Balgownie
174 Bridge of Carr
233 Cartland Bridge
260 Clachan Bridge
297 Craigellachie Bridge
411 Dundee, Tay Bridges
419 Dunkeld Bridge
576 Forth Bridges
592 Garvamore Bridge
1081 Rennie's Bridge
1094 Rumbling Bridge
1196 Stirling Bridge
1262 Tweed Bridge
1268 Union Suspension Bridge
1276 Wade's Bridge

SEE SCOTLAND AT WORK

11 Aberdeen, Crombie Woollen Mill
16 Aberdeen Fish Market
23 Aberdeen, Peacock Printmakers
31 Aberfeldy Distillery
32 Aberfeldy Water Mill
38 Achiltibuie Smokehouse
44 Airdrie Observatory
57 Peter Anderson
of Scotland Cashmere Woollen Mill
59 Antartex Village
87 Arran Visitor Centre
103 Balbirnie Craft Centre
126 Baxters Visitor Centre

134 Ben Nevis Distillery Visitor Centre
144 Blackwoodridge Pottery
145 Blair Atholl Distillery
146 Blair Atholl Mill
158 Borders Wool Centre
161 Borve Brew House
165 Bowmore Distillery
185 Buchlyvie Pottery Sop
189 Bunnahabhain Distillery
211 Caithness Glass, Perth
212 Caithness Glass, Wick
220 Caol Ila Distillery
222 Cardhu Distillery
234 Cashmere Visitor Centre/
Johnstons of Elgin
273 Clock Mill Heritage Centre
276 Clynelish Distillery
278 Coats Observatory
307 Creebridge Mohair and Woollens
311 Crieff Visitors Centre
320 Cruachan Pumped Storage Power
Station
339 Dallas Dhu Distillery
342 Dalwhinnie Distillery
345 Barbara Davidson Pottery
348 Dee Valley Confectioners
363 Dornoch Craft Centre
366 Dounreay Exhibition Centre
409 Dundee, Mills Observatory
410 Dundee, Shaw's Sweet Factory
425 Dunoon Ceramics
443 Edinburgh, Adam Pottery
458 Edinburgh, Crabbie's Historic
Winery Tour
461 Edinburgh Crystal Visitor Centre
465 Edinburgh, Fountain Brewery
502 Edinburgh, Royal Observatory
513 Edinburgh, Scottish Experience
and Living Craft Centre
528 Edradour Distillery
543 Fairways Heavy Horse Centre
556 Fear an Eich
561 Fettercairn Distillery Visitors'
Centre
563 Findhorn Foundation
569 Foggieley Sheepskin Rugs
588 Galloway Footwear Co-op Ltd
601 Glasgow, The Barras
661 Glendronach Distillery
662 Gleneagles Crystal
664 Glenfarclas Distillery
665 Glenfarg Silver
667 Glenfiddich Distillery
671 Glengoyne Distillery
672 Glen Grant Distillery
673 Glenkinchie Distillery
674 The Glenlivet Distillery
680 Glen Ord Distillery
683 Glenturret Distillery
689 Heather Graham Crafts
702 Grogport Organic Tannery
706 Russell Gurney Weavers
727 Highbank Porcelain Pottery,
Lochgilphead
729 Highland Fine Cheeses
731 Highland Line Craft Centre
735 Highland Park Distillery
736 Highland Stoneware
739 Highland Wineries
742 The Hirsel, Craft Centre
751 Anne Hughes Pottery
752 Hunterston Power Station
757 Hydro-Electric Visitor Centre
767 Inverawe Smokery
776 Isle of Mull Wine Company
802 Kilmory Workshop
834 Lagavulin Distillery
840 Laphroaig Distillery
864 Loch an Eilean Pottery
880 Loch Tay Pottery
891 Lovat Mineral Water
913 Mainsriddle Pottery
939 Mill of Towie
947 Moffat Pottery
965 Mull and West Highland Narrow
Gauge Railway
1004 North Glen Gallery

1008 Oatmeal Mill
1009 Oban Distillery
1011 Oban Glass
1024 Orcadian Stone Company
1033 Ousdale Weaving
1060 James Pringle Weavers
    of Inverness
1093 Royal Lochnagar Distillery
    Visitor Centre
1155 Scottish Wool Centre
1163 Selkirk Glass
1187 Speyside Cooperage
    Visitor Centre
1203 Strathisla Distillery
1206 Stuart Crystal Strathearn Glass
    Works
1213 Sutherland Pottery
1217 Talisker Distillery
1218 Tamdhu Distillery
1219 Tamnavulin-Glenlivet Distillery
1228 Thistle Bagpipe Works
1236 Tobermory Distillery
    Visitor Centre
1239 Tomatin Distillery
1241 Tombuie Smokehouse
1244 Tongland Power Station
1246 Torness Power Station
1274 Village Glass
1277 John Walker & Sons
1283 The Weather Centre
1298 Wild Wood Turnery
1303 Wooden Ewe

GARDENS AND PLANT NURSERIES

12 Aberdeen, Cruickshank Botanic
    Garden
14 Aberdeen, Duthie Park and
    Winter Gardens
35 Abriachan Garden Nursery
36 Achamore House Gardens
37 Achiltibuie Hydroponicum
62 Arbigland
68 Ardanaiseig Gardens
70 Ardchattan Garden
73 Ardencraig Gardens
75 Ardfearn Nursery
79 Arduaine Gardens
100 Sir Douglas Bader Garden
    for Disabled
116 Bargany Gardens
117 Barguillean Garden
132 Bell's Cherrybank Gardens
154 Bolfracks Garden
170 Branklyn Garden
176 Brodick Castle Garden
217 Cambo Gardens
238 Castle Kennedy Gardens
263 Clan Donald Centre
275 Cluny House Gardens
303 Crarae Glen Garden
304 Crathes Castle Gardens
332 Culzean Country Park
343 Damside Country Herbs
    and Arboretum
346 Dawyck Botanic Gardens
357 Dochfour Gardens
370 Drummond Castle Gardens
381 Duirinish Gardens and Nursery
394 Dundee, Barnhill Rock Garden
404 Dundee, Duntrune
413 Demonstration Garden
426 Dundee University Botanic
    Gardens
430 Dunrobin Castle and Gardens
437 Dunvegan Castle and Gardens
498 Earlshall Castle and Gardens
530 Edinburgh, Royal Botanical
    Gardens
546 Edzell Castle and Garden
565 Falkland Palace and Gardens
    Finlaystone
590 Galloway House Gardens
602 Glasgow, Botanic Gardens
614 Glasgow, Greenbank Garden

655 Glenarn
666 Glenfeochan House Gardens
684 Glenwhan Gardens
741 Hill of Tarvit
747 Hopetoun House
762 Inshriach Nursery
768 Inveresk Lodge Garden
769 Inverewe Gardens
784 Jura House Walled Garden
785 Kailzie Gardens
788 Kellie Castle and Gardens
798 Kildrummy Castle Gardens
801 Kilmory Castle Gardens
803 Kilmun Arboretum
804 Kiloran Gardens
805 Kilravock Castle
814 Kinlochlaich House Gardens
293 Kintyre Alpine Nursery
828 Kyle House
845 Leckmelm Shubbery and
    Arboretum
881 Lochalsh Woodland Gardens
887 Logan Botanic Garden
915 Malleny House Gardens
927 Meadowsweet Herb Garden
929 Megginch Castle Grounds
937 Mertoun Gardens
952 Monymusk Walled Garden
1022 Old Semeil Herb Garden
1051 Pitmedden Garden
1062 Beatrix Potter Garden and
    Exhibition
1058 Preston Tower and Gardens
1061 Priorwood Gardens
1186 Speyside Heather Garden Centre
1212 Suntrap
1231 Threave Gardens and Wildfowl
    Refuge
1247 Torosay Castle and Gardens
1255 The Tree Shop
1299 Winton House
1309 Younger Botanic Gardens

SCENIC AND NATURE INTEREST, CRUISES, ETC.

39 Achray Forest Drive
41 Aden Country Park
43 Ailsa Crag
51 Almondell and Calderwood
    Country park
76 Ardnamurchan Natural History
    and Visitor Centre
78 Ardtornish Estate
81 Argyll Forest Park
82 Argyll Wildlife Park
92 Auchingarrich Wildlife Centre
97 Ayr Gorge Woodlands
101 Badnaban Cruises
106 Balloch Castle Country Park
107 Balmedie Country Park
111 Balranald Nature Reserve
118 Barnaline Walks
120 Baron's Haugh
125 Bass Rock
129 Beecraigs Country Park
130 Beinn Eighe National Nature
    Reserve
133 Ben Nevis
188 Bullers of Buchan
190 The Burg
206 Caerlaverock National Nature
    Reserve
207 Cairngorm Chairlift
210 Cairnsmore of Fleet Reserve
213 Calderglen Country Park
221 Cape Wrath
231 Carsaig Arches
235 MV 'Cast-a-way'
243 Castle Semple Country Park
254 Chatelherault Country Park
288 Corrieshalloch Gorge
290 Corryvreckan Whirlpool
315 Crombie Country Park

332 Culzean Castle
    and Country Park
338 Dalkeith Park
354 Devil's Beef Tub
359 Dollar Glen
369 Drumlanrig Castle and Country
    Park
373 Drumpellier Country Park
389 Dunaverty Rock
393 Duncansby Head
398 Dundee, Camperdown House
    and Country Park
401 Dundee, Clatto Country Park
407 Dundee Law
412 Dundee, Templeton Woods
423 Dunnet Head
439 Eas Coul Aulin
448 Edinburgh, Calton Hill
450 Edinburgh, Cammo Estate
451 Edinburgh, Canal Centre
475 Edinburgh, Hermitage of Braid
476 Edinburgh, Hillend
531 Eglinton Country Park
534 Electric Brae
542 Fair Isle
547 Falls of Clyde Centre
548 Falls of Dockart
549 Falls of Glomach
550 Falls of Rogie
551 Falls of Shin
552 Farigaig Forest Centre
577 Fortingall Yew
579 Forvie Nature Reserve Visitor
    Centre
582 Fowlsheugh Nature Reserve
589 Galloway Forest Park
591 Gartmorn Dam Country Park
    and Nature Reserve
597 MV 'Gipsy Princess'
635 Glasgow, Rouken Glen
650 Glasgow, Victoria Park
    and Fossil Grove
653 Glen Affric
654 Glenan Bay
656 Glenashdale Falls
    and Giants' Graves
658 Glencoe and Dalness
660 Glencoe Chairlift
675 Glenlivet Estate
677 Glenmore Forest Park
678 Glenmuick and Lochnagar
679 Glen Nant Forest Nature
    Reserve
681 Glenshee Chairlift
682 Glentress Forest
686 Goatfell
694 Great Glen Cycle Route
700 Grey Mare's Tail
708 Haddo Country Park
714 Handa Island Nature Reserve
718 Harestanes Countryside
    Visitor Centre
719 Haughton Country Park
723 Hermaness National Nature
    Reserve
724 The Hermitage
726 Hidden Hills
760 Inchnacardoch Walks
772 Inverpolly National Nature
    Reserve
775 Isle of May
778 Jacobite Cruises
784 Jura House Walled Garden
787 Kelburn Country Centre
792 MV 'Kenilworth' Cruises
806 Kilt Rock
809 Kingfisher Cruises
811 King's Cave
817 Kintail
818 Kirk Yetholm
830 Kyles of Bute
832 Lady Margaret Restaurant Boat
833 Lady Rowena Steam Launch
842 Lauder Forest Walks
843 Laxford Cruises
849 Letham Glen
865 Loch-an-Eilean Visitor Centre

868 Loch Druidibeg National Nature
    Reserve
869 Loch Etive Cruises
870 Loch Garten Nature Reserve
878 Loch of Kinnordy Nature Reserve
879 Loch of the Lowes
873 Loch Morar
875 Loch Ness
884 Lochore Meadows Country Park
886 Lochwinnoch Nature Reserve
893 Lunderston Bay
908 Mabie Recreation Area
912 Maid of the Forth
923 Marwick Head Nature Reserve
931 Meikleour Beech Hedge
872 Loch Lomond
941 Millbuies Lochs
948 Monikie Country Park
960 Mugdock Country Park
961 John Muir Country Park
963 Muirshiel Country Park
988 Nevis Range Gondola
998 North Berwick Law
1005 North Hoy Nature Reserve
1007 Noss Nature Reserve
1019 Old Man of Hoy
1037 Palacerigg Country Park
1039 Parallel Roads
1040 Pass of Killiecrankie
1042 Pease Dean
1055 Polkemmet Country Park
1063 Puck's Glen
1064 Queen Elizabeth Forest Park
1066 Queen's View, Loch Lomond
1067 Queen's View, Loch Tummel
1069 Quirang
1071 Raiders Road
1074 Randolp's Leap
1078 Reelig Glen
1090 Rothiemurchus Estate Visitor
    Centre
1094 Rumbling Bridge
1112 St Cyrus Nature Reserve
1116 St Kilda
1124 St Mary's Loch
1139 Scapa Flow
1156 SS 'Sir Walter Scott'
1162 Scott's View
1158 MV 'The Second Snark'
1172 Skye Environmental Centre
1183 Smoo Cave
1189 Staffa
1191 Statesman Cruises
1198 Storr
1202 Strathclyde Country Park
1210 Summer Isles
1223 Tay Forest Park
1250 Torridon
1272 Vane Farm Nature Reserve
1273 Victoria Falls
1282 PS 'Waverley'
1302 Wood of Cree Nature Reserve
1307 Yarrow

ZOOS, FARMS,
ANIMAL
COLLECTIONS, ETC

   1 Abbey St Bathans Trout Farm
  42 Aigas Dam Fish Lift
 119 Barnsoul Farm
 143 Blackshaw Farm Park
 148 Blair Drummond Safari and
     Leisure Park
 150 Blowplain Open Farm
 158 Borders Wool Centre
 208 Cairngorm Reindeer Centre
 274 Cloverleaf Fibre Stud
 294 Craggan Fishery
 295 Craig Highland Farm
 316 Crook of Devon Fish Farm
 322 Crumstane Farm Park
 344 Darnaway Farm Visitor Centre
 349 Deep-sea World
 371 Drummond Fish Farms

399 Dundee, Camperdown Wildlife Centre
446 Edinburgh, Butterfly and Insect World
471 Edinburgh, Gorgie City Farm
526 Edinburgh Zoo
539 European Sheep and Wool Centre
543 Fairways Heavy Horse Centre
652 Glasgow Zoo Park
668 Glenfinart Deer Farm
670 Glengoulandie Deer Park
728 Highland and Rare Breeds Farm
738 Highland Wildlife Park
745 Holy Loch Farm Park and Highland Cattle Centre
763 International League for the Protection of Horses
782 Jedforest Deer and Farm Park
810 Kingspark Llama Farm
829 Kylerhea Otter Haven
888 Logan Fish Pond
914 Mallaig Marine World
956 Mossburn Animal Centre
1002 North East Falconery Visitor Centre
1028 Orkney Farm Park
1038 Palgowan Open Farm
1077 Red Deer Range
1103 St Andrews Sea Life Centre
1144 Scottish Centre for Falconry
1145 Scottish Deer Centre
1155 Scottish Wool Centre
1160 Sea Life Centre, Oban
1175 Skye Serpentarium
1186 South Bank Farm Park
1249 Torr Achilty Dam Fish Lift
1260 Tullochville Farm Heavy Horse Centre
1264 Tweedhope Sheep Dogs
1280 Waterfowl and Country Park

FOR CHILDREN

5 Aberdeen Amusement Park
8 Aberdeen, Beach Leisure Complex
14 Aberdeen, Duthie Park and Winter Gardens
16 Aberdeen, Fishmarket
19 Aberdeen, Jonah's Journey
24 Aberdeen, Maritime Museum
28 Aberdeen, Satrosphere, The Discovery Place
41 Aden Country Park
48 Alford Valley Railway
50 Almond Valley Heritage Centre
51 Almondell and Calderwood Country Park
61 Aquatec
89 Atholl Country Collection
95 Aviemore Mountain Resort
107 Balmedie Country Park
129 Beecraigs Country Park
132 Bell's Cherrybank Gardens
138 Biggar Puppet Theatre
156 Bo'ness and Kinneil Railway
176 Brodick Castle, Garden and Country Park
177 Brodie Castle and Gardens
213 Calderglen Country Park
314 Cromarty Courthouse
332 Culzean Castle and Country Park
337 Dalgarven Mill
338 Dalkeith Park
344 Darnaway Farm Visitor Centre
347 Dean Castle and Country Park
365 Doune Motor Museum
373 Drumpellier Country Park
383 Dumfries and Galloway Aviation Museum
398 Dundee, Camperdown House and Country Park
401 Dundee, Clatto Country Park
403 Dundee, Discovery Point
409 Dundee, Mills Observatory
410 Dundee, Shaw's Sweet Factory

444 Edinburgh, Ainslie Park Leisure Centre
445 Edinburgh, Brass Rubbing Centre
446 Edinburgh Butterfly and Insect World
459 Edinburgh, Craigmillar Castle
463 Edinburgh Experience
476 Edinburgh, Hillend Ski Centre
488 Edinburgh, Museum of Childhood
498 Edinburgh, Royal Botanic Garden
501 Edinburgh, Royal Museum of Scotland, Chambers Street
594 Giant Angus Macaskill Museum
597 MV 'Gipsy Princess'
598 Gladstone Court Street Museum
601 Glasgow, The Barras
615 Glasgow, Haggs Castle
626 Glasgow, Museum of Education
627 Glasgow, Museum of Transport
635 Glasgow, Rouken Glen
691 Grampian Transport Museum
708 Haddo Country Park
718 Harestanes Countryside Visitor Centre
734 Highland Museum of Childhood
744 Holmisdale House Toy Museum
766 Inveraray Jail
787 Kelburn Country Centre
793 Kerr's Miniature Railway
839 Landmark Visitor Centre
860 'Little Wheels'
876 Loch Ness Lodge Visitor Centre
934 Melrose Motor Museum
940 Mill on the Fleet
948 Monikie Country Park
953 Moray Motor Museum
960 Mugdock Country Park
965 Mull Railway
971 Museum of Flight
977 Myreton Motor Museum
990 New Lanark
1003 North East of Scotland Agricultural Heritage Centre (Aden Country Park)
1012 Official Loch Ness Monster Exhibition
1020 Old Mills
1037 Palacerigg Country Park
1062 Beatrix Potter Garden and Exhibition
1098 St Andrews Castle
1169 Skara Brae
1199 Storybook Glen
1205 Strathspey Railway
1211 Summerlee Heritage Trust
1225 Teddy Melrose
1227 Thirlestane Castle
1233 The Time Capsule, Monklands
1234 Timespan Heritage Centre
1256 Trimontium Exhibition
1306 A World in Miniature